The I Ching Revealed

Tap Into the Five Secret Patterns
Underlying the 64 Hexagrams

Bill Bodri

BILL BODRI

Copyright © 2023 William Bodri.

All rights reserved. No part of this book may be used or reproduced in any manner whatsoever the without written permission of the publisher, except in cases of brief quotations in articles and reviews. For information write:

Top Shape Publishing LLC
1135 Terminal Way Suite 209
Reno, NV 89502

ISBN: 978-0-9998330-9-4
Library of Congress Control Number: 2023938565

DEDICATION

Dedicated to the many translators, interpreters and students of the *Yijing*. These are only preliminary translations, a bit too hastily put together due to the pandemic, containing my insights to help seed the way for future translators and interpreters to produce better translations than this one. I hope that the patterns revealed within this book may produce more understanding of the structure of the *Yijing* and inspire even better *Yijing* translations in the future.

CONTENTS

	Acknowledgments	i
	Methodology	1
1	Hexagram 1 – Qian: Heaven, Yang Energy, Great Strength	17
2	Hexagram 2 – Kun: Earth, Yin Energy, Submissive Service	22
3	Hexagram 3 – Zhun: Difficult Beginnings, Initial Obstacles, Progress Impeded in Gathering Together	27
4	Hexagram 4 – Meng: Immaturity, Youthful Ignorance, Inexperience	31
5	Hexagram 5 – Xu: Getting Wet, The Drenching	36
6	Hexagram 6 – Song: Conflict, Grievance, Dispute, Contention, Litigation, Lawsuit	40
7	Hexagram 7 – Shi: An Army, The Troops	45
8	Hexagram 8 – Bi: Alliance, Joining Together with Others, Unification	50
9	Hexagram 9 – Xiao Xu: The Small Accumulates, Domestication	54
10	Hexagram 10 – Lu: Cautious Advance, Advancing with Care, Watching Your Step, Respectful Conduct	59
11	Hexagram 11 – Tai: Improvement of Status, Greatness	63
12	Hexagram 12 – Pi: Obstructions, Hindrances, Standstill, Stagnation, Overthrowing Obstructions, Overturning Blockages	68
13	Hexagram 13 – Tong Ren: A Fellowship of Men, Friendship, Companions Gathering Together, Fellowship With Others	72
14	Hexagram 14 – Da You: Great Wealth	76
15	Hexagram 15 – Qian: Modesty, Humility, Humbleness	80
16	Hexagram 16 – Yu: Repose, Contentment	85

17	Hexagram 17 – Sui: Pursuing	89
18	Hexagram 18 – Gu: Remedying the Spoiled Legacy, Rectifying the Inherited Decay	94
19	Hexagram 19 – Lin: Managing, Overseeing, Taking Charge, Leadership	98
20	Hexagram 20 – Guan: Observing, Viewing, Analyzing, Contemplation	102
21	Hexagram 21 – Shih He: Biting Through, Eradication	106
22	Hexagram 22 – Bi: Adornment, Ornamentation, Luxuriance, Elegance	110
23	Hexagram 23 – Bo: Stripping Away (Power and Influence), Flaying (an Individual), Destroying Someone; Dismembering Wang Hai's Body	114
24	Hexagram 24 – Fu: Returning, Turning Back, Retreat	121
25	Hexagram 25 – Wu Wang: The Unexpected, Unplanned Events	125
26	Hexagram 26 – Da Xu: Restraining Great Power, Taming the Strong	129
27	Hexagram 27 – Yi: Jaws, Hungry Mouth	134
28	Hexagram 28 – Da Guo: An Excess (Preponderance) of Greatness, Greatness (Yang) in Excess, Rejuvenation of Yang Energy	139
29	Hexagram 29 – Xi Kan: Danger, The Perilous Pit, Double Pitfall, Repeated Entrapment	143
30	Hexagram 30 – Li: Flaming Beauty, Flaring Radiance, Life	147
31	Hexagram 31 – Xian: Sexual Attraction, Rising Lust	151
32	Hexagram 32 – Heng: Holding Firm, Standing Fast, Duration, Constancy in the Midst of Change	155
33	Hexagram 33 – Dun: The Piglet	159
34	Hexagram 34 – Da Zhuang: Great Power, Using Great Force	163
35	Hexagram 35 – Jin: Advancing, Proceeding Forward	167
36	Hexagram 36 – Ming Yi: The Calling Pheasant, Injuring a Bright	171

Pheasant, Wounding Brightness, Brightness Obscured

37	Hexagram 37 – Jia Ren: The Family, The Household	176
38	Hexagram 38 – Kui: Estrangement, Alienation, Opposition, Disharmony	180
39	Hexagram 39 – Jian: Obstructive Hardship, Impasse, Stumbling, Limping	185
40	Hexagram 40 – Jie: Deliverance, Becoming Untangled, Liberation, Self-Purification	189
41	Hexagram 41 – Sun: Decreasing, Diminishing, Reducing, Lessening	194
42	Hexagram 42 – Yi: Gain, Increase, Advantage, Augmentation	199
43	Hexagram 43 – Guai: Resoluteness, Determination	203
44	Hexagram 44 – Gou: Meeting, Going to Meet	208
45	Hexagram 45 – Cui: Gathering Together, Assembling	212
46	Hexagram 46 – Sheng: Ascending, Rising and Advancing, Pushing Upwards, Advancement	216
47	Hexagram 47 – Kun: Burdened, Oppression, Exhaustion, Entanglement	220
48	Hexagram 48 – Jing: The Well	225
49	Hexagram 49 – Ge: Revolution, Transformation, Instituting Change	229
50	Hexagram 50 – Ding: The Cauldron, The Alchemical Vessel, Establishing the New, Transforming the Fortune	234
51	Hexagram 51 – Zhen: Thunder, Lightning Strike, Shock	240
52	Hexagram 52 – Gen: Mountain, Keeping Still, Stillness, Accumulation	245
53	Hexagram 53 – Jian: Gradual Development, Progressive Advancement, Step-by-Step Growth, Gradual Progress in Life	249
54	Hexagram 54 – Gui Mei: Marrying Maiden	254

55	Hexagram 55 – Feng: Affluence, Abundance, Seeking Prosperity	259
56	Hexagram 56 – Lu: The Wanderer, The Traveler	264
57	Hexagram 57 – Xun: Wind, Gentle Influence, Penetrating Influence	269
58	Hexagram 58 – Dui: Joyousness, Joyful, Happiness, Self-Indulgence; Peace Negotiations	276
59	Hexagram 59 – Huan: Dispersing, Dissolution	282
60	Hexagram 60 – Jie: Restraints, Regulations, Limitations, Boundaries	286
61	Hexagram 61 – Zhong Fu: Inner Sincerity, Inner Trust, A True Relationship	290
62	Hexagram 62 – Xiao Gu: Trying to Exceed One's Smallness	294
63	Hexagram 63 – Ji Ji: After Completion, After Fording the River	299
64	Hexagram 64 – Wei Ji: Before Completion, Not Yet Across the River	304
	Summary and Conclusion	309

ACKNOWLEDGMENTS

Many authors have influenced my own *Yijing-Zhouyi* researches and I am particularly indebted to the following works.

The basic *Yijing* translations I always reference and recommend for libraries include Edward Shaughnessy's *Unearthing the Changes*, *I Ching The Classic of Changes* translated with an introduction and commentary by Edward Shaughnessy, *Rediscovering the I Ching* by Greg Whincup, and Richard Rutt's *The Book of Changes*. I try to use the Mawangdui manuscript indications as much as possible.

When I am looking to understand hexagram lines I turn to the commentaries within *The Laws of Change* by Jack Balkin, *Yi Jing* by Wu Jing-Nuan, *The Astrology of I Ching* by W.K. Chu and W.A. Sherrill, and *The Authentic I-Ching* by Henry Wei. Some of these commentaries are real gems.

I am particularly impressed by the historical scholarship within Stephen Fields' *The Duke of Zhou Changes* and Geoffrey Redmond's *The I Ching (Book of Changes)*. I think future translators can be greatly helped by these two works as well.

All of these authors have greatly helped me develop my understanding of the *Yijing*.

METHODOLOGY

This translation of the *Book of Changes* (*Yijing* or I Ching) is for readers who already have some familiarity with the text but who are seeking another interpretation that will explain the hidden structure of the hexagrams, namely why certain images and phrases appear in each line. No one has previously done this fully because they were missing an important key, which is that the contents of each line reflects the symbolism of all the outer and inner trigrams overlapping the line, and the aggregate influence of all the trigrams impacting a line then becomes represented in the words and images used in the sentences.

Furthermore, you should not look upon the *Yijing* as something supernaturally mysterious because the sixty-four hexagrams are just a set of short commentaries on topics that touch people's lives, but its lines are written in an especially clever way that takes into account five or more special patterns. If you know these patterns then it becomes easier to decipher the *Yijing* and what each topic is about. Very often the lines are just recalling the history of the Shang and Zhou peoples.

This book is for experienced *Yijing* users so we need not go into long explanations on the history and structure of the *Yijing* but can instead focus on the meaning and structure of the hexagrams, which is what most people actually want. They collect versions of the *Yijing* in their libraries so that they can look up the interpretations of the lines within the hexagrams.

The portion of the *Yijing* within this book is properly the *Zhouyi*, but I will always refer to it as the *Yijing* because that's how layman audiences refer to the text. I titled this book as the "I Ching" instead of *Yijing* for the same purpose of easy communication even though I like "*Yijing*" better. I fully understand that not calling this the *Zhouyi* will peeve some academics, scholars and intellectuals but I want to establish a strong rapport with readers to communicate with them as easily as possible and they know this work as the I Ching.

These translations, because they reference the inner structure of the *Yijing* in terms of overlapping outer and inner trigrams, differ from most other *Yijing* translations and interpretations. As just one example, if you were to compare the traditional names ("tags") of several hexagrams against what I consider their meaning you would find a radically different interpretation. As you can see, these meanings greatly differ from the traditional interpretations proposed by many classical translations:

Hexagram 1 – "Heaven" – Rising Yang Energy
Hexagram 9 – "The Small Accumulates" – Problems Grow Between a Husband and Wife
Hexagram 23 – "Stripping Away" – Steps for Destroying a Powerful Person
Hexagram 27 – "Nourishment" – Military Objectives that Lack Sufficient Troop Capabilities
Hexagram 31 – "Attraction" – Sexual Attraction and Its Consummation
Hexagram 33 – "The Piglet" – Raising a Youth into Adulthood
Hexagram 36 – "The Crying Pheasant" – A Brilliant Official Who is Ignored
Hexagram 50 – "The Cauldron" – Changing Your Fate and Fortune
Hexagram 52 – "Keeping Still" – Resisting Sexual Desire
Hexagram 59 – "Dispersal" – Sacrificing Yourself and Your Self-Interests to Help Others During a Dangerous Situation

TWO BASIC HEXAGRAM PATTERNS

Unlike many scholars, I do not consider the lines within *Yijing* hexagrams as a collection of unrelated scraps that are independent of each other. Most hexagrams are like a story where each new line is a progression of the tale. There is actually a method in the madness as to why sentences with certain phrases appear, in the order in which they appear, and why they are worded as they are. A lot – which you will see – has to do with the inner and outer trigrams that intersect each line as well as the meaning of the hexagram and a general pattern from its first to top line.

The *Yijing* is not a set of Confucian moralistic teachings either, but simply a set of sixty-four commentaries on subjects that touch people's lives, and quite a few focus on geopolitical topics such as warfare and running a state. They are the issues that preoccupied the Shang and Zhou people, and in particular the leadership elite who might make use of it. The hexagrams often give sound advice, but they are very special because they are constructed in a very clever formulaic way in order to provide a commentary and guidance.

After decades of study I don't view the *Yijing* as a divination system although you can use it as one. I consider it as a set of commentaries on sixty-four independent topics where the commentary cleverly follows a basic pattern of rules. The sentences within each line cleverly follow a special structural pattern, and the hexagrams are so filled with common sense as to how events sometimes transpire for each topic that people later decided to make use of this set of commentaries for divination purposes. As they lost an understanding of the original meaning of many lines they slowly edited them so as to become lessons for moral guidance.

In other words, in my view the author of the *Yijing* would chose a specific topic for each hexagram due to its structure, perhaps what it even looked like because of its yin and yang lines. Next he would create a progressive story for the lines around that topic and make sure it progress from the bottom to the top line. The author wrote it in a special way in conformity with special patterns so it basically shows his cleverness in creating a dialogue that conforms to these patterns. If you become aware of potential problems cited by the *Yijing* this might help you avoid them but they don't have to happen nor happen in its articulated sequence. The *Yijing* is *not definitive* as to what one should always expect in a situation but simply gives one possible pattern that will would cause you to think about potential options for your actions.

The sentences in each line also reflect whether the line is yin or yang and the order of the line in the overall sequence of six yin or yang lines as well. The meaning of the sentences is impacted by the trigrams that overlap the line, which accounts for why certain phrases or images appear. Combining all of those influences together, the *Yijing's* author provides some pithy advice in line with these basic patterns while also following a progressive story line that encapsulates an overall theme or subject of the lines.

The hexagrams are therefore independent lectures on sixty-four topics where the author wanted to transmit some advice within a sequence of events related to the topic. The cleverness lies in how he follows a basic progressive story pattern that involves a sequence of increasing intensity from the lowest line to the top line, the fact that lines are yin or yang, the fact that each line reflects the symbolism ("influence") of the trigrams within which the lines are embedded, the fact that some lines reflect what is written in the equivalent lines of related hexagrams, and the fact that he offers some sound advice for each situation. It is rather clever to be able to mesh all these patterns together into a coherent story, and to sometimes use analogies that progress the story yet which don't seem related at all.

If one bases their translation on the Mawangdui silk manuscript (probably dating to around 190 BCE) it becomes much more clear that the author of the *Yijing* (*Zhouyi*) wanted to give a short lecture or commentary of insights on various topics. It is like a collection of essays or sermons that transmit the author's wisdom to readers. The sixty-four hexagram "essays" typically appear in two major patterns.

The first typical pattern is like a lecture that gives guidance to us by providing insightful commentary. In this case the author of the *Yijing* would pick a topic or theme for a hexagram based upon its sequence of yin or yang lines. Next, within the lines he would make commentaries on the theme of the hexagram where the bottom and top lines would represent the weakest and most extreme intensity of the theme, respectively. In addition to this gradient of progressive intensity, the sentences within a line would also incorporate whether the line was yin or yang, and would reflect the meaning of the external and internal trigrams that intersect the line within the hexagram.

> Five simple examples include hexagram 37 where the lines counsel us on how a family becomes rich. Hexagram 20 talks about observing and examining (analyzing) your own life and the lives of others to derive life lessons. Hexagram 43 is about the importance of maintaining determination and perseverance to pass through painful troubles, difficulties and obstacles. Hexagrams 41 and 42 provide counsel on the principles or events that lead to decrease or increase in people's lives.

The second typical pattern is a narrative story that starts in the first line of the hexagram (that encapsulates the beginning or earliest stages of something) and ends in the last line. Each successive line of the hexagram builds upon the story line and as before the images within the lines also follow other specific patterns that follow the principles of yin and yang, a gradient of progressive intensity, and the meaning of the external and internal trigrams within the hexagram. In other words, the phrases of the lines are not independent of each other as random scraps and snippets, but tell a linked story that progresses form one point to another.

> Five simple examples of this include hexagram 14, which tells the story of the necessary steps to becoming wealthy. Hexagram 30 speaks of the consecutive stages of human life and is reminiscent of the life phases revealed in the riddle of the Sphinx (where a baby crawls, a man walks on two feet, and old man walks with a cane). Hexagram 19 is about progressively becoming a better manager and then leader. Hexagram 1 is about the progressive increase of yang energy in a person's life, while Hexagram 40 is about progressively achieving liberation (release or dis-entanglement) from vices and flaws in one's personality and behavior.

To make the narrative story pattern clear, let's create a hypothetical hexagram on "warming" to illustrate this principle of a plausible commentary. Line one might be that water is icy cold. Line two might be that the water has warmed to become cool. Line three might be that the water has reached room temperature. Line four might be that water in a stove pot is getting hot whereas line five might be a description of water boiling and a comment that water always changes its state. Line six might be that the water turns into steam and evaporates away leaving nothing behind. In each of these lines the intensity of "warming" increases until we reach the top line of the hexagram, whose meaning can take several forms.

The top line of the hexagram is usually the most extreme (intense) example of the theme. It might summarize the hexagram theme in total while supplying advice for the hexagram as a whole, or offer a pithy commentary on its theme (while leaving the highest intensity of the theme to plateau in line five). However, it is often a destructive version of the theme where the subject matter reaches a peak and starts changing into something else because the hexagram is concluded and ready to transform into another, hence there is destruction. There are a variety of alternative ways in which the contents of the top line may go. Additionally, it is usually written in such a way to summarize the two trigrams that together compose the hexagram and its message.

Hence, each hexagram usually follows the sequence of a story that is laid out in lines one through six, or there is a commentary on the main topic of the hexagram where the intensity of the theme gradually increases from the bottom to the top line of the hexagram. In other words, there is some *gradient reflected through lines one to six that usually reflect the intensity of the theme.* However, the gradient can also be something different such as the length of the human body where the feet or toes are depicted in the first line of the hexagram and each successive line travels up through body parts until we reach the head in line six.

WHY PHRASES WITHIN THE SIX LINES CONTAIN THE CONTENT THEY HAVE

How did the author of the *Yijing* decide which phrases or images went into a specific line? Just as one must write poetry using the format of a certain rhythm structure such as iambic pentameter, there are several structural rules that guide the construction of *Yijing* sentences. Knowing these rules will help future translators create better translations and interpretations of the *Yijing* over time.

FIRST, each line of a hexagram is either yin or yang (broken or solid, a six or nine) in nature. The meaning of the line typically encapsulates the nature of yang or yin, namely good fortune or bad fortune, male or female, movement or non-movement, brightness or darkness, active or inactive, doing or thinking, warm or cold, fire or water, sun or moon, summer or winter and so on.

The meaning of some lines also reflects whether it is followed by several consecutive yin or yang lines, or is wedged in-between two yin or yang lines. Such patterns are often reflected in the lines with phrases such as "for three years" meaning three consecutive yang lines or "amidst" meaning that a line is wedged in between two others.

Another pattern is for the third line of a hexagram to refer to the entire subsequent upper trigram.

SECOND, the six lines of a hexagram usually tell a progressive story where the intensity of the main theme, topic or subject of the hexagram increases step by step throughout the consecutive lines, and that theme has its weakest form in the bottom line. While it may seem that consecutive hexagram lines bear no relationship to one another this is not the case because they typically continue a single story line and you simply cannot see the connection. Furthermore, usually there is (at least) one line within the six that contains specific words that reveal what the story is actually about when the overall meaning isn't too clear. If you reference the Mawangdui manuscript you will also often find that certain sentences were lost over the ages that once recovered would make the story line very clear. In particular, there often seems to be a break in continuity when some strange, unexpected step appears in the main story that seems unrelated to anything else. A superficial reading of the line will not reveal that it really *is* the next step in the story's sequence, but most people cannot see the connection.

THIRD, we also have the extremely important but commonly overlooked fact that the meaning of each line reflects the meaning of the trigram within which it is situated. The middle line of the trigram strongly represents its characteristic nature while the first line usually reveals the most weakened form of its meaning. The third or top line of a trigram is usually weaker than the middle line because it exhibits a tinge of destruction since it represents the termination of the trigram before it must change into another. A very general list on the meaning of the trigrams is as follows:

- **Qian** (Heaven) – great strength, strong action or force, king, creative, yang energy
- **Kun** (Earth) – acquiescence, acceptance, desire, attraction, massing, assembling, unification, corpses, burial, nurturing, docility, yielding, expansiveness, inner strength, royalty, yin energy, building, cities, walls, masses, assembly of people, royalty
- **Kan** (Water) – abyss, pit, water, danger, trouble, difficulties, downward, thieves
- **Li** (Fire) – brilliance, elegance, celebration, showing off, sun, shining, light, clarity, mind, intelligence, friendship, interrelationships, military fighting, destruction, robbers
- **Zhen** (Thunder) – motion or movement, agitation, shock, lightning, earthquake, destruction, action, pushing upwards, rushing forward, young men, initiative
- **Gen** (Mountain) – stopping or stopped, keeping still, restraint, non-movement, meditation, obstruction, accumulation, agglomeration, wealth, majestic or majesty
- **Xun** (Wind, Wood) – wind, wood, trees, vegetation, penetrating force, movement, destructive energy, dispersal, growing, entering or coming into, pliancy, merchants, kneeling
- **Dui** (Joy) – lake, marsh, water, mouth, head, drinking, talking, discussions, gossip, happiness, eloquence, pleasure or pleasing, confidence, young girl, breaking free, standing straight

<u>FOURTH</u>, the lines have a general positional meaning as follows:

- The **first line** or bottom line naturally reflects the meaning, flavor or influence of its trigram and usually has to do with beginning of some story or the earliest stage of a situation. It is typically the *lowest intensity* of some activity, topic or theme. It always signifies the very beginning of whatever story line, theme, or process the hexagram represents.
- The **second line** of the hexagram is in the middle of the bottom trigram so it sometimes represents being in the *middle or midst* of something. As the central line of the trigram it often represents the strongest possible flavor of the lower trigram's meaning but is altered by the one other inner trigram that overlaps it.

- The **third line** is the top line of the lower trigram that is the demarcation point between the lower and upper trigrams so it is usually dangerous or a stage of deterioration in some way. It often has this tinge of destruction to reflect the difficult crossing to the upper trigram that is coming where the bottom trigram loses its influence. Because there is a change of state coming the third line of the bottom trigram is typically harmful because it starts degrading. The third line *is also impacted by three overlapping trigrams* and their influences always appear within its sentences.
- The **fourth line** often shows a successful resolution of the difficulties seen in the third line, or a successful achievement of the hexagram's overall theme, because the fourth line has entered into the upper trigram that represents a change of state from the lower trigram. However, this successful accomplishment is not as perfect as in line five. The fourth line is also impacted by a total of three overlapping trigrams.
- The **fifth line** is in the middle of the upper trigram and is also the hexagram's ruling line. As the ruling line or "lord of the hexagram" the fifth line is most often auspicious, expresses the main message of the hexagram, and typically incorporates images of individuals of *high status* such as a cultivated individual or royalty. As the central line of the upper trigram it strongly expresses the major topic, theme, message or characteristic of the hexagram in general. To get a sense of the meaning of a hexagram you should immediately go to the fifth line because it usually presents a perfected form of the hexagram's main theme, and then you should look at the first and top lines since they represent the beginning and finale of the story, topic, situation or gradient. The fifth line is subject to the influence of the upper trigram and just one inner trigram.
- The **sixth line** or top line usually completes the story line of a hexagram, or portrays the most extreme intensity of the theme of the hexagram. It often symbolizes going too far. As the last line of the hexagram it sometimes indicates the end of its general theme (situation) and the beginning of another situation entirely, such as when yin turns to yang and yang to yin, so there is often a tinge of destruction to the line. Lastly, there is an aspect to the top line that most people miss: it *often* summarizes the meaning of the two compositional trigrams of the hexagram stacked on top of one another. In

other words, its sentences usually reflect the meaning of the hexagram's upper and lower trigrams, but not always.

FIFTH, the meaning of each line is usually influenced by the outer and inner trigrams that bound it. This is a fact that nearly everyone has missed when translating or interpreting the *Yijing*. For instance, line one is only influenced by the lower trigram since it is only impacted by the lower trigram. However, the second line is the middle line of the lower trigram and is also the bottom line of an inner trigram formed by lines 2-4. This hidden inner trigram has a weaker, secondary influence on the line but that influence often shows up in the image portrayed by the line. Hence, the line is impacted by the influence of two trigrams.

As to line three, it is the top line of the lower trigram, middle line of an inner trigram composed of lines 2-4, and bottom line of an inner trigram composed of lines 3-5. Here the inner trigram where it is a middle line will often have a very strong influence on the sentences or images of the line. The fourth line is the bottom line of the upper trigram, middle line of an inner trigram formed by lines 3-5 and top line of an inner trigram composed of lines 2-4. The fifth line is the middle line of the upper trigram and top line of an inner trigram formed by lines 3-5. The sixth line is simply the top line of the upper trigram and of the hexagram. Each line of the hexagram will be impacted by all the trigrams that overlap it.

The bottom and top lines of the hexagram should always be compared to one another as the bottom line often indicates the beginning of a situation and the top line its conclusion, or it makes a commentary on the situation as a whole. The bottom line is usually a lowest intensity situation while the top line is often a highest intensity situation. If one glances at the fifth line of the hexagram they will often see an ideal attainment or perfected actualization of the hexagram's main message.

Because the central lines of a hexagram have two or three trigrams throwing their influence on their contents, those two or three trigrams will "fight" one another in determining the final content of a line with the middle line of any trigram projecting a particularly strong influence and a top trigram line tending to be destructive.

Naturally, each line also has a meaning dependent on its progressive 1-2-3-4-5-6 gradient sequence within the hexagram such as the first line representing the beginning of a situation or lowest intensity of an activity while the fifth line represents a perfected form of the hexagram's meaning and the top line represents going too far.

There is also the possibility that the opposite hexagram (produced by making the yin and lines of a hexagram their opposite), reverse hexagram (produced by inverting the top and bottom trigrams of a hexagram and then transposing them), paired hexagram (where you flip over a hexagram), and future hexagram for a line are related to its meaning, but I have not studied this extensively. Some hexagrams seem to come in pairs (such as hexagrams 11 and 12) where their opposite hexagram is also their reverse hexagram, and in those cases the meaning of the lines is often related but not often enough for this to be a reliable principle to depend upon.

A SAMPLE HEXAGRAM INTERPRETATION

To understand how this all works together, let's examine the six lines of Hexagram 12 - "Overthrowing an Obstruction." From this example we can see how the content of each line incorporates these various influences. Here is the translation of the lines:

1. Pull up cogon grass and with it come the roots. Continuing onwards as you are doing is auspicious. Success.

2. Wrapped up by (bearing and enduring) what you have received (the circumstances that have happened to you). For an inferior man (to remain this way is) auspicious, for a great man not. Success.

3. Wrapped savory (sauced, spiced) meat offering.

4. An order (command) comes. No trouble. Blessings are attached to dividing up (splitting apart) a field.

5. Success against the obstruction (the standstill gives way). For the great man auspicious. What if it should fail, what if it should fail? Tie it to a bushy mulberry tree.

6. Overturning an obstruction (blockage). At first a blockage, afterwards rejoicing (happiness).

The hexagram is about trying to advance but having to deal with a blockage or obstruction, and the *Yijing's* general advice, which you might give to ordinary people on the topic, is to continue moving against obstructions to overthrow them otherwise you will come to a standstill. A superior man would not settle for a standstill but would push through the barriers inhibiting the attainment of his goals. This is the type of advice that the *Yijing* provides to readers.

In the first line you find an example of the mildest case of obstruction possible (pulling up a clump of weeds that gives you a tiny bit of resistance) while in the top line appears the greatest degree of difficulty involving a very great obstruction. Hence there is a gradient of intensity, weak to strong or low to high, in the lines about encountering obstructions in life and there is wise advice for how to deal with them.

The first line is the bottom line within the six-lined hexagram gradient and the bottom line of the Kun Earth trigram. As the bottom line of the hexagram we will see a very low level of obstruction. The Kun trigram represents the dense earth element and the roots of the cogon grass so it is throwing off the influence of obstruction that appears in the line. It is not that the cogon grass or earth element means that the Kun trigram is involved in the lines. It is that the Kun trigram is in the hexagram at this location and the influence due to its presence comes through as cogon grass and obstruction. The grass represents the Kun trigram.

The second line is the middle (second) line of the Kun Earth trigram and bottom line of an inner (hidden) Gen Keeping Still trigram that spans line 2 to 5. Therefore the image within this line should represent the influence of these two trigrams – a Kun trigram and Gen trigram. As the second and strongest (most representative) line of the lower trigram it should show a very strong influence of the meaning of the trigram. Because this hexagram is about "Overthrowing an Obstruction," the second line should also show an increase in the intensity of obstruction over the first line. Since this second line is the *middle line* of the Kun trigram it is in the middle or midst of something, which is why the individual is "wrapped up." It is also "wrapped up" since it is bound within two yin lines – one above and one below it. The Kun earth trigram also stands for pulling things together, massing them together in an assemblage, agglomerating them etc. so this is another reason that the sentences include "wrapped up," which is certainly an assemblage as well as obstruction. Furthermore, the Gen Mountain trigram projects the influence of Keeping Still, which is why a small man stays inactive (wrapped up) in this line (thus being obstructed) while a great man does not accept any restraints or settle for restrictions but pushes forward. The line provides wise counsel that individuals should not passively accept restrictive situations but should work through them.

The third line of the hexagram is at the top of the lower Kun Earth trigram. It is also the middle line of an inner Gen Keeping Still trigram and bottom line of an inner Xun Penetrating Wind trigram. These three trigrams – Kun, Gen, Xun – should therefore be reflected in the line since they all impact it. Thus the author of the *Yijing* constructed the sentence, **"Wrapped savory (sauced, spiced) meat offering,"** to take into account the influence of all three overlapping trigrams. The Kun Earth trigram represents the sauced meat, the fact that it is wrapped to prevent leaking shows the influence of the Gen Keeping Still trigram that represents accumulation or non-movement along with the Kun trigram once again (since it represents pulling things together), and the fact that there is sauce that might leak shows the presence or influence of the Xun Penetrating Wind trigram since this trigram often produces scattering and leakage. The sentence is therefore perfectly in tune with all three trigrams. A line will always show the influence of at least two of the three trigrams that surround it, but usually all three.

This is the secret structure of the sentences that most translators miss but after they recognize these principles it will become easier for translators to produce better *Yijing* translations going into the future. My own translation is by no means definitive because I put it together in a rather hasty fashion and am constantly finding new points and better ways of saying things when I edit it now and then. I am not aiming for perfection but simply blazing a trail to get it out as quickly as possible to show you the way.

The fourth line of the hexagram is an example of the *Yijing* author's brilliance. Overall this hexagram is about overthrowing obstructions that "wrap you up" and restrict you. In the lower trigram blockages were encountered but now we are at the first line of the new upper Qian Great Strength (Heaven) trigram, which has strength enough to overthrow or pierce through those blockages and obstructions. In terms of intensity, we have been encountering and working against increasingly difficult obstructions but now, within the upper trigram of Great Strength, we have the power to start obliterating them that is in part due to the history of past efforts in the lower trigram.

This fourth line is also the middle line of an inner Xun Penetrating Wind trigram and top line of an inner Gen Keeping Still trigram so Qian, Xun and Gen should all show an influence in the line. The line reads: **"An order (command) comes. No trouble. Blessings are attached to dividing up (splitting apart) a field."** An order is a command that comes that must be followed, which is a manifestation of the Qian Great Strength trigram. It reflects the fact that we have transitioned into a new trigram, which is the upper Qian trigram rather than the lower Kun trigram. The command involves cutting up a field, essentially dividing it into parts. This represents a combination of the influence of the Qian Great Strength trigram and Xun Penetrating Wind trigram that together cut through an obstruction, which is represented by the field. The field itself represents the presence of the Gen Mountain trigram, the blessings attached to this act are the majesty of the Gen trigram in its Mountain aspect, and this order/command only comes now because this is a new trigram. In any case, the influences of the three trigrams have once again perfectly cooperated to create the images in the line, and you will find this to be the case with almost all the lines of the *Yijing*. Most *Yijing* scholars and translators have missed this secret structure behind the construction of its lines, but this understanding would help with their translations. As previously stated, the fourth line of a hexagram often shows a degree of success in actualizing its main theme, which is overthrowing an obstruction, but a more perfected form of success is to be expected in the fifth line since the fifth line is the ruling line of the hexagram, also known as the lord of the hexagram.

The fifth line runs, **"Success against the obstruction (the standstill gives way). For the great man auspicious. What if it should fail, what if it should fail? Tie it to a bushy mulberry tree."** This line is the ruler of the hexagram so it should reveal a perfected form of the message of the hexagram, which is a great success against obliterating the obstructions and then moving forward with progress. It should also show the influence of the two trigrams that bound the line – the upper Qian Great Strength trigram and the fact it is the top line of an inner Xun Penetrating Wind trigram. The top line of a trigram, and especially the top line of the destructive Wind trigram, will usually manifest as some type of destruction or deterioration. Due to the Qian Great Strength trigram in line four the obstruction is overthrown, but here there is a worry about whether the success will last due to the negative, destructive influence of the inner Xun trigram that wants to blow it away, which is what the wind element does.

Most translators fail to take into consideration the inner hidden trigrams when trying to make sense out of the sentences in this line. They cannot fathom why the *Yijing* uses the images it does because they are missing these explanations. How do you counteract the destructive influence of the inner Xun trigram that should provoke worries since the Wind trigram is definitely going to throw a destructive influence on the situation? The *Yijing* even acknowledges this potential with the words, "What if it should fail? What if it should fail?" If you tie the success of overthrowing the obstacle to an alternative positive aspect of the Xun Wind trigram then you have one possible solution. The Wind element *is also the Wood element in Chinese culture* (the Xun trigram stands for the wind or wood element interchangeably), and hence we have the image of tying one's efforts or success to a bushy, *thriving mulberry tree* that is strong and hardy and grows easily. It represents a strong, positive Wood element! Once again the images within the line reflect the meaning of the trigrams that bound it, thus exerting an influence on those sentences.

The author of the *Yijing* must have had a fun time trying to create sentences, images or meanings for each line that reflected all the trigrams impacting the line as well as all the other relevant factors such as the story and its increasing intensity from top to bottom, yin and yang influences, and so forth. That is why it is so clever. Many lines even reference lines equivalently positioned in related hexagrams. He chose a topic for a hexagram and created a commentary in the lines to transmit to us some wisdom, and it comes to us in a very witty structure. It is not that his sequence of events has to occur. He simply created a story to fit in with the secret pattern I'm revealing.

Yet another possibility is to examine the meanings for the same lines that fortune tellers would use in the future hexagram (where the moving line is changed into its opposite), opposite hexagram (where yin and yang lines are reversed from this one) and reverse hexagrams (where the top and bottom trigrams of this hexagram are flipped and their positions transposed). At times I have used the indications of these lines to help determine an appropriate translation since I believe that the author wrote everything in an interdependent fashion so as to be as clever as possible. I have left it to future translators to extensively explore these correspondences to determine if there is any relationship and to improve the translations significantly if they can do so. As stated, during the COVID pandemic I just tried to produce and output this translation as quickly as possible.

In the sixth line of the hexagram we simply have some wise counsel about working to overthrow an obstruction – since that is the basic topic of the hexagram – and a reminder on what typically happens after success, namely some joy or celebration: **"Overturning an obstruction (blockage). At first a blockage, afterwards rejoicing (happiness)."** A summarizing and sometimes advice-laden comment like this often appears in the top line of the hexagram to encapsulate its total message. Since this sixth line is within a strong Qian Great Strength trigram, and since the top line of a trigram tends to be destructive, there is enough destructive power in the situation to "overturn an obstruction" for success.

As to the overall construction of the hexagram this also often appears reflected in the sentences of the top line, which again most translators have also missed. The hexagram is composed of two trigrams stacked upon one another so according to this pattern they should both be reflected in the words and images within the hexagram's top line. While translators have typically missed this pattern you can readily verify it for yourself. For instance, this hexagram is composed of a Qian trigram on top of a Kun trigram so we should see the meaning of these two trigrams in the sentences used for the top line. In this case we have the lower Kun Earth trigram representing blockage or obstruction and its overthrow by a great force represented by the upper Qian trigram. Thus we have "Overturning an obstruction (blockage)." Since the Qian Heaven trigram also represents success or joy at times due to being pure yang Qi, we also have the subsequent phrase, "At first a blockage (Kun trigram), afterwards rejoicing (Qian trigram)."

From this example of Hexagram 12 you can see how the sentences and images within each line of the hexagram reflects the influence of various trigrams, the gradient positions of the lines and the other factors already mentioned.

As to the line manifesting its good/bad fortune yin or yang nature due to whether it is a broken or solid (yin or yang, six or nine) line, this hexagram weakly follows this general rule while some hexagrams follow this rule extremely strongly. In this case, the sentences within the fourth through sixth lines reflect the yang nature of the line correctly. The third line's image of "being wrapped up" correctly reflects the yin nature of the line since that means inactivity, which is yin in nature. However, the second line contains both yin and yang elements in its imagery so it is hard to say that it accurately reflects the yin nature of the line, although one could argue that it does. It does reflect the phrase being "wrapped up" due to it being surrounded by two other yin lines. In the first line we find success, which is a yang quality whereas the line is yin because it is a broken line, and hence it does *not* reflect the yin-yang nature of the line correctly unless one were to argue that pulling up the grass and leaving an empty hole is yin in nature and thus characterizes the line.

THE INTERPRETATION

I believe that these structural principles you've just seen are a revolutionary revelation and can help your understanding of the *Yijing* grow significantly, *especially when you start spotting the influence of the inner trigrams upon the contents of the lines*. After studying this example, and then seeing the inner structure within several other hexagrams, in the future many students will discover for themselves the hidden order within its structure, and that understanding will help subsequent translators produce even better versions of this text.

The *Yijing* is actually a book you should be reading cover to cover rather than just looking up a topic. You should be reading the book rather than using passages for divination. It is a little like a public relations campaign for the Zhou dynasty because it keeps pounding away at a consistent theme along the lines of "Shang was bad, Zhou is good; Shang was evil, Zhou is virtuous."

As to my own interpretation of the *Yijing*, I have strived to prepare this text according to the principles I have laid out, and would certainly improve these interpretations given more time. However, recognizing my mortality during the pandemic I developed a strong determination to just get this book out as quickly as possible due to its unique and sometimes revolutionary contents in order to guarantee that they are not lost to the public.

For each hexagram there is a translation of the lines *as well as a more colloquial interpretation* in the explanatory section. Purists may criticize the offering of multiple translations for each line instead of one scholarly best choice, but your brain creates multiple meanings anyway so alternative translations for each line will help you train your brain to see a broader interpretation. I certainly don't consider my own efforts definitive because I improve upon translations all the time and sometime seven reverse myself. Such is the *Yijing*. Nevertheless this is the best I can offer at this time.

HEXAGRAM 1

Qian – Heaven, Yang Energy, Great Strength, Life Force, Great Force

Lower Trigram: Qian (Heaven) – great strength, dragon, sage, yang
Upper Trigram: Qian (Heaven) – great strength, dragon, sage, yang

The Judgment: Yang Energy. Supremely blessed. It is beneficial to keep on.

This hexagram, being composed of two Qian trigrams, is one of the eight doubled trigram hexagrams. It is about the force of yang energy and a tells what happens when yang Qi increases in an individual. At first your yang energy is submerged and does not stir. Next, your vitality starts arising and needs to be channeled correctly so you are advised to visit a wise man for guidance so you don't lose it. As its growth and development progresses the immature yang energy often wavers because it is still subject to the influence of yin energy. Eventually it grows in strength and purity so that it can triumph over any yin influences. The fifth line illustrates the perfection of yang energy in an individual where he can now reveal his full power and glory like a dragon soaring in the sky. Because yang turns into yin and yin into yang, the top line of the hexagram warns about the excess of yang that often symbolizes power, wealth, status and good fortune. The warning is not to become arrogant at the height of power, glory, riches or other yang phenomena otherwise pride, haughtiness or hubris will end in regret since an extreme of yang always turns to yin. What is the Judgment of the hexagram? When your yang energy grows it is extremely beneficial so keep cultivating it.

1. A dragon is submerged underwater. It does not act.

2. The dragon appears in the field. It is beneficial to meet with a great [wise] man.

3. The superior man is (creatively active and) vigorous all day long. In the evening he is apprehensive (cautious). There is danger but no

trouble.

4. The dragon is now jumping over the depths. There is no trouble.

5. The dragon is flying in the sky. It is beneficial to meet with a great man.

6. A haughty (arrogant) dragon. There will be regret.

All Lines Are Yang: Behold a flock of dragons without heads. Auspicious.

1.1: Yang at the first line at the bottom of the Qian Heaven trigram of great strength or power. **"The dragon is submerged [a hidden dragon]. It does not act."** The dragon is under water and while lying low *does not stir* (act). A dragon hidden underwater means that your yang energy does not yet arise and show itself. Therefore the next sentence is "It takes no action" or "It does not act" rather than "Take no action." This reflects the fact that the hidden dragon underwater – which is at the bottom line of the Qian Great Force trigram – does not stir since it is at a passive immature state. Perhaps this refers to the perineum of the human body, which is the *hai-di* (bottom of the ocean) where the Monkey King Sun Wukong obtained his golden staff that represents the use of his yang Qi. Your yang energy does not yet move because this is the first line of the hexagram that represents the lowest intensity of a gradient of growing yang force where the initial level is at its minimum represented by stillness.

1.2: Yang at the second line within the Qian Heaven trigram, and the bottom line of an inner Qian trigram as well, so the yang energy begins to arise. It begins to stir and is strong in this line. Thus a dragon, which represents yang energy, makes an appearance in a field because it is no longer submerged underneath water. It has risen from the bottom of the pelvis to a higher region such as loins or belly. **"The dragon appears in the field. It is beneficial [advantageous] to go to meet with a great wise man."** In this line a dragon represents the Qian trigram and so does the field (the three yang lines of the trigram) and a sage as well. Because the yang energy starts moving you should see an experienced wise man (sage) who can advise you on how to channel the arising power.

1.3: Yang at the third line of the hexagram, top line of the Qian Heaven trigram, the bottom line of an inner Qian trigram, and as the middle line of an inner Qian trigram. The yang energy is now active but subject to wavering because it reflects three different line positions. Hence it isn't stable because it is immature. Hence the sentences: **"All day long the**

gentleman is vigorously active [initiating]. At night he is apprehensive. There is danger but no trouble." The top line of the Qian trigram represents "night" in this line because the top line of a trigram means there is about to be a transition into a new trigram, and thus yang has the potential to change into yin. Thus the yang energy is full during the day (a time of yang) but there is the danger of loss at night since it is a time of yin. There are some commonalities here with the Chinese idea of cultivating your yang Qi and then carelessly losing it through sexual relations in the evening through self-gratification because the internal pressure is building and is so strong. Hence the line is translated as "At night he is apprehensive (of leakage). There is danger but no trouble" instead of "At night he is apprehensive as if there is danger, but there is no trouble." The meaning of these lines is that the yang energy is still ascending but subject to the potential of loss (through sexual activities if the man is not careful), which is due to conflicting positions within the Qian trigram and the fact that the top line of a trigram tends to be destructive (yin). If a man engages in sex during the evening he must be careful and stay alert (careful) so as not to lose his yang Qi through ejaculation, or he can just avoid sex entirely and prevent the problem by practicing celibacy so that his yang Qi keeps growing. In any case, this is an increase in the intensity of yang energy over the previous lines since in the first line it was hidden, in the second it finally starting appearing like a plant shoot, and now it is growing but is not yet fully mature.

1.4: Yang at the fourth line, and at the first line of the upper Qian Heaven trigram that shows a further development in the yang force. This is also the middle line position of an inner Qian trigram and top line of an inner Qian trigram too so three Qian trigrams overlap the line. **"The dragon leaps over the depths [waves]. There is no trouble."** Now the heavenly yang force has grown past its prior stage of immaturity tinged with yin energy, which is here symbolized by "depths of water" that represents the lower trigram. You might say this represents a disciplined triumph over sexual relations too. In the previous line the yang energy was wavering in an environment of yin symbolized by the night-time, which might even symbolize the sexual enticements of women, but at this higher stage of development it has no problem dealing with even stronger yin energies symbolized by water and waves, and hence can jump over or transcend them. This line can symbolize a refusal of sexual activities.

1.5: Yang at the fifth line, which is the lord of the hexagram, and in the middle of the Qian trigram and top line of an inner Qian trigram. **"The dragon flies in the sky [heavens]. It is beneficial [advantageous] to see a great [wise] man."** The fifth line is lord of the hexagram and shows a perfected form of its message, which in this case is a dragon flying in the sky and demonstrating its full yang powers. We're seeing an image of flying because the fifth yang line is strong in the middle of the Qian trigram and "flies" at the top of an inner Qian trigram. Thus the yang force finally is strong and resplendent; the yang energy has become fully mature so the dragon fully displays its power by soaring in the sky. Taoists would say that the man's yang Qi has permeated his body and ascended to his head. When your development is at this stage of yang fortune – at the heights of power, money, energy etcetera – you should seek the guidance of an experienced wise man (sage) in order that you do not go astray due to that great power. A sage or wise man represents mastery of internal yang energy and can guide you through the temptations of enjoying the fullness of yang Qi so that you don't succumb to errors.

1.6: Yang at the top line of the hexagram and of the upper Qian trigram. The top line will usually represent the most extreme degree of intensity of the principle of the hexagram. It could also contain some observation about the principal theme of the hexagram or a summarizing commentary on the meaning of the hexagram (in this case a lesson on yang energy), and it will usually be worded in such a way that reflects the hexagram's structure of two trigrams stacked upon one another. **"An arrogant (haughty) dragon will have regret."** In this sixth top line of the hexagram the yang energy has reached its peak. At this *highest extreme of yang energy* the dragon becomes arrogant and since the extreme of yang transforms into yin the great yang energy is about to turn to yin due to mistakes brought on by this arrogance and hubris. Yang will be lost, yin will arise (which is the next hexagram), and thus there will soon be regret. In general, the message of the hexagram is to cultivate yang energy, but since the extreme of yang becomes yin at its peak and the extreme of yin becomes yang, one should not let arrogance arise when you reach your peak otherwise the extreme of yang will turn to yin. Moderation and humility, since they avoid arrogance and hubris, are the recipe for dealing with the great power of yang energy at its peak.

As to the composition of the hexagram, the two Qian trigrams stacked upon one another naturally represent/produce power, an extreme of yang energy, as well as arrogance due to there being too much yang. Since the extreme of yang will transform into yin there will soon be regret because an eventual loss of yang energy and a turn of affairs is fated.

All Lines Are Yang: **"Behold a flock [company] of dragons without heads. Good fortune."** When all your yang energy has reached a state of excellence and its individual circulations within your body function together as a single unit, this is when the six dragons are not being guided by heads. It refers to a stage of emptiness attainment (empty mind) conjoined with body cultivation within the pathway of spiritual cultivation. When there is neither a set of minds or a single chief mind guiding the body's yang energy (because you have reached "a state of mental emptiness or no-thought") this refers to the highest state of physical good fortune and spiritual development because it means that all the yang energy inside your body circulates harmoniously. This is a state of high spiritual achievement.

HEXAGRAM 2

Kun - Earth, Yin Energy, Submissive Service

Lower Trigram: Kun (Earth) – ice, yellow, hidden, service, public, stillness
Upper Trigram: Kun (Earth) – ice, yellow, hidden, service, public, stillness

The Judgment: Yin Energy. It is beneficial to be constant like a mare. If a superior person takes the initiative he will go astray, but if he follows he will find guidance. Beneficial friends will be found in the south and west and friends lost in the north and east. Cultivating serene perseverance is auspicious.

This hexagram is the second of the eight doubled trigram hexagrams. It is composed of two Kun Earth trigrams. The earth element is considered an agglomeration of all five elements (earth, wind, fire, water and space/metal), thus it accepts them all into its fold as a single mass, unity or assemblage. However, the hexagram is about a progressive increase in yin energy by stages, and the yin energy is represented as a manifestation of human virtues such as the loyalty of a mare. In the bottom line the first signs of yin energy appear (at the lowest gradient level of intensity) so we know that more is coming. In the second line it manifests as positive human virtues. A greater yin situation is when you must humbly hide your talents while obediently serving another in a submissive role. A further increase in yin energy is to be so wrapped up in restraints (or stillness) that none of your virtuous qualities can show. In the fifth line, a perfect model of resplendent yin is demonstrated in the example of a minister who attains a high government position due to his service, and who represents the yin quality of selflessness. In the last line is the warning that the extreme of yin at its peak transforms into yang just as we saw in hexagram 1 where the peak of yang transformed into yin. This is why we see the yellow blood of a dragon develop a tinge of blue since this color symbolizes yang energy. The Judgment of the hexagram espouses that the nature of pure yin energy is to follow and serve rather than lead. Leading is the function of yang energy that takes the initiative. Hence this entire hexagram is about offering humble service to get ahead.

1. Treading on frost (means) hard ice will arrive.

2. Straight, square, great, and unique. There is nothing not beneficial.

3. Hiding (concealing) your abilities. Continue on this way. If you work in the king's service then claim no (credit for your) accomplishments but indeed complete them.

4. A tied-up sack. No trouble, no praise.

5. Yellow skirts. Supreme good fortune.

6. The dragon fights in the wild (wilderness). Its blood is yellow and black.

All Lines Are Yin: Beneficial to be persevering for the long-term.

2.1: Yin at the bottom line, which is at the bottom of the Kun Earth trigram. The Kun trigram represents the earth element, yin energy, agglomeration and acquiescence (passive acceptance of a situation) as well as receptivity. The first line: **"Frost underfoot means solid ice is coming."** This warning of coming ice (ice is solid water, hence it represents the Kun Earth-Solidity trigram that is all yin lines) offers the practical advice to be on the lookout for the signs of things going wrong (yin conditions) so that you can stop them and prevent problems from arising, or simply prepare for problems you know are coming because the initial signs of their arrival have already appeared. More importantly, this is the first yin line of six consecutive yin lines where each new line will symbolize a greater magnitude of yin energy. Hence, just as frost signifies that winter ice and snow will soon arrive, in this case the first yin line means more severe manifestations of yin energy (of progressively greater consecutive intensity) will appear in the subsequent lines. The bottom line of many hexagrams is often associated with human feet since they are the lowest part of the body (its "start"), and thus the feet can be used to represent the lowest magnitude of a gradient that embodies a rising intensity of characteristics.

2.2: Yin at the second line in the middle of the Kun Earth trigram, and as the bottom line in an inner Kun trigram. Being in the middle of the Kun Earth trigram it represents the fullness of earth element qualities that manifest as human virtues. In terms of surveying land the translation would be **"Straight, square, great, and unique"** which means that the three pure yin lines of this lower trigram are special, unique. This land analogy ties into the fact that opposite hexagram line 1.2 is about a dragon appearing in a field. In terms of people it would be, **"He is straightforward, foursquare, great, and unique. There is nothing not beneficial."** As the middle line within the wholly yin Kun trigram, this line about the resplendent qualities of land actually stands for human virtues and behavior whereas the first hexagram was about the physical body's energy. The earth element is traditionally symbolized as a square that represents being solid and grounded. Being straight in terms of human virtues means being honest, straightforward, and dependable just as the earth element is solid and dependable. Being great does not just stand for extraordinary excellence or abundance but also means tolerance because you are capable of accommodating everything, which is also a characteristic of the earth element. *An individual who is straight, square and great* is good enough to work for the king. The oldest *Yijing* or *Zhouyi* manuscript – the Mawangdui text – has the words "not repeated" after "straight, square and great" to denote that he is extraordinary and *unique*, which is why he can work for the king in line three. Basically, "Straightforward, foursquare and great" or "Straight, square and great" are character traits although some may say *these are characteristics of land that one is surveying because this is a doubled Kun Earth trigram*. The land might refer to a great plain but the characteristics apply to an individual too. The activities of such an individual will be in line with the principles of virtue and excellence and never not beneficial. Thus we have good fortune ("There is nothing not beneficial") for this yin line of resplendent virtues because anyone with such traits will create good fortune.

2.3: Yin at the third line at the top of the Kun Earth trigram, and at the bottom of an inner Kun trigram and middle line of an inner Kun trigram. Hence the line falls under the influence of three Kun trigram lines so the yin image should be strong. **"Hide [conceal] your abilities [talents, strategies, excellence]. Continue acting this way if you have a chance to serve the king. (With humbleness) Claim no credit for your accomplishments, but indeed complete your tasks."** The way the *Yijing* is constructed necessitates that this line must represent an increase in the magnitude of yin energy over the previous line of virtues and this means *hiding* your yang qualities. The Kun trigram virtues of selfless service to a group (assembly) include receptivity, submissiveness, humility, and self-effacement where you make yourself seem insignificant but still accomplish all that you must but without demanding recognition. This is the nature of yin, which does not promote itself due to its quality of passivity, receptivity and humility. Thus we have excellent abilities that are classified as yin because they represent selflessness, and self-effacing loyal service where modesty conceals one's contributions so that credit can be claimed by others.

2.4: Yin at the fourth line, at the beginning of the upper Kun Earth trigram. It is also the top line and middle line of an inner Kun trigram. Since we are now in the second Kun trigram we should see an even greater intensity or magnitude of yin qualities. **"A tied-up sack. No blame, no praise."** Line 1.4 has a dragon leaping over the depths so this line should be its opposite. It features an image where no yang activity can possibly show itself - a tied-up sack - that is a state of true yin stillness. This represents the yin qualities of passivity, stillness, submissiveness, silence, being reserved and being reticent. It also represents keeping your own counsel (keeping to oneself) and hiding your outstanding qualities as in line three so as not to provoke jealousy or envious attacks by others. Thus, no one can praise you because by remaining quiet and avoiding attention you also avoid attacks, blame and troubles. This is a further progression in yin that manifests as stillness or becoming hidden.

2.5: Yin is at the fifth line, which is the ruler of the hexagram, so we should see good fortune, a perfected message of the hexagram, and sometimes an individual of supreme rank. This is at the middle of the upper Kun Earth trigram (and top line of an inner Kun trigram) so we should see a resplendent example of the qualities of the Kun Earth trigram. **"Imperial yellow skirts (lower garments) are being worn. Supreme good fortune."** Yellow is the symbol of the earth element (Kun trigram) that represents moderation, humility, humbleness, sincerity, genuineness, loyalty and reverence. Skirts worn below the waist symbolize reserve and discretion and were worn during some rituals that involved reverence. Yellow is also the color of the robes worn by the nobility so at this line of doubled Kun we see the yellow color of the nobility. It means a promotion to becoming a high official due to service. The chief minister, who reaches his position because of his service to the king and country, also wore yellow skirts (imperial undergarments) and is at the right place in this fifth line since it usually involves a person of high status. In line 1.5 we have a dragon soaring because of its own brilliance but here we have the yin equivalent of a minister who is great because of selfless service. All of these examples represent the highest degree of perfected yin or selfless service on behalf of the country or public (Kun trigram). Hence, because of these virtues we see "Great good fortune." Some translators prefer "Yellow dragon" to "yellow skirts" in this line where the chief minister would qualify as a yellow dragon or the yellow dragon would symbolize the most powerful manifestation of yin force, however since the previous lines are about offering service the idea of an official (someone who wears yellow skirts) better fits the ongoing sequence.

2.6: Yin at the top line, at the top of the Kun trigram, and in this case it represents a sixth degree of magnitude in the progressive development of yin energy. **"The dragon fights [battles] in the wild. Its blood is yellow and black [dark blue]."** The sixth line is at the top of the hexagram, and so here a yellow dragon appears symbolizing the effulgence of yin energy. It starts fighting in the wilderness, which is the field of all six yin lines, and it sheds blood, which means it becomes wounded as a consequence of being too active and showy (since these go against its yin nature). What color is the blood? It is yellow, which is the color of yin, and also blue (or black or purple) to denote the beginning of yang. In Chinese culture the color blue is yang since it symbolizes the east where the sun and yang energy rises whereas black is often a northern color but can also represent yang or destruction. The message is that when yin reaches its zenith – represented by the top line of the hexagram – yang is sure to appear. In this case a yin dragon fights, spilling blood, showing that the pure yin of six lines is struggling to prevent a change of state but that change to yang is inevitable. That is why the blood shows a mixture of yin and yang colors, which means that the extreme of yin is already transforming into yang. I have switched the traditional translation of "black and yellow" to "yellow and black" with black at the end to denote the fact that there is destruction because yang is coming. The sentence simply reflects the fact that at the extreme of yang there arises yin and at the extreme of yin arises yang.

As to the composition of the hexagram, the two Kun trigrams stacked upon one another naturally represent strong yin energy that is represented throughout the hexagram as virtues such as selflessness and service. At this top line there are two dragons battling in the wilderness (the two Kun trigrams), and the yellow blood becomes dark because yin has reached its extreme of fullness and a new hexagram is therefore due to appear.

All Lines Are Yin: **"Beneficial to be persevering for the long-term."** The qualities of the earth element include perseverance because the earth endures and accepts everything despite whatever happens to it. This is a virtuous character trait for self-preservation. When a man encounters yin conditions everywhere (all six lines), which also means troubles and problems in practical life, he must accept everything but also undertake adjusting actions for self-preservation so that he can endure until the situation improves. Hence, the best yin traits to recommend during trouble are resilience and perseverance; you must persevere through yin conditions with persistence in the pursuit of long-term goals. You continue surviving through extreme yin conditions by adapting to situations with resilience while maintaining your perseverance.

HEXAGRAM 3

Zhun – Difficult Beginnings, Initial Obstacles, Progress Impeded in Gathering Together

Lower Trigram: Zhen (Thunder) – motion, agitation, shock, hunting
Upper Trigram: Kan (Water) – danger, trouble, difficulties, tallow, weeping

The Judgment: Difficult Beginnings. It is beneficial to persevere. Do not use this opportunity to undertake anything. It is beneficial to establish a feudal lord.

This hexagram is about the various difficulties that initially prevent people from coming together and how your personal efforts can be impeded when you are trying to gather support for yourself. Beneath the surface appearance it is mostly about the difficulties of getting married, namely finding the right spouse and getting her to acquiesce into marrying you. The theme is that this entails difficult beginnings. Progress in gathering people together first starts with someone who wastes their life in fruitless activities and then finally decides to settle down so they must meet a potential partner to marry. The Judgment mentions it is beneficial to set up a feudal lord, which means that one should get married and establish yourself as head of a household. In the second line you are warned that you may try to marry someone who refuses the invitation and only later, after much time, they might decide to join you. In the third line trying to make contact with a hard-to-meet individual (perhaps to make them a wife) is a useless pursuit if you lack an effective guide to help (you sometimes need a matchmaker as a go-between for introductions). In the fourth line we finally see that your efforts to establish a relationship with others is paying off because a man is finally about to get married. In the fifth line you are reminded that the marriage ceremony should be celebrated without stinginess or pettiness since it is a momentous affair and you should not hold back with a spouse but be generous in sharing everything. In the last line the wife dies, the groom sheds tears, and you are reminded that not only is it difficult to become a couple but difficult to stay together.

1. Around in circles (wheeling around making no headway). It is beneficial to become settled. It is beneficial to establish a lord.

2. Gathered together but halted (in delay). Horses and chariots stand arrayed (are lined up as on parade). They are not bandits but seeking marriage relations. The girl does not pledge herself to get married. After ten years she gets pregnant.

3. Hunting a deer without a forester. One enters deep in a forest. The superior man sees that it is better to desist (dispense with the pursuit). Going forward leads to distress.

4. Horses and carriage stand arrayed in formation (on parade). He is seeking marriage. Advancing is auspicious. Nothing is unfavorable.

5. Hoarding the tallow (fat). For someone small this is auspicious, but for someone great this is not.

6. Horses and carriage stand arrayed in formation. He weeps streaming tears of blood.

3.1: Yang at the bottom line at the beginning of the Zhen Thunder trigram is reflected in an image of confused movement, which represents a man's life before marriage where he runs around doing this and that – movement without any positive direction. **"Around and around in circles (making no headway). It is beneficial to settle down. It is beneficial to establish a feudal lord."** This line is about finally deciding to settle down because of establishing the intent to get married and start a household. You make this decision after years of fruitlessly running around in circles and wasting your life in useless activities that get you nowhere. Some might think that the first image of moving back and forth can also refer to an ancient Chinese marriage custom where the groom's family would dress as bandits and parade back and forth and proceed in circles around the bride's home but that interpretation is too early for the bottom line of this marriage hexagram because it would insinuate that a bride has already agreed to the match. However, the idea of establishing a feudal lord definitely means a man decides he should get married, settle down and establish a home.

3.2: Yin at the second line in the middle of the Zhen Thunder trigram. This is also the bottom line of an inner Kun Earth trigram (lines 2-4). **"Gathered together but halted in delay. Horses and chariots stand arrayed (are lined up as on parade). He is not a bandit but seeking** marriage relations (wants her to be his wife). The girl does not pledge herself (refuses) to get married. After ten years she gets pregnant." This is a line about trying to getting married but the girl will not accept the man. It is difficult to advance and there are all sorts of problems and delays. The seeking of marriage is a manifestation of the Kun Earth trigram that unifies disparate elements coming together, namely a future husband and wife. The Zhen Thunder trigram appears through the image of impatient horses and carriages arrayed and the fact that the girl says no. The groom and his friends surround the bride's house in a mock raid to steal the future wife. However, the girl does not want to marry the potential groom. She stays celibate. For ten years she refuses to marry, which is a substantial delay, and then she eventually gets pregnant which means that she consented to betrothal to another man and got married.

3.3: Yin at the third line at the end of the Zhen Thunder trigram, and thus we have a warning of danger and destruction that is typical of a thunderbolt. This is also the middle line of an inner Kun Assembly trigram (lines 2-4) and bottom line of an inner Gen Mountain trigram (lines 3-5). **"Hunting a deer without a forester [huntsman guide] will cause one to get lost in the (midst of the) deep forest. The superior man realizes that it is better to desist in chasing the deer. Going forward (and subsequently getting lost) would lead to distress [grief, trouble]."** Whereas in the first line the individual was going around in circles in life before deciding to marry, and in the second line the girl did not consent to the marriage, here the obstacle to marriage (gathering together) is not having a guide (proper help) to help you. The analogy is going into a forest chasing game and consequently becoming lost. This line refers to a man wanting to marry who does not seek the advice of other people or help of a go-between or matchmaker for introductions, and who is represented by the forester guide. In ancient China a man could not approach a maiden for marriage without the proper introductions and since the man doesn't have them he gives up the marriage pursuit, which is symbolized by giving up the pursuit of a deer. The desisting or halting of the chase is a reflection of the influence of the Gen Keeping Still trigram, hunting appears as a function of the Zhen trigram, and the *desire* to seek the deer is the Kun trigram.

3.4: Yin at the fourth line, at the beginning of the Kan Water trigram. This is also the middle line of an inner Gen Keeping Still trigram (lines 3-5) and top line of an inner Kun Earth trigram (lines 2-4). **"His horses and carriage stand arrayed on parade. He seeks a marital union. Advancing is auspicious [to go brings good fortune]. Nothing is unfavorable."** The fourth line of a hexagram is often an image of "almost perfect success," whereas "perfect success or accomplishment" of the hexagram's meaning often appears in the fifth line. The marriage is agreed because the groom's marriage party will visit the maiden's house to secure her as a bride, which is a manifestation of the Kun Assembly trigram that brings the two parties together in marriage. The fact that the horses and carriage are described as standing still in formation reflects the presence of the Gen Keeping Still trigram.

3.5: Yang at the fifth line, the center of the Kan Water trigram and also the lord of the hexagram. This is also the top line of an inner Gen Mountain trigram (3-5) that often stands for accumulation. **"Saving [hoarding] the fat (tallow). For someone small this is auspicious, but for someone great it is not."** In this line, the tallow or fat represents the Kan Water trigram. For someone with little resources the accumulation and hoarding of resources is proper due to the need to be frugal, which is an influence of the Gen Accumulation trigram. They should not spend too much on the wedding. However, for someone with great resources – someone who is "big" such as noble families rather than peasantry – one should not be miserly in spending on the wedding and should use their resources to lavishly celebrate the union. Hexagram line 22.5 also tells us not to be too stingy when trying to ornament an important occasion. In ancient China tallow was rare in peasant families and was used as a gift for the bride's family as it was used to make candles. In noble families a gift of tallow would have been considered insignificant and they would have used the more expensive commodity of silk as a gift. This line is basically just a reminder to spend appropriately on the wedding. The fifth line indicates a successful marriage, which is the theme of the hexagram, where the assembled people celebrate appropriately according to the level of the couple's wealth.

3.6: Yin at the top line of the hexagram, and the top of the Kan Water trigram. Thus there is an image of water in the line. **"Horses and carriage stand arrayed in formation. He weeps tears of blood that flow copiously like water."** This is the top destructive line of a Kan trigram so we should see some from of danger or disaster. Thus we see weeping and tears of blood probably because the wife has died. This hexagram tells the story of a marriage in steps where the couple marries in the fifth line, and now in the sixth line comes the reminder that death eventually happens to everyone including the wife. Death claims all so it is hard for a couple to stay together just as it is hard to become husband and wife. Thus the horse carriage (or cart) here stands arrayed for a burial.

In terms of the composition of the hexagram and how it is reflected in this line, a Zhen Thunder trigram (the horses and carts) is beneath a Kan Water trigram (tears of blood). Hence in this line we see that death struck the wife.

HEXAGRAM 4

Meng – Immaturity, Youthful Ignorance, Inexperience

Lower Trigram: Kan (Water) – folly, ignorance, woman, danger, trouble
Upper Trigram: Gen (Mountain) – trapped, still, stopping, accumulation

The Judgment: It is not we who seek the young fool [ignorant youth]. It is the young fool who seeks us. The first cast of milfoil stalks [divination augury] tells your fortune. A second or third cast is excessive and will not give you an informative answer. Persistence is beneficial.

This hexagram is about the ignorance of youth due to inexperience, and how to train young people so that they grow out of ignorance and mature into responsible adults who can support families (as in the previous hexagram) rather than become delinquents or criminals. There is an image of a mountain on top of water symbolizing putting structure or restraint (discipline) on top of danger, which means training youth. To grow out of immaturity young people need to acquire experience and shed their ignorance. The first stage of ignorant folly is represented by immature youth, but you can train them using discipline. In line two you become involved with youth to train them so that through your influence they will mature properly. As a result they will become responsible enough to marry and raise their own family. The third line states that one immature folly is to marry a woman who is only interested in your money. In line four, a higher degree of ignorance is to become involved with some sort of folly you cannot escape and then to suffer due to your ignorance. In the fifth line we see a prime example of forgivable ignorance in the pure naivete of children who innocently commit faults. A pithy reminder at the top line is that you might strike youth who commit misdemeanors in order to discipline them because your objective is to produce a good person rather than a robber. Applying punishments to youth is a way of "driving off robbers" by preventing them from becoming criminals due to uncorrected misdeeds.

1. To help youths discard folly (to educate or enlighten inexperienced youths) punishment is beneficial. However, one should remove shackles and fetters because continuing that way is distressful.

2. Auspicious to become bound with an ignorant youth. Auspicious to take a wife. The son can marry.

3. Do not marry a woman who, on seeing a wealthy man, loses herself. There is nothing beneficial (in this).

4. Trapped in ignorant foolishness. Distress.

5. Youthful ignorance (childlike folly). Auspicious.

6. Hitting an ignorant youth (callow youth engaged in misdemeanor or folly). It is not beneficial to be a robber. It is beneficial to drive off robbers.

4.1: Yin at the first line and at the beginning of the Kan Danger trigram, so there is an image of distress and a warning on training youths so that they do not ignorantly get into trouble, which is a manifestation of the Kan trigram. **"To cause youths to discard folly [to educate youths, to cultivate maturity in youths] punishment is beneficial. However, one should remove shackles and fetters [restraints] for continuing that way is distressful."** Youths are blind to danger and get into all sort of trouble due to their ignorance. They are just shrouded in folly. The meaning of the line is: "It is beneficial to use punishment (discipline) when educating youths so that they stay out of trouble." However, you should not use harsh, painful discipline (symbolized by manacles, shackles, and other overly restrictive restraints that are symbols of the Kan trigram). The degree of discipline must be appropriate and so shackles restricting a neophyte's normal development are excessive and should be avoided. "In order to educate youths (and free them from ignorance) you should remove their fetters and constraints because going forward that way is distressful." This is the lowest intensity or gradient level of ignorance.

4.2: Yang at the second line, in the middle of the Kan Water trigram representing danger. This is also the beginning line of an inner Zhen Thunder trigram. **"It is auspicious to take care of ignorant youth. Auspicious to take a wife. The son can marry."** This line tells us that it is a positive step to become a teacher of ignorant youths since that positive association will raise them out of ignorance. Although instructing ignorant youths is troublesome, which reflects the Kan Trouble-Danger trigram, this behavior will produce good fortune, meaning that a youth will reach maturity through the proper instruction of adults that includes the imposition of discipline (Zhen trigram). Besides associating with a youth by becoming his teacher (binding yourself to someone ignorant), "It is auspicious to become bound with a woman by marrying her." There is the reminder that the son of a marital union, which is shown in juxtaposition, will eventually become mature and responsible enough to marry and run a household himself, which is the success one wants from educating ignorant young people as per the first section of these lines. This is why the line says, "The son can marry." Hence, you might think of these lines as saying, "It is beneficial to become the teacher of ignorant neophytes because through your teachings they will grow up into fine maturity. Similarly, it is beneficial to become bound to a woman through marriage because that union will produce a son mature enough to be capable of running a household, which is what you want to happen when you start teaching seemingly hopeless youths."

4.3: Yin at the third line, and at the top of the Kan Danger-Water trigram that represents danger. This is also the middle line of an inner Zhen Thunder trigram and bottom line of an inner Kun Earth trigram. **"Do not marry a woman who, on seeing a wealthy man, loses herself. Nothing is favorable [advantageous] in doing this."** Due to the Kan Danger trigram and the prominence of the middle line of an inner Zhen trigram (that tends to be destructive) there is a warning against danger – a danger that arises from a more intense form of ignorance/folly than just being the clueless youth of previous lines. This line warns about marrying a gold-digger, which is a woman only interested in your wealth, and you know this because she loses control of herself when she sees your money. A gold-digger is only interested in your money so marrying her would be a big mistake but men lose their heads and do that out of ignorance. The third line of a hexagram is almost always dangerous or destructive like this. The previous line mentions marriage and advises you to teach ignorant neophytes, but here you are advised not to involve yourself with people who not sincerely interested in you. The image of marriage appears in this line because it represents the Kun Earth trigram that stands for agglomeration, assembly, massing or unity.

4.4: Yin at the fourth line at the beginning of the upper Gen Mountain trigram that symbolizes non-movement due to heavy restraint. Hence in this upper trigram we will see cases of individuals being stuck or trapped within ignorance. This is also the middle line of an inner Kun Earth trigram, which reinforces the influence of the mountain, and it is the top line of an inner Zhen Thunder trigram that causes trouble. **"Trapped [bound, confined] in ignorant foolishness [folly]. This produces distress [grief, trouble]."** This line should represent a higher level of ignorance over the previous three lines, and does. This is an individual who is *suffering from their ignorance* because they have become trapped in a heap of trouble due to ignorant foolishness. Their ignorance or inexperience is the cause of their suffering. They are now burdened with troubles, trapped due to their foolishness and ignorance. Being trapped in ignorance is due to the dual influence of the Gen Keeping Still trigram and Kun Agglomeration trigram, and the distress in the line is an influence due to the presence of the Zhen Thunderbolt trigram of destruction.

4.5: Yin at the fifth line, in the middle of the of the Gen Mountain trigram. This is also the top line of an inner Kun Earth trigram. **"Childlike folly [youthful ignorance or naivete, childlike innocence, innocent adolescence]. Auspicious."** This refers to the *innocent* ignorance of youth which is ignorance due to immaturity and inexperience. This line is the lord of the hexagram that normally shows a perfected form of its message, and in this case it paints the picture of innocent youthful folly where "Youthful Ignorance" is indeed the name and message of the hexagram. It refers to the folly of young adolescents who innocently fall into trouble or engage in innocent misdemeanors while having clean minds absent of guile, so in this case there are no mischievous notions. This is a greater degree of folly or naivete than all previous lines *because thinking is not involved in the mistakes so they are pure and innocent* in the sense of being devoid of any sort of ill-will or animosity. The mistakes are just part of growing up and learning such as getting burnt by matches for the first time and then learning that fire burns. This line represents the stage of natural innocent naivete rather than the destructive rebelliousness or overt stupidity of ignorant/inexperienced youth. The reason that the Gen Mountain is involved is because all young people are trapped in youthful innocence and get involved in follies until they mature, and the Kun Earth trigram is involved because they will certainly become engaged in (agglomerate) such experiences. There is yet another possible angle of translation – **"Innocent adolescent. Good fortune."** This translation would be stressing the great luck of having a child for they are all innocent as adolescents. To have a healthy, innocent child is a degree of good fortune worthy of the fifth line of the hexagram.

4.6: Yang at the sixth line, which completes the hexagram, and it is at the top of the Gen Keeping Still trigram. The entire hexagram is about training neophytes using discipline or restraint (Gen) so that they become more mature. **"Striking [hitting, punishing] an ignorant youth. It is not beneficial to be a bandit (who hits people in order to rob them). It is beneficial to defend against [oppose, ward off, drive off] robbers."** Striking an immature, inexperienced youth is a corrective measure for when they engage in misdeeds or avoidable folly. It is a punishment or type of discipline with the intent to stop wrong-doing from becoming a habit. The name of the hexagram is "Youthful Ignorance" and discipline is one way to correct it. However, it does not good to commit a violation when disciplining youth. If you beat children too much they can become violent, aggressive individuals themselves just as children who were abused often grow up to become abusive. Hence we have a warning to refrain from excessive physical punishment, which is the influence of the Gen Mountain trigram, and yet you want to discipline youth so that they do not become criminals. We want our children to grow up into mature adults and defend us against robbers, bandits and other criminals so they don't steal what we have accumulated (Gen trigram) so we punish their errant ways in order that they do not become wicked or evil.

In terms of the overall construction of the hexagram and how it appears in this line, there is a Kan Danger trigram below a Gen Keeping Still trigram. Thus, this line first shows an image of striking a youth in punishment along with robbers (Kan) before ending with the idea of defending against them to establish restraint (Gen).

HEXAGRAM 5

Xu - Getting Wet, The Drenching

Lower Trigram: Qian (Heaven) – great strength, perseverance, strong action
Upper Trigram: Kan (Water) – blood, pit, wine, danger, trouble, difficulties

The Judgment: Getting Wet. Sincerity brings shining success. Perseverance is auspicious. It is beneficial to ford the great river.

Some name this hexagram "Waiting," but it primarily deals with water images. It is composed of the Kan Water trigram over the Qian Heaven trigram, which is an image of a cloud in the sky, so "Getting Wet" seems more appropriate. If you prefer waiting as the meaning thyen you can replace the "getting wet" in each line with "waiting in." One should think of this hexagram as the story of making preparations to perform a difficult task and getting closer to doing it, such as preparing to ford a great river (where you will certainly get wet) or undertake a military campaign. You are progressively arriving at the undertaking that is itself a drenching. At first you are on the far outskirts of the river in line one, then you approach the river bank made of sand in line two, next you get stuck in the mud of the river in line three where your vulnerability temps robbers to come, who might represent soldiers, and finally you're wounded and bleeding due to fighting off the robbers while involved in the "bloody difficult" task of fording the actual river in line four. Fording a river was difficult in ancient China since boats were primitive but in this case you are using a cart so this river is shallow. After completing your crossing you can celebrate the accomplishment, which is line five. Now that you have crossed you enter into yet another pit or set of problems but some people unexpectedly come to assist you. A bit of wise advice at the top line therefore states that whenever people unexpectedly arrive who might help you should treat them kindly and gladly accept their assistance. The Judgment provides a good synopsis of the hexagram by stating that it is perseverance that produces good fortune when you want to ford a river.

1. Getting wet in the suburbs. Beneficial to persevere in one's purpose. There is no trouble.

2. Getting wet whilst on the sand. There is a little criticism. In the end auspicious.

3. Getting wet in the mud. This causes robbers to arrive.

4. Getting soaked with blood. Gets out of the pit.

5. Getting soaked with wine and food. Continuing this way is auspicious.

6. One enters a pit. Three unbidden guests arrive. Treat them with respect. In the end good fortune.

5.1: Yang at the bottom line and at the beginning of the Qian Heaven trigram that represents great strength, great force or a great movement forward. **"Getting wet in the suburbs [outskirts of the city]. It is beneficial to be persistent in one's purpose. There is no trouble."** You initiate the idea for an undertaking and then start preparations to perform the difficult task that is called "crossing a river," which is possibly a military expedition. Therefore you get wet in the suburbs far away from the river during this pre-commencement stage of preparation. The event of getting wet might come from a rain storm but probably just represents developing the idea to perform the great undertaking. Hence at this stage "there is no trouble" because you haven't really started yet. Since the deed is far away you must remain committed to your purpose and thus, "It is beneficial to be persistent in one's purpose."

5.2: Yang at the second line in the center of the Qian Heaven trigram, which represents a strong force. This is also the bottom line of an inner Dui Lake-Talking trigram. **"Getting wet whilst on the sand. There is a little criticism [small altercation, sharp words against you]. In the end auspicious."** Here you get closer to the river (starting the difficult undertaking) because you have now progressed to river sand (river shore) rather than remained in the far suburbs, so you have advanced due to the influence of the Qian Great Force trigram pushing you forward. "Getting wet whilst on the sand" is probably on the entry banks to the river instead of on a sandbar because the third line involves a progression into mud, which is an even wetter situation. As is natural, before the great task there is some criticism or small gossip about you and your efforts at this time due to the presence of the Dui Talking trigram.

5.3: Yang at the third line, and at the top of the Qian Heaven trigram. This is also the middle line of an inner Dui Lake trigram and bottom line of an inner Li trigram. **"Getting wet in the mud. This causes robbers to arrive."** Here you have gotten stuck in the mud of the river bottom (Dui Lake trigram). This obstruction is thwarting your efforts to cross the river, or slowing them down, and the standstill tempts robbers to arrive to steal your valuables. This could mean that enemy soldiers come to attack you during a river crossing. Basically, your situation is mired in difficulties, and this vulnerability has tempted robbers to come. The robbers appear due to it being the top line of the trigram, which tends to be destructive, and so a destructive great force appears. The mud is the influence of the middle line of the inner Dui Lake trigram and the level of trouble you now incur has increased from some second line criticism to an attack of bandits and the potential of great loss and injury. This is because you are getting closer to the deepest difficulties in crossing so trouble has indeed started.

5.4: Yin at the fourth line, at the beginning of the upper Kan Water trigram, so we should finally see the act of fording the river since the Kan trigram represents water and danger. This is also the middle line of an inner Li trigram and top line of an inner Dui trigram that also represents water or a mouth (the "pit"). **"Getting soaked with blood. He gets out of the pit."** This means he is wounded and bleeding profusely from the problems of line three such as fighting off the bandits (or soldiers). He successfully crosses the dangerous river that is under the influence of Kan Danger-Water-Abyss and Dui Lake trigrams, which is why the strong water problems appear. In this line you suffer trying to cross the river (accomplish a great deed), and hence we see the image of blood (Kan Water trigram) to denote the difficulties involved in actually accomplishing the task or fighting off the bandits/soldiers. After crossing the river, which means completing the task, "He emerges from the pit," which is the celebratory brilliance of the Li trigram.

5.5: Yang at the fifth line in the center of the Kan Water trigram. This line is the lord of the hexagram that often indicates success and good fortune, which in this case is celebration for successfully accomplishing the great undertaking. This is also the top line of an inner Li trigram that represents celebration. **"Getting soaked with wine and food. Continuing this way is auspicious."** The fifth line is the lord of the hexagram and illustrates a perfected form of the hexagram's message. You celebrate the successful river crossing by now getting drenched in (delving into) wine and food. The celebration symbolizes the Li trigram while the wine and "getting soaked" show the presence of the Kan Water trigram once again.

5.6: Yin at the top line of the upper Kan Water trigram completes the hexagram, and thus we see a summary of the situation. **"Entering into [falling into] a pit. Three unbidden [unexpected] guests arrive. If you**

treat them with respect [courtesy] then in the end good fortune will come." This hexagram symbolizes the process of attempting a great but also dangerous feat, which might even be a short military expedition where the bandits symbolize the enemy, and it is represented through the difficult task of crossing a river. Afterwards you enter a pit, which means that more difficulties are upon you after your crossing – a problem you cannot get out of such as a bigger attack. This is, after all, the top destructive line of the Kan Danger trigram. You cannot go backwards and you cannot move forwards. You need help. Next, "Three unbidden guests arrive. Treat them with respect [courtesy]. In the end good fortune." This line offers wise advice that when you are in trouble you should accept any unexpected help graciously. Take advantage of it and do not be afraid to accept it. The three guests might be the three yang lines of the lower Qian trigram that make their way through the upper Kan trigram to offer their assistance, such as reinforcements, or it might local allies in the territory you have entered. First, if you decide to undertake the difficult feat and help unexpectedly arrives you should make use of that aid with respectful appreciation. Second, the hexagram is constructed with a Qian Heaven trigram on the bottom – which symbolizes the three guests of great help since it is composed of three yang lines that slowly push their way to the top line – and the pit of difficulties (Kan trigram) is on top of it.

In this line, which reflects the structure of the hexagram as a whole, with great strength (Qian) you cross a river and then "enter into a pit" (Kan) and three guests arrive to offer the strength of help (Qian).

HEXAGRAM 6

Song - Conflict, Grievance, Dispute, Contention, Litigation, Lawsuit

Lower Trigram: Kan (Water) – grievance, lawsuit, danger, difficulties
Upper Trigram: Qian (Heaven) – king's command, winning, prize

The Judgment: Conflict. Be sincere. Maintain apprehensiveness (cautious alertness). At the midpoint (the situation is) auspicious but ominous in the end. Beneficial to see a great man. Not beneficial to cross a great river (attempt a major change or undertaking).

Think of this hexagram as the story of an individual who works for a superior such as a lord, and he has a disagreement or contentious argument with the lord or some other highly ranked individual. It is probably about a nobleman who terminates his service to the king because of some conflict with another lord. His grievance (dispute) is not resolved so he leaves the king's employ, suffers slander as a result, returns home to his estate (of three hundred families) to live off his accumulated wealth, but in the end returns after being called back to service. Eventually the dispute goes his way in the fifth line of the hexagram where this is probably the original grievance. However, the sixth line of the hexagram reminds us that you might be awarded position, wealth, rank or honor but they can just as easily be stripped away the same day so you might win a lawsuit or grievance but everything can just as easily be taken away from you. Thus this hexagram is about the troubles of trying to settle a conflict, grievance or dispute with someone also with great power, status or authority. As the Judgment says, you better be worried about the conflict (the pursuit of justice and the aftermath) and you better see a wise man for guidance because it isn't necessarily beneficial to pursue this case. It might seem that you are winning in the beginning but you might lose in the end; apparent victories can result in heavier losses. Remember that only one out of six lines in this hexagram is favorable. If you pair this hexagram with the previous fifth hexagram, trying to win this dispute is like the great undertaking of trying to cross a difficult river.

1. Not continuing his service (due to a grievance). There is a little criticism (slander against him) but in the end auspicious.

2. Unable to win the lawsuit. Retreating he returns home to his town of three hundred households. There is no calamity.

3. Feeding on (depending on) your old virtues. Continuing this way is dangerous but in the end auspicious. If he were to work in the service of the king he would achieve nothing.

4. Not successful in the (initial) lawsuit he returns (to the king's employ) to comply with the command. Changing (your attitude) brings peace and remaining that way is auspicious.

5. (He wins the) Lawsuit. Prime auspiciousness.

6. Someone awards you a leather belt (a symbol of a conferred rank or lofty position) but by the end of the morning it is stripped away three times.

6.1: Yin at the first line at the bottom of a Kan Danger-Water trigram. This means some trouble, and since it is at just the *beginning* of the Kan trigram it means that the trouble is at its lowest level of intensity so it is just starting. **"Not continuing in service (due to a grievance). There is a little criticism [slander or complaints spoken against him] but in the end auspicious."** The trouble is a dispute or grievance (Kan trigram) that causes you to quit working for a superior – to "cease perpetuation of your service." As a consequence of the conflict and quitting your service there is some criticism and slander spoken against you but the association ends, which is good. *It is not that the affair ends auspiciously, but that ceasing the employment is a good idea so that the situation does not become worse by spinning out of control.* Quitting enables you to withdraw from the strife and retreat. The hope is that things will calm down without too much bad feeling on all sides. You quit because of the conflict and the bad situation this creates, which are symbolized by the Kan Danger trigram.

6.2: Yang at the second line in the middle of the Kan Danger-Water trigram indicates danger and movement. This is also the bottom line of an inner Li trigram. **"Not succeeding in the lawsuit. Retreating he returns home to his town of three hundred households and thus escapes calamity [catastrophe, disaster, harm]."** In ancient China, grievances between the nobility were handled by a county magistrate in the capital city of a district, and the decision of this magistrate could be appealed to the duke's grand administrator located in the provincial capital. The only higher level of appeal was to the king. This individual is not able to resolve his grievance due to this second line of the Kan trigram being its strongest line, but he has a tinge of benefit from the presence of the Li trigram. Since he is in a weak situation without a position anymore he must escape the environment and flee to his support. Thus he returns to his fiefdom (estate) of three hundred households (which might possibly represent the three lines of the inner Li trigram) that enables him to escape the calamity of the Kan Danger trigram. Basically, you decide that the conflict is unwinnable so you give up and go home. Your resources there are limited but you escape disaster by returning home.

6.3: Yin at the third line, and at the top line of the Kan Danger-Water trigram, is represented by a dangerous situation and by the yin trait of humility. This is also the middle line of an inner Li Brilliance trigram, and bottom line of an inner Xun Wind trigram that will eat away at accumulated resources. **"Eating up (living on) your old virtues (your accumulated wealth and reputation). Continuing this way is dangerous but in the end auspicious. If you were to work in the service of the king you would achieve nothing."** Even though this is a yin line within the Kan Danger trigram, if you stay away from the conflict and rely on your accumulated wealth and reputation (Li trigram) this will become a line of good fortune. Using up your accumulated stock of merit (bounty) means living off your inherited estate – living off what you gained in the past. "Eating it up" is a function of the Xun Penetrating trigram that has the nature of destructively eating away at situations causing damage. Nevertheless this is the right way to live because this wealth is something you have was honestly gained and this is better than working for the king in a contentious situation. If you were to continue working for the king you would probably achieve nothing due to the unresolved dispute and not be able to gain credit for any accomplishments either, which is another influence of the Xun Wind trigram that disintegrates things and blows them away.

6.4: Yang at the fourth line at the start of the upper Qian Heaven trigram. This is also the middle of an inner Xun Wind trigram and top line of an inner Li Fire trigram. **"Unable to succeed in the dispute he turns back to following orders (working for the king). He changes his litigation-oriented attitude to peacefulness. Remaining in peacefulness (accepting the unresolved situation) brings good fortune."** At this line you would expect to be succeeding in the dispute (which probably continued while you were away) because this is the first line of a new Qian Great Strength trigram, but this is also the middle (strong) line of an inner

Xun Disintegration trigram that overrides its strength. The other party in the lawsuit or grievance is stronger than you therefore you cannot succeed against them. You cannot win the grievance, which is rejected, so you are unsuccessful in settling the matter to your satisfaction. The king commands you to come back to work and you do. You finally accept the situation and settle into acquiescence with peacefulness. Although burning inside with anger due to the inner Li Fire trigram, you must change your attitude in order to experience peace and contentment. A change will come in line five.

6.5: Yang at the fifth line, within the middle of the Qian Great Force trigram that typically represents great strength. This is also the top line of an inner Xun Wind trigram that in this case symbolizes the lawsuit, grievance or dispute since they are words (wind). **"He wins the lawsuit [conflict, grievance, dispute]. Supreme good fortune."** In the fourth line the nobleman returned to the provincial capital to work for the king again and found out that he won the lawsuit. The fifth line as lord of the hexagram typically displays a successful accomplishment of the theme of the hexagram, which is all about disputes, so in this line – which is at the center of the Qian trigram of great strength – the nobleman wins his initial grievance. Naturally this is great good fortune because it settles his grievance, preserves his reputation and vindicates his previous actions.

6.6: Yang at the top line, at the top of the Qian Heaven trigram, ends the hexagram and provides a lesson on conflicts and grievances in general. **"Someone awards [confers] you an honorary leather belt [rewarded as a symbol of rank or for some honor such as being the victor in a contest] but three times it is stripped away by morning's end."** Despite being vindicated in the previous line, the nobleman now suffers loss in other ways, which is due to the destructive nature of the top line of the Qian Great Strength trigram that now represents an oppositional party. Basically, you can win a lawsuit but opponents can screw you in other ways. A typical translation is that the honor you just won by winning the lawsuit will be stripped away three times by the end of the morning, and I am not familiar enough with the ancient Chinese legal system to know if it is possible to be awarded a belt and have it stripped away, awarded again, stripped away again, and so on. Perhaps this refers to a real historical case. Typically you cannot strip away something three times from an individual because you can only strip away something once unless it is each time given back. I would like to prefer "… three times as much can be stripped away from you" or "rewards earned three times can be stripped away" despite this not being accurate but my lack of historical knowledge prevents the best translation. Actually, it really doesn't matter because the lesson of this line is that you might win your dispute and win an honorary belt of rank but also lose it in the end because you are going against devious individuals who will slander you (as they did in 6.1) and try to find some way to screw you. You might lose more than anything you might gain by being disputatious with other powerful people, which is why the Judgment advises you to see a wise man (sage) for advice about a lawsuit before getting in deep. The Judgment of the hexagram states that things are auspicious at the midpoint (fifth line) but ominous in the end (sixth line) and that overall it is not beneficial to institute the lawsuit (cross a great river) even though one is sincere (righteous). In short, it is especially dangerous to be litigious with powerful people who have rank over you or are as powerful as you are.

This hexagram is constructed of a Kan trigram beneath a Qian trigram where the Kan danger eats away at the blessings of Qian, so the way this appears in this line is that your rewards (Qian) are stripped away (Kan) three times.

HEXAGRAM 7

Shi - An Army, The Troops

Lower Trigram: Kan (Water) – abyss, danger, trouble, war, death
Upper Trigram: Kun (Earth) – army, a mass of men, camp, corpses, a state

The Judgment: An Army. Requires perseverance and veteran leadership (for) Auspiciousness (and) No trouble.

This hexagram has the image of the earth holding water within itself, which means massing a great body of men together like an army. This hexagram is about the steps required to successfully launch a military assault against an opponent in order to defeat an enemy, conquer territory or even found a state. This requires an army of trained troops. Much of the story refers to the conquest of the Shang dynasty by King Wu (Ji Fa), second son of King Wen (Ji Chang) of *Yijing* fame. Ji Fa (King Wu) rises up with the help of the famous strategist Jiang Shang and defeats King Zhou (Di Xin) of the Shang dynasty at the famous Battle of Muye after which he established the Zhou dynasty, which also involved setting up a number of feudal states governed by his younger brothers and clan arrangements. This is mentioned in line 7.6. You can find most of the larger story in hexagram 17 and parts of the story in other hexagram lines here and there. The story of the Zhou state versus the Shang dynasty is predominant in the hexagrams because kings Wen and Wu helped create the hexagrams of the *Yijing* system. Since the launch of a military campaign is analogous to performing some great deed or undertaking you can also read many lines in this way as well. In the first line of this hexagram the troops must be disciplined before fighting a war and you can know they are well-drilled or not if when you observe whether they march in strict formation. In the second line it is fine to be just a regular army conscript out of which army officers and commanders are carefully selected. In the third line, you must understand that because this is war your army will suffer losses since many of your troops will be killed. Therefore, the fourth line reminds us that the army must take steps to avoid as much damage from the enemy as possible. In the fifth line, after winning a battle you must interrogate captives to derive military intelligence, and there is a reminder that winning battles requires experienced officers as leaders while the inexperienced officers should be assigned less critical tasks. If all goes well (sixth line) a prince becomes successful in his military campaigns, conquers new territory and can ultimately found a new state. This last line actually refers to King Wu conquering the state of Shang and founding the Zhou dynasty in its place.

1. Army troops set out in strict formation (ordered ranks). If (these be) not good it is ominous.

2. In the midst of the army (being among the troops). Auspicious. No trouble. The king thrice bestows commands.

3. Some troops will be carting corpses. Ominous.

4. The army camps to the left far away (from the enemy). It avoids harm (there is no trouble).

5. Hunting has resulted in a catch. Beneficial to interrogate captives to avert harm. The elder son commands (leads) the army. The younger son carts corpses. Persistence (with the casualty rate) is ominous.

6. The great prince has a mandate to found a state and establish feudal houses (hereditary families). Inferior men must not be used.

7.1: Yin at the bottom of the hexagram, and the beginning of the Kan Water-Danger trigram. Thus there will be an issue of danger in the image. **"Army troops set forth in strict formation (ordered ranks). If (their discipline is) not good it is ominous."** If an army is ready to set out on a military campaign but shows laxity in its troop formations then this is ominous (an omen of trouble) because the lack of order and discipline foreshadows losses. A lack of discipline, which can be seen in whether or not the troops move out in strict formation, reveals a lack of sufficient training, disunity, and poor command structure. *It's like a poker tell that lets you know the army has poor training and would therefore lose in battle.* Hence in the first line of the hexagram we have a warning of insufficient training and preparation which reflects the fact that the line is yin. The sentences are not warning that setting forth on a military campaign is a bad idea because the last line of the hexagram talks about the goal of establishing a state through the military's involvement. Rather it is saying, "If the army's discipline (training, drilling and preparation) is not good then this is ominous," which projects the "dangerous" meaning of the Kan trigram.

7.2: Yang at the second line in the middle of the Kan Water-Danger trigram. The yang line is in the middle of two yin lines, hence there is an image of being in the middle or *midst* of the army. This is also the bottom line of an inner Zhen Thunder trigram that also signifies army actions and surprising commendation. **"Being among the (middle of the) troops. Good fortune. There is no trouble. The king thrice bestows command."** The middle line of a trigram sometimes comes out as being inside or amidst something. The reason it is beneficial to be in the middle of the army is because this is a safe location. Danger surrounds the army since this line is within the Kan Danger trigram and also the first line of an inner Zhen Thunder trigram (lines 2-4) that represents striking thunderbolt activity like a military assault as well as the orders (commands) of the king which are given three times (three lines takes you into the next hexagram). During an attack the middle location would be safer than the perimeter so the safest location is *amidst* the troops. Furthermore, opposite hexagram line 13.2 says that you assemble with men at a gate and reverse hexagram line 8.2 says you seek alliance with insiders, so both these hexagrams refer to massing together with other people, i.e. troops. The commands by the king are a manifestation of the Zhen Thunder trigram and yang nature of the line where the yang activity appears as a positive benefit rather than assault or attack.

7.3: Yin at the third line completing the Kan Water-Danger trigram. The third line of a trigram usually reveals some destructive aspect of its nature since the trigram is about to change into another (meaning that its top line is prone to destructive change or deterioration), hence we should expect some bad fortune. This is also the middle line of an inner Zhen Thunder trigram (thus destructive) and beginning line of an inner Kun Earth trigram, which can symbolize burials or corpses. **"Some troops will be carting corpses. Ominous."** Soldiers who died in battle were usually buried on the battlefield (Kun Earth trigram) while noblemen and leaders were carried back by cart. This line therefore means many casualties, thus evidencing the danger aspect of the Kan trigram. This is also the second line of an inner Zhen Thunder trigram (lines 2-4) that represents an assault striking the army and producing casualties. The fact that troops are carting corpses is an omen of more deaths to come.

7.4: Yin at the fourth line at the beginning of the Kun Earth trigram. We just left the lower Kan Danger-Abysmal trigram and have entered the upper Kun Earth trigram. Thus we have an image of camping, whose settled nature represents the Kun earth element of the line. This is also the middle line of an inner Kun Earth trigram and top line of an inner Zhen Thunder trigram. **"The army camps to the left away (from the enemy). There is no trouble (it avoids harm)."** This line merely says that it is advantageous to position troops on the left, which might refer to the left side of your body since it represents your Qi and strength. However, this army battle may refer to the time King Wu of Zhou called together his troops to attack King Zhou Xin of the Shang dynasty ("King Zhou the Terrible") at Muye. King Wu camped in his own territory, which was on the left side of the river, before crossing the Yellow River at Mengjin. Because the left is also the side of retreat, an alternative translation preferred by many translators is that, "The army retreats. It avoids harm," which also makes sense because in the third line the army suffered many losses. In any case, this is the top line of an inner Zhen Thunder trigram (lines 2-4) that tends to be destructive so in order to escape the damage of thunderous assault ("to avoid harm") it says that appropriate precautions should be taken, and in this case those precautions entail camping safely due to two Kun Earth trigrams that symbolize an assembly or massing of men. This is what should be emphasized rather than "left side."

7.5: Yin at the fifth line, in the center of the Kun Earth trigram. This is also the top line of an inner Kun Earth trigram so there is a strong influence of the earth element, which in this case means burial. "**Hunting has resulted in a catch. Beneficial to interrogate captives to avert harm. The elder son leads the army. The younger son carts corpses. Persistence is ominous.**" This line is the lord of the hexagram so it should display a perfected form of its overall theme or message. The fifth line will also usually include an individual or situation of superior status. The line first says that hunting has been successful, which means that *the military assault was successful because the commanders attained the desired objective*. It then advises that enemy captives who were seized – which are akin to the game bagged in a hunt – should be interrogated so that the enemy's intentions can be known. This is beneficial because it can help minimize future losses and will certainly save troops from harm. It also advises that experienced veterans lead the army, which reflects the Judgment of the hexagram where attention is called to the advantage of veteran, skilled or mature leadership as symbolized by the elder son. Even though you obtained military intelligence and use veteran leadership it still says that the younger son will cart corpses, which are the bodies of the leaders and nobility (since troops are buried in the field) because *causalities are inevitable in war*. That is the message of the line: you gained what you set out to achieve and yet there will still be casualties anyway since this is war. *If you persist in having casualties then this is ominous*. Thus experienced officers should be used to lead the troops while inexperienced officers should be assigned to less important tasks. "The elder son leads the army and younger son carts corpses" may also refer to the battles against King Di Xin where Ji Fa (King Wu) commanded the troops and his younger brother, such as the Lord of Kang, transported his father's corpse because it is said that his body was taken into battle. I think that this was probably an ancestral tablet naming his father "King Wen" that was placed on a chariot and taken into battle but have also read of the actual corpse taken into battle. This fifth line falls under the influence of two Kun Earth trigrams composed of triple yin lines, hence there is the realization that your side will misfortunately suffer death and destruction no matter what since the Kun trigram represents burial and masses of men. There is no auspicious message that we would normally see in the fifth line since massive deaths are the consequence of war.

7.6: Yin at the top line completes the hexagram, which is the top line of a Kun Earth trigram. **"The great ruler has a mandate to found a state and establish a lineage and feudal houses (hereditary families). Inferior men must not be employed in doing so."** King Wen goes to war, starting at the first line, and eventually conquers the Shang dynasty (King Di Xin), which is the Kun Earth trigram of this line. Then he founds a new dynasty where he grants fiefdoms to his *superior* military commanders who in turn will establish feudal houses loyal to him. To become successful he did not use inferior people as military leaders, and in laying the foundations of the Zhou dynasty he cannot grant administrative positions or hereditary legacies to inferior men either. The entire hexagram has been about the steps required to send forth an army and conquer an opposing force in order to topple a king and found a new dynasty/state. As the Judgment said, it requires perseverance and veteran leadership for a good result in the end.

As to the construction of the hexagram there is a Kan Danger trigram beneath a Kun Earth trigram, and thus a dangerous war (Kan) was fought before founding a new state (Kun earth element), which is the message of this line.

HEXAGRAM 8

Bi - Alliance, Joining Together with Others, Unification

Lower Trigram: Kun (Earth) – trust, earthenware bowl, unification, alliance
Upper Trigram: Kan (Water) – outsiders, danger, trap, headlessness

The Judgment: Alliance. The original milfoil divination is excellent. The long-term prognostication is no trouble. People from regions of unrest will come. Those who tarry (latecomers) will meet misfortune.

In this hexagram is the image of water above the earth, which seeps into it so that the two become closely bound with one another and unify together. Whereas the previous hexagram was about launching a military assault to gain territory this hexagram is about alliances between men - political or military alliances. The principle of this hexagram is that alliances are necessary and beneficial and they can involve very trustworthy or untrustworthy parties so you must be careful. Various principles are stated such as the fact that even if the other party is a friend you cannot trust the alliance to last forever, and the best type of alliance is when people associate with you out of free will rather than because of coercion. In the first line you form alliances with trustworthy parties (like friends) but you are warned never to be too trustworthy because this is wrong in the long run. Trust in your ally but always continue to test your bonds of friendship and interdependence because situations will change over time. In the second line you make alliances with insiders who are parties close to you in some way perhaps because of shared interests. In the third line you make alliances with foreigners who are even less reliable as allies. In the fourth line you make alliances with parties outside of your normal associations. In the fifth line you make a wonderful alliance that is voluntary in all ways without any degree of coercion. In the last line you are warned not to make an alliance with another party that has no leader or that alliance will fail.

1. If there is trust allying with them produces no trouble. The trust is like a full earthenware bowl. In the end this will come to be harmful. Auspicious.

2. Allying with insiders. Continuing this way is auspicious (good fortune).

3. Allying with foreigners.

4. Allying with outsiders. Continuing this way is auspicious (good fortune).

5. A glorious alliance. The king (uses beaters and) drives game on only three sides, and spares the game that comes before him. Thus the citizens need not fear him. Good fortune.

6. Allying with parties without a head (leader). Ominous.

8.1: Yin at the first line and at the bottom of an Kun Earth trigram. Agglomeration or union is a quality of the earth element so there is an easy or trustworthy alliance (a unity from joining together) at this first level of alliances. **"There is trust. Allying with them produces no trouble. The trust [faith with one another] is like a full earthenware bowl. In the end this (trust) will come to be harmful [there will come to be harm]. Auspicious."** When there is natural trust or faithfulness between two friendly parties they can easily ally together with intimate interdependence without any major problems. That attraction for one another and unity of alliance is an influence of the Kun Earth trigram that represents assemblage or massing together. Trust, sincerity, and faith in one another are what alliances stem from. "Earthenware bowl" also appears in this line to reflect the presence of the Kun Earth trigram. This could be translated as a jar or pitcher without changing the meaning. However, if the trust "overflows like a full earthenware bowl" then the parties are too trusting of one another, and therefore the parties will eventually become careless and the alliance will develop dangerous cracks without people noticing. Alliances do not last forever and if there is too much trust you will abandon your caution, and *hence bad fortune will then arise from laxity due to an over-confidence of trust.* Nevertheless, one should establish an alliance anyway until it is no longer beneficial but should always monitor it as time goes on. That is why allying is "Auspicious" until the alliance someday ends because alliances do not last forever. An alliance is useful or profitable for as long as it lasts and hence an alliance is auspicious or good fortune.

8.2: Yin at the second line within the middle of the Kun Earth trigram. This is also the bottom of an inner Kun Earth trigram so we will see a double influence of agglomeration or unification. **"Allying with insiders. Continuing this way is good fortune."** This shows a different type of alliance that is a little bit more difficult to create than the easy one of the first line. The sentences speak of "insiders" because this is the middle line of the Kun trigram of three yin lines. In terms of history, the Zhou people around the time of the *Yijing's* creation were alliance makers who wanted to establish alliances with people within the Shang federation and outside it. At the time of its creation, "insiders" probably referred to the states within the Shang federation, namely parties with which the state of Zhou was associated in some way. Here it just means parties that surround you and are somewhat close to you.

8.3: Yin at the third line which is at the top of the Kun Earth trigram, and hence we should see a yin state since this trigram is all yin lines. This is also the middle line of an inner Kun Earth trigram and bottom line of an inner Gen trigram. **"Allying with foreigners [barbarians, non-humans, villains, evil people]."** In this line the image of barbarians fits the nature of the three yin lines in the Kun trigram. Yet another translation might be "foreigners" instead of "barbarians." Basically there is an alliance with non-Chinese tribes, such as people from *Guifang* the Land of Ghosts (Land of Gui, Demon's region) who are mentioned in later hexagrams. These "ghost people" were considered by the Chinese as barbarians ("non-humans") because of their cultural differences but they were just basically foreigners. In any case, this line represents a different type of partner than in the first two lines. In the first line you allied with people you trusted, in the second line with individuals who surround you in association but who are less trustworthy than good friends, and now you are aligning with individuals ("foreigners") even more different than you who are further removed from you and your interests. The reason you can even make an alliance with foreigners is due to two Kun Earth trigrams of assemblage or agglomeration pulling you together as well as a Gen trigram of Stillness or non-movement that helps keep the binding. In the next line the alliance will be of individuals even more removed from trustworthiness in some way.

8.4: Yin at the fourth line at the beginning of the upper Kan Water trigram. This is also the middle line of an inner Gen Mountain trigram and top line of an inner Kun Earth trigram. **"Allying with outsiders. Continuing this way is good fortune."** This is the topmost of four consecutive yin lines of the hexagram so it is the most external line of that group. Hence there is an image of outsiders. The alliance is good precisely because the Gen trigram and Kun trigram cooperate in making a trustworthy pact in the face of danger (Kan trigram). You've stepped out of the previous trigram hence we are dealing with outsiders (in the new trigram) who in history might refer to people outside of the Shang federation. Since they are outsiders they are even more removed from you in relationships than foreigners (*Guifang* tribes) and yet an alliance is still a good thing. The fourth line of a hexagram often shows a successful achievement of the hexagram's message where a perfect accomplishment is seen in line five, and that's what we have here.

8.5: Yang at the fifth line, within the Kan Danger trigram, and since it is a yang line there is an image of good fortune. This is also the top line of an inner Gen Keeping Still trigram. **"A glorious [illustrious] alliance. The king (uses beaters and) drives game on only three sides, and allows the quarry to escape (on the fourth side) in front of him. The citizens need not fear him. Good fortune."** The fifth line, being the lord of the hexagram, usually shows someone of noble status and typically demonstrates a successful accomplishment or perfect image of the hexagram's meaning. In this case we see a perfect alliance told through the story of a king who goes on a hunt using beaters who flush game towards him from three sides. He leaves one side open which allows some animals to escape by rushing out the opening and fleeing for their lives. The meaning is that the king does not try to grab everyone; if you don't want to ally with him then he'll leave you alone. You have to associate with him voluntarily. *He attracts people to him because of what he has to offer and only allies with those who want to ally with him voluntarily while letting the others leave. He does not coercively force an alliance on you.* Those who are not attracted to him he lets go like the animals that escape through the open side of the beaters, and he does not coercively force them into an agreement. *Thus the people "are not afraid of him" because he works through attraction rather than forceful coercion or punishment.* This is an ideal model of a good alliance because the parties associate with him for mutual benefit and not due to threats. The hunt for game appears in the sentences because it represents the dangerous Kan Danger trigram while the glorious alliance reflects the Gen Mountain trigram.

8.6: Yin at the sixth line, within the Kan Danger trigram, and thus the top line has no head since it is a broken line rather than yang leadership line. **"Allying with partners without a head (leader). Ominous."** Making alliances with others who have no leader (chief) will not work out. That is the same as putting trust in an unstable group consensus rather than in the word of another ruler. A ruler will be responsible for his decisions but a group will not. Hence you can predict the outcome of this bad state of affairs – ominous – which reflects the Kan Danger trigram.

In terms of the overall construction of the trigram and how it is reflected in this final line you have a Kun Earth trigram below and Kan Danger-Water trigram above. Thus in this sentence the unity of the earth element below, an alliance, is being dissolved by the power of water above (headlessness), which foretells danger.

HEXAGRAM 9

Xiao Xu - The Small Accumulates, Domestication

Lower Trigram: Qian (Heaven) – strong force, strong action, great strength
Upper Trigram: Xun (Wind) – emotions vanish, distribute virtue, cyclical

The Judgment: The small accumulates. Success. Dense clouds but no rain from our western outskirts.

There is an image in this hexagram of wind moving in the sky, which actually represents the talk between a married couple as well as their thinking and activity. This hexagram is actually about the trials and tribulations of marriage, and the process of becoming domesticated. In this hexagram a small force accumulates in increments and gradually grows larger without being discharged, which means that *slights grow between the spouses until there is some altercation that provides an opportunity to clear the air*. For instance, you should expect that clouds gradually grow larger in the sky, starting from nearly nothing, and eventually become so full with water that they discharge as rain to nourish the earth. If they do not discharge then things do not happen as expected. The growth of clouds is like the problems that grow within a marriage until there is an argument to clear the air. As small slights accumulate in a relationship without clearing matters the strength of the restraining force must grow until the accumulated disharmonies can no longer be restrained and there is an argumentative explosion or protest of some type. This is the cycle presented within the hexagram. In the first line a separated domesticated animal returns home on the road entirely of its own accord, which symbolizes a spouse resolving a dispute with their mate and repairing the disharmony by returning or agreeing. In the second line an animal is dragged back on a leash into returning home, which means a spouse is pulled back into agreeing with their mate. In the third line the force between going forward and returning is so large that a cart breaks apart and a married couple falls out with each one eyeing the other with contempt, thus splitting the harmonious unity of yin and yang. In the fourth line the two parties calm their emotions and restore their harmonious union after patching up the breach. The fifth line reminds us that the trust and sincerity felt between husband and wife binds them together; just as neighbors enrich one another through mutual assistance so do husband and wife. This helpfulness of neighbors symbolizes what the partners within a marriage do for one another. In the last line a rain cloud has finally discharged its rain to replenish the earth, and then the sky must restart the process of accumulation before there can be rain again. This is like issues within marriage that gradually come to a boil, erupt and then are resolved until eventually something new comes along. As long as there is trust and sincerity within the relationship the unity will hold despite the discharge of occasional disputes and disagreements. This is the meaning of the small accumulating; small slights and complaints will accumulate in a marriage until discharged and then the parties must maintain the healing peace as long as possible. During this time you should not initiate any behaviors that would cause enmity to arise again such as immediately launching into another altercation.

1. Returning by the road. How could this be trouble? Auspicious.

2. Dragged back in returning. Auspicious.

3. Cart and axle separate. Husband and wife glare at one another (fall out).

4. If there is sincerity then blood (anger) will vanish and fear give way. There is no trouble.

5. The captives are bound together. Neighbors enrich each other (neighbors become wealthy together).

6. The rain has fallen and settled, increase (accumulate) the virtue (once again) and then distribute it. The continuance of this (maintaining such a cycle) is dangerous for woman. The moon is almost full. If the superior man sets forth on an undertaking there will be misfortune.

9.1: Yang at the bottom line, and at the bottom of the Qian Great Strength or Heavenly Way trigram. **"(Voluntarily) returning by the road (of its own volition). How could there be any trouble in this? Auspicious."** In the Qian trigram, the intensity of any force will grow as you progress to the top line, which is the case for the hexagram as well. In this line a domesticated animal that was lost returns home of its own volition by following the road. *It does so voluntarily of its own accord* so the compelling force of return is small due to this natural inclination to return home (Qian Heavenly Way trigram). The *Yijing* is a book of symbolism, so another example would be a married couple who had a dispute that separates the two in opinion but is then naturally resolved, or one of them is involved in some activity of which the other disproves, catches himself and voluntarily ceases doing so without being told. Husband and wife return to harmonious union on their own.

9.2: Yang at the second line within the middle of the Qian trigram. This is also the bottom line of an inner Dui Joy trigram (lines 2-4). **"Dragged back in returning. Auspicious."** The middle line of the Qian Heaven trigram is stronger than its first line so the force involved in the returning or restoration is stronger; i.e. the person is *forced to return* because they are dragged back by a cord into submission. There is an image of animals on a leash being pulled to go home which is "dragged back into returning." A similar example of being pulled or dragged back is when a wife tells her husband not to do something, which would reflect the bottom line of the inner Dui Mouth trigram, and against his will he must reluctantly be drawn back into conformity with her wishes for good fortune. "Auspicious" (good fortune) is the end result because this is a yang line, harmony is restored, and because we have the presence of the Dui Joy trigram of happiness.

9.3: Yang at the third line, and at the top of the Qian Great Force trigram. This is also the middle line of an inner Dui trigram and bottom line of an inner Li trigram. **"Cart and axle separate. Husband and wife roll their eyes at each other (fall out)."** The force of pulling apart (Qian trigram) that we saw resolved in lines one and two is now so strong that it causes a cart and its axle to separate. Such a strong force can mean an argument between wife and husband who then separate from one another due to the strong disagreement. They almost get to quarrelling but since the dense clouds don't rain it doesn't turn into a big fight. Nevertheless the partners are exasperated with one another and roll or cross their eyes. The line represents an increase in the intensity of the Qian force pulling them apart, a verbal disagreement (Dui Talking trigram) and even fire in the relationship (their eyes roll due to the Li trigram). Eyes rolling is a sign of contempt showing that they are disgusted with one another.

9.4: Yin at the fourth line and at the beginning of the upper Xun Wind trigram. This is also the middle line of an inner Li trigram and top line of an inner Dui trigram. **"If there is sincerity blood will vanish and fear will give way [leave, diminish], and there will be no trouble."** Although husband and wife strongly disagreed in the previous line because the force of opposition was so strong, if there is a real attunement of sincerity, warmth, loyalty, trust or faithful allegiance between them then the disunity can be repaired. Most good relationships have an "us against the world" feeling that helps keep the partners together, they don't "talk shit" about each other, and they handle each other with care. The presence of an inner

Dui Joy trigram guarantees this core allegiance. The hexagram is about the small being tamed, and in this case an argument is tamed by the couple's inner regard for one another. Because of this inner unity/sincerity there will be no long-term trouble. Any blood (anger) in the face due to the Li Fire trigram, or any fear (the yin line of the Xun trigram) can disappear if sincerity (Dui trigram) between the two is renewed again.

9.5: Yang at the fifth line in the middle of the Xun Wind trigram. This is also the top line of an inner Li Brilliance trigram. **"Captives are bound (twisted) together. Neighbors enrich one another."** The statement that people are linked with one another, entangled together, bound or bonded together represents marriage *but the example used to represent this binding is neighbors who become united in friendship* through the mutual affiliation of trusting human relationships. Neighbors that enrich one another mean that husband and wife enrich one another. Neighbors represent marriage partners since husband and wife are like strangers at the initial stage of arranged marriages found in China. In a marriage the partners are considerate and loyal to one another rather than adversaries. They try to understand one another, don't take each other for granted, give each other complements, and work through their issues as they strive for a common goal. Psychologists think that the happiest marriages are of partners who are conscientious towards one another (in attunement), low in neuroticism (emotionally stable, easy going, peaceful and lacking a degree of chaos that would disturb the relationship), and are moderate adventurers rather than incessant novelty seekers. In this hexagram the "small accumulates" so the neighbors become wealthy together because they help one another just as do married couples. Marriage partners become bound to one another and end up enriching each other as good neighbors do. This line is certainly a veiled reference to marriage once again. It is the fifth line of the hexagram, and thus represents its perfected message that *while husbands and wives will often end up disagreeing with one another (as neighbors do) they are bound together and ultimately enrich each others lives despite those occasional differences*. This message is simply represented using the analogy of neighbors rather than spouses.

9.6: Yang at the top line, at the top of the Xun Wind trigram. This ends the hexagram and so here we have a summary lesson. **"The rain has fallen and settled, increase the virtue (once again) and then distribute it. The firm continuance of maintaining such a cycle is dangerous for woman. The moon is almost full. If the superior man sets forth on a new undertaking there will be misfortune."** All along a small force (of disagreements or complaints between husband and wife) slowly accumulated, which is seen through the image of a heavy cloud incrementally growing but not yet discharging rain despite becoming heavy.

For a long time the rain accumulates in clouds just as frustrations accumulate in a marriage. The accumulation of rain cannot last forever but must one day be discharged, just as husband and wife will eventually erupt into arguments. In this line the accumulation of small raindrops over time has ultimately caused a rain shower, the sky has cleared and the water has settled into the earth. Analogously, after a husband and wife argue they can clear the air of differences and start afresh again. Studies show that forgiveness is a key attribute to a sustainable, happy marriage and this is a time to clear the air and patch things up. Hence, "The rain has fallen and settled, accumulate the virtue (once again) and then distribute it." The rain cycle can be described as a cycle of accumulating virtue (cloud moisture) and then distributing it everywhere through discharge. However, "The firm continuance of this (this boom and bust cycle) is dangerous for woman" because women should be *continuously virtuous*; in terms of Chinese culture they should not be continuously argumentative or nag their husbands or build up resentments in a cycle. Next, "The moon is almost full" means that the yin force has reached an extreme when no new irritating actions or differences should take place otherwise it will cause trouble. After clearing the air you are on thin ice where one wrong move can get you in trouble again, so partners have to be gentle with one another and go through a healing phase. It has just rained so it is time for resting in peacefulness and clearing the air rather than a time to increase the seeds of conflict again. At this time a man should not initiate behaviors or undertakings that will cause any resentment to grow between the partners but should instead give attention to restoring harmony in the relationship. Hence, "If the superior man goes forward there will be misfortune." You could also say, "*Even if it were* a superior man any going forth at this time would result in misfortune." Psychologist John Gottman, a marriage and relationship expert, would say this is a time for repair and gentleness with one another. If a woman engages in a consistent cycle of continuously building up resentment and then discharging it in arguments, or if a man similarly keeps consistently performing conduct that that causes conflict with the wife then there will be trouble.

In terms of the hexagram's construction a Qian trigram (virtue) lies beneath a Xun Wind trigram on top, which means there should be a growing increase in virtue that is then distributed (Xun trigram).

HEXAGRAM 10

Lu – Cautious Advance, Advancing With Care, Watching Your Step, Respectful Conduct

Lower Trigram: Dui (Joy) – comfortable, pleasurable, mouth
Upper Trigram: Qian (Heaven) – tiger, resoluteness, strong action

The Judgment: Treading (stepping) on a tiger's tail without getting bitten. Success.

This hexagram is about carefully progressing (advancing, treading) through dangerous situations, i.e. making a cautious advance during some dangerous undertaking as in war. You might consider advancing with care as *respectful conduct*. In the hexagram each subsequent line entails advancing through dangers that are progressively greater with each line. Thus an individual must increase their level of caution in each subsequent line. In each line there is a different result from "stepping on a tiger's tail," which means encountering dangerous conditions. In the first line there is the act of ordinary walking that doesn't require any special caution or attention. In the second line there is walking in a cautious way to avoid problems. In the third line there is the ignorant act of advancing blindly and then stumbling into troubles as a consequence. In the fourth line you recognize your previous mistake in not paying attention and now you tread more carefully through dangers. In the fifth line you make the mistake of advancing with a bravado of over-confidence that abandons caution. The theme of the hexagram is not to be careless like this in advancing through dangerous territory. In the sixth line you have learned all these lessons and now cautiously watch where you step wherever you go. You are careful in advancing because you analyze the circumstances around yourself and take notice of whatever happens as you progress. Thus you can do as the Judgment advises, which is tread on a tiger's tail (advance through dangerous situations) without getting bitten.

1. Simple (plain) walking. There is no trouble.

2. Walking on a smooth, level road. Seclusion like that of a recluse is auspicious.

3. A blind man can see. A lame man can walk. He steps on the tail of a tiger and it bites him. Ominous. A military man acts on behalf of a great lord.

4. He treads on the tail of a tiger apprehensively. In the end auspicious.

5. Resolute walking (advancement). Persistently continuing in this way is dangerous.

6. He watches where he treads and inspects the signs (circumstances, results) within his circumference. Supreme good fortune.

10.1: Yang at the bottom line, at the beginning of the Dui trigram that represents joy. **"Simple, plain walking. There is no trouble."** Advancing is easy and requires no special wariness or precautions. This reflects the nature of the Dui Joy trigram where its talking aspect might in this case represent walking, or the (joyous) ease of not having to be cautious because the situation is comfortable or non-threatening.

10.2: Yang at the second line of the Dui trigram. This is also the bottom line of an inner Li Elegance trigram. **"Walking on a smooth and level road. Seclusion like that of a recluse (hermit) is good fortune (because it avoids troubles)."** Walking on a smooth road (the easiness of the joyous Dui trigram) means that the going is an easy path where there are no dangers. Seclusion is also an easy path lacking in dangers because a recluse, hermit, or solitary individual lives a peaceful life by entirely avoiding people and their issues. They don't get entangled in the affairs of the world and thus reduce any potential occasions for trouble by living peacefully (the Li trigram) by themselves. In the first line there is no trouble, but in this line *you avoid trouble*. You hide yourself away and avoid engagments.

10.3: Yin at the third line, which often represents bad fortune, and at the top of the Dui trigram that sometimes symbolizes a mouth (or in the case of this hexagram a biting tiger). This is also the middle line of an inner Li trigram that might be a tiger (due to its brilliant coat), and is the bottom line of an inner Xun Wind trigram that tends to be destructive. **"A blind man can see. A lame man can walk. He treads on a tiger's tail and it bites him. Ominous. This is like a soldier acting on behalf of a great lord."** The reference to a blind (or weak-eyed) and lame man show the influence of the inner Li trigram (seeing) and Xun trigram (walking). These two examples are of people who have limitations and can still function but not very well. These men cannot see clearly or walk properly so they must be careful. They might not be able to see things clearly or their abilities might not be up to the task. If they try to do things beyond their limited capabilities, and if they are not particularly careful, they could end up in trouble. In this case, being handicapped (either because he cannot see the tiger or cannot walk well) a man encounters trouble because he steps on a tiger's tail and he consequently gets bitten (inner Xun Destructive Penetrating Wind trigram). This is ominous because it foretells more troubles. It can be compared to a soldier acting on behalf of a great lord because a soldier is sent into battles where he must fumble around and never knows what will happen next (he is blind) and he faces danger everywhere where his abilities are taxed (he is lame). He never knows the full details of any situation and always encounters danger, which is why he steps on a tiger's tail. Since it bites him it is an omen or sign of more troubles to come.

10.4: Yang at the fourth line at the beginning of the Qian Heaven trigram representing a powerful force. This is also the middle line of an inner Xun Wind trigram and top line of an inner Li trigram. **"He treads on the tiger's tail apprehensively [carefully, with utmost caution and circumspection]. In the end auspicious."** In the previous line a person stumbled into trouble due to either not seeing the dangerous situation clearly or because of maneuvering clumsily due to lameness (where there abilities were inadequate). In this line you go into a situation *knowing that it is dangerous* and therefore act very carefully with great caution and awareness to avoid any trouble and this prudent circumspection results in good fortune. "He treads on the tiger's tail (Qian trigram) apprehensively (with great caution)" because he knows it is very fierce and can kill him (the destructive Xun trigram and strong Qian trigram) so he takes great caution and remains alert, careful and circumspect. It is a yang line of good fortune that also benefits from the Li trigram of mental acuity, so "In the end there is good fortune" if he acts this way.

10.5: Yang at the fifth line in the middle of the Qian Heaven trigram has an image of strength that reflects the power of the Heaven trigram. This is also the top line of an inner Dui Carefree Joy trigram. **"Resolute walking [advancement]. Persistently continuing in this way is dangerous."** This line must show strength because it is a yang line sandwiched between two other yang lines; it is the strong middle line of the Qian Great Strength trigram. Hence, now with *over-confidence* the individual engages in resolute bold walking (possibly in the face of danger) where there is no indication of any caution at all. "Resolute walking" means determined firm advancement but while doing so an individual often fails to remain aware of danger. There is only resoluteness and careless bravado (Dui trigram). There are "tigers" (dangers) around so being oblivious to that danger calls forth the warning, "Persistently continuing in this way is dangerous," which needs no explanation. Since this is the fifth line of the hexagram that should display its general theme the Judgment's warning comes through that you should tread (step) on a tiger's tail without getting bitten. However, you can only do this if you are cautious and circumspect rather than inattentive and careless with bravado. The advice of the hexagram is to be careful in dangerous situations because only then you can pass through them successfully. If this was a military initiative the idea would be to remain cautious while performing your mission.

10.6: Yang at the sixth line completes the hexagram, and it is the top line of the upper Qian Heaven trigram. **"He watches where he treads, and examines [analyzes, studies, inspects] the signs [auspices, circumstances] within his circumference [orbit]. Supreme good fortune."** He is cautiously looking before he takes his steps, watching where he treads, and he examines the situations around himself to assess what is happening and what to do for each step. This careful behavior will produce supreme good fortune because *this is the proper way to advance to avoid dangers and troubles*. Always watch where you are going and what you are doing, take notice of your surroundings, avoid problems, be careful if you encounter dangerous situations, and never abandon caution for bravado. This is a yang line within the upper Qian trigram that represents progressing forward, therefore the words "swirling" or "revolving" in the Mawangdui manuscript pertain to the circumstances, activities and events rapidly happening around the individual within the circumference of his vicinity. They pertain to rapidly changing changing situations (events or circumstances) within a perimeter around the individual.

In terms of the construction of the hexagram and how it manifests in this line there is a Dui trigram beneath a Qian trigram composing the hexagram. Hence there is a warning against oblivious carelessness (Dui) in the proximity of a situation of great force (Qian) that can hurt you, and if you can be circumspect then you can have good fortune (Dui trigram). Thus "he watches where he treads."

HEXAGRAM 11

Tai – Improvement of Status, Greatness

Lower Trigram: Qian (Heaven) – resistance, army campaign, perseverance
Upper Trigram: Kun (Earth) – neighbors, royalty, city wall, troops

The Judgment: Improvement of Status. The small departs. The great arrives. Auspicious. Success.

This hexagram has an image of heaven descending to the earth and intermixing with it, which means that humans receive heavenly help for their positive efforts. There is peace in the world due to this interaction. There are several major ideas contained within this hexagram. Its bottom half is the Qian Heaven trigram of Great Force that is slowly pushing its way upwards until the energy finally reaches the upper Kun Earth trigram. It embodies a great force that gradually rises and passes through difficulties including those in the upper trigram. In the upper Kun Earth trigram of three yin lines, which offers less resistance to its force, it elevates the status of those lines unless it is too destructive in the last line of the hexagram where it topples walls of earth. In each line there is also a unification of upper and lower status people that represents the union of the Heaven and Earth trigrams stacked upon one another. Thus there is a symbolism of the unity of Heaven and Earth (heavenly beings helping humans) within this hexagram due to its design. In this unity people who are weaker, "smaller" or of less status move forward together with those of higher status who take them with them, and thus they achieve elevation. In the first line grass roots, which we can consider "small" since they are hidden in the earth, are plucked along with their "higher" stems while a collection of men, great and small, similarly set out together on a military expedition. The grass is probably used for a sacrifice. In the second line the leftover grass is taken with you across a great river, which means you travel with some surviving men and you also get promoted among their ranks. In the third line an individual moves forward to achieve progress (elevation) by persevering through difficulties and thereby achieves wealth and status (sustenance). In the fourth line, despite an elevated position he goes back to visit his old neighbors (friends) out of a sincere longing to see them. In the fifth line the daughter of the king achieves elevation due to getting married. In the sixth line city walls fall into the moat due to the great strength of the Heaven trigram passing through the lines. In each line except for the last the status of "the small" was elevated to become greater. Thus the Judgment states that the small departs and the great arrives.

1. Pluck the cogon grass stems together with their roots. Marching forth on a military campaign (undertaking a venture) is auspicious.

2. Wrap the waste, use it to ford the river. Do not leave it behind. Although (some) friends will be lost one gains elevation amidst this group.

3. There is no plain (level ground) that does not lead to a slope. There is no going (trip) without returning. Continuing with perseverance through difficulties is blameless. Do not worry over one's trust (that this way is correct) for within this food (sustenance) are blessings.

4. Fluttering, fluttering (he flies down to visit). He does not use his affluence on his neighbors. He needs no admonition on sincerity.

5. The Sovereign Yi gives his daughter in marriage with felicitations. Supreme good fortune.

6. The city wall falls into the moat. Do not field the army troops. Issue commands (give orders) to the city. An omen of distress.

11.1: Yang at the first line bodes good fortune, and it is the beginning of the Qian Heaven trigram that indicates a strong force. **"Pluck the cogon grass together with the roots. Marching forth on a military campaign [advancing, moving forward, undertaking a venture] brings good fortune."** In this hexagram the Earth and Heaven trigrams are on top of one another so in most of the lines there is symbolism of the meeting of Heaven and Earth. Here the grass stalks represent Heaven while the roots represent Earth and the two are plucked together; when you uproot the grass stems they come up attached with their roots. The idea is that two groups – heavenly and earthly, superior and inferior, great and small – are pulled up together in a group because the roots are plucked together with the stems. Then the two advance together, which is symbolized by marching to war, so it means that different levels of people are conscripted for war and assembled together. The roots (the small) are being elevated because they are being taken along with the stems (the great or officers) and mixed together for a great effort. Cogon grass was used in sacrificial ceremonies, which would include an offering to Heaven asking for help and protection before a war.

11.2: Yang at the second line in the middle of the Qian Heaven trigram. This is also the bottom of an inner Dui trigram. **"Wrap the waste, use it to ford the river. Do not leave it behind. Some friends are lost but you will gain elevation [honor] amidst this group."** This line tells you to bundle the cogon grass of the previous line (which was used for sacrifices) and to take it with you when you undertake the difficult task of crossing the river (because the crossing will be difficult). Opposite hexagram line 12.2 says "Wrapped up by (bearing and enduring) what you have received (the circumstances that have happened to you)." Crossing the river (Dui trigram since it is water) is possible because of the great force of the Qian trigram that is all yang lines, but it will still require some luck or protection which is why you take the cogon grass leftovers with you, which also stands for fellow soldiers. After you ford the great river you will have left friends behind who will be lost to you forever, but in the midst of this new group you will gain elevation probably due to some type of promotion. Also, by associating with the uncultured the juxtaposition reveals your elevated status in another way too. This is why "One gains elevation in their midst," where "amidst" is mentioned because you are surrounded by two other yang lines. This line could mean fighting in a war where you embrace men of all types as comrades, you leave your friends at home when you are conscripted, and you lose some of your new comrades to death while you not only survive but are promoted (elevated).

11.3: Yang at the third line at the top of the Qian Heaven trigram. This is also the middle line of an inner Dui Mouth trigram and top line of an inner Zhen Lightning trigram. **"There is no flat ground that does not slope. There is no going (trip) without returning. Persevering through difficulties is blameless. Do not worry [be anxious] over trusting that this way is correct because within this food (sustenance) are blessings."** Once again images of both Heaven and Earth appear in a line because flat ground represents Heaven while a slope represents Earth. Travel has easy times (Heaven since it is all yang lines) and difficult times (Earth since it is all yin lines representing obstructions). You've been progressing through the Heaven trigram, as symbolized by the flat land, and now you will face the yin difficulties of the coming Earth trigram. You must persevere (Qian trigram) through those difficulties and must not doubt that pressing forward is the right thing to do because through the difficulties will eventually come blessings. For instance, *you fight in a righteous war, suffering difficulties, and win in the end.* You are told to trust that blessings (sustenance) will come through this difficult path that requires persevering through many hardships. This is how the small moves forward and becomes elevated in status.

11.4: Yin at the fourth line at the beginning of the Kun Assembly trigram. This is also the middle line of an inner Zhen trigram, and the top line of an inner Dui trigram. **"Fluttering, fluttering (he flied down to visit neighbors). He does not show off his affluence to impress his neighbors. He needs no admonition on sincerity."** This hexagram is about your status improving step by step, and within it there is usually the image of a heavenly (superior) status matching with the earthly lower status that corresponds to the masses of society. Hence, here the individual has passed through the troubles in line three and risen in rank and status because that happens in each line. He suddenly comes fluttering down (the Zhen trigram means fluttering and descending insinuates coming from a higher status such as from Qian Heaven), descending suddenly and unannounced like a bird flapping its wings to visit his old neighbors and friends (Kun Earth trigram) that he had left behind and did not forget. Perhaps this "fluttering about" mean he is now wearing the silk robes of an official and its sleeves flutter as he moves about, or it just means that this visit is a sudden random event that occurs without planning because the neighbors were not warned about his visit. In any case he now has a superior status but does not boast/flaunt his affluent position to his neighbors and thus Heaven and Earth mix together with sincerity. He doesn't need any lecture on sincerity because he has no motivation to visit other than to sincerely enjoy (Dui trigram) the relationship because this is an aspiration of his heart.

11.5: Yin at the fifth line in the middle of the Kun Earth trigram. This is also the top line of an inner Xun Wind trigram. **"The Sovereign Yi gives his daughter in marriage with felicitations. Supreme good fortune."** The fifth line is the ruler of the hexagram, and within this line there is usually a symbol of royalty or high status as well as the perfected message of the hexagram. Since this line is also in the middle of the Kun Earth trigram that is all yin we should see a strong image of yin, and thus we have the image of a princess. The high status we might expect comes from the fact that it is the king's daughter given in marriage, and the message of the hexagram is that the king united his family with that of a subordinate through marriage. Di Yi is the second to last ruler of the Shang dynasty who married his daughter to Ji Chang, Earl of the West (King Wen of Zhou), because he was becoming very popular and he wanted to join the two clans in marriage. The hexagram is about the small becoming elevated to a greater status which is happening here through marriage. Thus we then have a matching of Heaven (royalty) and Earth (the man of climbing status) again which we usually see in each line.

11.6: Yin at the top of the hexagram and at the top of the Kun Earth trigram, so there is an image of Earth and misfortune that represents the yin line. **"The city wall falls [collapses, tumbles] into the moat. Don't use the army. Announce commands [orders] within the city. An omen of distress."** Unfortunately, the great strength of the Qian Heaven trigram has finally reached the top of the hexagram with excessive force, thus collapsing the city walls composed of the earth element (Kun trigram). The city is now defenseless. Those walls, made of earth, represent the individual's ascension from a commoner of the masses to an official running a city but now there is an omen of decline. What was built up out of earth to touch the sky (city walls) now falls back into the water so the extreme of yang turns to yin that warns we will soon see a status reversal. The official does not muster the army troops because there is no external foe. Instead he issues commands to the people of the city (Kun trigram) to start making repairs. The man, who started out as a soldier in line one, is now an official who puts aside the military and issues orders to the common people thus demonstrating his high status. The last line of a hexagram usually has to do with reaching the end of the storyline, or going too far so that the situation turns into its opposite, and in this line yang is turning to yin. The ascension has turned into its opposite and there is now an omen of distress because the hexagram is over and will change into a new one. The omen is that the city or country is on the decline and its destiny is in trouble, and therefore the man's ascension is in trouble and due for a decline. Perhaps this reflects the fact that the next hexagram 12 means obstruction.

In terms of the construction of the hexagram being reflected in this line, the hexagram is composed of a Qian Great Strength trigram beneath a Kun Earth trigram, and hence this line embodies this composition via the image of city walls (Kun) collapsing into the moat due to the Qian Great Force.

HEXAGRAM 12

Pi – Obstruction, Hindrances, Standstill, Stagnation, Overthrowing Obstructions, Overturning Blockages

Lower Trigram: Kun (Earth) – cogon grass, obstruction, wrapped meat
Upper Trigram: Qian (Heaven) – a command, great force, overturning

The Judgment: Depraved (offensive) people are present (obstructing matters). The situation is not favorable (bodes ill) for the course of (upright) noble people. The great departs and the small arrives.

This hexagram has an image of heaven above the earth without them interacting with one another because they are both in their places, which means humans are not receiving heavenly help in their endeavors, thus humans face obstructions in their dealings. This hexagram is about your progress or advancement being blocked by powerful obstructions in which case you must accept that the situation has come to a *standstill* unless you overthrow the blockage. It should be titled "Overturning Obstructions" or "Overturning Hindrances and Blockages." In the first line you try to pull up grass but are thwarted (obstructed) by the roots offering some opposition, which is a mild form of opposition. In the second line you are really wrapped up by unfortunate circumstances and reminded that a superior individual will work through them while an inferior person will just give up and accept the blockages to then remain at a standstill. In the third line sauced meat is tightly wrapped up so that the sauces don't leak out, hence the wrappings are a type of obstruction that bind up everything. The wrapping represents an even greater intensity of blockages or obstructions over the previous lines because even liquid doesn't leak out. In the fourth line that is the beginning of the upper trigram you start making progress in cutting through obstructions because a command comes to divide a field, which represents cutting through a blockage or obstruction. In the fifth line you finally overthrow a powerful obstruction and because this was so difficult you try to secure your stage of progress so that it isn't lost. The last line offers the simple advice that in life you'll always encounter obstructions but after you eliminate or overthrow those hindrances you'll be happier. The hexagram is composed of the Qian Great Force trigram on top of the Kun Earth trigram, which symbolizes an obstructive earthly force being pierced through by a stronger force. The Judgment reminds us that brigands, "non-humans" or barbarians, oppress the people and must be eliminated (overthrown) with an example being the wicked ruler King Zhou Xi, the last king of the Shang dynasty who was overthrown because he was a tyrant.

1. Pull up cogon grass and with it come the roots. Continuing onwards as you are doing is auspicious. Success.

2. Wrapped up by (bearing and enduring) what you have received (the circumstances that have happened to you). For an inferior man (to remain this way is) auspicious, for a great man not. Success.

3. Wrapped savory (sauced, spiced) meat offering.

4. An order (command) comes. No trouble. Blessings are attached to dividing up (splitting apart) a field.

5. Success against the obstruction (the standstill is giving way). For the great man auspicious. What if it should fail, what if it should fail? Tie it to a bushy mulberry tree.

6. Overturn an obstruction (decrease the blockage). At first a blockage, afterwards joy.

12.1: Yin at the first line at the beginning of the Kun Earth trigram that symbolizes the earth element. **"Pull up cogon grass and with it come the roots. Continuing onwards as you are doing is auspicious [fortuitous, advantageous]. Success."** Here we see an image of grass and grass roots that represent the Kun trigram earth element. This also represents obstruction or hindrance because when you are trying to pull up grass you are inhibited by the roots that tug back at you. In ancient China cogon grass was used to thatch huts but it doesn't matter whether this is cogon grass, grass reeds or any other type of weed since that is not the important issue. We are at the beginning of the hexagram whose meaning is working against blockages of powerful forces and the humble roots at this stage of intensity therefore resist you. They represent the lowest gradient or stage of hindrance and opposition. Naturally you must continue to work away at hindrances because the true name of the hexagram is "Overthrowing an Obstruction" or "Hindrance Overturned" so "Continuing onwards as you are doing is fortuitous."

12.2: Yin at the second line in the middle of the Kun Earth trigram. This is also the bottom of an inner Gen Mountain trigram. **"Wrapped up by (bearing and enduring) what you have received (the circumstances that have happened to you). For an inferior man (to remain this way is) auspicious, for a great man not. Success."** This is a yin line surrounded by two other yin lines because it is within the center of a Kun Earth trigram. *Thus it is effectively wrapped by them.* The line is also obstructed, held in place, or trapped at the bottom of an inner Gen Mountain trigram that represents non-movement. Hence, "You remain wrapped up (obstructed) by what has happened, by the circumstances you have received." If you want to get through a standstill or obstruction you cannot stop and patiently comport yourself by accepting the standstill but must work through it. For an inferior man to accept obstructions and the cease of progress is okay. However, a great man (superior man) will not accept negative circumstances forcing him to come to a halt so a superior man will keep working to change or eliminate them.

12.3: Yin at the third line, which is at end of the Kun Earth trigram. This is also the middle line of an inner Gen Mountain trigram and bottom line of an inner Xun Penetrating Wind trigram. **"A wrapped offering of [sauced, spiced] meat."** This means that something good is bound or wrapped up, which is the sauced meat. It is wrapped so that it does not leak out just as in future hexagram line 33.3 a piglet is bound up to avoid harm while servants and concubines are taken care of. The meaning of the line is that an obstruction creates protection. The Kun, Gen and Xun trigrams all appear in this image because the meat is the Kun Earth trigram, its leaky saucy nature is the Xun Penetrating Wind trigram, and the fact that it is wrapped is the Gen Non-Movement trigram.

12.4: Yang at the fourth line and at the beginning of the Qian Heaven trigram of great strength or great force. This is also the middle line of an inner Xun Wind trigram and top line of an inner Gen trigram. **"An order (command) comes. No trouble. Felicitations are attached to dividing up (splitting apart) a field."** The fourth line of a hexagram often shows a successful achievement of its message where a more perfect accomplishment is seen in line five. Here an order arrives that you must obey and it leads to activity that helps you, which is why there are felicitations. Following the order entails carving up a field (representing obstructions), and the order is readily accepted by everyone so there is no trouble. He acts accordingly after receiving the command. Dividing up the field is a manifestation of the inner Xun Wind trigram since the wind element represents destructive penetration while the undivided field represents a large obstruction (Gen trigram). Due to the command you use force (Qian trigram) to start splitting up the obstruction so it is cut apart just as a single plot of land is divided. Thus the Xun trigram pierces the Gen trigram with a strong force (the Qian trigram) so there are "blessings" because of reducing a powerful force that has been blocking you.

12.5: Yang at the fifth line in the middle of the Qian Heaven trigram, so we would normally see good fortune and success, which in this hexagram would mean eliminating powerful obstructions. This is also the top line of an inner Xun Penetrating Wind trigram that usually represents destruction. **"Success against the obstruction (stagnation ends). Auspicious for the great person. It might be lost, it might be lost. Tie it to a flourishing mulberry tree."** The fifth line represents a perfected form of the message of the hexagram, hence in this line you have finally broken through the blockage because you have worked to eliminate it just as any great man would. That is the message of the hexagram. However, since hindrances, obstructions or oppression might return (due to the presence of the Xun trigram) the advice is to tie your success to a (growing) mulberry tree so that you don't lose it. Chinese tradition holds that the mulberry tree is sturdy and resilient with deep roots and fast growth. It also represents the Xun Wood trigram, but in a positive sense rather than as a negative influence. Mulberry trees were planted next to houses to protect them against the wind and provide shade. When its branches are cut the mulberry tree generates shoots that are sturdier than before so it is hard to kill. Hence, you must tie your success to its hardy sturdiness and strong growth tendencies to secure your progress while continuing at efforts to advance.

12.6: Yang at the top line and at the top of the Qian Heaven trigram. Here we therefore have the mention of good fortune. **"Overturn an obstruction (decrease the blockage). At first a blockage, afterwards joy [happiness, rejoicing]."** Since this line concludes the hexagram we have a lesson summarizing its overall theme, which in this case is advice to work through blockages, hindrances and standstills until you pierce through them and attain success. At first there was a hindrance, later there is happiness because you break through all the obstructions that blocked you. A strong force tends to suppress the weak and create a standstill unless it is overcome and when that finally happens there is rejoicing.

In terms of the composition of the hexagram and how it appears in this line there is a Kun Earth trigram beneath a Qian Heaven trigram. Therefore the construction of this line says there is an underlying "obstruction" or "blockage" (Kun) that has been overthrown (due to the force of Qian) and now there is happiness. The way this appears in this line is, "An obstruction is overturned … afterwards there is rejoicing."

HEXAGRAM 13

Tong Ren – A Fellowship of Men, Friendship, Companions Gathering Together, Fellowship With Others

Lower Trigram: Li (Fire) – brilliance, elegance, shining, light, clarity, mind
Upper Trigram: Qian (Heaven) – great strength, creative, strong action

The Judgment: Men gather together in the wilderness. Success. Beneficial to ford the great river. Persistently keeping onwards is beneficial for a superior man.

This hexagram highlights various stages involved in assembling together a great body of men who gradually grow together in *fellowship and brotherhood* because of the troubles they face. There is an image of fire below heaven so the hexagram involves military operations and the agglomeration of men as a body of troops to fight a war. Think of the lines of this hexagram as a story where there are increasingly larger gatherings of men who unify into progressively larger military forces. At first a few men assemble at a gate as a social occurrence in line one. Later there is some distressing news so a larger group of men meet at the ancestral temple in line two which is probably to discuss an upcoming military draft or the war news in general. After joining the army, in line three the enemy is seen hiding in the underbrush ready for battle so a large group of men ascend to higher ground to thwart them. Next, in line four they gather together with other troops within a city to create an even greater assembly, and they ascend to even higher fortifications by occupying the top of the city walls to defend it. In line five, this large body of men increases in size again by uniting with another battalion so that two large bands of men combine, which makes everyone rejoice. Finally the assembly of men proceeds past the city to its outskirts where the country folk can also participate in a ceremony of thanks for the conclusion of the war. These lines are all stages of men gathering together where they become companions in a growing assembly that develops into a larger unified force. The Judgment states that men gather together in the wilds to do a great deed (warfare) and should perseverance in their activity.

1. Gathering of men at the gate. There is no trouble.

2. Gathering of men at the ancestral temple. Distress.

3. (Enemy) Soldiers lie hidden in the tall grass. Ascend the high hill (so that) for three years they will not rise.

4. Mounting the city walls you cannot be attacked (because the fortified walls are unassailable). Auspicious.

5. The comrades first cry and weep, but later laugh. The great armies meet each other (and unite).

6. Gathering of men outside of the city (in the countryside). There is no regret.

13.1: Yang at the bottom line, and the beginning of the Li Fire trigram. **"Gathering [union, assembly] of men at the gate. There is no trouble [harm]."** This is the first level of gathering with other men at a time when there is no trouble at all – fellow men at the gate. This is symbolized by the fact that they socially gather together at a gate that symbolizes the entryway to something significant. The activity of men assembling together is symbolized by the Li Fire trigram, rather than the Kun Earth trigram, because this involves hustle and bustle, the social activity of talking to one another, excitement, activity and possibly war. The Li trigram also symbolizes military action.

13.2: Yin at the second line as the middle of the Li Fire trigram. This is also the beginning line of an inner Xun Penetrating Wind trigram. **"Gathering [assembly, union] of men at the ancestral temple [clan hall] because there will be trouble."** The yin of this line means we will see some bad fortune. Fellow men at the ancestral temple – this is a regretful or worrisome gathering at the clan hall where a community of men assemble together because they know trouble is coming, which is due to a destructive inner Xun Penetrating Wind trigram. They are now already a larger group, namely a village or clan. Preparing for trouble like this is a more urgent level of gathering than in the first line and more men assemble together too. The men assemble at the ancestral temple or clan hall in a distressful state of mind and will ask the ancestors for help for what is to come.

13.3: Yang at the third line, and the top of the Li trigram. This is also the middle of an inner Xun Wind trigram and bottom line of an inner Qian Great Force trigram. **"Enemy soldiers are crouching in the tall grass** [underbrush]. Ascend [climb] the high hill (because by doing so) they will not rise for three years."** In this line the men have already been drafted into the military, which is the Li Military trigram and Qian Great Force trigram. The enemy soldiers are also present as a reflection of the Qian Great Force trigram and dangerous Xun Penetrating Force trigram. However, this is the Li Fire trigram so there should be some sort of ascension (since fire rises) that should be helped by the Qian Heaven trigram. The enemy remains hidden in the grass but the fellowship of men can climb to a higher point to make camp, just as fire rises, because the Li trigram ascends and shows off rather than hides itself. Therefore the men ascend the high hill because by doing so the enemy soldiers can be watched and this will dissuade them from attacking. By occupying high ground you can observe an enemy's movements and thereby prevent them from making an assault. The "three years" without attack by enemy troops refers to the next three yang lines of the hexagram, which means the fighting commences in line five where it will probably be successful.

13.4: Yang at the fourth line at the beginning of the upper Qian Heaven trigram of great strength or strong force. This is also the middle line of an inner Qian trigram and top line of an inner Xun Wind trigram. **"Standing on the walls of the city [fortified battlements] you cannot be overcome (because the fortified walls are unassailable). Auspicious."** Since the upper Qian Heaven trigram is on top of the lower Li Fire trigram (fire burns and flares upward) we see an ascension in heights once again (which parallels the increase in the size of men assembling), which is also due to the influence of Qian and Xun. The men are unassailable because the third line said that the enemy troops don't attack for three years, because the men are on high ground once again (the fortified city wall), and because this line is located within two Qian Great Strength trigrams that indicate the men are strong enough to repel any attacks.

13.5: Yang at the fifth line in the middle of the Qian Heaven trigram of great force. It is also the top line of an inner Qian trigram as well, hence the line has great strength. **"The comrades first cry and weep [moan in misery], but later laugh. The great armies meet each other (and unite)."** When an army is being formed the men don't want to be conscripted but they eventually find brotherhood within the ranks and become close comrades. Thus there is sadness (moaning) at the beginning of conscription but a happy unity of fellowship afterwards. The fifth line is the middle line of a Qian Great Force trigram, and as the fifth line you would expect some image of perfection as to the assemblage of men coming together. It is also lord of the hexagram, so you might expect to find the image of a great personage of high status that in this case are great armies meeting together. The armies meet together because this yang line is surrounded by yang lines above and below and they were victorious enough to be able to meet. In the second line of the hexagram the men were distressed moaning about being drafted. Next they were fearful of ambush when they were scattered, but now they have assembled into a large force of comrades. This is the meaning behind, "The comrades first cry and weep." The most likely event for the soldiers to become happy ("but later laugh") is a reinforcement of troops where the group becomes larger in size. Because the military leaders are able to join their bands of separate troops together and rally them there is cause for joy.

13.6: Yang at the sixth line at the top of the Qian Heaven trigram. **"Fellowship [union, gathering] with men outside of the city in the suburbs [countryside, outskirts of the city]. There is no regret."** This line represents the next level of fellowship. At first you had a few people meeting at a gate, then more assembling at the ancestral temple, then more massing in a city, and then you finally gathered a large army. Now the situation returns to peace and the people want to give thanks for victory after a war. Therefore people gather together with the soldiers in the outskirts of the city that today we would call suburbs. This area is the cultivated land of the rural districts surrounding a city that involves a vast number of country folk people, and this is traditionally where troops would gather with the local inhabitants to make sacrifices to thank the spirits and protector deities after a victory. It is not a deep unity of fellowship like brothers in arms but a valuable get together of many people nonetheless.

As to the composition of the hexagram and how it is reflected in this top line we have the Li Fire trigram beneath the Qian trigram, and thus there is a gathering of celebration (Li Fire trigram) with a great multitude of people in the countryside (the three yang lines of the Qian trigram here represents a vast field and great force of people).

HEXAGRAM 14

Da You - Great Wealth

Lower Trigram: Qian (Heaven) – great force, duke, emperor
Upper Trigram: Li (Fire) – ostentation, blessings, brilliance, elegance

The Judgment: Great wealth. Supreme success.

The hexagram contains the image of the sun (or fire) high in the sky, and thus its brilliance shining everywhere is used to represent great wealth, possessions or holdings. This is a hexagram about accumulating great wealth told via a story of accumulating wealth in stages. Step one (first line) is that you avoid the harmful things that might drain your wealth so that even if you don't accumulate more money you don't lose what you already have accumulated. Step two, you get started at accumulating wealth or a great deal of possessions. In line three your wealth becomes so great from your efforts it is like important people of rank who can even host the Emperor. In line four there is a warning not to become too ostentatious because showing off your wealth will invite envy, jealousy and even attack. In the fifth line comes a reminder again that accumulating wealth involves tying up the factors that would cause loss such as robbers or military invaders. In the sixth line the ultimate lesson is that the greatest wealth is blessings from Heaven.

1. If there is no association with harmful things (that are difficult, dangerous or injurious) there is no trouble. If there is difficulty (if you must struggle) this is not harmful.

2. A great cart carrying freight is headed for its destination. There is no trouble.

3. A duke pays tribute to the Son of Heaven. An ordinary man cannot do this.

4. By avoiding ostentation (of one's great fortunes) there will be no error.

5. The captives are bound together in awe. Auspicious.

6. Blessings are granted from Heaven. Auspicious. There is nothing that is not beneficial.

14.1: Yang at the first line, and at the bottom of the Qian Heaven trigram, indicates good fortune. **"There is no association with harmful (difficult, dangerous or injurious) things. Therefore there is no trouble [trouble is avoided]. If you must struggle and endure difficulty there is no harm."** At this line you are at the start of your efforts to accumulate wealth and those efforts reflect the Qian Heavenly Great Force trigram pushing you to become wealthy. What is the first best step? To avoid association with harmful, injurious things that might cause you to lose money. *If you don't have any relationship with things that will cause loss then you will avoid loss/harm.* Therefore the first step is not to lose money (through harmful associations) or to stop losing money rather than to make money. As the billionaire Warren Buffett said, "The first rule of investing is don't lose money and the second rule of investing is don't forget the first rule." Most people must struggle through hardship and experience difficulties to accumulate wealth so you should not consider such difficulties trouble because this is just the natural way of things. In other words, as you struggle to accumulate wealth you will suffer hardship but this should not be considered trouble but just the ordinary way things work such as the fact that saving money involves voluntary deprivation.

14.2: Yang at the second line in the middle of the Qian Heaven trigram that is all yang lines. This is also the bottom line of an inner Qian Heaven trigram. **"A great cart carrying freight [used for transport] is headed for its destination. There is no trouble."** The doubled Qian trigram manifests in the fact that you have been successful in accumulating wealth, which is now symbolized by a large cart carrying goods to some destination. This yang line must certainly signify good fortune since it is surrounded by other yang lines, and it also signifies the active movement or transport of the large cart carrying one's accumulated wealth. It is similar to line 13.2 where a large group of men assemble together whereas in this case one's wealth is accumulated and then carried in carts.

14.3: Yang at the third line at the top of the Qian Heaven trigram. This is also the middle line of an inner Qian Heaven trigram and bottom line of an inner Dui trigram. Since this has the influence of two Heaven trigrams the high status of a duke and emperor are both involved in the image: **"A duke pays tribute (offers gifts) to the Son of Heaven. A lesser individual (a man in an ordinary position) cannot do this."** Sometimes this is translated as the duke sacrifices to the Son of Heaven, makes an offering to the Son of Heaven, makes banquets for the Son of Heaven, but we'll summarize these as paying tribute to the Son of Heaven. In this line you have already successfully accumulated wealth. The analogy of your riches is like a duke who can pay homage to the king by offering him a feast (the Dui Mouth-Joy trigram), but of course you don't have such a high status yourself. Only a duke can feast the Emperor while an ordinary individual cannot due to having lesser status but the idea is that you have really become wealthy. Hence, "A duke pays homage to the Son of Heaven while lesser men cannot."

14.4: Yang at the fourth line that is at the beginning of the upper Li Fire-Brilliance trigram. This is also the middle line of an inner Dui trigram and top line of an inner Qian trigram. **"By avoiding ostentation (of one's fullness of fortune) there will be no error."** Not being arrogant and not boasting of your great wealth will prevent misfortune because not showing off will prevent envy and jealousy. The Li trigram represents elegance, brilliance and showing off since fire shines brightly. Here it is on top of the lower Qian Heaven trigram so it is showing off, especially due to the joy of the Dui trigram, and this is detrimental to your prosperity because displaying your fullness invites attack whereas in reverse hexagram line 13.4 you do the opposite and climb the city walls to occupy high ground (which is like showing off) so that you are not attacked. Showing off commonly produces envy and jealousy so the message of this line is to reject boastfulness and ostentation. People will want to attack show-offs but if you avoid pride and don't boast about or show off your wealth you can prevent troubles from occurring.

14.5: Yin at the fifth line in the middle of the Li Fire trigram. This is also the top line of an inner Dui trigram. **"The captives are bound together in awe. Good fortune."** In this hexagram the Li trigram is above the Qian Heaven trigram so there is fire above the sky that all can see. People are thus captivated and awed into allegiance. They become captives of your awesomeness. The fifth line usually shows a perfected form of the message of the hexagram, and it usually involves a person of significance. That person is either the Emperor from line four, or you because *you now have wealth and tremendous power that makes you awe-inspiring. People are captivated by your status thus fulfilling the requirements of a fifth line.* In future hexagram line 1.5 we have "The dragon is flying in the sky, it is beneficial to meet a great man," which similarly contains two examples of seeing a power that should awe you. Here we have captives bound together who view someone with awe, symbolizing that you have become so awe-inspiring that you captivate people who thus become bound. Due to the Li Brilliance trigram you have the power, wealth or prominence that awes (Dui trigram) people into following you or regarding you with renown.

14.6: Yang at the sixth line, and at the top of the Li Brilliance trigram. **"Heaven grants you blessings. Good fortune. There is nothing unfavorable."** One is blessed by Heaven, which is to go beyond material wealth and possessions. How can this not be good fortune? At the sixth line we often find the final part of a story that held throughout the lines, a summary of the hexagram's message, an example of the highest degree of the hexagram's main principle, an example of going too far, a message reflecting the two trigrams that composed it, or some pithy comment related to the hexagram's main message. In this case the message is that being blessed by Heaven is highest form of wealth or abundance.

In the hexagram the Li trigram is stacked on top of the Heaven trigram, and this is reflected in this line via the message that "Blessings (Li trigram) come from Heaven (Qian trigram)."

HEXAGRAM 15

Qian - Modesty, Humility, Humbleness

Lower Trigram: Gen (Mountain) – modesty, humility, accumulation
Upper Trigram: Kun (Earth) – humility, neighbor, city and state

The Judgment: Modesty brings success. The son of the lord (high-born) carries affairs through to completion.

The image within this hexagram is that in the midst of the earth is a mountain rising up and towering above others, and because the mountain stands out there is a reminder to cultivate modesty. This hexagram is about modesty, humility or humbleness and is the only hexagram where all six lines represent good fortune. In particular, it is about being especially humble when building a state so that you don't call undue attention to yourself and invite attacks from neighbors on account of envy or worry (where they don't want a powerful neighbor on their border so they must block its ascension). Even though the presence of some negative inner trigrams indicate that there should be some cases of misfortune in this hexagram we have good fortune in all these lines. The implication is that the virtue of modesty, humbleness or humility is so wonderful that it can enable people to change their fortune to a more positive note. In the first line of the hexagram, extreme humility enables a high-born individual to embark on a great undertaking even if conditions are unfavorable. In the second line he cultivates favorable conditions for himself by continuing to display modesty (being humble) everywhere despite his rank of nobility. In the third line he continually humbly labors away at hard work so that he successfully completes whatever he is doing, which entails building the state. In the fourth line the circumstances have finally become very beneficial and advantageous (from all the previous labor) so he should display his humility even more so as to dissuade attacks from others. In the fifth line your prosperity is blocked by a neighbor and your humility fails to influence them. An example is the case where Japan's vital import resources necessary for growth were cut off (blocked) by the United States, thus forcing it to declare war in WWII. The U.S. keeps trying to cut off Russia's access to world markets in order to provoke it into war as well thus illustrating this line. The fifth line states that the only option for removing the neighbor's obstruction is to launch a military expedition. In the sixth line the king launches the required military campaign with justification because he wears a mantle of humility and the moral authority of righteousness. The Judgment reminds us that even though one is high-born they must put aside any arrogance and then, through humbleness, they will be able to carry their affairs to completion.

1. Modesty, modesty (extremely humble). The lord's son herewith fords the great river. Auspicious.

2. Radiating humility (and then one's modesty becomes well-known). Continuing onwards this way is auspicious.

3. Laboring humbly the lord's son carries affairs through to completion. Auspicious.

4. There is nothing that is not beneficial. Therefore radiate humility even more.

5. You don't prosper on account of your neighbor (who is blocking your prosperity). It is advantageous to invade (with a military expedition) and attack. There is nothing that is not beneficial.

6. Radiating humility (his humility has become recognized). It is favorable to dispatch the army to campaign against city and state.

15.1: Yin at the first line at the bottom of the Gen Mountain trigram. **"Modesty, modesty [Great humility]. By virtue of this the son of the lord crosses the great river. Auspicious."** Great humility is symbolized by the fact that this is the lord's son rather than a lord. The lord's son is symbolized by the bottom line of a majestic mountain, which is the Gen Mountain trigram. The hexagram is about humility so the first line should be the most humble line of the hexagram gradient, and thus here we see doubled humility ("modesty, modesty"). The line states that one should start out on a difficult venture or great undertaking with a great degree of humility because its natural accompaniment is caution, carefulness and preparation. You want to work towards your objectives quietly, diligently and effectively without calling undue attention to yourself (such as by trying to impress others) but just get things done. Discipline and perseverance will allow you to succeed. Humility is the proper attitude for undertaking great deeds because it helps you prevent errors. Because this line involves the lord's son the undertakings have something to do with building up the state and he also represents individuals such as you or I with less power than the top elites. One can expect good fortune when you launch an undertaking after first intensifying your humility *and concern*. You should expect stillness (non-movement) rather than an undertaking in this line because it is within the Mountain Keeping Still trigram but it is precisely because of the great virtue of humility that one can proceed against these influences.

15.2: Yin at the second line in the middle of the Gen Mountain trigram. This is also the bottom line of an inner Kan Danger trigram but danger is avoided in this line because of humility. **"Radiating modesty (and it thereby becomes well-known). Continuing onwards this way is auspicious."** If you cannot be humble then appear humble. By always acting with humility the modesty of your character will eventually become well-known. Radiating humility is auspicious and represents the strong middle line of the Gen Mountain trigram since it is a yin line within a trigram of majesty where overt or "loud" yang activities would be suppressed. To act with modesty brings good fortune despite the danger of the inner Kan trigram because humility helps you be careful and avoid misfortune.

15.3: Yang at the third line at the top of the Gen Mountain trigram. This is also the middle line of an inner Kan Danger trigram and bottom line of an inner Zhen Thunder trigram. **"Hardworking [laboring, toiling] humbly the lord's son carries affairs through to successful completion. Auspicious."** This is a yang line so there is an image of toiling away at labor. The lord's son is toiling away so this means building up the prosperity of the state. Toiling means labor that is a struggle, which is what one would expect within the Gen Keeping Still trigram that can represent obstructions within a task. However, even though the Gen Mountain trigram symbolizes non-movement, an individual is able to complete his affairs successfully by slowly but continually laboring away with humility in the face of Kan Danger and foreign attacks (Zhen Thunder trigram). This is the message of the hexagram, which is that by slowly toiling away with modesty and humility you will always eventually attain success in your endeavors even under precarious conditions. Despite there being five yin lines in this hexagram that would normally show different forms of misfortune, and despite the fact that this line is the center of an inner Kan Danger-Pit trigram, this is the only hexagram where all lines are favorable due to the fact that one cultivates humility. *It can help you grow and build without being arousing the enmity of others who might then attack in response to block your rise in power and prosperity.* This is referring to the work of the state of Zhou in building itself up without attracting attacks from the Shang dynasty.

15.4: Yin at the fourth line, and the beginning of the upper Kun Assembly

Trigram. This is the middle line of an inner Zhen Thunder trigram and top line of an inner Kan Danger trigram. **"Nothing is unfavorable. Therefore rouse your humility by extending it everywhere."** The lord's son has just entered the upper Kun Assembly trigram of neighborliness on top of the Gen trigram activity that laid a previous foundation of accumulation, but he should take care that his head does not swell from that accumulated success. *Since there is nothing that isn't now beneficial and everything is advantageous he should stir up his humility even more and extend it everywhere rather than flaunt his growing abundance. Otherwise he will attract enemies due to his growing prosperity.* Thus, with everything he does he gestures with humility. If he cannot be truly humble then he should still strive to appear humble to avoid attacks. The problem is that the Zhen and Kan trigrams suggest an attack or assault of danger, perhaps from Kun neighbors, but by expressing humility everywhere this will override any negative influences from the Zhen and Kan inner trigrams that would cause disturbance. The opposite hexagram line 10.4 speaks of treading on a tiger's tail cautiously and the strategy of displaying modesty to an even greater degree is to neutralize danger.

15.5: Yin at the fifth line within the Kun Assembly trigram. This is also the top line of an inner Zhen Thunder trigram whose presence is reflected in the advice to launch an attack. **"You don't prosper on account of your neighbor. It is advantageous to invade and attack. Nothing is unfavorable."** The translation of this line is problematical. However, if we turn to reverse hexagram line 16.5 we find an individual suffering from a long-lasting illness that doesn't kill him, which in this case is similar to not being wealthy. In the future hexagram line 39.5 an individual similarly suffers from great lameness, which is also similar to not being wealthy. In opposite hexagram line 10.5 we find resolute walking is dangerous, which is akin to a military expedition launched for subjugation. *Therefore a reasonable translation is that you don't prosper on account of your neighbor - you are not rich because the neighbor is somehow blocking you - but using modesty to influence them as your tool (so that they change their ways) won't work.* There is no need to be humble when misfortune descends on you from your neighbor and being modest and respectful does not work on him. Rather, it is favorable to invade and attack to remove their blocking influence. There is a historical precedence for this which is that the state of Zhou was unable to prosper because of the Shang state, and only after King Wen allied with his neighbors and attacked Shang did he profit at the expense of Shang. Therefore the line is telling us to use our strength assertively to break the blockage, and hence it will be profitable to employ invasion and attack to do so. The neighbor is a manifestation of the Kun trigram, and attacking them is a manifestation of the Zhen trigram. The message of this line is that modesty only works up to a certain point in protecting you as your affluence grows, and then you must use other methods to advance such as force. The Judgment states, "The son of the lord (high-born) carries affairs through to completion" which includes building up the state peacefully with modesty *and* using military might.

15.6: Yin at the top line of the Kun Earth trigram and sixth line of the hexagram, and thus the lesson of the hexagram. **"Radiating humility (it has been recognized). It is favorable to launch an army to campaign against city and state."** Here the history of your humility has become well-known and attracted people to your cause, but it is useless for influencing your neighbor to cease their obstructive ways against you. *That is one of the messages of the hexagram, which is that modesty or humility can help you ascend but it does not help in all situations. Sometimes you must put it aside and use force to get your way, but you must still use it as part of your justification for assertive actions like war.* Being humble proves that you were reasonable or suffered unjustly. The *Yijing* teaches that a leader cannot wage war without sufficient support and a ruler can win the necessary support of the populace through personal modesty and humility. Chinese history cites many cases where a ruler patiently cultivated an image of righteousness, which is here represented by humility and modesty, in order to be able to rally their troops to launch a *just* military expedition. If a leader is publicly viewed as righteous then they will have the necessary moral authority to launch a just war. Hence, someone known for extreme modesty or righteousness, such as Ji Chang (King Wen) who attacked the state of Shang after being mistreated, will have the moral authority to send forth the army to cities and states, which are manifestations of the upper Kun Earth trigram. After Zhou defeated the Shang it also expressed modesty by announcing that its small nation did not dare to seize power from Shang on its own but was only able to defeat Shang due to Heaven's glorious power because Heaven had decided not to leave power in the hands of a deceitful dynasty. In the fifth line was the decision for attack and in this line is the activity of Ji Chang and his sons attacking the Shang dynasty.

In terms of the construction of the hexagram and how it is reflected in this line, the Gen Mountain trigram represents humble majesty while the Kun Earth trigram above appears as cities and states. The way this appears in this line is "Humility has become recognized (Gen). It is favorable to launch the army to campaign against city and state (Kun)."

HEXAGRAM 16

Yu – Repose, Contentment

Lower Trigram: Kun (Earth) – rock, desire
Upper Trigram: Zhen (Thunder) – illness, motion, agitation

The Judgment: Enthusiastic Pleasure. Beneficial to establish a lord and set the army in motion.

The hexagram has an image of thunder rolling and shaking the earth, which is like desire for enjoyable indulgences arising and then shaking your peaceful equanimity. This hexagram is about overly enthusiastic yearning for pleasurable enjoyments – being beset with strong desires – and then finally indulging. In the first line you start out in a start of equanimity or complete contentment. In the second line you start to feel desires and are strong enough to refrain from indulgence but your willpower wavers even though abstinence is the best course of action. In the third line you start longing for an enjoyable pleasure, which is called reposeful gazing because you aren't yet acting upon the longing, and though you stir up the inner turmoil of desire you refrain from indulgence that then produces internal discomfort. In the fourth line you are advised to become your own source of pleasure or inner contentment rather than chase after desires and then friends will rush to join you due to sensing the inner peace you radiate. They will want to experience the same thing. However, line five warns that even if you cultivate inner contentment there will still be times that desires afflict you – they will always afflict you like a sickness that never goes away – but you won't die from them. The big lesson appears in line six, which is that you might lose yourself within an indulgence of enjoyable pleasures for some time but that's okay *if* you return to normal afterwards because then it's only a temporary indulgence rather than a permanent habit or addiction where you always lose control of yourself. Through the analogy of establishing a lord before launching a war, the Judgment reminds us that it is beneficial to make yourself your own master first (to gain control of yourself before indulging), and only after mastering self-control should you pursue pleasurable indulgences.

1. Radiating contentment (harmonious equanimity). Ominous.

2. Firm as a rock, but not till the end of the day. Continual persistence is auspicious.

3. Reposeful gazing (with longing for pleasure) produces regret. Tardiness (tardy action) will (also) produce regret.

4. Being a source of inner contentment. Great will be the gains. Do not doubt that friends will gather around you just as a hair clasp gathers hair.

5. Long-lasting (chronic) illness, but you will not die.

6. Lost within the indulgence of pleasure. If you can change after it's over there will be no trouble.

16.1: Yin at the first line, and at the bottom of the Kun Earth trigram. **"Radiating contentment. Ominous."** This is the lowest line of a hexagram on enjoyment so the beginning state or lowest gradient is that of contentment. This matches with the fact that this is the first line of the Kun earth element that is in harmony with itself. In reverse hexagram line 15.1 you similarly start out as "Extremely modest (humble)." Now yin turns into yang so a state of balanced harmony must change and thus a balanced state of equanimous contentment is an omen of disharmony to come, which refers to the other lines of the hexagram. The lower Kun Earth trigram also stands for attraction or desire because the earth element is an agglomeration of all the other elements pulled together. The attraction or pulling together nature of the earth element means that it also symbolizes desire. Strong desire is stilled in this first line but it is eventually sure to arise. Yin will change to yang at an extreme like this state so being in this state of yin (extreme contentment) is an omen that the disturbance of desire will occur.

16.2: Yin at the second line within the middle of the Kun Earth trigram. At this strong middle point the line should fully reflect the earth element so we'll find the image of a rock tinged with an influence of whatever other trigrams overlap. This is also the beginning line of an inner Gen Mountain trigram that exudes an influence of stillness, non-movement, firmness or inaction. **"Firm [unmoved, steady, strong] as a rock, but not till the end of the day. Continuous perseverance brings good fortune."** Desire has started to rise as forecast in line one. However, despite the pull of this disturbance you refrain from indulging in pleasure, which is a manifestation of self-discipline due to the unwavering Gen Keeping Still trigram.

However, your willpower is insufficient to reject the *pull to pleasure* all day long and thus your desires cannot be continuously ignored. However, if an individual perseveres in resisting the pull of desires this will produce good fortune since restraint is wise and accords with the trigram influences impacting the line.

16.3: Yin at the third line, which is at the top of the Kun Earth trigram. This is also the middle line of an inner Gen trigram as well as the beginning line of an inner Kan trigram. **"Gazing reposefully (longing for pleasure) produces regret. Delaying action also brings regret."** There are two negative factors here. The first is gazing longingly without acting upon the desire, which is enthusiastically thinking about satisfying your desires but doing nothing. This produces unrest or distress because your desires are not fulfilled so you experience regret. The desire comes from the Kun trigram, the fact you don't act (are reposeful and simply gaze at what you want) is an influence of the Gen trigram, and the discomfort you consequently feel is the Kan trigram. Unfulfilled, desirous gazing (the Kun trigram represents desire that wants to unite) creates a strain that causes discomfort. Opposite hexagram line 9.3 had a similar situation where an axle separated from a cart due to straining and a husband and wife rolled their eyes at each other. The second negative issue is that "Tardiness in delaying your indulgence will also bring regret." Once again, since at this third line you delay your actions and don't indulge the waiting produces discomfort and regret (the Kan trigram). Both this third line and the previous second line are the beginning and middle lines of an inner Gen Mountain trigram of non-movement, which is why there is no indulgence in pleasure at this time, but in the next line you will leave the Gen trigram and escape its influence.

16.4: Yang at the fourth line that is the beginning line of the upper Zhen Thunder trigram. This is also the middle line of an inner Kan trigram and top line of an inner Gen trigram. **"Being a source [fountain] of real inner contentment. Great will be the gains. Do not doubt [be confident] that friends will gather around you like hair gathered together by a hair clasp."** Rather than running after pleasures and enthusiastic delights you should "Be a source of real contentment and great will be the gains." This is similar to reverse hexagram line 15.4 where you are told to be very humble while opposite hexagram line 9.4 says that because of sincerity between people any anger between them will vanish. Here, if you become an example of real contentment (real happiness and joy) with the result that friends will gather around you due to the attractiveness of your inner peace. Since this is the start of the upper Zhen Thunder trigram you will represent the source of energy that is an inner peace and contentment – rather than the pull of desire – that attracts people. Friends will gather because the Gen trigram represents great accumulation. You should not doubt that you will find gain in doing this rather than by satisfying desires. In fact, the results will be so valuable to others that, "Friends will certainly rush to gather around you (to also bathe in your energy) just as a hair clasp gathers hair."

16.5: Yin at the fifth line in the middle of the Zhen Thunder trigram, and as the top line of an inner Kan trigram. **"Long-lasting (chronic) illness, but you will not die."** This is the top yin line of an inner Kan trigram so it is destructive and manifests as illness. The strong middle line of the Zhen Thunderbolt trigram is also there constantly throwing off its influence. This means that desires will constantly be biting at you and causing you discomfort in life while you are trying to ignore them, yet though they are uncomfortable like a chronic sickness you won't die from this. They disturb your inner peace, contentment and repose but this is the way of life. Hence, "Long-lasting illness, but you will not die." A long-lasting illness means you will constantly suffer afflictions. They appear due to the presence of the top destructive line of an inner Kan Danger-Trouble trigram and the Zhen trigram that causes desires to strike you now and then.

16.6: Yin at the sixth place at the top of the upper Zhen Thunder trigram. The top of the Thunder trigram tends to be destructive so here we have a warning. **"Losing oneself within the indulgence of pleasure. If you can change after it's over [after you finish with it], there will be no fault."** This lesson at the top line of the hexagram summarizes the pursuit of pleasurable indulgence. You can indulge, of course, but don't stay too long under water. Hedonism, which is a constant indulgence in pleasure, is not something that Chinese culture recommends but here the *Yijing* says that it is okay to *temporarily* enjoy yourself now and then with *deep pleasurable indulgence*. Everyone in life engages in pleasurable pursuits now and then but you should not chase after them constantly and forever be seeking indulgences. You should never continuously seek extravagant, excessive delights or develop addictions to satiations. After obtaining satisfaction in a pleasurable indulgence you must let go of the experience and move on.

In terms of the construction of the hexagram we have a Kun Earth trigram (desire) beneath a Zhen Thunder trigram (the act of indulgence), so this line warns that you can indulge in pleasurable desires (Kun) but then you must abandon them (Zhen) after you are done.

HEXAGRAM 17

Sui – Pursuing

Lower Trigram: Zhen (Thunder) – motion, agitation, pursuing
Upper Trigram: Dui (Joy) – clear conscience, happiness, mouth, talking

The Judgment: Pursuing. Supreme success. It is beneficial to continue with persistence. No trouble.

In this hexagram is the image of thunder within a lake, which symbolizes a growing revolt (thunder) amongst a great mass of people (lake) although that great power is initially submerged beneath the surface. This is not a hexagram about following or allegiance but about rebellion against a corrupt political order and then the pursuit of conquering (capturing) it rather than remaining its obedient vassal. The hexagram disguises the story of the drive to conquer the Shang dynasty by the vassal state of Zhou that then founded what Confucius considered the righteous Zhou dynasty of benevolent monarchs. This concerns Ji Chang, later known as King Wen, who is said to have helped create the *Yijing*. In the first line a governance or administration changes (which is the conquest of your territory by the state of Zhou) and you agree to follow along with the policies of the new rulership without any type of rebellion and just go about your daily life. In the second line, the threatened Shang king Di Xin becomes worried about the growing conquests of Zhou and considers holding as hostage the son of Ji Chang, the leader of Zhou, to secure his allegiance, but if he does so he'll truly lose the allegiance of Zhou. This is symbolized by tying up a young boy and thereby losing an adult. In the third line King Zhou of Shang imprisons Ji Chang instead, which in response sets the state of Zhou on a clear road to conquer the Shang kingdom. This is tying up the adult instead of the young boy with the result that the state of Zhou becomes determined to conquer the Shang kingdom. In the fourth line Zhou conquers the Shang kingdom and everyone is happy about this conquest after the pursuit (warfare) because the cause has been a righteous one so everyone's conscience is clear. In the fifth line everyone is extremely happy because this great conquest of Shang was successful and they toppled a wicked leader. In the last line many nobles of Shang are captured and then bound in allegiance to the new rulership of Zhou, which is being trussed up twice, and the king offers a sacrifice to Heaven in thanks for the conquest. The Judgment reminds us that pursuing a great objective can only be accomplished through perseverance at the task.

1. There is a change of governance (administration). Following it is good fortune. Going out the gate to interact (freely associate) with others has success.

2. Tie up the little son, lose the senior man.

3. Tie up the senior man, lose the small son. By pursuing you will gain what is ought. It is beneficial to occupy a settlement.

4. If one pursues there will be a capture. Persistent continuation is ominous (brings misfortune). There is sincerity in this course. Having brightness (a clear conscience) what trouble is there?

5. Triumphant (joyous) capture. Auspicious.

6. Capturing and tying them, and then further trussing (binding) them. The king presents offerings on the western mountain.

17.1: Yang at the first line as the bottom of the Zhen Thunder trigram usually indicates movement or a bolt of action. **"There is a change of governance (administration). Following along is good fortune. Going out the gate to associate and interact with others attains meritorious accomplishment."** The influence of the Zhen Thunder trigram appears as a new government or administration perhaps because of a new leader replacing the old one, because of the state being conquered, because of the establishment of a new dynasty, etcetera. Being new the ruling powers want to consolidate their control over the populace. In this line the government dramatically changes the administrative policies for conducting public affairs due to the influence of the shocking Zhen Thunder trigram. You are advised that you should just *follow along with the new administration* and its changes rather than become a rebel or resistor. Just go along with their changes and then go about your regular business in life, which is represented as "Going out of the gate to interact with the public." Later we will see that this new governance could be the capture of a territory by Ji Chang (King Wen) who was expanding his territory through military activities and political alliances, and who thereafter established good policies that encouraged agriculture and improved the economy in those annexed regions.

17.2: Yin at the second line, which is the middle line of the Zhen Thunder trigram. This line is also the bottom of an inner Gen Mountain trigram, hence we see in the line an image of keeping still manifested as captivity or it could represent a member of royalty (majesty). **"If you tie up the small son you will lose the adult man."** Most translators feel that the meaning of the line is that by becoming preoccupied with little things you will miss the bigger issue, e.g. focusing on the small boy rather than on the adult means focusing on trivialities rather than important stuff and thus you will lose the big thing. However, this line and the entire hexagram probably refers to a historical situation where the last Shang king, Di Xin or King Zhou of Shang, was seeking to restrain the rebellious western vassal state of Zhou that kept expanding and threatening its leadership. He was considering taking Bo Yikao, the eldest son of Ji Chang (the Duke of Zhou or "Duke of the West" of the Shang dynasty) as a hostage to guarantee Zhou's allegiance (Ji Chang had ten sons and one daughter by his wife and another eight sons with concubines), which was a common procedure for feuding states in ancient China. However, if he did this then the Shang King Zhou Xin risked losing the loyalty, allegiance and following of the Zhou state forever. By seizing the son as a captive he would lose the loyalty of his father and the state of Zhou (the "adult man"). The other alternative was to tie up Ji Chang, the adult man, and forget his son, the little boy. Losing the adult man is a result of the Zhen Thunder trigram while tying up the boy is the influence of the Gen Keeping Still trigram. Later King Zhou imprisoned Ji Chang and executed Bo Yikao, turning his body into meat cakes and feeding them to Ji Chang while imprisoned in Youli. Bo Yikang's horrible death solidified the will of the Zhou people to rebel and overthrow the Shang dynasty, hence by King Zhou executing the son Yikang he actually lost the adult, meaning the allegiance of King Wen and Zhou.

17.3: Yin at the third line of the lower Zhen Thunder trigram. This is also the middle line of an inner Gen Mountain trigram and bottom line of an inner Xun Wind trigram. **"Tie up the adult man and lose the small son. By pursuing you will gain what is sought. It is beneficial to occupy a settlement."** Most translators think that binding the adult while ignoring the small boy means focusing on a big issue (adult) by ignoring the insignificant ones (small boy). This is in some ways similar to throwing back a small fish so that you can catch a big fish … whatever a "fish" might be in terms of objectives. However, what is more probable is that this is a continuation of the story of the last Shang king Di Xin (King Zhou) who ended up imprisoning Ji Chang instead of any of his sons, so he "tied up the adult man and (neglected) the son." Ji Chang is eventually released to return home after many years as a prisoner and plots the overthrow of Di Xin. Ji Chang strategically conquers about two-thirds of the Shang kingdom through direct possession or through sworn allies, and then moved his capital city from Mount Qi to Feng. This is why the hexagram talks about occupying a settlement or land. Bo Yikao's younger brother Ji Fa (the second son of Ji Chang) rises up (with the help of the famous military and political strategist Jiang Shang) and defeats King Zhou of Shang at the famous Battle of Muye after which he established the Zhou dynasty, which also involved setting up a number of feudal states under his young brothers and clan arrangements. Eventually Zhou also created and constructed a new capital city too, which is also occupying a settlement. It then becomes clear about the meaning of the line: "By pursuing (attempting to defeat King Zhou Di Xin) he gained what he sought." Ji Fa through conquest of the Shang dynasty thus becomes King Wu of Zhou. In terms of the trigrams showing their influence in the lines, the third destructive line of the Zhen Thunder trigram produces the attack against Shang, which is "pursuing what you seek," while the Gen trigram represents the royalty of Ji Chang, and the conquest of territory is a reflection of the Xun Penetrating Wind trigram together with the Gen Great Territory trigram as well.

17.4 Yang at the fourth line, and at the bottom of the upper Dui Joy trigram. This is also the middle line of an inner Xun Wind trigram and top line of an inner Gen Mountain trigram. Hence, **"From pursuit there is a capture. Persistent continuation is ominous. There is sincerity in his course. With brightness [a clean conscience] what trouble is there in this?"** In the lower trigram there was the pursuit of overthrowing the Shang dynasty and now there is joy because it was successful - there is the capture of the state of Shang. This is a hexagram about pursuing and then obtaining something, and in this line you have pursued (Xun trigram) the conquest of the Shang kingdom and captured it instead of remaining a subservient vassal state. The pursuit is ominous because many people will die in battle. Once you have captured the kingdom you should cease the military campaigns for more territory, which is the stilling effect of the inner Gen trigram. "There is sincerity in his path [confidence in this road]" means there has been nothing but righteousness in overthrowing the Shang regime. King Zhou is often negatively represented as an evil man and wicked ruler and centuries later even Mencius commented, "Men who abuse humanity are crooked; men who abuse righteousness are villains. They are both merely vulgar men. I have only heard that King Wu killed a vulgar man named Zhou, but I have not heard that King Wu (Ji Fa) ever killed a sovereign." Your mindset regarding rebellion is that this is a proper path of righteousness or rectitude: "With brightness, what trouble (blame) could there be in this?" This attitude is the influence of the Dui Joy trigram. In summary, the pursuit is a manifestation of the Xun trigram whereas the admonition to stop annexing territories after the conquest of Shang ("mission accomplished") is the Gen trigram, and the sincerity of one's course in overthrowing the wicked ruler Zhou Di Xin with a clear conscience of brightness in one's heart is the Dui Joy trigram.

17.5: Yang at the fifth line that is the middle of the Dui Joy trigram. This is also the middle line of an inner Xun Wind trigram. **"Triumphant capture (The capture is joyous with celebration)."** In the fifth line of a hexagram we will usually see a perfected form of its main message, and we do: "Joyful capture." Here you successfully gained what you were pursuing so you are extremely happy. For instance, you already established in the fourth line that your pursuit is correct and here you have succeeded by capturing what you sought so you are pleased about the accomplishment. *You overthrew the Shang dynasty*, but the analogy used is just capturing something. The joy of the line appears due to the Dui Joy trigram and the pursuit of conquest reflects the Xun Wind trigram.

17.6: The sixth line of the hexagram is yin, which produces an image of criminals being arrested and bound after being successfully hunted. This is also the top line of the upper Dui Joy-Talking trigram. **"Catching and binding them, and then further trussing (binding) them. The king presents offerings on the western mountain."** The state of Shang was captured, including many of its nobles and generals who in addition to being "caught and bound" were then secured ("further trussed") because they were given positions within the new Zhou dynasty. They were captured, which was the first binding in this line, and then secured or trussed again by being offered important vassal positions. This included Weizi, the big brother of King Di Xin. After King Wu's victory over the Shang he divided the territory into three parts and appointed his brothers Guan Shu and Cai Shu as two of the regional rulers. King Wu granted Shang's capital city to the late King Du Xin's son, Wu Geng, to rule along with all the surrendered people there, but Wu Geng rebelled years later with the lords of some other states and was defeated again. This is also why the sixth line speaks of binding (capturing or conquering) individuals and then further securing them (by making them subordinates). Once you acquire what you have been seeking it is time to give thanks to Heaven so the new King Wu made offerings to Heaven on a western holy mountain of the original Zhou state, which is probably Mount Qi since it was the site of the ancestral temple of the lords of Zhou.

Since the hexagram is composed of a Zhen trigram beneath a Dui Joy trigram the sixth line mirrors this construction because the prisoners are first caught and bound, which embodies the meaning of the Zhen trigram below, and then there are the sacrificial offerings afterwards which reflect the Dui trigram on top.

HEXAGRAM 18

Gu - Remedying the Spoiled Legacy, Rectifying the Inherited Decay

Lower Trigram: Xun (Wind) – wood, motion, deteriorated legacy
Upper Trigram: Gen (Mountain) – accumulated riches, stopping

The Judgment: Remedying what has been spoiled. Supreme Success. Beneficial to ford the great river. Before *jia* (the first day of the 10-day heavenly stem week) three days, after *jia* three days.

Note: The first day of the Chinese celestial stem week was called *jia*, the third day before *jia* was called *xin* and three days after *jia* was the day called *ding*. *Ding* and *xin* were considered lucky days.

There is an image of wind below a mountain in the hexagram which symbolizes an attempt to impose structure or organization (the mountain) over a decaying situation (wind). This is a hexagram about inheriting spoiled or lousy circumstances that have became deteriorated and then fixing what has been spoiled. You can think of these circumstances as problems left behind by someone and now they are troubles *you* must deal with. Hence, the hexagram is about lousy conditions you inherit that you must fix and the degree or intensity of inherited ill conditions increases for each subsequent line. In the first line a departed father leaves behind troubles that his surviving son must clean up. In the second line a departed mother leaves behind messy troubles that must be remedied. In the third line it is recounted that a deceased father's legacy of problems he left behind don't require any great effort to remedy. In the fourth line the troubles are abundant so fixing them causes distress. In the fifth line praise is given for remedying whatever problems the father has caused. The sixth line offers a pithy comment that it is better that you don't need to spend your time remedying the troubles or ills caused by someone else – including problems caused by your father or even a lord or king – but to work on accomplishing your own goals in life instead.

1. The deceased father's legacy of troubles. There is a capable surviving son. There is no trouble. Danger but in the end

auspicious.

2. The deceased mother's legacy of troubles. One cannot be too insistent (harsh or inflexible).

3. The deceased father's legacy of troubles. There is a little regret but no great trouble.

4. The legacy of troubles caused by a prosperous deceased father. Going to see them is distressful.

5. Correcting the legacy of troubles caused by the deceased father. One wins praise.

6. Serving neither a king nor lord. His service is more elevated.

18.1: The first line is the start of the Xun Wind trigram, and as a yin line bodes trouble. If we paraphrase the line we get: **"The deceased father made mistakes (He left behind troubles, namely corrupted or spoiled conditions that he created). A surviving able son can rectify/correct them (and thereby free his father from blame). These are troublesome or grave conditions but there is good fortune in the end."** The idea is that even though a deceased father left behind problems he will be blameless if he has a surviving son who, because he is capable, can remedy whatever problems the father created and left behind. The idea of spoiled conditions being inherited is due to the destructive nature of the Xun Penetrating Wind trigram, but the extent of spoiling or destruction isn't serious because this is just initial line of the Xun trigram so a son can easily remedy the problems since the gradient is so low. This hexagram may be making historical references where the deceased father is King Wen whose son, King Wu, founded the Zhou dynasty. King Wen died before overthrowing the Shang in battle but his son, King Wu, conquered the Shang and established the beginning of the Zhou dynasty. Thus as the surviving son he had to rectify the incomplete business of his father.

18.2: Yang at the second line in the middle of the Xun Wind trigram. This is also the bottom line of an inner Dui Young Woman trigram, which explains why we will see a woman in this line. **"Remedy (undoing) the mother's legacy of problems [troubles, mistakes, deteriorated conditions] she caused. One cannot be too insistent [serious, harsh or inflexible]."** In this line the woman is one's mother so one cannot be too critical of her problems. One must be more forgiving because of affection for one's mother and because women, being more emotional, are entitled to more leeway than men. You must approach correction with tenderness and moderation rather than with a stubborn strictness as you would do with a man. You must be flexible due to the changeability of the Xun Wind trigram and due to the Dui Joy trigram that symbolizes being a bit yielding and gentle. If this hexagram is making historical references then the deceased mother might refer to the Lady of Shen, Taisi, who was the wife of King Wen and mother of King Wu.

18.3: Yang at the third line at the top of the Xun Wind trigram. This is also the middle line of an inner Dui Joy trigram and bottom line of an inner Zhen Thunder trigram. **"Rectify [handle, correct, solve, remedy] the troubles caused by the father. Slight regret but no great harm [trouble] from doing this."** The wind element here indicates both troubles and movement so there is trouble and the busyness of remedying (handling) those problematical issues. A little effort/action is involved here due to the inner Zhen Thunder trigram but there is not much trouble in fixing things since the inner Dui Joy trigram reduces any regrets. In the first line the problems were such that a son fixed everything easily, then the problems were greater but forgivable when caused by a woman, and now they are even more serious but remedied with only just a little trouble and regret. In terms of historical references this hexagram may be referring once again to King Wen who died before conquering the Shang.

18.4: Yin at the fourth line, and the start of the upper Gen Mountain trigram. This is also the middle line of an inner Zhen Thunder trigram, and top line of an inner Dui Joy trigram. **"The troubles caused by a prosperous deceased father. In seeing them there will be distress."** The fourth line of a hexagram often shows a successful resolution of the difficulties seen in the third line (the problems caused by a deceased father) or a successful achievement of the hexagram's message where a perfect accomplishment is seen in line five. A rich man has the potential to cause more troubles than a poor man, and that is what we see in this line. The Gen Mountain trigram usually represents an accumulation so the father's legacy of troubles are large, and in seeing them there will be distress not only because they are great but because this is a yin line and the next line is yin as well. Seeing them will be a shock because of the influence of the Zhen Thunderbolt trigram. The conditions are so terrible they cannot be tolerated. There is no mention of fixing the problems because the middle line of the Zhen Thunder trigram predominates over (is stronger than) the Dui Joy trigram, and to experience such good fortune would be yang but this is a yin line. If this hexagram is making historical references then the deceased father may be King Wu (Ji Fa), who conquered the Shang and thereby founded the Zhou dynasty. However, King Wu died soon afterwards and his young son Prince Song became King Cheng of Zhou. King Cheng of Zhou had trouble inheriting the throne due to a rebellion by three uncles so he had difficulties in securing his reign and pacifying the Shang who had been conquered. Thus the "prosperous deceased father" is King Wu and there is the "distress" of handling the rebellion of the Shang after being conquered that included three of Wu's brothers.

18.5: Yin at the fifth line in the middle of the Gen Accumulation trigram. This is also the top line of an inner Zhen Thunder trigram. **"By rectifying [remedying, correcting, undoing] the troubles that the deceased father caused one gains praise [recognition]."** This line is the lord of the hexagram and should show a perfected form of the hexagram's overall message. In this line one remedies inherited, accumulated troubles of the deceased father and this demonstration of filial piety thereby wins praise and approval from others. One gains praise (an unusual manifestation of the Zhen Thunder trigram as an exaltation) because of fixing many accumulated problems (the Gen trigram of accumulation). This line exhibits the hexagram's Judgment: Remedying what has been spoiled is proper and so it is favorable to set out to accomplish this great task. If this hexagram is making historical references then the deceased father may be King Wu who conquered the Shang. A lot of time was spent gaining control over the Shang people after King Wu's death. One individual who spent much time rectifying matter was the Marquis of Kang who is mentioned in hexagram 35.

18.6: Yang at the sixth line, and at the top of the Gen Mountain trigram of non-movement as well as majesty and loftiness. **"He serves neither a king nor a lord [nobles, princes]. He serves more elevated, loftier purposes [goals or pursuits]."** This is at the top of the Gen Keeping Still trigram so he is not serving someone of high status like a king or lord. His service is even loftier so it is comparable to the lofty majesty of a mountain. In serving more elevated purposes other than taking care of someone's mistakes this summarizes the hexagram's lesson in general: *It is better to be working on your own goals and elevate your virtue rather than become preoccupied with fixing other people's problems.* This line might also refer to King Wu's son, Prince Song, who ruled as King Cheng of Zhou for over forty years, because his reign was a time of peace during the Zhou dynasty and peace would accord with the wishes of Heaven.

In terms of how this hexagram's composition is reflected in this sixth line, the hexagram is composed of a Xun Wind trigram below a Gen Mountain trigram. Serving a lord is a subsidiary position like the wind (Xun trigram), and the more elevated, loftier purpose is symbolized by a majestic mountain (Gen trigram).

HEXAGRAM 19

Lin – Managing, Overseeing, Taking Charge, Leadership

Lower Trigram: Dui (Joy) – mouth, eloquence, talking, managing, guiding
Upper Trigram: Kun (Earth) – group leadership, nurturing, docility

The Judgment: Overseeing. Supreme success. It is favorable to keep on. When you reach the eighth month it will be ominous.

This is a hexagram on management, leadership and overseeing activities or people. Therefore it is called "overseeing." Each subsequent line of the hexagram represents a progressive improvement in management skills. By degrees you learn how to manage well (such as not being lax in responsibilities) so that you gradually become a good manager, then leader, and then the highest form of leader that is a great lord or ruler who practices benevolent leadership. The first line of the hexagram contains an example of good management. The second line repeats the first line stressing comprehensive management, which means attending to all details, and this duplication of message means that the continuous application of good management is the important principle. In the third line is a warning about not being lax in one's management responsibilities because then it is not "comprehensive" management anymore. In the fourth line your management skills have grown so much that you become a leader. In the fifth line there is an example of very good management, which is the wise management appropriate to a lord. In the sixth line is a yet higher level of management, which is the benevolent management style that we typically attribute to a sage. The Judgment reminds us that it is beneficial to continually manage affairs well but there will always come a time when things will go wrong and problems arise (represented by the eighth month) despite your very best efforts, and then you will have problems managing your way through those difficulties.

1. Overseeing (leading, managing) comprehensively. Continuing this way is auspicious.

2. Overseeing (leading, managing) comprehensively. Auspicious. There is nothing not beneficial.

3. Sweet (lax, easygoing) overseeing (leadership, management). Nothing is beneficial in this. If you are concerned over this (and self-correct) then there will be no trouble.

4. Arriving at (attaining) a position of overseeing (leadership, management). There is no trouble.

5. Wise overseeing (leadership, management). This is appropriate for a great lord. Auspicious.

6. Benevolent overseeing (leadership, management). Auspicious. No trouble.

19.1: Yang at the bottom line, and at the beginning of the Dui trigram that represents young women, joy and talking. As the first line this will be the lowest level of management competency for overseeing others. **"Overseeing [leading, managing] comprehensively [completely]. Continuous perseverance produces good fortune."** The basic idea is that comprehensive, competent, good management will produce good fortune. Comprehensive management entails being all-inclusive and fully taking care of all details. Management involves talking to people with persuasion (instead of just ordering them about), educating them, getting them to readily do things without complaint through your influence and then making sure their performance meets all standards. Therefore the Dui trigram is used to represent the persuasion, influence and management techniques that produce good guidance over situations.

19.2: Yang at the second line within the middle of the Dui Talking trigram. This is also the bottom line of an inner Zhen Thunder trigram. **"Overseeing [leading, managing] comprehensively [completely]. Auspicious. Everything is beneficial."** In this case the injunction to manage affairs comprehensively is now reiterated a second time to strongly emphasize the importance of *continuous competent management*. This is especially important since the second line now receives an influence from an inner Zhen thunder trigram that tends to strike with disastrous assault, but here the middle line of the Dui Joy trigram is stronger than the beginning line of an inner Thunder trigram (lines 2-4). Thus the joy aspect comes through as competent management during any potential troubles so that nothing goes wrong. Everything will be advantageous even if there are difficulties.

19.3: Yin at the third line, and at the top of the Dui Joyous trigram. This is also the middle line of an inner Zhen Thunder trigram and bottom line of an inner Kun Earth trigram. **"Sweet (lax, easygoing) overseeing (leadership, management). Nothing is beneficial in this. If you are concerned [worry with reflection, grieve, have regret] over this then there will be no trouble."** Here the management is no longer comprehensive or *strict*. It has become too lax. Normally the Dui trigram symbolizes joyousness and even sweet-talking but in this situation it indicates that the quality of management (leadership) has become too loose, careless or complacent, especially since this line also comes under the influence of the inner Kun Earth trigram that symbolizes acquiescence or ready acceptance. Hence we have sweet, easygoing or lax management in this line where errors can easily slip in because you aren't strict about standards anymore. *"Sweet leadership" means putting aside standards and becoming too lax and easygoing so that errors can occur.* "Nothing is beneficial in this" because this is not the way of good management. However, if you catch your mistake and worry over this lapse with regret (due to the potential danger of the Zhen trigram) so that you change your ways then there will be no trouble because you will fix your errant behavior. Whenever you catch personal errors and correct your behavior you will return to the right way.

19.4: Yin at the fourth line at the beginning of the Kun Earth trigram. This is also the middle line of an inner Kun Earth trigram and top line of an inner Zhen Thunder trigram. **"Arriving [reaching] at a position of overseeing (leadership, management). There is no trouble."** Here you are promoted to a higher level of management responsibility and a higher level of professional achievement. Similar to this is the fact that in reverse hexagram line 20.4 your status rises enough that you gain an audience with the king and can survey the kingdom's glories, while in opposite hexagram line 33.4 a piglet's size is finally deemed "good enough" as it is used to symbolize the capabilities of a (young) superior man. The fourth line of a hexagram often shows a successful achievement of the hexagram's message or theme where a more perfect accomplishment is seen in line five, and that's what we have here regarding the attainment of a skillful level of management. In this new upper trigram we see a higher level of management capability than everything previous and because it is the fourth line we almost see a case of perfect management. In this line an individual (who was probably a manager) reaches a higher position of leadership where he can issue orders (Zhen trigram). The higher position of leadership is due to the strong influence of the doubled Kun Earth trigram, which symbolizes solidity and agglomeration capabilities over a group.

19.5: Yin at the fifth line at the rulership position of the hexagram. This is also the middle line of the upper Kun Earth trigram and top line of an inner Kun Earth trigram. The Kun trigram represents a great multitude of people, or assembly of people, who are wisely managed in this line. **"Wise leadership [overseeing, management]. This is appropriate [suitable] for a great lord. Auspicious."** The theme here means truly *knowing how to manage*. The fifth line usually illustrates some perfected version of the message or theme of the hexagram, which in this case is good management, and as the lord of the hexagram often involves a dignified personage such as the great lord found here. In this line the leadership position and the method of leading or managing is the highest of all previous lines. As the best type of overseeing or leadership it is intelligent and wise because it embodies reason and is good enough for running a country. You use the right people and delegate the necessary authority to them.

19.6: Yin at the sixth line, and top of a Kun Earth trigram that thus completes the hexagram. This line represents the highest type of management and also summarizes the hexagram. **"Benevolent [sincere, high-minded] overseeing (leadership, management). Auspicious. No trouble."** This is the highest form of leadership, which is the level of a sage who is magnanimous, helpful and beyond personal ambition. The message of the hexagram comes down to the principle that the best form of leadership or management embodies beneficence in yourself and benevolence in looking after people just as a sage does. This is how to proceed properly.

As to the composition of the hexagram being reflected in this top line we have the Dui Joy trigram below the Kun Earth trigram in its construction, so management (Dui Mouth-Talking trigram) is nurturing the multitude (Kun Masses trigram) who accept the leadership and guidance. Thus we have "Benevolent leadership. Auspicious. No trouble."

HEXAGRAM 20

Guan - Observing, Viewing, Analyzing, Contemplation

Lower Trigram: Kun (Earth) – acquiescence, observation
Upper Trigram: Xun (Wind) – country's activities, thinking, contemplation

The Judgment: Observing. The ablution has been made but not yet the sacrificial offering. There is the sincerity of reverence.

There is an image in the hexagram of winds moving over the earth, meaning that you use thinking (wind) to gain wisdom or a broader perspective and wider vision or view by contemplating the conditions of life and the world. This hexagram tells us to observe other people, analyze their lives, and then engage in the contemplation of self-reflection and self-correction so that you avoid their errors such as blameworthy deeds. As with most hexagrams the quality of the main theme – observation and contemplation – starts at a minimum amount but gradually increases in intensity, quality and refinement. The first line starts with the image of a child gazing at something, which represents a childish or immature view of situations. The second line shows a maiden who clandestinely peeks from behind a door to spy on what is going on so she can only obtain a fractional, incomplete view of a situation. In the third line there is an improved level of observation, examination and analysis of other people's lives. In the fourth line the level of observation and reflection has risen again because there is now examination or analysis of the country's doings made possible by becoming a guest of the king where you can observe great matters. In the fifth line you observe your own life in personal self-reflection, which is the most important type of contemplation. In the sixth line you look at the lives of other people to derive further life lessons and see that those who acted ethically and morally are the ones without blame.

1. A childish (immature) way of viewing things. For an inferior man there is no blame but for a superior man (such immaturity) will cause distress.

2. Peeking (a brief clandestine look of furtive viewing) to obtain a view. Beneficial to continue this way if it is (merely) a woman.

3. Looking at the advances and setbacks of my own life.

4. Contemplating the glories of the kingdom. It is beneficial (therefore) to have an audience with the king.

5. Looking at my own life. For the noble man there is no blame (there are no major faults).

6. Contemplating the lives of others. For noble men there is no blame (there are no major faults).

20.1: Yin at the bottom line at the beginning of the Kun Earth trigram. This line represents the lowest level of observing or contemplation, which is the immature view or mindset of a child. **"Looking at things in a childish (immature) way. This is blameless for inferior people but blameworthy [inappropriate] in a superior man [more cultivated individual]."** This trigram reflects the Kun trigram of the earth element that just watches (and absorbs) without doing anything. It doesn't engage in activity so the Kun trigram is used to represent observation in the hexagram. Here we have the example of a child's observations that are immature, of course, because they are superficial. They are insufficient in terms of thoroughness, wisdom, or depth of analysis. You can surely criticize an adult if they were to stay at this level of childish observations.

20.2: Yin at the second line in the middle of the Kun Earth trigram. This is also the bottom line of an inner Kun Earth trigram. **"Peeping briefly (a clandestine observation) to observe. Advantageous if this was just a woman."** Here we should see an improvement over a childish view, namely an increase in the quality of observational, contemplative skills because we've reached the strong middle line of the Kun trigram and an inner Kun trigram also intersects the line. The example provided is of the contemplative powers of women, which are used since there are three yin lines in the trigram and this is the central line. The woman can only see inside her home and not enough of the outside world. Peeping or peeking means just a fractional observation of a situation, namely an incomplete or uneducated view. This line therefore represents narrow observation and understanding.

20.3: Yin at the third line completes the Kun trigram of earth. This is the middle of an inner Kun Earth trigram and the bottom line of an inner Gen

Mountain trigram. **"Contemplating [observing, analyzing] the advances and setbacks (ups and downs) of my own life."** In this line you are analyzing your life, evaluating matters, determining how to behave better and deciding what path to take going forward in life. To review your life is a type of *introspective contemplation* (contemplative meditation) that reflects the receptive yin nature of the line, and that stillness of self-reflection also reflects the Gen Mountain trigram, which also corresponds to a higher view or vantage point.

20.4: Yin at the fourth line at the beginning of the Xun Wind trigram. This is also the middle line of an inner Gen Mountain trigram and top line of an inner Kun Earth trigram. **"Contemplating [beholding, analyzing] the glories of the country [kingdom]. It is therefore advantageous [favorable, propitious, beneficial] to be a guest of the king (to do so)."** The many glories of the country – so many activities – represent the Xun wind element of incessant movement. The Gen Mountain trigram in this line represents something majestic that has been accumulated and the Kun Earth trigram represents a great assemblage or mass of people. It is advantageous to be a guest of the king in order to observe the glories of the kingdom because that is the best vantage point to encounter its most outstanding individuals and hear discussions on national events and policies. The outstanding men that surround the king represent the brilliance of the state and you can observe them by being his guest. Furthermore, by having an audience with the king you will be able to hear about the best things within the country with all its internal doings and accomplishments that are its movements symbolized by the wind element. Your perspective becomes enlarged from being exposed to all these things.

20.5: Yang at the fifth line in the middle of the Xun Wind trigram. This is also the top line of an inner Gen Mountain trigram. **"Looking at [observing, contemplating, analyzing] my own life course. For the superior person there is no blame [he has no regrets, is without fault]."** The fifth line is the lord of the hexagram and often represents some type of high status individual who attains a perfected form of the meaning of the hexagram. The meaning of this line is to introspectively contemplate the course of your own life (Gen trigram) just as you might observe and analyze the glories of the country or kingdom in line four. It is by scrutinizing your past behavior that you attain self-knowledge and with that new understanding can act better going into the future. If you contemplate (observe and analyze) the life of a superior person you won't find any great faults (Xun trigram) because those men were careful not to commit any big errors and never abandoned moral rectitude in their actions, which is what made them noble individuals (superior people). This is the main theme of the hexagram. A superior person *regularly contemplates his own behavior throughout life* by reviewing it regularly and he then rectifies (corrects) himself whenever he finds himself going astray. Thus, even if he makes errors he immediately corrects himself so that later he has nothing to be ashamed of. By following a moral code throughout life he becomes a superior man, which is *a man of consummate conduct*. Therefore his life is without blame due to having continuously followed a path of reflective self-correction along the way. In essence, this line mimics what Shakyamuni Buddha once said to a group of his monks: "Mendicants, an ethical person who has fulfilled ethical conduct need not make the wish, 'May I have no regrets.' It is only natural that an ethical person has no regrets."

20.6: Yang at the sixth line at the end of the hexagram and top of the Xun trigram. **"Contemplating [analyzing] the lives of others. For superior men there is no blame [they are without fault]."** The major principle of this hexagram is the advice to observe, contemplate or analyze the lives (behaviors) of others - and especially oneself - in order to derive the success factors for life. You scrutinize the behavior of others and your own to find faults (Xun trigram) and then work to reduce those errors in yourself. You act to cut off or avoid errors after *awareness* allows you to spot them. In observing the lives of others you will find that the superior, cultivated individuals cannot be highly criticized. And why? Superior people regularly practice introspection or inner contemplation in order to institute self-correction and by doing this they avoid great errors in life because they always correct themselves (see *Color Me Confucius*). Hence they don't have any great regrets and cannot be blamed for any great errors in their life. In the previous line you examined your life and character to see if it was impeccable. In this line you examine more people in general and find that superior men have less faults and troubles than others because of their impeccable character, conduct and activities. You discover that *character is destiny so behavior is destiny*.

In terms of the composition of the hexagram, the Kun Earth trigram is beneath the Xun Wind trigram, and thus in this line you are "contemplating the lives of the masses" (Kun trigram) and finding no large destructive tendencies (Xun) in the lives of superior men because they police their own behavior and engage in self-correction.

Hexagram 21

Shih He - Biting Through, Eradication

Lower Trigram: Zhen (Thunder) – motion, agitation, biting, damaging
Upper Trigram: Li (Fire) – brilliance, dried, bronze, gold, thinking

The Judgment: Biting Through. Success. Beneficial to administer justice.

In the hexagram is the image of thunder and lightning, which means strong forces are being applied to a situation. The name of the hexagram is biting, which means closing the mouth and eradicating an obstruction. The hexagram actually looks like an open mouth (hexagram 27 Jaws) with an obstruction at the fourth line. The obstacle represents a need for justice and reform. I originally thought this hexagram was related to hexagram 40 (Becoming Untangled) that is about an individual's work at self-purification to free themselves of errant traits and tendencies but then realized that criminals would not be reading the *Yijing* for such advice. Hence this hexagram is probably addressed to officials whose difficult job is to administer the justice system. The Judgment basically states it is beneficial to apply the penal code to correct someone's criminal activities and dissuade them from further wrongdoing. Enacting the penal code is a powerful way to deter people from evil and dissuade wrongdoings in society. In the first line of the hexagram someone is walking in shackles that cut their feet, which means they are being criminally punished to dissuade them from further wrongdoing. The punishment should motivate them to reform. In the second line there is the image of biting deeply into the flesh where the nose becomes mutilated, which means that force must be applied to a rough and unruly criminal individual. The third line is an image of biting into dried meat and becoming poisoned, which refers to judges who suffer the hardship of the difficult job (encountering poison) of righteously applying the law to hardened criminals (the dried meat). The fourth line is an image of biting into dried meat on the bone and being lucky enough to find a bronze arrowhead, which symbolizes a judge working through his cases properly and achieving good fortune for society from this righteous activity (being awarded a bronze arrowhead). Perhaps the arrowhead also means that some criminals become reformed. The fifth line is an image of biting into dried meat as in line three, and you find a piece of gold which means you use discernment to find the truth (honest testimony in the dried meat) of situations and render just decisions when dealing with difficult cases. In the sixth line we see a man wearing a cangue that cuts off his ears or his ear is already cut-off. This symbolizes that he gets into trouble because he did not listen to previous warnings to change his criminal behavior.

1. Walking in fetters that cut his feet. There is no trouble.

2. Biting into flesh and cutting the nose. There is no trouble.

3. Biting into dried (preserved) meat and meeting poison. Small distress. There is no trouble.

4. Biting into dried meat on the bone and obtaining a bronze arrowhead. It is beneficial to persist through difficulty. Auspicious.

5. Biting into dried meat and obtaining yellow bronze. Persistence is dangerous. There is no trouble.

6. Carrying a cangue on his shoulders with a cut-off ear. Ominous.

21.1: Yang at the first line at the beginning of the Zhen Thunder trigram. This means that the image must somehow incorporate movement. Hence, **"He walks shackled in leg-fetters that mutilate the feet (because they cut into the skin). There is no trouble."** Here the power of the Zhen Thunder trigram has damaged the feet. This line describes a person who has committed a criminal offense for the first time. Only a mild punishment is needed so he is punished by having to wear shackles. This symbolizes that he is being prevented from walking in the wrong direction, which means his punishment is an attempt to correct his wrongdoing tendencies. He is caught, punished by the penal code, and will probably learn his lesson and not commit any further crimes. The shackles painfully cut the flesh of the feet so they will motivate a person to reform their behavior.

21.2: Yin at the second line of the Zhen Thunder trigram. This is also the bottom line of an inner Gen Mountain trigram, which represents a nose in this line. **"Biting flesh that cuts the nose. There is no trouble."** The next four lines speak of "biting through" so they are metaphors for the reform or eradication of problems in individuals or society. Biting the flesh (Zhen) and cutting the nose (Gen) means applying violence to an unruly criminal. You bite through tender meat and the nose becomes submerged. This degree of penetration is greater than your skin getting cut due to wearing shackles on your feet. If this is a judge applying the law or enforcer of the law then the message is probably that he is dealing with an unruly tough fellow and must apply drastic or violent measures to restrain him. The punishment must be severe enough with a penetrative effect on the criminal to cause future deterrence otherwise crime will not be suppressed. "There is no trouble" means that this is the right course of action.

21.3: Yin at the third line at the top of the Zhen Thunder trigram, and here the force of the thunder is felt because he strikes something like a jolt of lightning. This is also the middle line of an inner Gen trigram and bottom line of an inner Kan Danger trigram, which is why the individual gets sick from poison. **"He bites through dried [preserved, cured] meat and encounters poison. Some indisposition [small regrets]. There is no trouble."** For this line an individual bites (Zhen trigram) through dried meat (Gen trigram) and strikes poison (Kan trigram). If the line concerns administering justice then the dried meat represents a hardened criminal or repeat offender. For legal officials who must administer the law to hardened criminals the job of administering justice fairly at all times is a challenge or hardship, which takes a toll on the official (who is constantly encountering poison). Thus there is some indisposition but this is the correct way to do things so there is no trouble. Legal officials might feel brutal for the penalties they must impose, but repeat offenders require a strict application of the penal code to deter further violations otherwise crime would run rampant in society.

21.4: Yang at the fourth line and the beginning of the upper Li Fire trigram. This is also the middle line of an inner Kan trigram, which accounts for the difficulties, and top line of an inner Gen trigram. **"He bites through dried meat on the bone and obtains a bronze arrowhead. It is beneficial to persist through difficulty. Auspicious."** As an individual who finds a bronze arrowhead (Li trigram) after biting through dried meat (Li trigram) is like someone getting a prize like recognition for their efforts or just feeling they did a good job for reducing crime in society. *Preserved meat sticking to the bone (Gen trigram) is even harder than simply dried meat so it represents dealing with more difficult cases* or the job in general to obtain this prize. In terms of the justice system this line means that a law officer must steadfastly persist in the duties of his difficult job that are like chewing through something very tough - like dried meat on the bone - but it will lead to good fortune for themselves and society. That is why they will obtain a bronze arrowhead of reward and recognition from this difficult but righteous path. Criminal punishment, which is *making an undesirable event contingent on an unwanted action*, is highly effective in eliminating unwanted behavior and is probably the most effective tool in behavioral modification.

Hundreds of psychological studies prove this, but it is often an ugly job for those who must administer justice.

21.5: Yin at the fifth line, which is the lord of the hexagram within the Li Fire trigram. Hence we have a symbol of striking gold that is a symbol of the Li trigram. This is also the top of an inner Kan Danger trigram, which is why you must still bite through dried meat along with advice to be persistent through difficulties. **"He bites through dried meat and obtains yellow bronze (gold). Persistence is dangerous. There is no trouble."** The fifth line represents a perfected message of the hexagram. There are two possibilities. Law enforcers who must apply the law should remain high-minded and pure in their rulings like gold. They must use discernment to get at the truth accurately in each case and must render just decisions biting through the dried meat of dealing with difficult cases. Then they will obtain gold (or yellow bronze) for society. As long as they continue applying the criminal law fairly and appropriately, regardless of how stern or cruel the punishments may seem, "there will be no trouble." However, danger arises from becoming lax in personal standards or applying the law (especially in difficult cases), slipping and then making wrong decisions and punishments. There are various other possible interpretations of this line and I have only provided just one because all of them are speculative.

21.6: Yang at the top line, the end of the Li trigram and completion of the hexagram. **"Shouldering a cangue with a cut-off ear. Ominous."** The cangue was a large wooden device, three or four feet square, worn around the neck as a punishment given to convicted criminals. Either his ear is already cut-off, meaning he didn't listen to advice and now is punished with the cangue, or a cangue cuts off your ears ("the ears disappear") so you cannot hear. This line basically symbolizes that you didn't listen to the previous warnings of the court or other people regarding your crimes and didn't amend your ways so you got into trouble again, are being punished by wearing the cangue, and this is ominous because it is indicative of future problems too. In the first line only a mild punishment was needed but this line represents an incorrigible person unwilling to reform so he is punished more severely.

The bottom trigram of Zhen Thunder trigram in the hexagram represents criminal tendencies and punishment, and the top trigram of Li Fire trigram represents the destruction they cause, so in this sixth line someone shoulders a cangue (Zhen trigram) that cuts the ears and causes misfortune (Li trigram).

HEXAGRAM 22

Bi - Adornment, Ornamentation, Luxuriance, Elegance

Lower Trigram: Li (Fire) – elegance, glistening, light
Upper Trigram: Gen (Mountain) – hill top, majestic, keeping still

The Judgment: Adornment. Success. Slight (small, minimal) adornment is beneficial in going somewhere.

There is an image in this hexagram of a fire below a mountain, which is a picture of elegance and grace. The message is that by adorning yourself – by making yourself attractive – you are able to advance. Specifically, this hexagram is about a groom who adorns himself in order to get married. The overall lesson is that adornments can run to the elaborate, luxurious and splendorous but simple plain adornment, such as dressing in white, is just fine. The simplicity should not cause any shame at all. In the first line the man adorns his feet because he wants people to notice them. In the second line he adorns his face, namely his beard. In the third line he makes his adornments as elegant as possible and if he continues staying this way it will be fortunate for seeking a bride. In the fourth line he is getting married so the adornments are magnificent. In the fifth line is an admonition not to be too stingy with adornments when getting married, which is the very same advice we saw in line 3.5 (about not saving the fatty meat). However, if you cannot afford elaborate adornments then any shame you feel for their paltriness will pass. In the last line is an admonition that despite the possible beauty of splendorous adornments plain white is without fault.

1. He adorns (decorates) his feet (makes them elegant). He abandons his carriage and walks on foot.

2. He adorns (makes luxurious) his beard.

3. Adorned (elegant) and glistening. Long-term persistence (in such handsome grooming) is auspicious.

4. Adorned as white as snow and like a white horse that has wings. He is a not a robber but a suitor who seeks a matrimonial alliance.

5. Adornments on a hill-top garden, the bolt of white silk is paltry. Distress but in the end auspicious.

6. (Simple) white adornment is without fault.

22.1: A yang line at the bottom, and the beginning of the Li Brilliance-Elegance trigram. **"He adorns [decorates, ornaments] his feet. He discards the carriage and walks on foot."** In this hexagram the brilliance and elegance aspect of the Li trigram stands for adornment or ornamentation. In particular, at this first line you ornament yourself with the lowest level of adornment which is symbolized by adorning your feet for a wedding (or just to make yourself more attractive). The adornments or ornamentation might be embroidered shoes or shoes made of silk brocade. A man gets out of his carriage – "He discards the carriage and walks on foot" – in order to meet the bride and her assembled party by walking. He does this *so that everyone can see his shoes* – his attractiveness – which he wants to show off since this is the nature of the Li trigram.

22.2: Yin at the second line in the middle of the Li Brilliance trigram. This is also the first line of an inner Kan Water trigram. **"He adorns [graces, makes luxurious] his beard."** In this line you adorn yourself higher up in the body – at your face – which befits the showing off aspect of the Li trigram. This represents a superficial degree of brilliance or adornment such as washing, trimming or plaiting his beard. Due to the presence of the Kan Water trigram the image is that a man washes his beard and hair, but due to the Li trigram perhaps his beard also becomes braided or tied with ribbons. These are just another level of superficial beautification.

22.3: The third line is yang and it completes the Li Elegance trigram, so now the brilliance of the Li trigram fully appears. This is also the middle of an inner Kan Water trigram and bottom line of an inner Zhen Thunder trigram. Thus, **"Adorned and glistening [bedewed]. Long-term continuance [in handsome grooming] will bring good fortune."** "Glistening" reflects the presence of the inner Kan Water trigram and means that the adornment or ornamentation is sparkling, luxuriantly glossy or bedewed like water. The man is really clean from line two but the influence of the Zhen Thunder trigram is fleeting due to its temporary nature. Hence the hexagram advises that "Long-term continuance of bedewed adornment (Water trigram) will bring good fortune." This is because *staying well-groomed equates* with higher admiration from others and a higher chance of getting married. The principle is that by adorning yourself – by making yourself attractive – you will be able to advance.

22.4: The fourth line is yin and it is at the beginning of the upper Gen Mountain trigram that symbolizes non-movement. This is also the middle of a Zhen Thunder trigram and top of an inner Kan Water trigram. **"He adorns himself with snowy whiteness and appears like Pegasus, a lofty white horse furnished with wings. He is not a robber (seeking plunder) but a suitor seeking to marry."** Once again the level of adornment surpasses the previous lines and because of the Zhen Lightning trigram is almost startling in brilliance. The reason for the majestic elegance is because the man is getting married. The reference to robbers appears due to the presence of the Kan Danger trigram and refers to a common custom in ancient China of fictitious bride stealing where the groom's party would masquerade as bandits to abduct the bride from her home village.

22.5: The fifth line is yin in the middle of the Gen Mountain trigram. The yin of the line manifests as some misfortune or error. This is also the top line of an inner Zhen Thunder trigram. **"Adornment of a hill-top garden, the bolt of white silk is too paltry [meager, small, insignificant, non-magnificent]. Distress [humiliation, shame] but eventually good fortune in the end."** The location of the *hill-top* garden reflects the presence of the Gen trigram since Gen represents a mountain or hill. This line should also represent greater ornamentation than in the previous fourth line but since it is yin in nature there is some sort of deficiency. The fifth line is the ruler of the hexagram that reveals its message and here you are told not to be too stingy or deficient when trying to ornament an important occasion, which is like the advice given in hexagram line 3.5. At each stage you were progressing through increases in ornamentation but now when they should be maximally resplendent those adornments (or even betrothal gifts) are inadequate. The lack of magnificence causes some shame (which is the destructive aspect of the Zhen trigram) but in the end everything goes well because everything is still acceptable.

22.6: A yang line at the top, thus completing the Gen Mountain trigram and the hexagram. The overall lesson of the hexagram is often found in the fifth or sixth line, and in this case the message is: **"Being adorned in simple, plain white - naturalness without decoration - is without fault [error, trouble]."** In other words, simple natural adornments (like a Gen Mountain), rather than elaborate ornamentation, are without fault. They are a sign of natural grace and beauty. Hence, *if you don't have the money for fancy adornments then simple white adornments are good enough and without shame*. It is not that simplicity is best but that simplicity is fine - without any faults - so one need not make the mistake of many cultures which insist that individuals spend excessively on fashion or style at weddings. If one is sincere there is no need to be elaborate especially since finances will limit anyone's ability to adorn themselves. As the Judgment says, "Slight (small, minimal) adornment is beneficial in going somewhere."

As to the overall composition of the hexagram there is a Li trigram (adornment) below a Gen mountain trigram (natural majesty or beauty) so the combination of the two is reflected in this line as the mountain itself - naturalness without fault or blame.

HEXAGRAM 23

Bo - Stripping Away (Power and Influence), Flaying (an Individual), Destroying Someone; Dismembering Wang Hai's Body

Lower Trigram: Kun (Earth) – acquiescence, acceptance, nurturing, docility
Upper Trigram: Gen (Mountain) – stopping, keeping still, accumulation

The Judgment: Stripping Away (someone's power and influence). It is not beneficial to go on a journey (have somewhere to go).

This hexagram is extremely problematical so I will offer two interpretations of the lines. From this hexagram you will see that many of my interpretations, and those of other translators, are fallible. Nevertheless I've done my best just as all translators have, yet some hexagrams remain mysteries because the true meaning seems shrouded beyond one's abilities of decipherment. Understanding this should be instructive, which is why I hope many new translations will appear based on the principles revealed in this book. This first translation will be based on the traditional *Yijing* text that most people would find in their libraries and the second will be based on the Mawangdui manuscript (which is what I normally use). I will do this dual approach only one more time using hexagram 58. You'll see that this first interpretation is probably not correct because of analyzing events from the aspect of the trigrams! Thus you'll see how useful the trigrams are for developing translations of the *Yijing* and for eliminating plausible interpretations.

This hexagram has the image of a mountain resting upon earth, its support, and speaks in analogies of the earth being removed beneath it so that its majesty collapses. This hexagram is a set of step-by-step instructions for how to destroy and remove someone by stripping away their power, which happens when their support is cut out from beneath them. The step-by-step means of destroying someone powerful is designed to overthrow someone, or we can say someone is being overthrown in this hexagram. The target is an individual who is like a mountain (upper Gen Mountain trigram) attached to the earth (lower Kun Earth trigram) in that they have assembled some power and resources that other people want to grab. If an individual with some power has their support stripped away from them then he will fall and that is what we see happening in this hexagram through destruction of their support and reputation. At first an individual's support is stripped away just as if someone cut off the legs of a couch or bed. Next, their character is cut apart though criticism and arguments. In the third line, now that the individual's support and character have been stripped away through attacks the act of going after them using all sorts of character assassination methods (flaying them) is easy. In the fourth line people increase their attacks and continue stripping away at the individual's accumulation of good fortune, namely the history of their past accomplishments. In the fifth line the palace officials celebrate that an influential target has been stripped of their power or prestige. They try to swallow their power, possessions, position or other resources (divide the spoils) as the entire purpose of the stripping away was to remove their power and influence. The last line offers a pithy comment that really big individuals are hard to destroy but can even gain through circumstances of attack whereas little men are stripped apart and can lose everything.

1. Stripping away (cutting off) the legs of the bed. Bearing such destruction with perseverance is ominous.

2. Stripping (cutting apart) the frame of the bed. Persevering through such losses is ominous.

3. Stripping away. There is no trouble.

4. Stripping away at the bed and depriving it of its surface (skin). Ominous.

5. A string of fish. Eaten by the people of the palace. There is nothing not beneficial.

6. A large fruit remains uneaten. The superior man acquires a carriage while the inferior man is stripped of his house.

23.1: Yin at the first line at the bottom of the Kun Earth trigram bodes ill fortune. **"Stripping away (cutting off) the legs of the bed. Bearing such destruction with perseverance is ominous."** This hexagram is almost entirely yin lines that portend destruction except for one yang line at the top. Each line symbolizes a progressive degree of attack against someone's power. In this line the lowest gradient of stripping away someone's power removes their support, which is symbolized by cutting off the legs of a couch or bed so that what is firm and sound will be destroyed. Those who persevere through this will eventually be destroyed so the start of the process is an omen of disaster, which means more is to come. If an individual has their support cut away from underneath them then it is an omen of more attacks coming. The individual's power in the bottom trigram is symbolized by the Kun trigram that represents an assembly of the earth element. However, the image is of a bed or couch (wood element) that has the legs cut away, and this is usually represented by the destructive penetrating wind element yet the Xun Wind-Wood element doesn't appear here and is nowhere to be found. As a result, perhaps there is the insinuation that the individual doesn't even see where the attack is coming from … or perhaps the second translation is better.

23.2: Yin at the second line in the middle of the Kun Earth trigram, and as the bottom line of an inner Kun Earth trigram. In this hexagram the earth element symbolizes someone's power base because it is an assembly or massing of various elements congealed together. **"Stripping (cutting apart) the frame of the bed. Persevering through such losses is ominous."** A yin line usually indicates bad fortune and because this is the middle of the Kun trigram of three yin lines, and this is also the bottom line of an inner Kun trigram, there should be an increase in the intensity of destruction or deterioration. Here the stripping away has proceeded to attack the character of the individual, presumably through criticism or arguments that the *Yijing* typically calls disputes. Also, persevering through such losses is ominous because they mean that more is to come. The easiest way to destroy someone is to attack their character, namely their "goodness" that is a symbol of the center of the Kun Earth trigram.

23.3: Yin at the third line, at the top of the lower Kun Earth trigram, as the center line of an inner Kun trigram, and as the top line of an inner Kun trigram. **"Stripping away [cutting apart, flaying, skinning]. There is no trouble."** The activity of stripping away the individual's power encounters no obstructions because this line reflects the presence of three intersecting Kun trigrams. There is no problem in cutting down someone's power or reputation at this stage because their support has already been reduced through the prior attacks in lines one and two. The three overlapping Kun trigrams of total yin lines means there is a stripping away of power. The Kun trigram also symbolizes corpses.

23.4: Yin at the hexagram's fourth line, at the bottom of the upper Gen Mountain trigram, as the middle of a Kun Earth trigram, and as the top of an inner Kun trigram. **"Stripping away at the bed and depriving it of its surface (skin). Ominous."** The intersection of two Kun trigrams at this line continues the bad fortune. Here the Gen Mountain trigram represents the accumulation of someone's good fortune along with majesty, and it is being stripped away. In this case the destruction of the individual's power has increased because attackers now try to attack his accumulated (Gen) accomplishments. They are attacking everything about the individual like stripping a bed to its skin. A saying aptly runs, "Those whom the gods wish to destroy must first be vilified."

23.5: Yin at the hexagram's fifth line, which is lord of the hexagram, the center of the upper Gen Mountain trigram, and the top of an inner Kun Earth trigram. **"A string of fish. Eaten by the people of the palace [eaten from the steamer of the palace courtiers]. There is nothing not beneficial."** "A string of fish" could also be translated as "Strung fish" without really changing the interpretation. Since this is the lord of the hexagram we should see some indication of individuals with superior status involved in the line, and this manifests in the image of courtiers or palace residents. As palace residents they belong to the Gen Mountain trigram. We should also see a successful accomplishment of the meaning of the hexagram, which in this case is stripping someone of power (Kun trigram). In this line the progressive destruction of the individual has reached an extreme and is represented by a string of dead fish, whose bodies are eaten by the inhabitants of the palace. Eating the fish symbolizes either having killed the powers and glories of the once powerful individual and split it into pieces, or consuming (distributing) his power and position amongst themselves. Thus, "Nothing is unfavorable" to those who did the stripping.

23.6: Yang at the hexagram's sixth line, and the top of the upper Gen Mountain trigram. **"A large fruit remains uneaten [not destroyed]. The superior man acquires a carriage while the inferior man is stripped of his house."** The hexagram is composed of all yin lines except for the top line, which is the large fruit that remains uneaten. This may symbolize a superior or eminent individual (Gen Mountain trigram) who cannot be destroyed through the shenanigans targeted against other influential men who weren't strong enough to protect themselves, and who therefore lost everything including their homes. A superior man is wise so he might actually be able to gain when people attack him. During crisis periods a superior man might see it as full of opportunities, and thus he acquires a carriage because he profits while "the house of the inferior man is split apart [destroyed]." The five previous lines were all yin, and were like the walls of a house where this yang line is its roof. For an inferior man the roof is ready to cave in because the destruction poured against him enveloped him, but a superior person might find opportunity in this situation due to his greater fortune. Even so, stripping away is a dangerous time and as the Judgment says, does not make it beneficial to go anywhere or undertake any great deed.

As to the overall composition of the hexagram and how it is reflected in this line, there is an Kun Earth trigram underneath a Gen Mountain trigram to serve as the support of the mountain. Thus an inferior person (loose earth) can lose something in this situation because they are not strong enough (their resources can be disassembled to go to others) while a towering superior person can gain.

- - o - -

For the second translation, which is based on the Mawangdui manuscript, this hexagram probably tells the story about how the body of the ancestral Shang king, Wang Hai, was cut up as punishment for having an adulterous affair with the queen of the King of Yi. The story of King Wang Hai, said to be the Chinese father of animal husbandry because he raised livestock and tamed horses and cattle, appears in many places in the *Yijing*. Despite his remarkable achievements as the ancestor of the Shang people (such as inventing the double-shaft ox cart for trade) he was killed for having an adulterous affair. Thus his story throws dirt on the entire morality of the Shang dynasty that was eventually toppled by the Zhou people in response to the depravity of King Zhou Di Xin. The *Yijing* commonly criticizes the unethical behavior of King Di Xin through the retelling of the story of Wang Hai, his brother, and their moral lapses. Because they were the founders of the Shang dynasty this basically insinuates that the rest of the dynasty is immoral as well, and especially King Zhou Di Xin who was overthrown by the Zhou. Retelling the story was a way to reiterate that the Zhou people were justified in overthrowing the "evil" Shang. The consistent message within is the *Yijing* is that Zhou is virtuous and Shang is bad. As to the story, basically King Hai and his younger brother Heng crossed the Yellow River to pasture their flocks in the state of Yi in Hebei where he and his brother were treated like dignitaries by Yi's King Mian Chen. Hai had an affair with Mian Chen's queen and was killed as a consequence. His body was cut into eight pieces that ended up representing eight bird totems. In this hexagram is the punishment story of cutting up his body (and the bed) into pieces. His brother Heng escaped by fleeing to his homeland but Mian Chen appropriated their flocks. The Shang people supported Wang Hai's son Jia Wei as the new leader of the Shang tribe and he raised an army to kill King Mian Chen and capture Yi four years after his father's death. This hexagram tells the story of Hai's dismemberment as punishment for his affair.

1. Cutting up (splitting apart) the bed together with the feet. The augury about losses is ominous.

2. Cutting up the bed together with the knees. The augury about losses is ominous.

3. Cutting it up. There is no trouble.

4. Cutting up the bed together with the skin. Ominous.

5. A string of fish. Eaten by the people of the palace. There is nothing not beneficial.

6. A large fruit remains uneaten. The superior man acquires a carriage while the inferior man is stripped of his house.

23.1: Yin at the first line at the bottom of the Kun Earth trigram. **"Cutting up the bed together with the feet. The augury about losses is ominous."** The Kun Earth trigram represents a corpse. Here the feet of Wang Hai are being cut off, which is the first of the eight pieces. This is an omen of tremendous loss to come.

23.2: Yin at the second line in the middle of the Kun Earth trigram, and as the bottom line of an inner Kun Earth trigram. **"Cutting up the bed together with the knees. The augury about losses is ominous."** Here the body is being dismembered at the knees. There are two Kun Earth trigrams that represent a corpse. This is an omen of more loss to come.

23.3: Yin at the third line, at the top of the lower Kun Earth trigram, as the center line of an inner Kun trigram, and as the top line of an inner Kun trigram. **"Flaying it (cutting it up). There is no trouble."** Here the body is being dismembered in general. Since there are three overlapping Kun Earth trigrams, which is the maximum possible, there is no trouble in doing so.

23.4: Yin at the hexagram's fourth line, at the bottom of the upper Gen Mountain trigram, as the middle of a Kun Earth trigram, and as the top of an inner Kun trigram. **"Cutting up the bed together with the skin."** Here the flesh and skin are being cut off. Naturally we have the corpse representing the Kun trigram and perhaps the Gen trigram represents some other part of the body.

23.5: Yin at the hexagram's fifth line, which is lord of the hexagram, the center of the upper Gen Mountain trigram, and the top of an inner Kun Earth trigram. **"A string of fish. Eaten by the people of the palace. There is nothing not beneficial."** This line is problematical. The fish symbolize abundance and fertility so perhaps they refer to the fact that

King Mian Chen kept the flocks belonging to Wang Hai. Hence all the residents of the palace accordingly benefited.

23.6: Yin at the hexagram's sixth line, and the top of the upper Gen Mountain trigram. **"A large fruit remains uneaten. The superior man acquires a carriage while the inferior man is stripped of his house."** The large fruit that remains uneaten is probably the wife (consort) of the King of Yi who remains unscathed, whereas King Jia Wei comes in later to conquer Yi as the superior man while King Mian Chen is toppled as the inferior man.

HEXAGRAM 24

Fu - Returning, Turning Back, Retreat

Lower Trigram: Zhen (Thunder) – motion, agitation, harm
Upper Trigram: Kun (Earth) – country, ruler, army

The Judgment: Returning. Success. One goes out and comes back in (exits and enters) without harm. Friends arrive without troubles. Turning around and reversing (returning to) one's path the course repeats itself. On the seventh day comes the return. It is beneficial to have somewhere to go (to have a goal or destination).

This hexagram deals with the issue of returning from some journey and many interpretations are problematical because they might, or might not, refer to short military excursions where at times you had to turn back from completing your mission. The difficulty of each trip tends to progressively increase with each new line. In the first line you make a short trip that isn't too distant and the return trip has no incidents. In the second line there is an ordinary and successful trip without any incidents and hence the return is ordinary. In the third line the individual repeatedly returns from a trip due to dangers and he thereby avoids trouble. In the fourth line he sets out on a journey with others and in the middle he returns alone. In the fifth line the trip (or military mission) was successful and in exaltation he magnanimously returns in a fantastic mood because he profitably accomplished whatever he wanted to achieve. In the sixth line the return is confused and calamitous like the scattered retreat of an army where there are many casualties.

1. Returning from not far. There is no harm or trouble. Supreme good fortune.

2. A successful return. Auspicious.

3. He makes repeated returns due to (there being) danger. There is no trouble.

4. Returning alone in the middle of the journey (before the journey is done).

5. Magnanimous (exalted) return. No regrets (no occasion for repentance).

6. Returning he loses the way (a confused return). Ominous. There will be disasters and calamities. If one fields an army it will end in a great defeat with disaster for the ruler of the country. Ominous. For ten years you won't be able to repair the disaster (recover to attack again).

24.1: Yang at the bottom line at the start of the Zhen Thunder trigram. Since this is the start of the Zhen Thunder trigram there is a quick, sharp movement together with the yang nature of the line that produces good fortune. **"Returning after not going very far. There is nothing to regret (there is no harm or trouble). Supreme good fortune."** He doesn't go far but then has to turn back. He suffers no troubles returning home. Thus there are no special troubles or harm even though the Zhen trigram tends to be destructive. Here the line simply represents either a short trip that is interrupted with a safe return, or a quick completed full trip and again an event-free return (probably in the face of danger since there is the presence of a Zhen trigram). This line represents the shortest type of round trip - a foray of a short distance - because it is the bottom line of the hexagram so the journey's return is rather simplistic.

24.2: Yin at the second line within the Zhen Thunder trigram. This is also the bottom line of an inner Kun Earth trigram. **"Successful [fine] return. Auspicious."** The second line represents an increase in the length of the trip and return. The first journey was short and not far away. As to this regular journey it could have been complicated or dangerous due to the harmful effects from the Zhen Thunderbolt trigram but was successful. The traveler was spared any difficulties on his return due to the inner Kun Earth trigram of natural attraction and assemblage. Also, the future hexagram line 19.2 says that management was comprehensive, meaning excellent, so analogously there was a successful complete trip.

24.3: Yin at the third line at the top of the Zhen Thunder trigram, which tends to be destructive. This is also the middle line of an inner Kun Earth trigram and bottom line of an inner Kun Earth trigram. **"He returns repeatedly. Danger. He avoids trouble [harm]."** He returns repeatedly (against his will) because there is a barrier or danger after a certain point. This comes from the fact that this yin line is surrounded by yin lines. In the reverse hexagram, line 23.3 shows the stripping away of a bed or individual which means damage, and in opposite hexagram line 44.3 someone is wounded on the forehead which suggests that the repeated returns are made to avoid danger. The danger in this line appears due to it being the destructive top line of the Zhen Thunder trigram (before the trigram changes into the upper Kun trigram) but by returning the traveler avoids harm. This line probably means multiple attempts to go somewhere but having to return each time due to danger, and then starting out again and returning again. He avoids harm despite the Zhen Lightning Strike trigram due to the blessings of the two Kun Earth trigrams that represent assemblage or massing of people.

24.4: Yin at the fourth line at the bottom of the upper Kun Earth trigram. This is also the middle line of an inner Kun Earth trigram and top line of an inner Kun Earth trigram. **"He returns alone in the middle of a journey."** The man starts off with others since he is in the middle of five yin lines that represent a group of individuals. He is moving right in the center/midst of other yin (divided) lines and has just entered the upper trigram, but now he must turn around and return home. This line also has three overlapping Kun trigrams composed of all yin lines, but the next fifth line has only two overlapping Kun trigrams and the final sixth top line has only one solitary Kun trigram (and is one solitary yin line). The third line has two overlapping Kun trigrams and second line has one. He returns in the middle of his trip (since there are no forward yang lines) while losing his companions along the way, and thus returns alone. Perhaps this refers to the death of comrades due to war (since the Kun trigram represents corpses and burial) where the journey is a military expedition. In that case the lower Zhen trigram would represent the danger of assaults or military attacks. Opposite hexagram line 44.4 states that a packet has no fish to represent the absence of vital energy or men, so perhaps the objective cannot be completed due to the loss of comrades.

24.5: Yin at the fifth line in the middle of the Kun Earth trigram. This is also the top line of an inner Kun Earth trigram. **"Magnanimous (exalted) return. No regrets."** This line is problematical because the translation options for the return are that it is noble, noble-hearted, generous, thick, magnanimous, urgent, involves great sincerity of heart, is for some high purpose, etcetera. Let's see if we can figure this out. Here the line captures the influence of two Kun earth element trigrams that nurture people, accept all influences, and represent an agglomeration of wealth, people or even royalty. The reverse hexagram line 23.5 shows a string of dead fish so it makes sense that in this line one retains the booty of the trip. All these relationships push us towards the idea of a generous, magnanimous or *exalted (highly successful)* return which would mean that the complete trip was successful – the objective was achieved. Since this is the fifth line that is the lord of the hexagram, which normally indicates a perfected form of the hexagram's theme or message along with a respected individual, a "generous (magnanimous)" or "exalted" return means a highly successful trip (Kun trigram of blessings), and this also accords with the Judgment where friends arrive. Thus a "magnanimous" or "exalted" return means it is definitely successful and perhaps the traveler is big-hearted and generous on his return because of the good fortune in achievement.

24.6: Yin at the top line, and at the top of the Kun Earth trigram, ends the hexagram and summarizes the general message of returning. **"Returning he loses the way (a confused return or retreat). Ominous. There will be disasters and calamities. If one mobilizes an army it will end in a great defeat with disaster for the ruler of the country [king]. Ominous. For ten years you won't be able to repair the disaster (recover to attack again)."** To understand this hexagram you must look at it as a whole. The hexagram has one yang line at the bottom, which is akin to launching a military campaign, and five yin lines on top of that yang line constitute potential troubles where people can die. The top line is at the extreme of these yin lines and thus represents a confused return, *which in the military would be a scattered retreat that is an omen of more losses*. Opposite hexagram line 44.6 says that two parties lock horns and engage in an aggressive tug of war while future hexagram line 27.6 says that from using your teeth comes danger. Hence this line is pregnant with negative military implications since this is the top destructive line of the Kun Earth trigram that represents mass deaths and burials as in hexagram 7. All the lines of the hexagram are yin so the message is that a military attack or expedition launched (like thunder) in line one would ultimately result in disasters and calamities, and even harm to the king is mentioned because he is royalty represented by the (top line of the) upper Kun trigram. With five yin lines in a row representing defeats the total calamity would be momentous and it would take years to repair matters.

In terms of the overall construction of the hexagram and how it is reflected in this line, the Zhen trigram is beneath the Kun Earth trigram, and so there are disasters and calamities (Zhen) eating away at to the land/country (Kun) since they are beneath it. This is why it is hard to recover again.

HEXAGRAM 25

Wu Wang - The Unexpected, Unplanned Events

Lower Trigram: Zhen (Thunder) – motion, agitation, unexpected
Upper Trigram: Qian (Heaven) – great strength, perseverance

The Judgment: The Unexpected. Supreme success. It is beneficial to persevere. Not being correct will result in calamity. It is not beneficial to initiate an undertaking.

The image of this hexagram is of thunder rolling under the sky causing unexpected problems everywhere. Like a lightning strike this hexagram is about unexpected, unplanned events that result in problems through no fault of your own. Within such dangers the Judgment states that it is not beneficial (the right circumstances) to initiate a big undertaking. The lines of the hexagram are like a journey through life with unexpected problems and troubles that often happen to people. In the first line is the lowest level of unplanned events: you must unexpectedly go someplace and it turns out well. In the second line you receive an unexpected opportunity of good fortune. In the third line there is an unexpected disaster of loss due to no fault of your own. In the fourth line you are advised to persevere to pass through the trouble of the loss. In the fifth line you unexpectedly get ill but then get well without need of any medicine or special efforts. In the last line, which represents the extreme of unexpected troubles, some actions on your part unexpectedly cause disaster.

1. Unexpected journey (going). Auspicious.

2. Not plowing (sowing) yet reaping (harvesting a crop), not clearing raw land but it becomes cultivated (planted). It is beneficial to undertake something.

3. Unexpected calamity. Though the ox was tethered it became a passerby's gain and the villager's loss.

4. If one is able to persevere (despite the calamity) then there is no trouble.

5. Unexpected illness is cured without medicine. Then there is happiness (again).

6. Unexpectedly walks into (produces) disaster. There is nothing beneficial.

25.1: Yang at the first line of the Zhen trigram of shock or thunder, which usually symbolizes agitation or a burst of motion while yang typically symbolizes good fortune. **"Unexpectedly goes (unexpected journey). Auspicious."** Here you are setting forth unexpectedly due to the influence of the shocking Zhen Thunder trigram. Hence it is an unanticipated journey without any idea of gain (there are no expectations) and there is good fortune because it is a yang line. Opposite hexagram line 46.1 says he is indeed ascending.

25.2: Yin at the second line in the middle of the Zhen Thunder trigram, and the first line of an inner Gen Mountain trigram that can indicate an accumulation. The interpretation is problematic. **"He reaps (a harvest) without having plowed the land, the fields produce a harvest without having been cultivated. It is beneficial to have a destination."** A possible first interpretation is that one shockingly receives unexpected good luck – an unexpected bounty from Heaven. This accords with the fact that most of the lines have to do with something unexpected, and this boon accords with the Gen Accumulation trigram that can represent an accumulation of riches. Hence, *here everything is done for you and you unexpectedly gain a harvest without sowing the land*. An alternative interpretation involves the standard advice not to count on achieving a result for your actions - **"Do not count on a harvest while plowing (sowing) or expect a ripe field when cultivating raw (fallow) land."** However, although this idiom is commonly preferred by many translators the meaning doesn't match with the hexagram. The first interpretation of unexpected good fortune is therefore preferred and is somewhat analogous to future hexagram line 10.2 where a recluse, who doesn't do anything (like in this interpretation), experiences a smooth life as a consequence. In the first line you advanced unexpectedly and now in this second line *you have fortune given to you without having had to work for it*. You reap without having ploughed and gather in produce without having cultivated it. *The path ahead has already been prepared for you without you having had to work for it*. You need only to take advantage of the unexpected opportunity so "it is beneficial to undertake something," meaning to seize it.

25.3: Yin at the third line of the Zhen Thunder trigram, and in this line the thunder strikes to produce loss (yin), which is typical of destructive third lines of trigrams. This is also the middle line of an inner Gen Mountain trigram and bottom line of an inner Xun Penetrating Wind trigram that often produces loss as well. **"Unexpected disaster. Though the ox was tethered it became a passerby's gain and the villager's loss."** The Judgment says, "Not being correct will result in calamity" but in this line you do nothing wrong. Nevertheless, an unanticipated loss still occurs despite your blamelessness and the loss is significant. This situation is that a tethered ox (the Gen Keeping Still trigram) is taken away by a traveler because of theft or because the ox escaped and some passerby found it and took it away. It is an unexpected loss caused by the Zhen Thunder trigram together with the Xun Penetrating Wind trigram that both tend to be destructive.

25.4: Yang at the fourth line at the beginning of the upper Qian Heaven trigram of great strength. This is also the middle line of an inner Xun trigram and top line of an inner Gen trigram. The yang nature of the line indicates good fortune. **"One who is able to persevere (despite the calamity) is without trouble [error]."** You just experienced a great loss, but if you are able to persevere you will get through that difficulty. The new upper Qian trigram gives you great strength to persevere as does the Gen Keeping Still trigram that keeps you on course while the Xun Wind trigram plays with your emotions or tries to make you lose direction. The trouble that might be caused by the Xun Wind trigram is held in check by the combination of the Qian and Gen trigrams exerting their influence against it. The basic idea is the theme of the hexagram that you need to persevere through unexpected calamities.

25.5: Yang at the fifth line at the center of the Qian Heaven trigram. This is also the top line of an inner Xun trigram. **"An unexpected illness. It is cured without resort to medicine, and then there is happiness (again)."** At the fifth line that is the lord of the hexagram we should see a perfected form of the message of the hexagram, which is that *unexpected bad fortune occurs but if you just keep plowing forward you can recover from most problems.* Most unfortunate situations will turn out well in the end without any major effort needed on your part. Therefore the image is that without using medicine to treat an unexpected illness you become well again ("there will be happiness"). *Many unfortunate situations resolve themselves or you simply adapt and get used to them and then continue moving forward with life.* This is a yang line within the upper Qian trigram of great strength so we should naturally expect the individual to recover from an unexpected illness. The only negative influence impacting the situation is the destructive top line of an inner Xun Penetrating Wind trigram, which is what causes the illness. The wind element can cause illness because it represents a force of penetration, disassembly, disintegration, deterioration or destruction but this force is also being countered by the strong middle line of the upper Qian Great Strength trigram. Without making any attempt to get rid of the destructive wind element (sickness) it will naturally go away.

25.6: Yang at the sixth line at the top of the Qian trigram completes the hexagram and this line summarizes its meaning. The bad fortune is due to the Qian Strong Force trigram producing actions that unexpectedly produce disaster, so the extreme of yang turns yin. **"Unexpectedly walks into (produces) disaster. There is nothing beneficial."** Line 46.5 of the opposite hexagram similarly says, "Ascending in the dark," which means climbing or acting in darkness where you do not know what will happen because you cannot see anything. Here motion, movement and just activity in general unexpectedly leads to disaster so the individual unexpectedly encounters calamity. The top of the Qian trigram represents great strength at its peak but the extreme of yang turns to yin at its peak. Hence we have a yang line deteriorating and turning destructive at the end of the trigram and producing the yin result of misfortune to match with the "unexpected" message of the hexagram.

The overall construction of the hexagram overall is that a Zhen Thunder trigram is beneath the Qian Great Strength trigram so that there is lightning and thunder in the sky. The way this appears in this line is that we have "unexpected actions (lightning strikes) that produce disaster."

HEXAGRAM 26

Da Xu – Restraining Great Power, Taming the Strong

Lower Trigram: Qian (Heaven) – great force, strong action, horse
Upper Trigram: Gen (Mountain) – stopping, horn guard, majesty

The Judgment: Restraining Great Power. It is beneficial to persevere. Not eating at home is auspicious. It is beneficial to ford the great river.

This hexagram incorporates an image of a mountain above the sky and is about the growth of power and how to tame or restrain it so that it does not become harmful. In this hexagram you are restraining the strong, i.e. restraining great power. The lessons revolve around putting strength under control and the analogies that illustrate this principle are methods of controlling powerful animals that might hurt people if steps aren't taken to restrain them. In the first line there is danger ahead because of some powerful force so you are advised to offer sacrifice and ask for protection from Heaven. In the second line a cart stops moving because an axel-strut that channels its power of movement breaks loose. In the third line a team of capable horses are being chased and arranged defensively to protect against some external danger. In the fourth line the power of a young bull is restrained by using a headboard that protects everyone from its horns. In the fifth line a (powerful) boar has been gelded to protect people from its ability to cause harm and destruction. In the top line you are advised to follow the way of Heaven by submitting to Heaven's pattern of fate rather than your own egoistical demands, which is a path of humility that will restrain your errant energies and the usage of your power.

1. There is danger. It is beneficial to offer a sacrifice.

2. A cart throws off its axle-strut.

3. Fine horses (race forward) being chased. It is beneficial to persevere through difficulties. Arrange the carts defensively and then it is favorable to advance.

4. A young bull has a headboard (horn guard) put on his horns. Supreme good fortune.

5. A gelded boar's tusks (remain, but it cares little to use them). Auspicious.

6. Following the way of Heaven. Success.

26.1: Yang at the first line at the bottom of the Qian Heaven trigram that symbolizes great strength. **"There is danger. It is beneficial to offer a sacrifice."** The danger exists because of an immature but growing power that exists due to presence of the Qian Great Force trigram which is as yet unchanneled and untamed. The presence of this danger requires you to ask Heaven for help for the blessing of protection. At this stage of immaturity you want to take the right actions to check this growing power so that it does not become dangerous or harmful. You need guidance from Heaven on how to do this and to make sure nothing unfortunate happens in the meanwhile. A popular alternative translation is "It is beneficial to stop (desist, bring activities to a halt)" rather than "It is beneficial to make a sacrifice." Here the idea is that with danger at hand it would be wise to bring one's activities to a halt and cease one's efforts of advancing at this time. To decide between the two translations, note that this is the first line of the Qian trigram that would push you forward while any danger is weak, and by stopping you would not move forward to any subsequent lines. The reverse hexagram 25.1 has "Unexpected going" while the opposite hexagram 45.1 has estranged friends meeting. Hence the most probable translation is to go but make a sacrifice asking for help to handle all the powerful forces coming, which also accords with the sixth line's reference to follow Heaven's way since the first and sixth lines are often related to one another.

26.2: Yang at the second line in the middle of the Qian Great Strength trigram. This is also the bottom line of an inner Dui Talking trigram that also symbolizes breaking free or stepping forward. **"The cart drops an axle-strut (therefore he stops his advance)."** A cart becomes separated from its axle-strut means that the cart loses the fitting that holds it to the axle and therefore it cannot go forward. An axle part breaks and this stops the carriage. There are all sorts of alternative translations for this part such as axle strap, axle box, axle holder, axle bracket etc. but the basic message is that the cart or carriage loses some type of axle part that channels its power of movement and therefore the cart stops advancing because of this separation. You cannot advance so your great power in moving forward is restrained. The break is due to some type of great force due to the presence of the Qian Great Force trigram, and the accident causes a stop to all forward movement. So the power of movement was stopped because one part became separated from all the others.

26.3: Yang at the third line, which is at the top of the Qian Great Strength trigram. This is also the middle line of an inner Dui trigram and bottom line of an inner Zhen Thunder trigram. **"Fine horses (gallop) being chased. It is beneficial to persevere during difficulties [hardship]. Arrange the carts defensively and then it is favorable to advance."** Horses normally gallop and chase one another which is a manifestation of the Zhen Thunder trigram. In this case, the horses are either being chased as a team, or their power is harnessed together and they are used as a team in a chase. It is most probable that the individual is being chased and urging his way with galloping horses because "defensive" is mentioned in the lines. It is certainly beneficial to have available the strength (Qian trigram) of capable, galloping horses but that is possible – steeds galloping in companionship with a power useful to you – *only if their power is arranged and harnessed in an appropriate way*. Future hexagram 26.3 warns against losing a man from a group of three while reverse hexagram 26.3 warns against losing an ox, which means that the horses need to be harnessed together appropriately. Next, "Arrange the carts defensively and then it is favorable to advance." You should arrange the horses in a way that unites their powers where they are under your control and the military should arrange its carts to protect against any forces that might attack so that you don't lose any. If you arrange your carts defensively then it will be favorable to advance. In the subsequent lines four and five of the hexagram you restrain animals in various ways, and *the basic idea is to somehow restrain their great power in order that it doesn't go out of control*. In this line you do so by arranging the positioning of the horses (your power). In other words, use the power of galloping horses to proceed through difficulties, but this power must be channeled in a safe formation that protects you instead of just letting them run wild. You also must arrange your carts so that you are not vulnerable to external attacks. Controlling your own defensive powers through proper positioning will be favorable for the attainment of goals. The horses in a chase represent the Qian Great Strength and Zhen Thunder trigrams, and the fact that there is a chase is the Dui Joy trigram of happiness since the horses can give full expression of their spirits through galloping. The possibility of attack that requires defense is also the Zhen Thunder Strike trigram.

26.4: Yin at the fourth line, and at the bottom of the Gen Mountain trigram that symbolizes restraint and non-movement. This is also the middle line of a Zhen Thunder trigram and top line of an inner Dui Joy trigram. **"A young [growing] bull gets a headboard put on his horns. Supreme**

good fortune." In ancient China, when a young bull grew horns then a board was typically fastened across their tips to protect its owners and other animals from injury. The board shapes the growth of the horns and prevents goring. Hence, a horn guard tied to a young bull minimizes the danger that comes from such wild power and is highly beneficial. It is a way to restrain the bull's powers and prevent problems from happening. This *precautionary measure* restrains increasingly substantial power. Such a restraint is the influence of the Gen Stillness trigram while the potential danger of goring represents the Zhen Thunder trigram. *The headboard is a method of avoiding danger by dealing with potential problems when they are small and easy to manage.* The result of protecting the breeders and other cattle from harm by restraining the bull's power in this way is "Supreme good fortune." The fourth line of a hexagram often shows a successful achievement of the hexagram's message where a more perfect accomplishment is seen in line five, and that's what we find here.

26.5: Yin at the fifth line in the middle of the Gen Mountain trigram. This is also the top line of an inner Zhen Thunder trigram. **"A gelded [castrated] boar's tusks. Auspicious."** The fifth line is the lord of the hexagram and usually involves a man of dignity or high status, but in this case it is a strong boar. The lord of the hexagram also typically shows a perfected example of its main message. In this line the power of a wild boar has been restrained through castration, which symbolizes preventing problems by taking steps to curb power before it can grow out of control. The *Yijing* states that this preventative measure represents great good fortune. This line entails potential trouble greater than that of the young bull in line four, and it uses even greater preventative restraint as well. In both lines it is difficult to restrain animals after they grow into adulthood and become very strong. For instance, a boar is a strong *wild animal* with a violent temper and its dangerous tusks can harm people. In this case a boar has been castrated to control that power because after being gelded it becomes docile and easier to manage. Its tusks remain, but the boar cares little to use them and hence disasters can be avoided by gelding.

26.6: Yang at the top line, and the top of the Gen Mountain trigram that symbolizes restraint. **"Following the way of Heaven. Success."** A very accurate translation of the line is "Carrying (according with) Heaven's crossroad (the highway of the sky)," but few people would understand what this means. In Chinese culture Heaven's crossroad is a section of the night sky consisting of four stars in Scorpio, which marks the point where the celestial equator and ecliptic intersect. The phrase usually means not following your own way but putting yourself in tune with Heaven, which is considered the highest mode of beingness. It means going along with the flow of Heaven's patterns since Heaven is considered the highest exemplar of virtue. Thus you submit to Heaven's way rather than your own egotistical pursuit of power or dominance, which is a discipline imposed by the Gen Stillness trigram. If you follow the way of Heaven, which is a path of humility, you will be rechanneling your errant energies and powers and thereby protecting yourself. Hence, this is the highest method of majestic restraint.

In terms of the overall construction of the hexagram composed of the Qian and Gen trigrams, you are constrained to follow the path of Heaven because the Gen Mountain trigram sits on top of the Qian Heaven trigram, thus restraining your actions to its path. The way this appears in this line is that you "follow the Way of Heaven."

HEXAGRAM 27

Yi – Jaws, Hungry Mouth

Lower Trigram: Zhen (Thunder) – motion, chewing, surprise
Upper Trigram: Gen (Mountain) – stopping, keeping still, jaws

The Judgment: Jaws. Perseverance is auspicious. Observe the jaws and determine for yourself the state of the teeth.

This hexagram has the image of thunder below the mountain where despite having great power the thunder cannot conquer it. Using the analogy of worn teeth this hexagram discusses whether or not your soldiers (teeth) are strong enough to undertake a military expedition to gobble up more territory (nourishment) and make it your own where your men and resources have already been reduced in strength (your teeth have been whittled away). You have a hungry mouth in this hexagram so you certainly want to do this. It symbolizes militarily biting into a conflict because you think a successful result/conquest will make you stronger and nourish/feed you but your abilities are inadequate to take on the task. Thus the Judgment says to observe the jaws (inspect your troops) and the food you seek (the territory you want to conquer). This hexagram says that due to diminished military strength and resources (teeth), you can only look at conquering new territory with hunger but cannot do it. In the first line you are reminded not to use divination to foretell the future for something as important as war but to just carefully examine the condition of your troops for yourself and then the answer will become immediately obvious. Using the analogy of teeth, in the second line you are reminded that you cannot undertake a military expedition if your men and equipment are worn down. In the third line you are warned that in a state of weakened resources, such as when all your teeth are worn down, it is neither recommended or even possible to launch a military assault. In the fourth line is the observation that it is still feasible to think about achieving some military objectives when you still have some viable resources and abilities (when the teeth are not totally gone). In the fifth line, which uses chewing as an analogy, there is a reminder that you must seek nourishment to restore the strength of your army/resources, which means that you must drill the troops and bide your time in your home territory before launching any attack. In the sixth line is the reminder that using your teeth (e.g. force or military resources) is always a perilous undertaking (because they can crack or wear down or you can encounter something unwholesome) but there can be good fortune in the end.

1. You put aside your numinous tortoise and look up at my drooping jaws (the ailing condition of my teeth in the jaws). Ominous.

2. Jaws without front teeth, chewing using the wisdom molars. A military campaign is ominous.

3. Jaws without teeth, chewing using the gums ("scraping the jaw"). To continue this way is ominous. For ten years you cannot put them to use. There is nothing beneficial.

4. Jaws without front teeth. Auspicious. A tiger stares fearsomely with covetous craving. There is no trouble.

5. Chewing one's food (masticating in order to separate inedible items). Persevering in your territorial residence (camp) is auspicious. It is not appropriate to cross the great river.

6. From using the jaws (teeth) comes danger and then good fortune. It is beneficial to ford the great river.

27.1: Yang at the first line at the beginning of the Zhen Thunder trigram where in this case it represents something shocking. **"You put aside your numinous tortoise and look up at my drooping jaws [the ailing condition of teeth in my jaws]. Ominous."** A "numinous (magic) tortoise" is either an elderly tortoise or an old (dried up) tortoise shell used for divination purposes. The analogy to the aged, hard turtle shell is aging broken teeth. "Drooping jaws" refers to the weakened muscles and the poor condition of teeth in the jaws, many of which are missing, and this poor condition is represented by the old tortoise shell. This represents the dilapidated state of a beaten up army. The line tells you to put aside the magic tortoise shell used for divination and instead look at the misfortunate condition of the man's teeth (within his drooping jaws) for yourself, which is *actually inspecting the situation*, and from this you will know what he can or cannot do with his mouth. You don't need to resort to any divination – just inspect things for yourself. You cannot bite into a difficult situation if your teeth are poor which means that that your military capabilities are not up to the situation at present. Typically before a military invasion (Zhen trigram) one would divine using a tortoise shell, but this line says that you should put it aside. Why? You can know for yourself if you are capable just by looking at the condition of your troops and equipment. Just look at the situation of your troops and equipment and you will know that your military force is not strong enough, which is the meaning of ominous.

27.2: Yin at the second line of the Zhen Thunder trigram so we would typically see some type of bad fortune. This is also the bottom line of an inner Kun Earth trigram. **"Jaws without teeth, chewing using the wisdom molars. A military campaign is ominous."** In this line the progressive teeth loss has increased but there are still molars (Kun Earth trigram) remaining. In previous lines the teeth were aged and in bad condition from heavy usage. However, in this line the crowns of the wisdom molars are not yet worn down so you still can bite (Zhen trigram) using the back of the jaws, but it isn't a very strong bite. Therefore you still cannot set out on a military expedition (chewing) because the soldiers (teeth) are too few or weak (not fit for the task). The state of the teeth (troops) is ominous foretelling defeat in any military campaign. The Kun trigram or earth element is strong in these lines and represent the teeth while the Zhen trigram shows its presence as chewing and a military expedition.

27.3: Yin at the third line ending the Zhen Thunder trigram, and thus we have more misfortune since its top line tends to be destructive. This is also the middle line and bottom line of two inner Kun Earth trigrams. **"Jaws without teeth except for worn-down molars [scraping the jaw because the mouth is mostly just gums]. Continuing this way is ominous. For ten years do not use them. There is nothing beneficial in this."** In this line there is a further progression of losing teeth where the intensity of deterioration has increased again. The striking damage of the Zhen trigram on the two Kun Earth trigrams, which symbolizes military engagements, is represented as the wearing down of teeth from chewing including the molars. You cannot keep subjecting yourself to such destruction but must desist. For an army the analogy is that almost all your troops have been destroyed and the remaining troops are worn out. The advice to the military leader is that you must not take any more action because it will not be in any way advantageous. The army must stop to retreat, rebuild and replenish its strength, and such assemblage is due to the Kun Earth trigram.

27.4: Yin at the fourth line at the beginning of the upper Gen Mountain trigram. This is also the middle and top lines of two inner Kun Earth trigrams so we will still see teeth involved in the image. **"Jaws without teeth (but molars are present). Auspicious. A tiger watches fearsomely with persistent (covetous) craving. There is no trouble."** At this stage some molar teeth (Kun Earth trigram) still exist so because of your hunger for conquest you still want to do something with the little strength you retain. The military analogy is that the army is still in good enough shape to launch an attack so it is like a hungry, fearsome tiger who is eyeing potential prey. A hungry tiger that covetously eyes its prey waiting for a chance to strike represents the stillness of waiting that is the Gen Non-Movement trigram. The message is that when you don't have many forces available you should remain in readiness but not act and then you will thereby avoid harm or trouble.

27.5: Yin at the fifth line, in the middle of the Gen Mountain trigram, and thus we will see an image of non-movement in not crossing a river. This is also the top line of an inner Kun Earth trigram that symbolizes the threshing or chewing of food. **"Chewing one's food. Persevering in your territorial residence is auspicious. It is not appropriate to cross the great river."** This is the fifth line or lord of the hexagram and thus it should present a perfected form of the hexagram's message: you must abide/dwell where you are and spend your time drilling your troops and restoring their strength rather than trying *to undertake* any great military assault, which is represented by a dangerous river crossing. Your mouth might be hungry for food, which means you might want to attack some city or conquer some territory, but you should spend your time in your home territory drilling your troops (chewing your food) instead. People use their teeth to "thresh the warp," which means masticate the food and separate the good from the bad. You chew your food completely to separate inedible items and prevent non-masticated food from being swallowed. You are still in a situation where your resources are poor so you should focus on drilling your troops to identify the bad and train them to restore your strength (through nourishment) rather than move forward. It is not appropriate to cross the great river because the condition of the mouth is in a weakened, inferior state. *The message of the entire hexagram is that when your army is weak and worn down you should continue drilling the troops and try to restore your military strength, resources and abilities rather than to launch an expedition with weakened forces.*

27.6: Yang at the top line of the Gen Mountain trigram, which symbolizes teeth in the hexagram. **"From using the jaws (teeth) comes danger [difficulties, peril, adversity] and then good fortune. It is beneficial to cross the great river."** From using the army (your jaws with teeth, namely troops) comes danger and then conquest (good fortune). The idea of cautiously using your teeth to chew to provide yourself nourishment, and the reminder that teeth deteriorate over time, should be extended to other things you use that deteriorate over time as well. Good fortune comes from their preservation. With teeth (resources and ability) you can eat food, i.e. cross a river. Without teeth you cannot eat food; i.e. cross a great river. An army without good soldiers, for instance, cannot possibly launch military expeditions and win battles.

In terms of the composition of the hexagram the Zhen Thunder trigram is underneath the Gen Mountain trigram and so chewing food (the Zhen trigram that means a military assault) must be done carefully for success in a great undertaking (Gen trigram). With caution it will be beneficial to cross the great river (perform the undertaking).

HEXAGRAM 28

Da Guo – An Excess (Preponderance) of Greatness, Greatness (Yang) in Excess, Rejuvenation of Yang Energy

Lower Trigram: Xun (Wind) – wood, grass mat, popular tree, ridgepole
Upper Trigram: Dui (Joy) – lake, mouth, wife, pleasure, shallows

The Judgment: An Excess (Preponderance) of Greatness. The ridgepole bends (sags). It is beneficial to have a destination (an undertaking). Success.

This hexagram is actually about the rejuvenation of the human body because of a gradual increase in internal yang Qi (due to spiritual cultivation), and so the yang energy progressively increases in each line of the hexagram that analogously looks like a ladder. Its first rung is a yin line to represent meditation or spiritual practice where you empty the mind, and the last rung is a yin line that is empty because a man loses his great accumulated energy through sex. In the first line the level of a man's internal Qi is humble as he starts engaging in spiritual reverence (ceremonial offering), which represents spiritual cultivation that normally increases your Qi energy. In the second line that energy becomes stronger in intensity and starts rejuvenating an older man, who is represented by a withered popular tree. In the third line it keeps growing and the analogy of "a ridgepole that sags" implies that the accumulated energy is lost through sexual activities since the man was feeling rejuvenated. In the fourth line the man's strength recovers, which means that the ridgepole becomes stronger again due to restraint (celibacy as the power inside him grows), and he is warned that if he loses his yang energy again (through more sexual dissipation) this would be bad. In the fifth line the man feels rejuvenated because of his returning or ascending Qi (remember that the hexagram is in the shape of a ladder) and then starts having more frequent sex with his wife. In the last line is the image of falling into water over your head, which is another reference to overindulgence in sex. The overall lesson of increasing yang Qi (due to spiritual cultivation of the first line) is to use it productively rather than expending it through the outlet of sexual activities. Thus the Judgment states it is beneficial to have a destination (an undertaking) other than to employ growing yang energy in sexual activity where the ridgepole ends up bending.

1. For the ceremonial offertory mat use white cogongrass. No blame.

2. A withered poplar tree grows shoots. An old man takes a young wife. There is nothing not beneficial.

3. The ridgepole sags. Ominous.

4. The ridgepole arches upward. Auspicious. If harmed there will be distress.

5. The withered poplar tree blossoms (produces flowers). An old wife gets a young husband. No blame - no praise.

6. While wading (the shallows) the water goes over his head. Ominous, but no trouble.

28.1: Yin at the bottom line, and the beginning of the Xun Wind trigram. **"For the ceremonial offertory mat use white cogongrass. No blame."** As the lowest gradient of the hexagram this line represents the most humble stirring of wind, which represents yang Qi, rather than a very strong force. A humble offering using white grass (white = pure, wood/grass = wind element or Qi) as the offering mat instead of an altar represents a humble beginning of yang energy that normally arises when a person engages in reverential (spiritual) activities. This line represents pure spiritual activities that cultivate your yang Qi. When yang Qi arises in a body it rejuvenates it. Thus, "Nothing blameworthy."

28.2: Yang at the second line in the middle of the Xun Wind-Wood trigram and bottom line of an inner Qian Great Strength trigram. **"A withered poplar tree grows shoots. An old man takes a young wife. There is nothing not beneficial."** The Xun trigram stands for the wind element or Qi energy that is our life force. Here we see images of a tree (wood) being renewed where the tree (wood) is another symbol for the wind element. We also see an old man regaining his sexual vitality (virility) due to the renewal powers of rising yang Qi represented by the Qian Great Strength trigram and Xun Life Force trigram. When you increase the yang Qi of your body, which you can usually accomplish through spiritual cultivation as symbolized in the first line, it causes rejuvenation.

28.3: Yang at the third line, at the top of the Xun Wind trigram, as the middle line of an inner Qian Great Strength trigram and bottom line of yet another inner Qian Great Strength trigram. **"The ridgepole sags. Ominous."** Here the yang energy has become extremely full due to the presence of two Qian trigrams. What does a man do when his energy becomes full? He engages in sexual activities and then loses his energy. Afterwards "his ridgepole bends." The preponderance of great yang energy is then lost. Why did this happen? The top line of the Xun Wind trigram is destructive and represents leakage. Opposite hexagram line 27.3 similarly says that the jaws have lost all their teeth. Ordinary translations will say that a sagging ridgepole is a weak, old ridgepole and a sign that the roof may possibly fall in, especially with two Qian Great Strength trigrams sending power through it and causing the ridgepole to bend. The bending is ominous because if it cannot bear the force any longer it will break. The true symbolism escapes most translators – the rejuvenated man who has accumulate yang Qi then engages in sex and after consummation his ridgepole is bending rather than rigid, which is the normal reaction, so the sagging is a sign of no more good fortune for the immediate future – ominous.

28.4: Yang at the fourth line, at the beginning of the Dui Lake trigram, as the middle of an inner Qian Great Force trigram, and as the top line of yet another inner Qian Great Force trigram. **"The ridgepole arches [curves, bows] upward. Auspicious. If harmed there will be distress."** The previous line of the hexagram was under the influence of the top destructive line of a Xun Penetrating Wind trigram. It caused the man to experience loss in the presence of his increasing vitality. Here we have two inner Qian trigrams again so due to celibacy the man's vitality has recovered and he is full of Qi again as well as happy or blissful, which is represented by the Dui Joy trigram. The Dui Joy trigram sometimes symbolizes standing straight which is also represented here via the ridgepole. This yang line is particularly strong because it is wedged in between other yang lines and it receives the influence of two inner Qian Great Strength trigrams to give it power. An ordinary translator might say something like "if the ridgepole wasn't strong enough then there would be a disaster (distress) because the beam would break and the roof would fall in. However, the fact that it arches upward shows that it is strong, or that possibly there is a new roof." Actually, the ridgepole becomes strong again after some time because a man's vitality becomes restored due to the discipline of celibacy and restraint. However, if he loses his energy again through sexual leakage then there will be distress. Opposite hexagram line 27.4 mentions a hungry tiger that stares but does not pounce on his prey, which has connotations of being beset by sexual desire but not indulging, and that is what is happening here. Let's see how the man uses his recovering energy in the fifth line.

28.5: Yang at the fifth line within the middle of the upper Dui Joy trigram (that often symbolizes water and women) and as the top line of an inner

Qian Heaven trigram of great force. **"The withered poplar tree blossoms (produces flowers). An old wife gets a young husband. No blame - no praise."** The fifth line of a hexagram portrays a perfected form of its overall message, and in this case we see rejuvenation where an almost dead tree comes to life again and an older woman obtains a younger husband. The meaning is that her husband becomes rejuvenated so he is now like a younger man (husband) with renewed sexual virility and interest, and the "popular tree blossoms" because they begin having frequent sexual relations again (the Dui Joy-Lake trigram) due to his returned vitality. Hence, "The withered poplar tree blossoms (produces flowers). An old wife gets a young husband." This is "Not blameworthy, not praiseworthy" because this sudden frolicking is temporary and a woman's fertility cannot return so the flowers are a temporary burst of useless glory as compared to young shoots.

28.6: Yin at the sixth line of the hexagram and at the top of the upper Dui Lake trigram that accounts for the usage of a water image in this line. **"Wading the shallows the water goes over the top of his head. Ominous, but no trouble."** The image used is that you are crossing some shallows, you accidentally drop into some deep water where you temporarily sink but you get out of the trouble. The superficial meaning of this concerns encountering a force stronger than you can handle (it's over your head) and then landing in a troublesome but not fatal difficulty. Actually, this line is a veiled reference to sexual intercourse again where the man, feeling full of his renewed vitality, "slips" and has an orgasm again. This is a natural calamity so there is no error or harm in this. This line thus indicates a man's yang energy reaching an extreme and then deteriorating rather than continually enlivening or rejuvenating the man.

In terms of the construction of the hexagram there is a Xun Wind trigram stacked beneath a Dui Water trigram, and hence this final line is constructed in such a way to represent a strong life force moving (Xun trigram) through water (Dui trigram of sexual intercourse) where you slip and lose your head.

HEXAGRAM 29

Xi Kan – Danger, The Perilous Pit, Double Pitfall, Repeated Entrapment

Lower Trigram: Kan (Water) – abyss, pit, precipice drop, danger, trouble
Upper Trigram: Kan (Water) – pit, wine, earthenware, imprisonment

The Judgment: Double Pitfall. Maintaining faithfulness in the heart (a optimistic, positive attitude) and calm mind leads to success. Along the way there will be elevation.

In this hexagram there is an abyss piled upon an abyss so that there are two pit-traps or dangerous situations. Hence misfortune is far more probable than a favorable success. This hexagram means entanglement in a difficult situation or danger where you can make the situation even worse so you must especially remain careful, calm and endure troubles as you wait for help. It instructs us to handle dangerous, perilous situations by remaining calm rather than struggle uselessly otherwise you might make the situation worse and fall into deeper entrapment. Naturally you should avoid dangers in the first place so that you avoid the peril but here you fall into trouble and are counseled how to *avoid a double pitfall*. The hexagram points out that the best strategy for handling extreme danger like this is calmness, but if you fall into a double pitfall there will be no way to get out of the troubles easily. In the first line you fall into the opening of a pit, which is a misfortunate event that represents getting into some type of trouble. In the second line you can climb back up towards the pit's opening just a little bit even thought the pit has steep sides; you remain in difficulty despite your efforts to extricate yourself. In the third line your efforts to escape cause you to slip and fall deeper into the pit hitting its bottom; your problems have become greater in size. In the fourth line someone sends you some food (assistance) as a helpful relief to sustain you but you still don't escape. In the fifth line you are advised to remain calm to get through the difficulties. In the sixth line the situation is compared to being bound as a captive while also inside a prison of thorns where you cannot escape the double (multiple) troubles for years. All these lines symbolize getting into some type of trouble where you are warned not to make the difficulty worse by getting into even more trouble (falling into a second pit), and where you should remain calm until you can receive aid or get out of the trouble.

1. There is a pit within a pit. He enters into the pit opening. Misfortunate.

2. The pit has a drop (precipice). In seeking there is little gain (of the deliverance you seek).

3. Bam-bam, thudding hard you hit the bottom. The pit is steep and deep. Don't go down into the (second) pit opening.

4. A goblet of wine and two bowls of rice. Use plain earthernware vessels. Pass them in (by rope) through the pit's opening. In the end there is no trouble.

5. The pit is not filled (with water). Blessings will come from remaining calm. There is no trouble.

6. He is tied with rope and cords, and imprisoned in a thicket of thorns. For three years he will not get out (attain release). Ominous.

29.1: Yin at the first line of the Kan Abyss trigram, which suggests misfortune. **"There is a pit within a pit. He falls into the pit opening. There is misfortune."** The beginning of trouble starts here. "There is a pit within a pit" represents two potential degrees of trouble because the hexagram (situation) has two Kan Abyss trigrams stacked upon each other. They represent two possible pitfalls of danger. The subject falls through the opening of the first pit to encounter the first danger because this is the first line of the hexagram, and thus just the beginning of a misfortunate situation that *is not yet super serious* at this lowest line of intensity.

29.2: Yang at the second line within the Kan Abyss-Danger trigram indicates just a tiny bit of good fortune, just a tiny bit of gain or deliverance within the peril. This is also the bottom line of an inner Zhen trigram. **"The pit has a precipice. In seeking you will obtain only a little gain."** You are at the very middle line of the Kan Danger-Abyss trigram so you are surrounded by danger, yet this is a yang line so there is a little bit of good fortune due to it being there. But you still cannot get out of trouble. You can only attain some small relief, small gain, because the middle Kan line is the one that most represents the pit and it is tinged a little bit by the presence of the dangerous Zhen Thunderbolt trigram. With a Zhen trigram there who knows what could happen next since you have not hit absolute bottom yet.

29.3: Yin at the third line completes the lower Kan Danger trigram. This is also the middle line of an inner Zhen Thunder trigram and bottom line of an inner Gen Keeping Still trigram. **"Thudding hard you hit the bottom"** of the first pit because this is the end of the first trigram. Next, **"The pit is steep and deep. Don't go down into the second pit opening."** You hit the bottom of the first pit and then stop. You fell because of the Zhen Thunderbolt - your efforts from line two made your situation worse. Now you are at the top and most destructive line of the Kan Danger-Abyss trigram. Another pit, or Kan trigram, lies ahead in the second half of the hexagram. To avoid further danger you are told not to go deeper and enter into the second pit. Hitting bottom in the first pit is not only due to being at the end of the first Kan trigram but also reflects the influence of the Gen Keeping Still trigram that halts further dropping. The warning not to go into the second pit is commonsense but is also telling you to resist the dangerous motive force of the Zhen Thunder trigram that might push you into trying something stupid that causes further misfortune.

29.4: Yin at the fourth line at the beginning of a second Kan Water-Abyss-Danger trigram. This is also the middle line of an inner Gen Mountain trigram and top line of an inner Zhen trigram. **"A goblet of wine and two bowls of rice carried in plain earthernware vessels. Send them in (by rope) through the pit's opening to those who are stuck. In the end there is no trouble."** Here the individual in the pit (second Kan trigram) attains a bit of relief during their dangerous dilemma. The surprising (Zhen trigram) assistance of wine, grain and the earthenware vessels pick up the symbolism of both the water of the Kan trigram and the earth element of the inner Gen Mountain trigram. The pit's opening is mentioned due to the picture made by the two consecutive yin lines three and four.

29.5: Yang at the fifth line in the middle of the Kan Danger trigram indicates a little bit of good fortune. This is also the top line of an inner Gen Keeping Still trigram. **"The pit is not filled (with water). Blessings will come from remaining calm. No trouble."** The fifth line, or lord of the hexagram, usually represents a perfected from of the message of the hexagram. In this case, the fifth line represents the strongest level of danger because of your deep location within the pit, but there is no trouble at this line if you follow the advice to remain calm to handle the danger, which is the "keeping still" influence of the Gen trigram. This is the message of the hexagram, which is *to remain calm during emergencies and troubles*. If you are in a dangerous situation then calmness is the best mental state to cultivate as you wait for help or try to work out your own escape because calmness allows you to engage in clear thinking for possible salvation.

29.6: Yin at the sixth line completes the hexagram, which is at the top of a Kan trigram. This line represents the extreme of the hexagram, and summarizes the meaning of two Kan trigrams on top of each other that indicate double trouble or danger. **"He is tied with rope and cords, and imprisoned in a thicket of thorns [thorn bushes]. For three years there is no release. This is bad fortune."** "He is tied with rope and cords" represents the troubles of the first Kan trigram, and "being imprisoned in a thicket of thorns" represents the second Kan trigram. Entering into such a doubly dangerous situation is extremely bad fortune. If you enter into such a dangerous, troublesome situation you will not be able to easily escape despite heroic efforts.

Since both trigrams are described in this line we need not elaborate on how the hexagram's construction appears in its sentences.

HEXAGRAM 30

Li – Flaming Beauty, Flaring Radiance, Life

Lower Trigram: Li (Fire) – brilliance, yellow light, sun
Upper Trigram: Li (Fire) – brilliance, flaring, military, king

The Judgment: Flaming Beauty. It is beneficial to continue. Success. Raising a cow brings good fortune.

This hexagram has a flaming brightness flowing into a flaming brightness above it, which represents stages of human life. Using the progression of the sun rising, shining brightly and then setting, this hexagram symbolizes the progression of a human life that is born, "flares up," passes away and is then mourned in passing. Hence it can also be called "Flaming Beauty" or "Flaring Radiance" rather than "Radiant Beauty." Life is a flaming radiance that only lasts a short while, and the Judgment says that it is beneficial to beget children during life ("raise a cow") since they will give you joy, take care of you in old age and continue the family lineage. This hexagram has parallels to the riddle of the sphinx where a man walks on three legs (crawls) in the morning, two legs in the afternoon (life flares up), and three legs in old age (the sun sets), and then dies and is mourned. In the first line, a toddler walks with confused steps and must respectfully obey adults in order to safely grow. In the second line the sun appears and shines radiantly symbolizing the fullness of young adult and adult life. In the third line the sun sets and elders sigh that life is nearly over. In the fourth line there is a summary of life in general: it appears, flares up, dies and then is discarded. In the fifth line people mourn the passing (death) of an individual. In the sixth line a king sets forth on a military expedition, executes defiant chieftains and captures their followers. The king represents the maximum power, position and status one can possess in life akin to the all-powerful radiant sun whereas in the opposite hexagram line 29.6 we find the inverse image of someone inundated with inescapable troubles.

1. Walking with confused steps. Adopt the attitude of respect (tread respectfully) and there will be no trouble.

2. Yellow light (net of radiance). Supremely auspicious.

3. In the light (net of radiance) of the setting sun you do not drum on the pots and sing but the great elders sigh. Ominous.

4. Something suddenly comes up, it flares up, it dies out and is discarded (forgotten).

5. One sheds tears in a torrent and grieves in sorrow. Auspicious.

6. The king goes out on a military campaign. He is happy to (succeed in) cutting off the heads (of chieftains) and capturing their followers. No trouble.

30.1: Yang at the first line at the beginning of the Li Fire-Light trigram. **"Stepping with confused steps. Adopt the attitude of respect and there will be no trouble."** This line actually represents a young toddler (the first stage of becoming an adult) and also youth who walks with tottering, confused steps until he grows older, and who must respectfully listen to adults in order to develop properly. Analogously, in this line the sun's light is just dawning rather than at full strength since this is only the first line of the Li Sun trigram, hence the toddler/youth can only take confused or uneven steps. This line definitely represents childhood where, symbolically speaking, at the very beginning of your life your steps are confused and fumbling until you grow up, mature and develop mental clarity. Adults must guide you until then so the advice is to tread more carefully by "Adopting the attitude of respect (to elders) and then there will be no trouble." The Judgment says that raising a cow brings good fortune because at the beginning stages of your life you are like a simple-minded cow that must be cared for and raised by others.

30.2: Yin at the second line in the middle of the Li Brilliance trigram. This is also the beginning line of an inner Xun Wind trigram. **"Yellow light [radiance, brightness]. Supreme good fortune."** Here we have an image of the light of the sun shining brightly – a *yellow net of light*, radiance, brightness, etcetera - because this is the strong central line of the Li Fire trigram. This is the sun's brilliance at its best that is probably noontime since this is the middle line of the Li trigram. The line is tinged with an influence from the inner Xun Wind trigram but the wind element feeds the fire element so the fire should shine more brightly. Hence we have strong yellow brightness. The physical analogy of the sun having risen and shining with glory is like *the mid-life of human beings when they are at their peak strength*. Since the light of the sun is strong in this line there is great clarity, health, activity and yang Qi energy to reflect the positive aspects of the inner Xun wind (growth) trigram. Being at the middle of the Li trigram *this line symbolizes the middle age period of a person's life where life is vibrant and full of energy and activity.*

30.3: Yang at the third line that ends the lower Li Light trigram. Now the lower Li trigram is ending so the light is fading. This is also the middle line of an inner Xun Wind trigram, which also usually produces disintegration, deterioration or destruction, and this is the beginning line of an inner Dui Joy-Talking trigram that will also show its influence. **"In the light of the setting sun you do not drum on the pots and sing but the great elders sigh. Ominous."** Life is a radiant beauty, which is the name of the hexagram, but it eventually passes away. Here the sun is now setting so the light is dimming where the sunset is a metaphor for old age. You cannot rejoice at such an event as your life force is declining; something you have depended upon is about to end, namely life. Thus you are not drumming and singing in joy (the Dui trigram). Instead the elderly are sighing in lamentation. This line is "ominous," which means it is a sign of coming bad fortune since it is the end of the Li trigram. The line represents the fact that life is almost over and death is coming.

30.4: Yang at the fourth line at the start of the second Li Fire trigram that is stacked on top of the previous one. The image should therefore be one of fire or light in some way. This is also the middle line of an inner Dui Joy trigram and top line of an inner Xun Wind trigram. **"Something suddenly appears, flares up, dies out and is discarded (forgotten)."** The first three phrases summarize the previous trigram - the sun appeared, it rose in the sky, it fell at sunset and then disappeared … which means someone was born, grew up into a mature adult, reached old age and then died. That entire sequence is summarized in this line which outlines the course of a human life in general. The inner Dui Joy trigram appears as the fact that the sun appeared in its glory for awhile, and the Xun Wind trigram gives birth to the phrase that "something … is discarded" since the wind element will blow it away.

30.5: Yin at the fifth line in the middle of the Li Light trigram. This is also the top line of an inner Dui Lake-Talking trigram. **"One sheds a flood of tears [in a flood like heavy rain] in grief and despair, and grieves with sorrow. Auspicious."** This line is the lord of the hexagram and instead of the glory we would expect from two Li trigrams stacked upon one another we instead unexpectedly have sadness. This is because it is a yin line (so misfortune is expected) and because the hexagram is commenting on the temporary, transitory, impermanent nature of the radiant beauty of life. In the fourth line something was given birth, flared up and then passed out of existence, meaning that a life has passed away into death. In this line the people cry in sorrow to recognize the passing, which reflects the yin nature of the line.

30.6: Yang at the top of the Li trigram and hexagram, and summarizing its overall nature. Here we see a king - who represents the Li Brilliance trigram of elegance, power and high status - going out and doing great things with his energy as befits his supremacy. **"The king launches a military [campaign] expedition. He is happy to succeed in capturing the masses and cutting off the heads of the chieftains. No trouble."** The doubled Li Sun-Fire trigram is like a glorious king who demonstrates his high position and power by launching military campaigns to conquer his enemies, and because he represents the sun he succeeds in victory. How could he not succeed when he represents the bright glory of the doubled Li trigram? The king, with his power, destroys the ringleaders but spares the followers. This hexagram in general encapsulates the phases of a man's life where this line represents the maximum you could possibly ever achieve, which is to become a king with glory and power who can launch punitive expeditions against rebels and capture the followers who must then submit to you. You are at the absolute top of all dominance hierarchies.

In terms of the composition of the hexagram, "the king launches a military expedition" is the bottom Li trigram and his happy celebratory success is represented in the top Li trigram.

HEXAGRAM 31

Xian - Sexual Attraction, Rising Lust

Lower Trigram: Gen (Mountain) – stopping, remaining stationary
Upper Trigram: Dui (Joy) – lake, mouth, pleasurable sex, kissing

The Judgment: Sexual Attraction. Perseverance is beneficial. Taking a wife is auspicious.

This hexagram has a lake in the mountains where in its line image you have two legs (the mountains) that intersect in the lake, which is your sexual organs. Therefore this hexagram describes the initial onset of sexual desire (the initiation of sexual attraction) and its culmination in sexual relations. At first you feel a little bit of sexual attraction, it progresses to a stage where sexual desire afflicts you strongly, and eventually you finally engage in sexual relations. In the first line you feel just a little bit of sexual desire that we might call an inkling or impulse (symbolized by a feeling within the toes) that prompts you to take some initiative in that direction. In the second line your desire increases but the timing is not yet beneficial for indulgence. In the third line sexual desire has reached the point where it torments you like torn flesh. In the fourth line your "friend" accords with your longings and the two of you enjoy sexual relations. In the fifth line you are holding each other in embrace and the sixth line shows an image of kissing. Each line of the hexagram was therefore matched with a increasing degree of sexual desire and a higher part of the physical body because it is used in the hexagram as a gradient for lust. As the Judgment states, when sexual desire strikes it is beneficial to persevere (in abstinence or celibacy) but to solve the problem it states that marriage is the solution.

1. Sensation in the toes.

2. Sensation in the calves of the legs. Ominous. Remaining as you are is auspicious.

3. Sensation in the thighs. Grasping the torn flesh (sexual desire torments you). Going will produce distress.

4. With determination advancing brings good fortune. Regrets disappear. Tremblingly going and coming back and forth (sexual intercourse). A friend (companion) follows your longing.

5. Sensation in the back. There are no regrets.

6. Sensation in the jaws, cheeks and tongue (kissing).

31.1: Yin at the first line, which is the beginning line of the Gen Keeping Still trigram. **"Sensation in the toes."** A stimulating influence begins to stir but it is small. This is the beginning of a tiny impulse of sexual desire that is symbolized by the movement of toes or a sensation (feeling) within the toes since this is the lowest part of the body. The toes represent just a slight *inkling* of sexual desire, and the Gen Keeping Still trigram keeps you from acting on the inkling.

31.2: Yin at the second line of the Gen Keeping Still trigram so the line accordingly states that movement is unfavorable. This is also the bottom line of an inner Xun Wind trigram that tends to prompt movement or cause disturbance but the Gen trigram overrules it. **"Sensation in the calves of the legs. Ominous (because sexual desire is difficult to bear). Staying as you are (not indulging) will bring good fortune."** You feel the sexual desire rising (due to the Xun Life Force trigram), but you cannot or should not engage in sex at this time because the middle line of the Gen Keep Still trigram throws a strong influence on non-advancement. Basically, the degree of sexual desire has grown greater than in the first line.

31.3: Yang at the third line at the top of the Gen Keeping Still trigram. This is also the middle line of an inner Xun Wind trigram that causes a strong disturbance and the bottom line of an inner Qian Strong Force trigram that also produces a great stimulation of yang energy. **"Sensation in the thighs you grasp the torn flesh (sexual desire assaults you). Going (to follow it) produces distress."** Sexual desire has advanced yet further, and has reached the point where it is now really bothering you with discomfort. It has become a strong force (Qian trigram) that disturbs you greatly with physical and mental distress (Xun trigram). However, this line is within the Gen Keeping Still trigram and subject to its influence so you still cannot indulge at this time. You are impelled to pursue a partner but you should remain in your place rather than seek sex with another, otherwise advancement will cause regrets. Hence you unfortunately suffer the uncomfortable promptings of sexual desire with distress.

31.4: Yang at the fourth line, at the start of the upper Dui Happiness trigram. This is also the middle line of an inner Qian Great Strength trigram and top line of an inner Xun Wind trigram. **"Continuing is auspicious. Regrets disappear. Tremblingly going and coming back and forth (sexual intercourse). A companion (friend) follows your longing."** In this line you give in to your sexual desire due to the influence of all three trigrams, especially the arrival of the Dui Happiness trigram. Some translations of this line include, "His thoughts go back and forth but his friend follows his ideas," "Wavering, wavering, coming and going," "His mind vacillates but his friend follows his thoughts," "Coming and going ceaselessly," ... Actually, the line is about sexual intercourse but most translators miss this entirely. This activity is happening because the Dui trigram represents joy and a young woman, the Qian trigram represents the exercise of great strength (intercourse) and yang energy, the Xun trigram represents the penetrative movement of life energy, and of course in the progression of lust up the lines we finally arrive at a stage of sexual relations.

31.5: Yang at the fifth line in the middle of the upper Dui Happiness trigram. This is also the top line of an inner Qian Great Strength trigram. **"Sensation in the spine. There are no regrets."** This is just a play on the hexagram lines reflecting a gradient of body length where the first line represents the feet, second line represents the lower calves, third line represents the thighs, fourth line represents the loins, fifth line represents the back and sixth line represents the mouth. As one progresses upwards from the feet the sexual desire grows until consummation in the upper trigram. In this line we must reference something higher than the hips, so the man's hands are wrapped around his partner's back in embrace and the spine is also twisting and turning in active sexual relations. As the lord of the hexagram, this line represents a greater degree of sexual intimacy than line four that only involves physical sex because you are holding your partner and talking to one another (Dui Mouth trigram) as a couple normally does, you are exerting more playful twisting than in just the hips, and thus there is sensation in the spine.

31.6: Yin at the sixth line, the end of the upper Dui Mouth-Talking trigram and the end of the hexagram. The Dui trigram also represents lake water, happiness or joy while the top line of the hexagram, in terms of a body gradient, represents the head or mouth. Hence we have the following image: **"Feelings in the jaws, cheeks and tongue,"** which is a description of kissing. Because this hexagram represents sexual desire and sexual congress, kissing is the correct explanation not only due to this activity matching the description but because the top line of the hexagram often represents the head or mouth.

In terms of the composition of the hexagram in general, the lower Gen Mountain trigram comes through as the jaws while the upper Dui trigram comes through as the mouth, or cheeks and tongue.

HEXAGRAM 32

Heng - Holding Firm, Standing Fast, Duration, Constancy in the Midst of Change

Lower Trigram: Xun (Wind) – wood, motion, penetrating, destructive
Upper Trigram: Zhen (Thunder) – motion, agitation, pushing upwards

The Judgment: Holding Firm. There is no trouble. It is beneficial to persevere. It is beneficial to have somewhere to go.

The hexagram has thunder riding the wind, which are both tumultuous forces, so the message is about the benefits of persistently holding to principled behavior throughout volatile circumstances and the changes of life. The universe continuously changes but you can adhere to principled behavior throughout these changes if you remain determined. This is called cultivating duration or constancy of character. In other words, you can cultivate a constancy of behavior while passing through dramatic changes that might tempt you to abandon your principles. Holding to ethical principles or simply maintaining a steady course of action is called maintaining constancy, and this hexagram is about maintaining your virtues and principles throughout life. In the first line an individual persistently behaves in a certain way or consistently stands firm without changing direction and this fixity is producing a bad outcome. In the second line regret disappears because either the situation improves or the individual's behavior changes and the situation then consequently improves. In the third line other people view an individual's behavior ("virtue") as inconstant, and his unreliability is seen by others as a disgrace. In the fourth line people therefore avoid him; he goes hunting in a field but catches nothing because there isn't any game. In the fifth line is a reminder that it is always proper for a woman to remain virtuous in following her husband but a man must decide what to do according to the situation, and adapt as appropriate, so constancy is not expected. The last line is the opposite of the first line because there is now a state of continuous changefulness ("agitation") rather than constant behavior, and the continuous changefulness is a harbinger of troubles.

1. Deep constancy. Being steadfast (continual persistence in one's behavior) is inauspicious. There is nothing beneficial.

2. Regret disappears.

3. If inconstant in virtue you may meet with disgrace (be shamed). Continued persistence (in such a deviation) will result in distress.

4. In the field there is no catch (during hunting).

5. Constancy in the virtues is auspicious for a woman but ominous for a man.

6. Constant changefulness (continuous trembling). Ominous.

32.1: Yin at the first line, and at the beginning of the Xun Wind trigram that signifies movement and sometimes destruction. **"Fidelity to deep constancy (firm fixity in behavior – deeply constant). Being steadfast (continual persistence) is inauspicious. There is nothing beneficial."** Due to the message of the fifth line about your behavior this line most probably is spotlighting incorrect fidelity to some sort of prolonged behavior that produces unfortunate results. Reverse hexagram line 31.1 says "Sensation in the toes" that suggests an impulse is pushing you, which accords with this conclusion. Opposite hexagram line 42.1 says, "Beneficial to begin a great undertaking," which means to change the behavior you are holding onto with constancy. The Xun trigram represents destructive behavior you've been engaging in and you don't want this destructive influence to continue long-term. You must change what and you are doing things.

32.2: Yang at the second line in the middle of the Xun Wind trigram, and at the bottom of an inner Qian Great Force trigram. **"Regrets [remorse, disappointments] disappear."** In the first line you were being steadfast in some way and it was producing bad results. Now your regrets vanish because the amount of perseverance you use is appropriate to the situation, or perhaps circumstances have changed. Hence there is no longer any cause for regrets. Circumstances have probably changed because the Qian trigram will now provide a tinge of "great strength" against any Xun destructive tendencies, so there may be a positive improvement in the situation causing any destructive influences to abate. This is all speculative, however, because there isn't a lot of information to go on. Opposite hexagram line 42.2 says, "Someone increases him, and it is as if receiving ten pairs of tortoise shells," which we might take as an unexpected benefit from the Qian trigram in circumstances getting better to match with your behavior.

32.3: Yang at the third line and the top line of the Xun Wind trigram. This is also the middle line of an inner Qian trigram and bottom line of an inner Dui Mouth-Talking trigram. **"If inconstant [without duration] in virtue you may meet with disgrace (be shamed). Persistent continuation of unsteadiness in virtue will lead to grief."** Previously constancy of behavior caused problems, and now the problem is inconstancy (changefulness) of behavior. As a moral lesson, inconstancy of character brings shame; you should give duration to virtuous behavior in order to avoid disgrace in life. The top line of the Wind trigram has volatile tendencies that can be greatly destructive. You must be steady in character ("give duration to your character") despite being subject to negative wind influences otherwise people may slander or insult you for lapses in virtue, and this criticism would reflect the Dui Mouth trigram. Hence, if your virtue is unreliable (you are unsteady in your character and conduct) then others will deem this as shamefulness and you will probably end up suffering from humiliation, disgrace and grief due to criticism or insults from others. The Wind trigram is sure to push you into a departure from virtuous constancy so you should remain strong and steady (the inner Qian trigram) otherwise you will reap the products of the Wind trigram – strong criticism and insults (wind) from someone's mouth (Dui trigram) that can result in shame or humiliation.

32.4: Yang at the fourth line is the beginning of the upper Zhen Thunder trigram indicating movement. This is also the middle line of an inner Dui trigram and top line of an inner Qian trigram. **"In the field there is no catch; he hunts and gets nothing."** This translation is preferred to "No game in the field" or "The field has no game" because the Zhen and Qian trigrams symbolize the actual activity of hunting. In line 31.4, which is the reverse hexagram of this one, the man finds a sexual partner but here due to inconstancy of virtue he finds no correlate at all – just people avoiding him. The subject goes hunting, which is a yang action representing the Thunder trigram, but he hunts and gets nothing. The attempt at gain fails. Perhaps his inconstant virtue has resulted in no one wanting to deal with him and so he cannot come to any type of arrangements or relationships with others because no one trusts him, which would then be the meaning of not being able to catch any game despite his efforts.

32.5: Yin at the fifth line in the middle of the of the Zhen Thunder trigram. This is the top line of an inner Dui trigram. **"Constancy in the virtues is good fortune for a woman but ominous for a man."** This line is the lord of the hexagram so it should represent a perfected form of its message, which is that a man should *not* be absolutely unchanging in his behavior because he needs to adapt to situations in times of need. The lesson on fixity of behavior is not to be too fixed. The fifth line is under the strong influence of the Zhen Thunder trigram and a bit under the influence of the Dui trigram that represents a young woman. Yin is bad for a male but good for a female so a man should flexibly adapt to thunderous yang activity while a woman should match with the submissiveness of yin where she follows the lead of her husband. This is the meaning of a woman being constant in virtue, which is accepting her husband's lead. *A man, on the other hand, is not supposed to be a yes-man or unquestioning follower but an independent thinker who takes actions according to the dictates of the situation.* A woman's main job in Chinese culture is to follow her husband and show kindness in creating an environment suitable for the rearing of children and comfort of adults, and her primary virtue is her fidelity to her husband. Hence, "Constancy (steadiness) in the gentle virtues is fortunate for a woman but misfortunate for a man." A man has to decide what is right according to circumstances and alter his behavior accordingly while sticking to his principles as much as possible and keeping his long-term goals in mind.

32.6: Yin at the top line at the end of the Zhen Thunder trigram, so we should expect misfortune due to the destructive top line of this shaking trigram that appears as constantly changing one's course. **"Continuous changefulness (trembling) results in misfortune."** The idea is that constant changefulness in one's behavior produces misfortune as opposed to line one where you never change your behavior and thereby produce misfortune. This is the end of the hexagram at the top of the Thunder trigram, which is a destructive yin line, so we see a lesson on the extreme of constantly changing one's ways. Some interpret this line as suffering constant agitation like an attack: "Constant (long-lasting, prolonged) agitation (quaking) results in misfortune" because continuous excitement, restlessness, or agitation destroys peacefulness that then causes harm. However, a more appropriate interpretation is in accordance with line 42.6 of the opposite hexagram ("He does not keep his intentions constant.") where *you are constantly changing your mind and ways* – one moment virtuous and the other moment not – where "shaking your constancy" produces misfortune. Constantly flipping back and forth in either mind or behavior is definitely a situation of turmoil that makes you undependable. Inconstancy of behavior – constantly changing it – is misfortunate.

In terms of the construction of the hexagram and how it appears in this line we have the Xun Wind trigram underneath the Zhen Thunder trigram. The Xun Wind trigram is constantly empowering (throwing its influence on) the destructive Zhen Thunder trigram, hence we have agitation producing a "prolonged inconstancy" that results in destructive "misfortune."

HEXAGRAM 33

Dun - The Piglet

Lower Trigram: Gen (Mountain) – stopping, tethering, binding
Upper Trigram: Qian (Heaven) – excellence, fine pig, great strength

The Judgment: The Piglet. Success. Persistence in (managing) small matters is beneficial.

The hexagram has a mountain trigram that rises into the sky, and the message is about the growth of human beings when you educate and train them so that they grow up and become outstanding individuals – like mountains that rise into the sky. On the surface this hexagram is about a piglet that gradually grows bigger and bigger. The piglet actually represents a youth who slowly grows into a responsible adult, and the lessons within this hexagram are metaphors for training the young to the point where they become mature. Hence we have the Judgment that persistently educating youth as they grow ("managing small matters") is beneficial. The first line uses a piglet's tail to represent a small child who should not go anywhere or do anything on his own. The second line uses a tethered piglet to emphasize the importance of disciplinary rules for raising a child. The third line warns that tying up a piglet will cause them affliction and you should keep rearing them before you do so just as you take care of servants and consorts where you teach them and tell them what to do. The fourth line says that some young adults are very mature and can handle important matters but most cannot so you have to wait until they grow older. In the fifth line we have a praiseworthy piglet that represents a youth who has grown into a fine young man. The sixth line uses a fat piglet to represent an individual who has grown up and become an admirable adult from all this prior care and training.

1. A piglet's tail. Danger. Do not try to go anywhere.

2. Tether (the piglet) using the hide of a yellow ox. Nothing will succeed in tearing it loose.

3. A tied-up piglet. Affliction. Danger. Rearing servants and concubines is fortunate.

4. A good (sized) piglet. Favorable for a superior man but negative for an inferior man.

5. A fine (excellence) piglet. Persistence in a correct course is auspicious.

6. A fat piglet. There is nothing not beneficial.

33.1: Yin at the first line, which is at the bottom of the Gen Keeping Still trigram that symbolizes restraint so we will see a warning not go anywhere. **"A piglet's tail. Dangerous. Do not try to go anywhere."** We are starting very small in the first line, as usual, which is symbolized by a piglet's tail. "A piglet's tail" means that we aren't even talking about a piglet yet but only a tiny tail. This represents someone extremely small and weak because this is not a whole piglet but just a tail. Hence this is a baby or a very young child. "Dangerous" means that their situation is perilous because they are immature and cannot protect themselves. An immature youth is unable to handle any matters of significance so they must be protected. They are too small to be responsible for any undertakings hence "Do not try to make a forward move in any direction." This interpretation is in tune with the meaning of the Gen trigram since it symbolizes keeping still.

33.2: Yin at the second line within the middle of the Gen Keeping Still trigram, and thus we see another image of restraint. This is also the bottom line of an inner Xun Wind trigram that will try to move things. **"Hold the piglet fast using the hide of a yellow ox. Nothing will succeed in getting it loose."** The back feet of piglets are often hobbled (tied) together so that they cannot wander off and escape. You can do this using rope but rawhide is stronger so the restraint being used to bind the piglet's back feet is ox hide that no one can break. The piglet wants to wander because of the Xun wind element prompting it to move around so you must bind him with restraint, which is a reflection of presence of the Gen Keeping Still trigram. The meaning is that to keep raising a piglet (child) safely you must restrict their movements rather than allow them to freely roam everywhere; you cannot allow young children you are raising to run wild but must subject them to discipline and oversight. They must be subject to disciplinary rules, which is why the color yellow is used together with the ox hide image since it symbolizes moderation. A young piglet being restrained has the analogy that a youth should be disciplined as he grows through rules or restrictions that teach moderation.

33.3: Yang at the third line at the top of the Gen Keeping Still trigram that symbolizes being stationary. This is also the middle line of an inner Xun trigram (which represents a penetrating danger or destructive force) and bottom line of an inner Qian Heaven trigram. **"A piglet bound (tied) up. Affliction [sickness and adversity]. There is illness. Danger. Rearing servants and consorts is fortunate."** When a teenager or young adult, youth often go through a stage of recklessness that is like a sickness where they tend to get into trouble because they cannot control their energies and impulses. Teenage boys tend to do stupid, dangerous things and you need to impose discipline on them just as you would tie up a piglet (in order to prevent it from running around) to prevent troubles, but you should not overly tie them up or this will be an affliction. For instance, in reverse hexagram line 34.3 it is said that an inferior man uses force and a ram butts its head against a hedge and damages its horns. This is the same story as a teenager getting into trouble. Similarly, opposite hexagram line 19.3 warns that managing people too sweetly or laxly is not beneficial, and future hexagram line 12.3 states that sauced meat must be wrapped up (in restraint). Hence, a young man will pass through a stage, like a sickness or affliction, where he gets into trouble due to not controlling his energies and you should impose discipline on him just as you should bind a piglet at this stage of growth, but not tie him up too tightly or that will cause its own set of problems. Insurance companies finally decrease car insurance rates at age 24 because by that time the human brain has finally developed enough and individual has gained enough experience that prudence becomes a personality characteristic. The binding of the piglet is the Gen Keeping Still trigram because of the danger of the Xun trigram, which represents rising yang Qi energy. Two things that are normally of lower subservient status are manservants and handmaidens (concubines), which symbolize young boys and girls that you order about as well as the first two lines of the trigram. "Rearing them, maintaining them or taking care of them is fortunate" means that you should still be taking care of them just as you would take care of a piglet because they are not yet adults and can get into trouble if you do not watch them, instruct them, impose rules, and give them responsibilities to keep them out of trouble.

33.4: Yang at the fourth line, and the beginning of an auspicious upper Qian Heaven trigram. This is also the middle line of an inner Qian Heaven trigram and top line of an inner Xun Wind trigram. **"A good sized piglet. Beneficial for a superior man but negative for an inferior man."** The fourth line of a hexagram often shows an almost perfect achievement of the hexagram's message where a perfect accomplishment is seen in line five, and that's what we have here. The growth of the piglet has reached a sufficient stage of maturity because the hexagram has transitioned to the first line of the new upper Qian trigram. *This means childhood is over (the lower trigram) and the individual has reached young adulthood (the upper trigram).* "Beneficial for a superior man but negative for an inferior man" means that a superior individual has already reached maturity at this initial trigram line, but an inferior individual must still grow some more before reaching a stage of maturity. A superior kind of person is wise and mature at a young age so they can start out in the world to do things much earlier than an inferior individual who will need much more time to mature. The immature man must therefore grow and develop a bit further. This explains, "It is sufficient for a superior (wise) person, but an inferior person still needs more time to grow and develop." The doubled Qian trigram comes through in this line as the well-grown fat piglet and superior man while the Xun Wind trigram comes through as the inferior man.

33.5: Yang at the fifth line at the center of the Qian Heaven trigram. This is also the top line of an Inner Qian Heaven trigram. **"A fine [excellent, praiseworthy, admirable] piglet. Continuing in a correct course is auspicious."** The fifth line is the ruler of the hexagram and represents a successful achievement of its message. Here the growth of the piglet has finally reached a very fine stage of excellence that reflects two overlapping Qian trigrams. The stage is that of "A fine praiseworthy piglet," which is excellent! Now the individual should continue developing even further as a fine adult. How did he get to this level of mature excellence? Because his parents followed the advice of the Judgment: "Persistence in managing small matters is beneficial," which means they carefully raised the small piglet into a big pig, i.e. they taught/trained their child as he grew so that he became a virtuous, outstanding individual. Hence the line suggests for the future, "Persistence in a correct course is auspicious."

33.6: Yang at the sixth line and the top of a Qian trigram. Because this is the top line of the hexagram it talks about the image of the hexagram in total. **"A fat piglet. Nothing is unfavorable."** We have seen success in growing a piglet by using restraint (discipline) until it develops into a fine plump piglet, which represents the top line of the Qian trigram. We want to see all human beings similarly develop so that they all become exemplary human beings with bright futures.

In terms of the hexagram's construction and how it is reflected in this line, the Gen Accumulation trigram at the bottom represents accumulation that appears as the "*fat* piglet," and the Qian Heaven trigram on top comes through as a big, strong pig and "nothing unfavorable."

HEXAGRAM 34

Da Zhuang - Great Power, Using Great Force

Lower Trigram: Qian (Heaven) – military campaign, persistence, ram
Upper Trigram: Zhen (Thunder) – motion, wounding, butting

The Judgment: Using Great Force. Persistence is beneficial.

The name of the hexagram is Great Power or Great Strength, and it is an image of thunder in the sky. Using the analogy of a military expedition the lessons within this hexagram are about using great power or strength in situations. The main theme is to use moderate force rather than powerful (great) force since it tends to be destructive. At the initial stage of this hexagram (the first line) you are wounded so you do not have enough strength to start out on a military campaign. In the second line you start persistently using moderate force and make some progress. In the third line you are warned that the superior way is not to use too much power but to stay reserved otherwise you could damage yourself or your situation. In the fourth line you exert a moderate force to push through opposition and as a result those obstructions part without getting destroyed. In the fifth line you stop using aggressive force wildly. In the sixth line you become entangled in an obstacle due to your use of force but you eventually break free. The Judgment of the hexagram counsels that you must be persistent in the application of power in order to accomplish goals.

1. Wounded in the foot. Military campaigning would be disastrous. This is certain.

2. Persistence is auspicious (brings good fortune).

3. The inferior (lesser) man uses force. The superior man does not. Determination is dangerous. A ram that butts against a hedge damages (injures) its horns.

4. Persistence is auspicious. Regrets will disappear. A hedge will part open without being broken when wounded by the axle-strut of a

great chariot.

5. Loses a ram in the Kingdom of Yi. There are no regrets.

6. A ram butts against a hedge. It is not able to withdraw nor advance (pull out or push through). Nothing is beneficial. Difficulties and then auspiciousness.

34.1: Yang at the bottom line, which is the initial line of the Qian Great Force trigram. **"Wounded in the foot. A military expedition would be disastrous. This is certainly true (unavoidable)."** This is the lowest stage of force intensity (great strength) in the hexagram. At this stage you are weakened because your foot is wounded, and because healthy feet are necessary for marching you should not be trying to project force on anyone. To go ahead at this time would incur misfortune. Reverse hexagram line 33.1 says "A piglet's tail (which means that you are too weak). Do not try to go anywhere." A military expedition (undertaking a venture) would therefore be disastrous. You cannot march to war because your foot is injured so the first line simply says that your own strength isn't yet good enough to proceed so don't apply yourself to force. You are told "this is certain" or "be confident of this" because this is obvious but you have to be reminded of this fact because you want to go since the Qian trigram wants to push you forward towards engagement. That's why you must be reminded with this warning. You cannot set forth on a project, campaign, new venture, undertaking etc. that requires great strength when you are wounded. You should not be trying to project great force at this moment. Wait and heal first.

34.2: Yang at the second line of the Qian Great Strength trigram. This is also the bottom line of an inner Qian Great Strength trigram so we should see a strong emphasis of great force due to the doubled Qian influence. **"Persistence is auspicious."** Persistence is beneficial and brings good fortune because it is a manifestation of the doubled Qian trigrams. Rather than using an excessive amount of great power to accomplish deeds you persistently apply a steady level of pressure to achieve your objectives so persistence brings good fortune. That persistence reflects the influence of the two Qian Great Strength trigrams that overlap this line. Their influence manifests in a continual application of moderate force to achieve progress, which we normally call persistence.

34.3: Yang at the third line, completing the Qian Great Strength trigram. This is also the middle line of an inner Qian trigram and bottom line of an inner Dui Joy trigram. **"The inferior man uses force (strength). The** superior man uses nothing [is reserved, behaves otherwise]. The determination to use power is dangerous. A ram butts against a hedge and damages [injures, breaks] its horn."** The inferior man wants to use lots of force due to falling under the influence of two Qian trigrams. However, using excessive force is dangerous because you can hurt yourself – especially as the top Qian line can be destructive – so the superior wise man does otherwise and holds himself in check. The superior man remains reserved so that he does not hurt himself from using too much force. He refrains from forceful actions otherwise he will damage himself like a ram that butts against a fence with its power and injures its horns in consequence. The image of the ram's head and horns in this line reflects the Dui trigram that often represents a head, mouth or in this case horns. The entire bottom trigram is about not getting carried away in using force to achieve your goals but instead to continue using moderation with persistence to avoid harming yourself.

34.4: Yang at the fourth line, and at the bottom of the upper Zhen Thunder trigram that represents a bolt of force and motion. This is also the middle line of an inner Dui Joy trigram and top line of an inner Qian trigram. **"Persistence is auspicious. Regret then disappears. A hedge parts open without being broken, wounded by the axle-strut of a great chariot [by the wheel-spokes of a large wagon]."** The persistent application of moderate force achieves your goals without harming anything because this is a good fortune yang line fueled by the influence of the Zhen and Qian trigrams. Whether it is by the wheel-spokes of a large wagon or axle-strut of a large carriage, the idea is that the continued application of moderate force finally weakens and then parts any powerful obstacles blocking you *without destroying them* (or harming you). The strength you apply with persistence will weaken obstacles so that you can press through them without destroying them. In this line the presence of the Zhen trigram is responsible for the hedge parting open, the disappearance of regret is due to the Dui Joy trigram, and the Qian trigram is represented by the persistent application of force.

34.5: Yin at the fifth line in the middle of the Zhen Thunder trigram. This is also the top line of an inner Dui Joy trigram. **"Loses a ram in the Kingdom of Yi. There is no regret [remorse]."** The purpose of using great force is to get to a place where you no longer need to use any force and can abandon aggressive tendencies. This is one of the themes of this hexagram. Thus the line refers to the Kingdom of Yi and the ancestors of the Shang dynasty. The famous story is that King Hai was the leader of a nomadic people and he is often said to be the first domesticator of cattle and sheep in ancient China. Along with his brother Heng, King Hai led their flocks across a river to pasture them in the state of Yi where he and his brother *started living an extremely carefree life* because they were treated like dignitaries by Yi's king. One of the rams from their great flock becomes lost which means losing the desire to impulsively use one's energy in aggression. The usage of moderate force in the previous lines has enabled someone to reach this state. Opposite hexagram 20.5 says, "Looking at my own life – for a superior person there is no blame." This line is the lord of the hexagram where, although not mentioned by name, King Hai is the individual of status that we normally see in the fifth line. *The message of this line and the hexagram is that success is reached when you no longer use any aggressive force. However, when you become too carefree or abandon moderation this will lead to problems such as loss.* In the third line the hexagram taught that a superior man should not use excessive force but just be persistent. During the persistent application of moderate force in the fourth line a man achieved some success in moving forward without destroying anything. In this line you no longer have to use force at all but you shouldn't become too lackadaisical either but that's not right either. Losing a ram is a result of the destructive power of the Zhen trigram while the lack of regret or remorse is a function of the Dui Joy trigram.

34.6: Yin at the top line, completing the Zhen Thunder trigram and the hexagram. **"A ram butts against the hedge. It is not able to withdraw nor advance (pull out or push through). There is nothing beneficial. Difficulty, but followed by auspiciousness."** This top line should represent the highest intensity of using force due to the gradient principle of hexagrams. In this line the application of great power against an opposing force is like a ram butting against a hedge and getting entangled. Eventually it gets free of the difficulty which suggests that the usage of force succeeds in the end. Using force entails difficulty but when properly employed it can help you break through obstacles, which is the message of the hexagram in general.

In terms of the overall construction of the hexagram and how it appears in this line, the Qian Great Strength trigram at the bottom comes through as the ram using his great power and getting stuck by a strong oppositional force (the hedge) while eventually breaking through to obtain release appears as a reflection of the upper Zhen Thunder trigram.

HEXAGRAM 35

Jin - Advancing, Proceeding Forward

Lower Trigram: Kun (Earth) – masses, acceptance, royalty
Upper Trigram: Li (Fire) – military attack, rebellion, destruction

The Judgment: Advancing. The Marquis of Kang was awarded with many horses. During the day there were three (winning) engagements.

The hexagram is composed of a sun rising over the earth, which represents the principle of advancement. This hexagram is about advancing (progressing forward) when there is opposition against you so in order to move forward you must gain the trust of other people and win their confidence. Only then you can make progress without much difficulty. This is different from the previous hexagram 34 where you advanced just using persistent moderate force. Here to advance you must also win over the people. The hexagram overall is a veiled reference to the military troubles of the Marquis of Kang as he tried to crush a rebellion by three of his brothers against the rightful heir and ruler of the Zhou dynasty, King Wu's young son Prince Song (King Cheng of Zhou). In the first line of this hexagram your desire to advance is driven back because you encounter people who have no confidence in you. In the second line you advance even though there is this resentment or opposition against you, and your progress is achieved due to some higher level womanly assistance. In the third line the great masses come to accept you and now look at you favorably which will pave the way for subsequent advancement. In the fourth line you advance like a rat that runs from here to there scurrying around trying to do everything in a scattered fashion. In the fifth line you finally attain a momentum where you should just keep proceeding without any regards to gains or losses and everything is then beneficial. In the final line advancement requires force but you can use military force on special occasions. The hexagram refers to the story of the Marquis of Kang (Ji Zhao) who was the ninth son of King Wen given the fiefdom of Kang after the Zhou victory over the Shang state. He later led one of six armies to crush a rebellion led by three of his brothers and tirelessly strengthened his dukedom in order to help the king. He expanded the Zhou territory in the North and in the West. Hence the Marquis frequently met with the ruler and was awarded many horses for his loyalty and military accomplishments including the important fiefdom of Wei whereby he also gained the title of the Marquis of Wei. The idea presented here is that you must push through many troublesome situations to eventually gain success and (imperial) recognition just like the Marquis. The theme is that the Marquis did not try to advance himself by joining the rebellion but made his contributions of service and waited patiently for advancement to be given to him.

1. Advancing but driven back. Persistence is auspicious. If there is no confidence (trust) in you respond with liberality. No trouble.

2. Advancing, but in sadness. Persistent determination is auspicious. He receives great blessings from the Queen mother.

3. The masses are loyal (trust him). Regrets disappear.

4. He advances like a large rat. To continue on like this is dangerous.

5. Regret vanishes. Do not worry about gains or losses. Going forward is auspicious. There is nothing not beneficial.

6. Advancing using horns to attack a city. Danger but auspicious. There is no trouble. Continuing on this course is distressful.

35.1: Yin at the first line, which is at the bottom of the Kun Earth trigram that symbolizes acquiescence or passive acceptance. **"Progressing but pushed back. Persistence will bring good fortune. To respond to a lack of confidence (trust) in you entails no error."** Forward progress is rebuffed and pushed back because of the presence of the Kun Earth trigram that represents a mass of people congealing or assembling together to offer obstruction. Military advancement is slow at this time and requires persistence. The *Yijing* counsels to keep pressing forward and advises that you dissolve any opposition against you. If you are not trusted (by the party thwarting you) then you should respond with liberality to counter their lack of confidence that has produced opposition. In history this line seems to state that the Lord of Kang's initial attacks against the rebellion were rebuffed and he had trouble winning acceptance by the people.

35.2: Yin at the second line, and at the center of the Kun Earth trigram. This is also the bottom line of an inner Gen Mountain trigram. **"Proceeding (though) with sadness. Persistent determination is auspicious. He will receive great blessings from the royal mother (the king's mother)."** Since the bottom Kun trigram is composed of three yin lines we will see strong yin images in this line such as women or yin emotions like sorrow. which appear here in the strongest middle line of the Kun trigram. Sadness appears due to progressing through so many yin lines, such as the first line where you were pushed back, but you successively continue advancing through those obstructions although you are "proceeding with sadness." The message is that you must hold to your ambitions and continue trying to advance despite the people being against you. Hence, "Persistence will bring good fortune" despite your sadness. Next we have the image of the Queen Mother, who appears because of the middle line of the Kun trigram (which often represents royalty) combined with the presence of the majestic Mountain trigram. She offers assistance to the Marquis which demonstrates that yin conditions can help you progress. In this line you have trouble advancing on your own but eventually you receive help and become able to advance. In terms of the history of the Marquis of Kang, his military forays were accompanied by sadness because he was fighting against his brothers and the public was not fully with him. Naturally the Shang population was opposed to him but he "received a boon from his royal mother" because she was a Shang princess given in marriage to his father King Wen by the last Shang King Di Xin, which gave him some legitimacy in the eyes of the Shang subjects. After his defeat of the rebels he was given a new fief at Wei where as ruler he presided over the remnants of the Shang. The eventual fiefdom might also be partially credited to his mother as well because in accepting him as their lord the people would be swearing allegiance to one of their princesses.

35.3: Yin at the third line, and at the top of the Kun trigram. This is also the middle line of an inner Gen Mountain trigram and bottom line of an inner Kan Danger trigram. **"The masses are loyal (trust him). Regrets disappear."** The consensus of the common people is that they now trust him and approve of him; everyone trusts him. The Kun trigram represents (an assembly of) the common masses and the Gen trigram represents accumulation, thus their trust is accumulated. In short, the Marquis has won the people's loyalty and because of this approval they will not thwart his further advancement. The upper trigram will therefore have a winning character different than the delays and disappointments in the lower trigram. In terms of history this line simply indicates that the Shang people eventually gave the Marquis their allegiance, possibly due to some legitimacy being passed to him due to his mother. Once he had gained the trust of the people the trouble between the Zhou and remaining Shang nobles declined.

35.4: Yang at the fourth line is also at the beginning of the new upper Li Fire trigram. This is also the middle line of an inner Kan Danger trigram and the top line of an inner Gen Mountain Stillness trigram. **"He advances** like a large rat. To persist (in rat-like behavior of scurrying and stopping to advance) is dangerous."** Rats and other animals like voles or squirrels move by scurrying around in all directions, which is by stopping and then starting again, running and then halting everywhere in a scattered manner. Their movements are rarely smooth and continuous. They are also timid and run away easily by scurrying to safety. For you to continue like this is errant because there is a Li trigram for blazing military advancement. The scurrying like a rat reflects the presence of the Kan Danger trigram while the halting reflects the presence of the Gen Keeping Still trigram. This line refers to the military maneuvers of the Marquis for which we have no records to comment on any correspondences.

35.5: Yin at the fifth line and in the middle of the upper Li trigram that indicates brightness, elegance, intelligence and success. This is also the top line of an inner Kan Danger trigram. **"Regret vanishes. Gains or losses are not important. To go on (advancing) is good fortune. Nothing is unfavorable."** This fifth line should portray a perfected example of the meaning of the hexagram, which is that you should be working at advancing whether or not there is gain or loss because you just have to keep moving forward. To go on is good fortune. The Marquis of Kang required three years to crush the rebellion of his brothers. Here his patient military persistence, perseverance and determination are rewarded with eventual success. At this line persistent military efforts are due to the strong presence of the Li Military trigram while the Kan Danger trigram indicates destruction to enemies. Thus advancing is successful in the end.

35.6: Yang at the sixth line at the top of the upper Li trigram. **"Advancing using horns to attack a city. Dangerous but good fortune. There is no trouble in doing this but persistent continuation of this course is distressful."** The top line of the Li trigram might represent military fighting or destruction, and the advice is to use destructive military force carefully rather than recklessly or ruthlessly. A special pincer move (where two military forces converge on either side of a enemy position) is used to subdue a city, but to have to keep doing this is distressful. This maneuver is mentioned probably because the Marquis of Kang employed it to conquer or destroy cities.

In terms of the composition of the hexagram and how it appears in this line, the Kun Earth trigram is beneath the Li Fire trigram. Here the Kun trigram of earth represents the city and the Li trigram appears as a harsh, angry attack against it. You are advancing but not in a friendly way.

HEXAGRAM 36

Ming Yi – The Calling Pheasant, Injuring a Bright Pheasant, Wounding Brightness, Brightness Obscured

Lower Trigram: Li (Fire) – brilliance, pheasant, flying, southern chief
Upper Trigram: Kun (Earth) – belly, royalty, courtyard

The Judgment: The Calling Pheasant. In difficulty it is beneficial to persevere.

The hexagram is an image of the sun (or light) beneath the earth when darkness reigns, and the theme is that of a brilliant official whose advice is totally ignored by his lord so he becomes emotionally injured and dispirited. The hexagram uses the imagery of a crying (calling) pheasant to represent an official who tries to give advice to his ruler but whom the ruler ignores. Thus this hexagram is also known as "Brilliance Injured" because the official's honest advice is rebuffed. The image of a pheasant is used because the bird's bright plumage is reminiscent of the fine robes of officials, so a pheasant naturally represents the Li trigram in this hexagram. In the first line of the hexagram an individual (the official) hurriedly travels on a road, without even stopping to eat, in order to give advice to his ruler. In the second line he is emotionally injured, perhaps from being rebuffed by his ruler, so his self-esteem and confidence need to recover and heal. In the third line he travels south on a military foray and conquers the chief of a tribe that had been periodically troubling the Shang borders. In the fourth line his ruler finally listens to him and understands what he has been saying – perhaps because of the southern chief situation. In the fifth line we see that Prince Jizi is held up as the example of a crying pheasant that all should emulate because even though his wise advice was always rebuffed he persevered in trying to correct the king. In the sixth line one is reminded that the life of an official has both highs and lows, both favoritism and then rejection by the ruler. What should one do? The Judgment simply says that an official should persevere with persistence.

1. The calling pheasant is in flight, its wings drooping. The nobleman (traveling) on the road does not eat for three days. There is someplace to go (in order to have words with his ruler). The ruler

grumbles.

2. The calling pheasant is wounded in the left thigh. Treat a horse's wound to maintain (hold aloft) its vitality. Auspicious.

3. The calling pheasant during a southern hunt gets a great chief. One cannot continue to accept affliction (illness).

4. He penetrates into the left side of the belly and captures the calling pheasant's heart just as he is leaving through the courtyard and gate.

5. A calling pheasant like Prince Jizi. Beneficial to remain persistent.

6. Not bright but dark. Initially it flies up to Heaven, afterwards it falls down to earth.

36.1: Yang at the first line, and the bottom of the Li Fire trigram representing brilliance and display. **"A crying pheasant is flying on a drooping wing. A nobleman travels three days without eating a thing in order to get to a destination. The ruler grumbles at his words."** A pheasant is used in this hexagram to represent an *upright official*, and itself is a symbol for the Li Brilliance trigram. Pheasants give flight only when they are startled due to danger, so an official is trying to run to his ruler because of some emergency where he has something to say (perhaps admonition) or he has been urgently summoned for advice. The noble man (superior man or upright official) is traveling to reach a destination speedily to talk to his lord, and his journey and advice will parallel the pheasant that cries when it gives flight. A pheasant flying on a drooping or wounded wing represents this man's traveling in haste without food for days to reach the ruler because his counsel is so important. However, the ruler does not receive his advice with appreciation but with criticism.

36.2: Yin at the second line. This line is at the center of the Li Fire trigram so we still have the image of a crying pheasant but it is injured because this is a yin line. This is also the bottom line of an internal Kan Danger trigram that comes through as injury. **"The calling pheasant is injured [wounded] in the left thigh. Treat a horse's wound to maintain its vitality. Good fortune."** To understand this line you must know that the left side of your body symbolizes your yin Qi while the right side symbolizes your yang Qi. Also, a strong horse symbolizes human spirit or human energy. If an official gets injured (rebuffed, criticized, embarrassed, etc.) because of offering honest opinions to his ruler in line one then his ego and self-esteem become wounded, which would be a hit to the left side of his body. Hence the calling pheasant would be injured on its left side. The message is that the official's spirit and emotions become injured after speaking to his lord, who probably rebuffed him for the advice that he hastily traveled to offer. The *Yijing* says he should certainly try to recover from the emotional injury, which is symbolized by treating a horse's injury because the horse represents human Qi or spirit. In this line the injury is due to the presence of the Kan trigram while the pheasant, symbolizing the official, appears due to the presence of the Li trigram.

36.3: Yang at the third line, completing the bottom Li trigram of brightness. This is also the middle line of an inner Kan Danger trigram and bottom line of an inner Zhen Thunder trigram. **"The calling pheasant goes hunting in the south and captures a great (rebel) chieftain. One cannot continue to accept affliction [sickness, illness]."** In the previous line the official was rebuffed by the ruler when offering his advice. Such a conscientious official is upset that his leader does not listen to him, especially when he is upright and honest. *The ignored official goes south on a military expedition to fix an affliction* (problem affecting the Shang state) and conquers a great chief, which means a local great leader of a Chinese tribe who was periodically attacking the Shang people but should have been someone with whom the Shang allied. Reverse hexagram line 35.3 indeed says that "The masses become loyal to him." The south direction is used in the line because it is the direction traditionally associated with the Li Fire trigram, which also represents both the great chief in the south, the pheasant and a military expedition. The affliction is a manifestation of the Zhen Thunder trigram.

36.4: Yin at the fourth line, and the beginning of the new upper Kun Earth trigram that represent acquiescence. This is also the middle line of an inner Zhen Thunder trigram and top line of an inner Dui Joy trigram. **"He penetrates into the left side of the belly and captures [bags, snares, grasps] the calling pheasant's heart just as he is leaving through the courtyard and gate."** The image within the line is that of someone (the official symbolized by the pheasant) who has consistently been trying to get his lord to listen to him without any luck, but now there is a meeting of minds. Opposite hexagram 6.4 says that a noble was unable to succeed in a dispute (the admonition of this hexagram) but finally turns back and works for the king, while future hexagram line 55.4 says that the curtains have been so thick and situation so dark that you could see the Big Dipper at noon but now he "meets his lord." These lines finally speak of a heartfelt communication where the ruler begins to understand the official whereas in the past the lord usually rejected him. Thus someone – probably the ruler –

comes to the official, pierces through his upset feelings (left side) to grab his heart and leaves with it, meaning leaves understanding him and captures his loyalty again. This finally happens as the ruler is leaving the courtyard and gate, which means after leaving the lower trigram. This unexpected event appears as an influence of the Zhen Thunder trigram while the words that must have been spoken reflect the influence of the Dui Talking trigram.

36.5: Yin at the fifth line, at the center of the Kun Earth trigram and as top line of an inner Zhen Thunder trigram. **"A crying pheasant like Prince Jizi. It is beneficial to remain persistent."** This line is the lord of the hexagram and therefore it involves a prince to represent the high status of the line. Prince Jizi is mentioned, who was a righteous minister and virtuous relative to King Di Xin (last king of the Shang dynasty) who often admonished the king for his cruelty and immorality. He was a "calling pheasant" or official always offering honest advice to the King but was imprisoned as a mad man for remonstrating against his misrule so his "brilliance was injured." After the Shang were conquered by King Wu, who founded the Zhou dynasty, Jizi gave Wu advice on how to rule. He eventually moved to northwest Korea and became known in history as a virtuous man who was punished for remonstrating with the last king of the Shang dynasty. He reminds me of the loyal official and reformer Qu Yuan from the Warring States period for whom the Dragon Boast Festival was started. In this line, King Wu obtained a brilliant official – a calling pheasant like Jizi. The message of the line appears in the example of Jizi and the Judgment which states, "In difficulty it is beneficial to persevere," which is essentially instructing officials about the story of Jizi who maintained his principles before, during and after his imprisonment and who always promoted good policies in order to help the country. It is not surprising to find Jizi's story in this line because many *Yijing* hexagrams focus on retelling the story of Zhou's overthrow of the Shang dynasty. The Kun Earth trigram in this hexagram represents royalty, which is Jizi since he was the uncle of the Shang king, while the Zhen Thunder trigram appears as the remonstrance and admonition that the Shang ruler didn't want to hear – the crying of the pheasant. There are insufficient details of Jizi's life to confirm the correspondence with a southern chief and so on.

36.6: Yin at the sixth line, the top of the Kun Earth trigram. **"Not bright but dark. Initially it flies up to Heaven, afterwards it falls down to earth."** The hexagram was composed of the Li Fire trigram that rises (flies) upwards and the Kun earth trigram that represents the ground, and both trigrams are seen in this line which summarizes the life of an official with its ups and downs. You may reach heights of glory because the ruler listens to you and you obtain influence, but eventually you will fall to earth once again after you lose your influence and status.

In terms of the construction of the hexagram there is a Li Fire trigram at the bottom and Kun Earth trigram above, which together represent a Calling Pheasant encountering obstructions around the ruler. The Li Fire trigram below and Kun Earth trigram on top explains the phrase "not bright (fire) but dark (earth)" as well as the phrase that it (Li Fire trigram below) flies up to Heaven but later falls back down to earth (the Kun trigram).

HEXAGRAM 37

Jia Ren - The Family, The Household

Lower Trigram: Li (Fire) – cooking meals, frivolity, intelligence
Upper Trigram: Xun (Wind) – family Qi, motion, trust and respect

The Judgment: The Family. A woman's perseverance is beneficial.

This is a hexagram about the various steps that will increase a family's wealth so it is ultimately about creating prosperity within a family. The first step to increasing a family's wealth is "plugging leaks" by guarding the household to prevent thieves from taking away what you already have accumulated. Then you must get to work at increasing the family wealth and maintain the discipline to preserve it. If you follow these steps then a family will gradually attain prosperity over time. Hence, in the first line a family uses a gate to protect the household from theft and in the second line the wife stays centered in devoting herself to household duties like preparing the food; the family stays productive rather than pursues worthless distractions. In the third line there is a reminder that a family must maintain a certain level of discipline to become prosperous because frivolity will open the door to loss and decline. In the fourth line is the attainment of wealth and prosperity for the family. In the fifth line is the example of a king returning to his family to help the household rather than control its members. In the sixth line is the reminder that a truly wealthy family is a unified family where everyone harmoniously gets along with one another.

1. The household has a gate (the home is enclosed). Regrets disappear.

2. She shouldn't be following after other activities. Remain centered inside (keep the household) and prepare meals for the family. Perseverance will bring good fortune.

3. The family freely laughs *ha ha*. Regretting (the dangers of lax discipline) brings good fortune. When women and children giggle foolishly *hee hee* (are so frivolous and garrulous that they lose the

standards of discipline) then in the end there will be distress.

4. A wealthy family (household). Greatly auspicious.

5. The king joins his family. Do not worry. Auspicious.

6. There is trustworthiness and respect (among the family members). In the end auspicious.

37.1: Yang at the first line at the bottom of the Li Intelligence trigram, so there is an image of good fortune. **"The home is gated (to establish security and protect the family). Regrets disappear."** The family uses a gate to make the household secure since gates guard houses by enclosing the space, thus discouraging robbers. "Regret disappears" because now protection has been established so wealth can be safely accumulated without the danger of theft. The gate prevents robbery hence the gate plugs leaks. Once again this is a reminder of Warren Buffett's strategy of wealth accumulation: "The first rule of investing is don't lose money and the second rule of investing is don't forget the first rule." This strategy is a reflection of the brilliance and intelligence of the Li trigram.

37.2: Yin at the second line at the center of the Li Fire trigram, and this is the bottom line of an inner Kan Danger trigram. **"She shouldn't follow after her fancies (whimsical distractions of no worth). Devote yourself to (household duties like) preparing meals for the family. Perseverance in acting this way will bring good fortune."** By attending to the household duties that must be daily performed a family can build up its prosperity, which it cannot do if it is engaged in pursuing all sorts of trivial pursuits – "nothing done of worth." In this line the Kan Danger trigram comes across as chasing after whims and desires so as to veer off course while cooking (and remaining centered in one's responsibilities) reflects the middle line of the Li Fire trigram. The idea is to attend to one's immediate responsibilities, duties and obligations in running a household rather than acting impulsively and following one's whims in other directions. If you put your energy in unproductive activities you cannot move forward.

37.3: Yang at the third line at the top of the Li Fire trigram, and as the middle line of an inner Kan trigram and bottom line of an inner Li Fire trigram. **"The family members freely laugh *ha ha*. Regretting the dangers of lax discipline brings good fortune. If women and children giggle foolishly *hee hee* (play too much rather than retain discipline) then in the end there will be distress."** At this point when prosperity is finally being built a warning comes not to put aside your discipline. Discipline cannot be too severe and it cannot be too lax. Since this line is embedded within two Li Fire trigrams, which can symbolize exuberant celebration like an ebullient fire, the reminder is not to lose oneself in playful activities if you want to build a prosperous household. Play is the opposite of being productive. This is why the Judgment states that a woman's perseverance (attention to work) is beneficial. Here the danger (Kan) to wealth is a loss of discipline especially as the top line of the Li trigram can have a destructive tinge of going too far with too much ebullience.

37.4: Yin at the fourth line at the bottom of the new upper Xun Wind trigram. This is also the strong middle line of an inner Li Brilliance trigram and top line of an inner Kan Danger trigram. The wind element will feed the brilliance of the fire element, and hence the brilliance of fire will flare up in display. Hence, **"A wealthy family. Greatly auspicious."** Wealth has finally manifested, which is the symbol of good fortune. The family has become enriched by following the advice of the previous lines in the lower trigram. The fourth line of a hexagram often shows a successful resolution of the difficulties seen in the third line or a successful achievement of the hexagram's theme where a perfect accomplishment is seen in line five, and that's what we find here.

37.5: Yang at the fifth line within the center of the Xun Wind trigram. This is also the top line of an inner Li Brilliance trigram. **"The king approaches his family (household). Do not worry, good fortune."** The fifth line, or ruler of the hexagram, will involve a personage of high status and reveal a perfected form of its message. Thus a king (rich man) approaches his family, rather than is with his family, because this line is comes under the influence of the Xun Wind trigram of movement. He doesn't come to stress his authority but to interact with his family members and hence no one is worried about his arrival. Because he is a king this is a symbol of public and domestic happiness. He represents a wealthy man who comes home to enjoy time with his family. The king and good fortune are both a reflection of the Li Brilliance trigram.

37.6: Yang at the top completing the Xun Wind trigram and the hexagram. **"There is trustworthiness and respect (unity among the family members). In the end auspicious."** This is the real wealth of a family. The hexagram is about the steps necessary for a family to become prosperous, but real prosperity is a matter of harmonious family unity rather than money. In this case the top line of the Xun trigram, or wind element, does not represent destructive wind but yang Qi.

The two trigrams of Xun (Wind) and Li (Fire) composing the hexagram are reflected in this final line because the emotions of the family members, or wind element, reach a harmonious state of brilliance ("In the end auspicious"), which is the fire element. Just as air feeds fire, the Wind and Fire trigrams harmoniously cooperate in this last line to produce auspiciousness for a family.

HEXAGRAM 38

Kui - Estrangement, Alienation, Opposition, Disharmony

Lower Trigram: Dui (Joy) – lake, mouth, eloquence, pleasure, talking
Upper Trigram: Li (Fire) – brilliance, elegance, shining, light, clarity, mind

The Judgment: Estrangement. Small affairs. Auspicious.

In the previous hexagram 37 a family became wealthy, but in this hexagram it splits apart (or at least one individual becomes estranged) due to contrary viewpoints among its members. This hexagram is about the alienation someone will suffer when they become separated from others due to having different opinions - conflicting, oppositional viewpoints. Some common examples include argumentative differences with others over politics, religion or how to use money that then cause you to fight and argue. In the first line things go astray when you disagree with someone but at this weakest stage of conflict you shouldn't worry about this too much. The differences are minor and the discomfort is like the feeling you get from seeing a deformed man that makes you feel uneasy and uncomfortable inside but which really doesn't amount to trouble, and the situation will return back to normal just as if a horse runs away but later returns. In the second line you settle your differences in private, and in the third line of suffering opposition you temporarily encounter some ugly situations due to your estrangement that eventually pass. In the fourth line you meet someone of similar mentality who has high status and he helps you because he shares the same views, but you have to be careful how you handle this relationship. In the fifth line, despite your alienation and disharmony with others (to the extent that you have become estranged from them), family members have gathered together at the ancestral temple for some type of get-together celebration. You are welcomed into joining them, which means that you are accepted despite the past conflict. In the sixth line, having been isolated and estranged for so long, you imagine oppositional enemies everywhere so you immediately mistake a marriage party as a cart full of demons instead of seeing it for what it is. This response shows what happens from prolonged separation from others due to the opposition of different views (where you immediately imagine everyone to be an enemy), but "rain" can wash those wrong perspectives away.

1. Regrets will disappear. Do not chase after a run-away horse. It will return of itself naturally. If you see an ugly man there will be no trouble.

2. He meets (encounters) his lord in a narrow lane. There is no trouble.

3. He sees a cart being dragged, its ox has one horn upturned and one downturned, its driver is branded on the forehead and his nose is cut off. There is no beginning (it seems this situation has been going on forever) but there is an end.

4. Persevering in solitude (estranged and lonely/isolated), he meets a great man. They can interact (associate) with sincerity. Dangerous, but no trouble.

5. Regrets disappear. At the ancestral temple they are eating meat. In going (choosing to proceed) what trouble is there?

6. Persevering in solitude (isolated and estranged), he sees a pig bearing on its back a load of mud and a cart full of the men of *Gui* (fiends that are his ruler's enemies). First you draw your bow (getting ready to shoot) and then you lay it down. They are not robbers but marriage suitors. Going forward it is good fortune if you encounter rain (to wash away your destructive thoughts)

38.1: Yang at the first line at the bottom of the Dui trigram, which often represents a mouth, head, talking, criticism, joy, pleasure, young woman, lake or breaking free. **"Regrets will disappear. Do not chase after a run-away [straying] horse. It will return of itself naturally. If you see an ugly [disfigured, hideous, horrible] man there will be no trouble."** Minor disagreements and misunderstandings often occur between people where arguments sometimes cause minor estrangements that are upsetting but just temporary. Hence those "regrets will (naturally) disappear." In this line a horse runs away but your sorrow is also temporary because the horse will return on its own just as relationships will naturally heal. The ill feeling of loss, however, is as if you unfortunately see an evil or ugly person (unfortunate situation) that arouses inner discomfort, but the feeling is temporary so you can shake it off. You expect to see your horse but instead you see an ugly face. The message is that conflict may cause a *temporary* separation between you and others but pay no heed to the bad feelings. Issues will naturally resolve themselves at their own pace without need of any efforts to produce a reconciliation. You are bound to encounter uncomfortable feelings when you disagree with others and encounter opposition but they will disappear naturally so "Disappointments will disappear."

38.2: Yang at the second line within the center of the Dui Mouth trigram. This is also the bottom line of an inner Li Brightness trigram. **"He bumps into his lord in an alley-way. There is no trouble."** The estranged subject who has a difference of opinion with his ruler comes upon his lord in an alley. If you encounter your lord in a narrow lane it means there is no way to avoid him. The meeting might be uncomfortable because of his higher status but there is no way to avoid him so you must meet your lord with humility in this informal place outside the palace and interact in a polite fashion. Based on the presence of the Dui Mouth-Joy trigram and Li Brightness trigram there is talk between you two and most probably reconciliation where you clear the air and resolve your misunderstandings, which *you certainly would not be able to do in a formal public environment like the palace*. The idea of the line is that when misunderstandings or differences of opinion have estranged you from others you might be able to reconcile your differences if you *meet privately*. In this line the prince is a reflection of the Li trigram while meeting him and subsequently discussing any matters (with happy reconciliation) is the Dui trigram.

38.3: Yin at the third line at the top of the Dui Mouth trigram, the middle line of an inner Li trigram and the bottom line of an inner Kan Disaster trigram. **"One sees a cart being dragged, its ox has one horn downturned, and its driver is branded on the forehead with his nose cut off. There is no beginning but there is an ending."** There is a halted ox cart where the driver bears all the mutilation marks of a criminal punishment and who no doubt is therefore socially shunned. The driver represents how others look at you because of your estrangement. People now treat you with disrespect because of your prior disagreements and view you like a criminal. The strange sight of the mutilated man arouses ill feelings inside just as in the first line but these feelings will pass as your situation improves. The situation represents troubles you will encounter as you work through the estrangement but the troubles will eventually end. In the first line you had a fall out with individuals but you didn't have to worry about the estrangement. In the second line you made up with a superior and healed your differences. In this line you encounter an unfortunate situation where other people (don't know you healed your relationship with your superior in line two since it happened in an alley so they) treat you with disrespect. However, if you persevere things will pass. In this line the adversity encountered is the Kan trigram, the disfigured driver is the Dui Head trigram, and the eventual end to the problem is the Li trigram.

38.4: Yang at the fourth line, and at the beginning of the upper Li Fire trigram that often represents good fortune and celebration. This is also the middle line of an inner Kan trigram and top line of an inner Li trigram. **"Persevering in solitude [estranged and alone], he meets a prime individual. They can associate with each other sincerely in good faith. Dangerous, but no trouble."** You have been estranged in opposition like an orphan persevering in solitude. Although alone, through the continuance of your efforts you finally transition to the upper trigram where your bad fortune can change for the better as you encounter the upper Li trigram. You end up meeting helpful influences including the like-minded individual of this line – a "prime man" who represents the Li trigram. He shares your opinions so you are no longer alone. Thus, "He meets a helpful person and they exchange trust (have an affinity) with one another." Accordingly they can associate or interact with each other in good faith or sincerity. "Dangerous, but no trouble" is the result. The situation is dangerous, meaning not totally trustworthy, but if the subject acts prudently then he can gain some mental relief and the situation may slowly improve. In this line the prime individual with whom you can share trust is a reflection of the two Li trigrams, but the danger of the situation is due to the fact that the Kan Danger trigram is still present.

38.5: Yin at the fifth at the center of the Li trigram of brilliance and celebration. This is also the top line of an inner Kan trigram. **"Regrets disappear. At the ancestral temple relatives are eating meat. In going what trouble is there?"** This line is the lord of the hexagram and represents a perfected form of the message. In this line your family is eating together at the ancestral temple and nothing prevents you from joining them despite the estrangement you have been going through. Now is a time for drawing together again and healing divisions because they have made the first move towards reconciliation by biting into tender meat. You will be accepted by your relatives despite your differences so you can celebrate with them (Li trigram) as a unified family again. Regrets disappear in that you are now accepted. Hence the message of the hexagram as represented in this line is that estrangement from family members can be healed. They are willing to accept you and you just have to go forward to make it happen.

38.6: Yang at the top line of the Li trigram, which appears as a wedding, and the hexagram is concluded. **"He is isolated (due to opposition) and estranged. He sees a pig covered with mud and a cart carrying the enemies of his ruler. First he draws his bow (getting ready to shoot) and then he lays it aside. They are not bandits but bridegrooms seeking to woo (seeking marriage). If one goes forward and encounters rain it will be good fortune."** Alone in estranged isolation for quite some time you have experienced many feelings of inner turmoil because of the opposition against you. You have experienced many fears and difficulties due to your estrangement and now, due to your habit energy, you illusorily see enemies where there are only people. Because of your past struggles you reflexively, unthinkingly believe people are against you and take a marriage party (yang) as a wagon of outlaws or ghosts (yin) where you instinctively become defensive and get ready to fight. This is all an illusion that has arisen because you've lost your perspective on the situation after being isolated due to opposition and estranged for so long. However, after you recognize your error, stop imagining injuries, adopt more realistic attitudes and relax then the danger will pass. It's time to recognize that the people you considered enemies or you were angry with were not evil people as you imagined, and they meant you no harm. If you encounter a little bit of rain that clears the air and washes the past away then there will be good fortune.

In the construction of this hexagram as a whole there is the Dui Joy trigram below and Li Fire trigram above, so in this line you were ready to fight (Li trigram) some imaginary oppositional enemies that turned out to be suitors seeking a marriage relationship (Dui trigram).

HEXAGRAM 39

Jian – Obstructive Hardship, Impasse, Stumbling, Limping

Lower Trigram: Gen (Mountain) – stopping, keeping still, difficulty moving
Upper Trigram: Kan (Water) – trouble, difficulties, lameness, stumbling

The Judgment: Obstructive Hardships. The southwest is beneficial, not the northeast. It is beneficial to see a great man. Perseverance is auspicious.

This hexagram is an image of a mountain obstruction impeding the flow of water, which therefore has trouble going forward. The hexagram uses lameness to symbolize an inadequate ability to deal with troubles, obstructions, difficulties, hardship, severe impediments, and so on. In the first line you go forth, meet with obstructions and difficulties, and then retreat since you cannot overcome them. In the second line an official takes on overwhelming hardships and difficulties for the benefit of the ruler; he becomes crippled in handling these affairs so we know they are large but he did not cause the troubles through any fault of his own. In the third line an individual starts advancing, encounters obstructions, and then ceases his efforts because he realizes he is not equipped for the task so he retreats. In the fourth line an individual goes forward and then withdraws from some effort after recognizing his inability to handle the obstructions, and he returns to recruit allies and helpers before he tries again. In the fifth line an individual suffers lameness (great hardship) but luckily friends come to help him. This is what we all hope to happen for us in life. In the sixth line an individual is still inadequate for handling a situation or achieving some objective so he ceases his efforts. However, he develops a firm conviction that success may be possible so he goes to a wise man to ask for advice.

1. Going results in lameness (meets with difficulties that cause stumbling due to the obstructions). Coming back is praiseworthy.

2. The king's minister suffers lameness but not through his fault.

3. Going he becomes lame so he (turns around and) comes back.

4. Going results in lameness (stumbling ahead because of obstructions). He comes back to form associations (find useful connections of associates who can help him).

5. Great lameness (considerable difficulties). Friends come (to aid).

6. Going results in lameness (stumbling, obstructions). He comes back with firm confidence. Auspicious. It is beneficial to see a great man (for advice).

39.1: Yin at the first line at the first line of the Gen Keeping Still trigram that represents obstruction, stoppage or non-movement. **"Setting out results in lameness (he stumbles ahead because of obstructions). Coming back (returning) is praiseworthy."** At this initial minor level of lameness or stumbling we have an individual setting out to go somewhere (handle a situation). He encounters difficulty and then comes back rather than continues to proceed. Since advancing is difficult and the achievement of the task is implausible then giving up that quest is praiseworthy because a strategic retreat is the wise thing to do. Hence, "Going forth is difficult; coming back is commendable."

39.2: Yin at the second line within the center of the Gen Keeping Still trigram. This is also the bottom line of an inner Kan Danger trigram. **"The king's minister suffers lameness (meets with difficulties and obstructions) but not through fault of his own."** On behalf of the king a minister becomes involved in trying to solve some state difficulties. He would like to avoid the troubles but because it is for the king and country he advances and does not retreat from facing them. In handling those difficulties he becomes lame or crippled, which means beset with problems – difficulty upon difficulty. His difficulties, suffering and consequential lameness are not his personal fault, and he valiantly works to fix things. Because he is inundated with overwhelming problems we say he becomes injured – becomes lame – as a result of his struggles to fix matters. The lameness (difficulty walking) and obstructions in this line appear as manifestations of the Gen Keeping Still trigram and the Kan Danger-Difficulty trigram.

39.3: Yang at the third line at the top of the Gen Keeping Still trigram. This is also the middle line of an inner Kan Danger trigram and bottom line of an inner Li trigram. **"Going forth (advancing) he becomes lame (stumbles from meeting obstructions) so he (turns around and) comes back."** This line is the opposite of line two. Going leads to obstacles, obstructions and problems you cannot overcome because you are handicapped (deficient or lame) in some way, so you stop advancing and come back. You avoid troubles by retreating unlike in line two where the minister must face them. This is the final line of the Gen Keeping Still trigram, which represents non-movement, so it is apt that there is no forward progress. The individual stops because the obstructions (Kan trigram) are too large so he realizes (Li trigram) his inability to complete his objectives and turns back to obtain relief (Gen trigram).

39.4: Yin at the fourth line at the beginning of the upper Kan Danger trigram. This is also the middle line of an inner Li Interdependence trigram and top line of an inner Kan Danger trigram. **"Going forth results in lameness (moving ahead is difficult and he stumbles because of obstructions). Coming back he forms associations (forges useful connections of associates who can help him)."** "Lameness going forward (advancing)" means being handicapped, not being prepared, not being adequate to the task, lacking the required abilities or skillfulness or necessary resources, meeting great obstructions or difficulties, etcetera when trying to handle the situation. If you try to take on the problem singlehandedly you will suffer defeat because of two Kan trigrams so the individual turns back to find helpful associates with the intent that a useful collection of allies might help him succeed. Meeting difficulties where you make no headway and must turn back is due to the influence of doubled Kan trigram while the subsequent search for useful allies is an influence of the Li trigram that represents interconnectedness, brilliant mental clarity and energy.

39.5: Yang at the fifth line, in the middle of the upper Kan Danger trigram so we are likely to see great lameness since this is the central line of the Kan trigram. This is also the top line of an inner Li trigram that often represents celebrations or friends. **"Great lameness (considerable difficulties). Friends come to aid one."** The fifth line usually represents a perfected form of the message of the hexagram and often represents the height of good fortune. In this line someone experiences severe troubles and obstructions, and while in great trouble friends come to their aid. The meaning is that when you encounter great problems or difficulties then friends will come to help you, which is how we all want to be treated in life so this is the perfected message of the hexagram. "Great lameness" means severe personal impediments, great inadequacy for the situation, inability to handle tasks, and so on as well as great difficulties, great hardship, severe troubles, obstructions, etcetera. Due to this great lameness you cannot move forward, or you can move forward but only with great difficulty. The lameness is due to the line being the middle (strongest part) of the Kan Danger-Abyss trigram. However, there is some good fortune because friends arrive to help due to the Li trigram that shows its influence in the phrase, "Friends come (to help)." One of the morals of the hexagram is that when you are suffering great difficulties it is your friends who will help you.

39.6: Yin at the top line, finishing the Kan Danger trigram, and summarizing the hexagram. **"Going results in lameness (leads to stumbling). He comes back with firm confidence. Auspicious. It is beneficial to see a great man (for advice)."** The meaning of this line is that you make progress in some project or effort but start stumbling, which means you lack sufficient skills, ability, resources, etcetera. You are proceeding against the top line of a Kan Danger trigram that tends to be destructive and thwarts success so going leads to obstruction, difficulties and troubles. You return non-victorious but with a confidence that success (good fortune) is possible but not yet achieved. Thus you should go to a man of many accomplishments and ask for advice for how to proceed: "It is beneficial to see a great man (for advice)."

In terms of the construction of the hexagram and how it is also represented in this line there is a bottom Gen Keeping Still trigram below a Kan Trouble trigram. Hence, you cannot make forward progress but turn back (Gen trigram) because of the Kan difficulties.

HEXAGRAM 40

Jie - Deliverance, Becoming Untangled, Liberation, Self-Purification

Lower Trigram: Kan (Water) – abyss, pit, danger, trouble, difficulties
Upper Trigram: Zhen (Thunder) – motion, agitation, pushing upwards

The Judgment: Liberation (from Non-virtuous Qualities). The southwest is beneficial. There is no place to go to so his coming in return is auspicious. If there is someplace to go then going early is auspicious.

The hexagram is an image of thunder and the release of rain that clears the air, which symbolizes the great effort required to free yourself of faults and shed yourself of non-virtuous qualities to purify yourself. Basically the hexagram is about the pursuit of self-perfection and the struggle to free yourself from non-virtuous qualities such as bad habits, faults or character flaws. The lines tell the progressive struggle to become free of personality faults and errors, which we can call becoming liberated from, purified of or untangled from non-virtuous qualities. The technical term is "self-cultivation." The principle being transmitted is that through personal effort you can indeed rid yourself of faults and bad habits and achieve self-purification or deliverance. This idea is transmitted through the image of becoming untangled, namely becoming untangled from one's faults, flaws and bad qualities. In the first line you start out on the path of self-purification to free yourself of bad qualities which is never a wrong decision. In the second line you start making progress in getting rid of your bad qualities, which is as valuable as finding a metal arrowhead (since this was precious in ancient times). In the third line you prematurely put on airs due to this small progress in purification and try to act like a high-status individual while carrying luggage on your back, thus inviting attacks from others (criticism) due to the gap between appearance and reality. In the fourth line you let go of some bad traits or habits you were holding onto, and in cleansing your personality you thereby acquire friends. In the fifth line you attain true release from your passions, faults, and other bad qualities and because of this cleansing (being "untangled") are able – due to your ethical purity or admirable character – to influence even uncultivated individuals just as a saint does. In the sixth line, having become a superior person due to your previous self-cultivation, you can now eliminate even the difficult-to-change inferior elements in your psyche that have been hard to eradicate, and which are symbolized by a duke shooting a difficult target on a high wall.

1. There is no error (without fault).

2. During hunting he bags three foxes and obtains a golden (yellow bronze) arrowhead. Determined perseverance (keeping on) will bring good fortune.

3. Carrying a load (of baggage) on your back while riding inside a carriage causes robbers to arrive. Persistence (in your behavior) will lead to distress.

4. He releases his thumbs. Friends come whom you can trust.

5. The superior person (nobleman) becomes untangled (achieves release). Good fortune. Small men now trust (have faith in) him.

6. The duke herewith shoots a hawk on top of a high wall bagging it. There is nothing not beneficial.

40.1: Yin at the bottom and the first line of the Kan Water-Trouble trigram. **"There is no error."** While this is a yin line it does not show any bad fortune nor does it show any trouble, error or fault despite the influence of the Kan trigram. The reason is because when you start upon the road of self-improvement, which entails striving to free yourself of faults and non-virtuous qualities, this pursuit is excellent. You cannot fault it and hence, "There is no error." There is no fault or error in getting started at eliminating your faults to achieve deliverance from flaws and non-virtuous qualities, which are a reflection of the Kan Danger-Trouble trigram.

40.2: Yang at the second line of the Kan trigram, and the bottom line of an inner Li trigram. **"While hunting he bags three foxes and obtains a golden (yellow bronze) arrowhead. Determined perseverance (keeping on) will bring good fortune."** Here we see a progressive advancement in self-purification, and thus good fortune. In Chinese culture foxes are tricky, crafty animals and the "three foxes" typically represent greed, ignorance and fear. Thus they symbolize the Kan trigram. In this line you have overcome some of your negative tendencies because you slayed the three foxes, and thus you have reduced some of the internal troubles in your life. While hunting you also find either a yellow bronze or golden arrowhead, which represents obtaining something valuable (the Li

Brightness trigram), and the difference over bronze or gold doesn't matter since metal arrowheads had significant monetary value in ancient days. If the arrowhead was made of gold, which is improbable, this meant even greater value. In ancient Chinese culture, a golden arrow was an award given to someone only when they accomplished something great, so the meaning is that by eliminating your negative traits such as greed you will obtain something valuable in return. In this second line the great accomplishment is conquering the three poisons of greed, ignorance and fear *or other negative qualities* because you are trying to get rid of the bad qualities in yourself. You make progress through introspection in hunting for and then slaying your faults or vices, and hence you obtain a golden award. The counsel being transmitted is that you should keep on this path of self-perfection, which is why we have the line, "Determined perseverance [continuing to do this] will bring good fortune."

40.3: Yin at the third line at the top of the Kan Water-Danger trigram. This is also the middle line of an inner Li trigram and bottom line of an inner Kan trigram. Due to the influence of two Kan trigrams there is a strong image of danger in this line. **"Carrying a load [baggage] on your back while riding inside a carriage tempts robbers to come. Persistence in this will produce distress [misfortune, regret]."** Here an ordinary person carrying a heavy burden on his back rides in the carriage of an aristocrat, which is the brilliance or showing off aspect of the Li trigram. He should have stowed the luggage with the rest of the baggage on top of the carriage, but he draws attention to himself by riding inside the carriage with the luggage remaining on his back. Therefore he creates problems for himself because "to carry on one's back and also to ride" is an anomaly that invites robbers to come. The robbers are a manifestation of the doubled Kan Danger trigram. It is not that pretending to be something you are not – the aristocrat (who is free of faults and vices) – leads to the *attacks* and misfortune. What invites misfortune is continuing to cling to non-virtuous qualities (carrying the luggage on your back) while trying to pretend you are a higher status (virtuous) individual free of such faults. To further improve yourself and progress up the ranks of moral purity you must not pretend that you are now free of faults and represent virtue with the little progress that you have made. You still possess many undesirable traits (symbolized by the two Kan trigrams).

40.4: Yang at the fourth line, which is at the beginning of the upper Zhen Thunder trigram. This is also the middle line of an inner Kan trigram and top line of an inner Li trigram. **"He unloosens (releases) his thumbs. Friends come whom you can trust."** You achieved progress in the lower trigram and now progress to the upper trigram free of various faults. There is a reference to thumbs in this line because the subject has been holding onto either his luggage or some non-virtuous qualities he dislikes (Kan trigram). He finally lets go of those errant traits and habits – unloosens his thumbs – which will produce the yang of good fortune because he stops trying to put on airs and pretend being what he us not, so the attacks stop. When he finally lets go of these faults or his luggage, which belong to the self of the lower trigram, then his personality will change and friends will come to him (the Li trigram) whom he can trust just as they gather around a sage who has cleansed himself and achieved inner purity by freeing himself of non-virtuous traits. Thus, "He unloosens (releases) his thumbs. True friends will come." Reverse hexagram line 39.4 says that going forth leads to lameness (the robbers attack) so he comes back and forms associations (friends arrive). The personality is becoming so clean and pure due to moral progress that friends are naturally attracted to him just as moths are attracted to lamps.

40.5: Yin at the fifth line at the middle of the Zhen Thunder trigram. This is also the top line of an inner Kan Danger trigram. **"The superior person becomes untangled (achieves release). Good fortune. Small men now trust (have faith and confidence in) him."** The fifth line usually involves an individual of superior rank as well as a perfected form of the message of the hexagram. The individual has been cultivating to rid/purify himself of unwanted faults, and as a reflection of the Zhen trigram of discharge he finally achieves release in the fifth line: "The superior person becomes untangled by achieving the release he seeks. Good fortune." This is a sign of perfection, and it means throwing off the negative aspects of the Kan trigram in his personality and behavior. Because of finally achieving a stage of higher virtue, "His sincerity (now) gains the trust and confidence of inferior people." In other words, the subject worked hard at self-perfection and cleansed, purified or transformed his personality enough to now naturally attract people who admire him. This is what happens to sages because people gather around them after they purify themselves and achieve enlightenment. His personality has become so purified of faults that he can now influence individuals around him including petty or low-class people, which are a reflection of the Kan trigram that he now conquers.

40.6: Yin at the sixth line at the top of the upper Zhen Thunder trigram. **"The duke shoots a hawk on top of a high wall bagging it. Nothing is unfavorable."** The "hawk on a high wall" symbolizes inferior elements that have achieved a high position in someone's psyche and been difficult to eliminate thus hindering one's moral progress. However, here the subject has become a superior person – a duke or prince – and he shoots at the hawk and kills it, which is a manifestation of the Zhen Thunderbolt trigram.

The hexagram's meaning is that you can gradually, progressively free yourself from your own inferior elements – faults and flaws and non-virtuous tendencies – but it takes cultivation effort to achieve that purification. As you purify yourself you will win the regard of people, and at the utmost excellence you will finally become able to eliminate even difficult non-virtuous tendencies in yourself. This is a stage of a purified personality and consummate conduct.

In terms of the construction of the hexagram and how it is also represented in this line, there is a Kan Water trigram beneath a Zhen Lightning Strike trigram, and thus a duke shoots an arrow (Zhen) at a hawk (Kan) to kill it.

HEXAGRAM 41

Sun - Decreasing, Diminishing, Reducing, Lessening

Lower Trigram: Dui (Joy) – drinking, mouth, pleasure, talking
Upper Trigram: Gen (Mountain) – tortoise shells, accumulation

The Judgment: Decreasing with Sincerity. Supreme good fortune. There is no trouble. One can continue this way. Beneficial to have a destination. What is the use of only two small bowls? They are sufficient for making an offering.

The meaning of the hexagram concerns how somehow reducing your affairs is a reduction that can actually produce gain for you rather than loss, and how a state of deficiency (or being the underdog) will sometimes turn into accumulation. The entire hexagram is actually about how the state of Zhou slowly gained allies over time while Shang lost allies and friends before it was conquered by Zhou. The main idea is that being of lower status makes advancement possible and you should try to bring about increase without using force. Also, the point is made that living in an inferior state is okay because the Judgment states that when you are sincere then just two small bowls are enough for a sacrifice to Heaven; you don't need to make a big show of things but just need to be sincere. The hexagram is most probably a veiled reference to the story of King Wen that appears in hexagram 7 and 17, but the focus is on how he gradually enlarged his allies and prosperity (from an initial state of inferiority or deficiency) without resorting to warfare. In the first line the principle of reduction is demonstrated through the example of finishing affairs quickly. For a state this means becoming more productive and not wasting money with the consequence that you experience greater prosperity. In the second line the counsel is to stay determined (to conquer the Shang dynasty) but not to launch a military attack at this time because you will not decrease the enemy but end up increasing (strengthening or enlarging) them. In the third line you are reminded that you might lose companions but a solitary existence can also gain companionship. This means that you can slowly gain allies. In the fourth line you suffer a temporary decrease due to illness and then eventually get well, which means you rebound again. This might refer to King Wen's imprisonment and then release. In the fifth line a state of deficiency is reversed when you unexpectedly receive some great good fortune. This could be a large number of soldiers who now follow you, new allies or the conquest of territory. In the sixth line you do not diminish (weaken) others but increase (strengthen) them because they know you are getting ready for war so they strengthen themselves in preparation, but this is to be expected.

1. Finishing the sacrificial service quickly. There is no blame. Decrease the amount of your toasting (enjoyment).

2. Determined (unwavering) persistence is beneficial. Military campaigning is ominous. Rather than decrease (weaken) them you will increase (strengthen) them.

3. If three men travel together they will lose one man. If one man travels alone he will find a companion.

4. When his illness subsides (decreases) his happiness will return quickly. There is no trouble.

5. Someone enriches him with ten pairs of tortoise shells. It cannot be refused (he cannot decline). Supreme good fortune.

6. Rather than decrease (weaken) them you will increase (strengthen) them. No error (in this). Continuing is auspicious. It is beneficial to have somewhere to go (advantageous to advance). He gains a servant who has no family.

41.1: Yang at the first line at the bottom of the Dui Joy-Mouth trigram that often indicates joy, water, drinking, pleasure and talking. **"Finishing (completing) the sacrificial service and leaving quickly [hurrying away]. There is no blame. Decrease the amount of your toasting (enjoyment)."** For a hexagram about reduction we start off with a simple example of diminishment that involves speeding up. At the bottom line of the hexagram the mild example used is ending your affairs and leaving quickly. Service libations would then be reduced so you decrease your drinking (which manifests the Dui Joy-Water trigram). The idea is to speed up and spend less. Put aside fun, non-essentials and start preparing. You are told to make a hasty departure since speeding things up reduces the time it takes to complete anything. This advice probably refers to a government administration becoming more productive and not wasting money in order to produce greater prosperity. It means reducing non-essentials because this hexagram tells the story of the state of Zhou preparing for war.

41.2: Yang at the second line in the middle of the Dui trigram. This is also the bottom line of an inner Zhen Thunder trigram. **"Determined (unwavering) persistence is beneficial. Military campaigning (marching to war) is ominous. You won't decrease (weaken) them but increase (strengthen) them."** We are told it is beneficial to remain strongly determined, which is the Zhou state's determination to topple the Shang despite its inferior condition. However, it also says that at this time you should scale back any plans to set out on a "military campaign" (Zhen trigram), which the *Yijing* typically uses to symbolize a long journey, large project, new undertaking and most often war itself since this was an important topic to the Zhou people who fought to overturn the Shang dynasty. This basically means to cut out any plans for great undertakings at this time, including any military assaults, where refraining from doing so is another type of diminishment or reduction. In other words, don't go to war – don't use that strategy thinking it will increase you. Opposite hexagram 31.2 and future hexagram line 27.2 also say to stay where you are and avoid campaigning. Basically, you should not start any new ventures, and certainly no military campaigns *because the subsequent three coming lines are yin.* At the moment you should stay determined to defeat your enemy but refrain from taking the offensive because "Campaigning (advancing, moving forward) will bring misfortune." Paraphrasing, the line states, "Instead of decreasing others due to your attacks they will be enlarged (strengthened)." The historical example is King Wen's refusal to start a presumptuous war with the Shang state when he wasn't strong enough because he lacked sufficient allies, yet he kept his determination to topple its regime. If he had attacked too soon the Shang state would have had its allies join in an assault on the Zhou, but by waiting and cultivating allies himself eventually King Wen was able to increase his own strength and reduce the loyalty of others to the Shang.

41.3: Yin at the third line at the top of the Dui Joy trigram, which symbolizes pleasure and talking. This is also the middle line of a Zhen Lightning trigram and bottom line of an inner Kun Group Assembly trigram. **"If three men travel together, their number decreases by one [one will leave]. One person walks [sets forth, travels] alone, he finds a friend [companion]."** The Zhen Lightning trigram issues a strike that accounts for losing one individual from a group of three (Kun Assembly-Massing trigram). This yin line is followed by many others until it hits a single yang line, or "friend," at the top line of the hexagram. Hence the individual who travels alone, which refers to this yin line, will eventually meet a companion. The overall idea is that reduction is often followed by eventual increase, but in the next line there is a carryover of the reduced condition. This line is probably referring to the fact that King Wen slowly found allies in his determination to topple the Shang King Di Xin while Di Xin slowly lost loyal allies. At first King Wen was put in prison, so his group lost him, but after his release he gained more loyal allies. Another analogy is that some army comrades are killed in war whereas new conscripts develop comrades.

41.4: Yin at the fourth line at the beginning of the upper Gen Keeping Still trigram. This is also the middle line of an inner Kun Earth trigram and top line of an inner Zhen Thunder trigram. **"When his ailment [illness, faults or problems] diminishes [subsides, decreases] then joy will come quickly. There is no trouble."** This line is ruled by the Gen Keeping Still trigram that indicates the continuance of a condition. The yin aspect of this line manifests as sickness due to the carryover of a deficiency condition from the previous line and the presence of the Zhen trigrams. When the sickness of this initial line of the upper trigram diminishes and turns to wellness then the peace of the upper Gen trigram can make itself felt. The idea is that diminishment is often just a temporary affair. This line is probably a veiled reference to the time King Wen was in prison (temporary ailment) and then launched a military assault against Shang some time after being released.

41.5: Yin at the fifth in the middle of the Gen Mountain trigram of majesty and accumulation. This is also the top line of an inner Li Celebration trigram. **"Parties increase your wealth with ten pairs of tortoise shells, and accept no refusal. Supreme good fortune."** As the ruling line of the hexagram, the fifth line often represents a perfected form of the meaning of the hexagram. In this line a state of deficiency or reduction disappears, even though this is a yin line, because now you experience an unexpected increase of great good fortune. Ten pairs of tortoise shells, which was considerable wealth in the ancient Shang and Zhou dynasty cultures that birthed the *Yijing*, come to you. The fortune is exceedingly large and so large you are not able to refuse it. The most probable thing is that the large number of tortoise shells this is a veiled reference to *army troops* willing to fight on your side. It could also mean a extensive aid from allies, prosperity arising from the good administration of your state, and the least likely interpretation is conquest of territories through military means. The most probable meaning of *tortoise shells is that they represent an army of troops*. The Gen Mountain trigram could also refer to new territories or allies since it means accumulation and the Li trigram to happiness for what one is given.

41.6: Yang at the sixth line and the end of the Gen Mountain trigram and hexagram. **"Rather than decrease (weaken) them you will increase (strengthen) them. No error (in this). Continuing is conducive to good fortune. It is beneficial to have somewhere to go (advantageous**

to advance). He gains a servant who has no family." This line is at the top of the Gen Mountain trigram that also stands for accumulation. Here you have received the troops in line five and decide to fight. This will cause the Shang forces to strengthen. This is to be expected so "there is no error in this approach." Continuing onwards in this way brings good fortune so it is favorable to advance to war. Why does it say, "He gains a servant who has no family"? It is probable that this refers to new allies who have no relationship with the Shang. A servant without a family, which is submissive support without clannishness, is represented by the first two empty yin lines of this upper Gen trigram whose top line represents the servant. The idea is that you gain helpful support from a person in a state of *deficiency* since the servant has no wife or family, and they help you. Once again, this probably means soldiers but most likely allies. You increase your household by one person and the servant who had no family gains you. The reduction hexagram of an inferior status is over and now it is time for increase, which is the next hexagram 42 in sequence.

The entire hexagram is about the need for the Zhou state to slowly gain allies before attacking the Shang dynasty, while the Shang state lost allies before it was conquered. This hexagram is composed of a Dui Lake trigram beneath a Gen Accumulation trigram, so you increase your enemy (the water of Dui) but gain allies (Gen trigram).

HEXAGRAM 42

Yi - Gain, Increase, Advantage, Augmentation

Lower Trigram: Zhen (Thunder) – initiation, surprise, destructive harm
Upper Trigram: Xun (Wind) – move, start a family, generosity, attack

The Judgment: Increase. It is beneficial to have a destination (go ahead with plans). It is beneficial to cross a great river.

This hexagram is about augmentation or gain and is paired with hexagram 41 on decrease. It is about *using force* to secure gain in your life and how the ambitious use of force for advancing turns to its opposite in the end. It is most probably a veiled reference to military designs for conquest. In the first line the principle of increase or gain appears at minimum strength through the analogy of a new undertaking that is just beginning, which might be a military campaign. In the second line your good fortune is increased by an exceedingly large amount which might be wealth or command of a large army. In the third line, you experience increase or gain by making use of an unfortunate event that might be the death of an important individual. In the fourth line you are given audience by individuals with higher rank who follow your advice, and therefore your status rises. In the fifth line you cultivate a benevolent heart of kindness that provokes others to respond, and this elevates your inner life that is a type of increase or gain. In the sixth line the extreme of yang starts turning to yin so instead of gaining you now become a target and are attacked.

1. Beneficial to begin a great undertaking (undertake a great enterprise). Supreme good fortune. No trouble.

2. Someone increases him with ten pairs of tortoise shells. He cannot refuse. Determined (unwavering) persistence is auspicious. The king makes an offering to the Supreme Lord of Heaven. Auspicious.

3. He gains (is benefitted) by making use of unfortunate circumstances. No harm. Of only middle rank he reports with a

jade *gui* (jade tablet) to the duke.

4. Although of middle rank he reports to the duke who accepts (follows) his advice. Beneficial to start a family and to move the capital.

5. He gains from having a kind (benevolent) heart. You need not question this. Supreme good fortune. The sincerity and trust (confidence) of people will reward your virtue.

6. No one increases him but someone strikes him. His established intentions are not kept constant. Inauspicious.

42.1: Yang at the first line at the bottom of the Zhen Thunder trigram. **"Beneficial to begin a great undertaking [undertake a great task, undertake a great enterprise]. Supreme good fortune. No trouble."** To *begin* a great undertaking means that you start out at the lowest gradient level of increase, which is "gain" at its beginning stages. The impulse to move forward by undertaking a new venture is due to the influence of the Zhen Thunderbolt trigram so it might possibly represent a military campaign. The basic message is that there will be great good fortune (increase or gain) if you start some great undertaking.

42.2: Yin at the second line in the middle of the Zhen Thunder trigram that is also at the bottom line of an inner Kun Earth trigram. **"Someone increases him with ten pairs of tortoise shells. He cannot refuse [deflect it]. Determined (unwavering) persistence is auspicious. The king makes an offering to the Supreme Lord of Heaven. Auspicious."** This is the second line so its level of gain should be greater than in the first line, and you are indeed increased tremendously from the undertaking you started in line one. Most people translate this as "Someone increases him with ten pairs of tortoise shells" but I prefer this more generalized interpretation that captures the idea of being increased greatly but not necessarily by tortoise shells because they could represent men/soldiers since both are the Kun trigram. You might be given the basis of an army. One should stay determined in the undertaking, which might be a war or founding of a dynasty. A king (Kun Royalty trigram) making an offering is probably giving thanks for the great gift or possibly a successful military invasion that would also represent the Kun Earth trigram. A possible story: you receive a large number troops (tortoise shells), you cannot refuse them, you are persistent during the course of a military invasion, it is probably successful (due to the hexagram being about increase) and the king gives thanks for the conquest.

42.3: Yin at the third line at the top of the Zhen Thunder trigram, which is usually destructive. This is also the middle line of an inner Kun Earth trigram and bottom line of an inner Gen Accumulation trigram. **"He gains advantage through making the most of unfortunate circumstances. No harm. Of only middle rank he reports with a jade *gui* (jade tablet) to the duke."** He takes advantage of misfortunate circumstances for gain, which might be due to someone's death (or military failure) due to the presence of the destructive Zhen Thunderbolt trigram in conjunction with the Gen Burial trigram and Kun Corpse trigram. When unfortunate events happened in ancient times an official would report them to the king and other states to request help, and he would carry a jade *gui* or tablet symbolizing truthfulness and sincerity. Someone of lower rank does not normally report big events because it is a task beyond their station, but this individual of only middle (moderate) rank is protected from punishment due to their sincerity. In any case they gain in status; their ability to report to the duke despite a low status demonstrates the principle of increase. As stated, here the destructive nature of thunder appears due to this being the top line of the Zhen Thunder trigram, but the Gen Mountain trigram stands for accumulation (and possibly its stillness feature of not getting punished) while the middle line of the Kun Earth trigram stands for the assemblage of people or even death (corpses and burial). This line could actually represent someone reporting to the duke about the results of a military assault since these are unfortunate events that encapsulate the Zhen Attack trigram and Kun Burial trigram.

42.4: Yin at the fourth line at the start of the transition to the upper Xun Wind trigram that symbolizes penetration, the wind element and thus talking. This is also the middle line of an inner Gen Mountain trigram and top line of an inner Kun Earth trigram. **"Although of middle rank he reports to the duke [lord, prince] who accepts his advice [follows]. Beneficial to start a family and to move the capital."** Here we have transitioned out of the lower Zhen Military Assault trigram and are now in the upper Xun Wind trigram, which can represent growth or movement so a war may be over. The fourth line of a hexagram often shows successful achievement of the hexagram's message where a perfect accomplishment is seen in line five. Here the individual is of middle rank because this is a yin line (in the upper trigram) having two yang lines above it, thus the man (this line) has lower rank. Even so, the prince follows his advice so this shows an increase in his status. "It is favorable to start a family and to move the capital" represents the Xun wind element that causes movement and growth and represents the hexagram's principle of increase. Moving the capital is advised because the site is no longer fortunate. It previously corresponded to the bottom Zhen trigram (subject to attack) but now it must move in order to grow. The capital is mentioned in the line due to the presence of the Gen Mountain trigram and Kun Earth trigram. For instance, King Wen moved the capital of Zhou to Feng prior to the battle with Shang, and King Wu moved to capital to Hao after he attained the throne. Starting a family is also a representation of Xun but the time to do so is when war is over, which is what this line probably represents.

42.5: Yang at the fifth line at the center of the Xun Wind trigram, as the top of an inner Gen Majestic trigram, and this is the ruling line of the hexagram. **"Benefits accrue from having a kind heart. You need not question this. Supreme good fortune. The sincerity and trust (confidence) of people will reward your virtue."** In paired hexagram line 41.5 you are benefitted by a monetary gift. However, in this line you are benefitted (increased) from kindness in your heart because others recognize your virtue and respond with sincerity and trust. You are kind to others and they respond to you in a positive fashion. The fifth line of a hexagram usually indicates a man of high status or rank along with a demonstration or achievement of the main principle of the hexagram. Here the principle of gain has manifested as kindness rather than wealth or territory because kindness uplifts your heart, elevates your life and makes the world a better place. This is a genuine gain so by focusing on this virtue the *Yijing* is emphasizing that real gain has nothing to do with money, power or status but virtue and its effect on others who respond in kind.

42.6: Yang at the sixth line of the hexagram at the top of the Xun Wind trigram. **"No one increases him but someone strikes him. His established intentions are not kept constant. Inauspicious."** The hexagram overall is about personal gaining but the process of increase ceases at this top line where the hexagram ends, hence you are no longer gaining so someone now attacks *you* since the extreme of yang turns to yin. The top line of a Xun Wind trigram is very often destructive which appears as someone striking you. Also, "He does not keep his established intentions constant. Inauspicious." You must switch from offense to defense now just as the wind changes directions. Opposite hexagram line 32.6 also says, "Continuously changing your behavior results in misfortune," which can also mean you must now go on the defense.

In terms of the overall construction of the hexagram and how it is reflected in this line, the presence of the lower Zhen Thunder trigram appears in the fact that "someone attacks him" and the upper Xun Wind trigram appears as his "established intentions are not held steadfast."

HEXAGRAM 43

Guai - Resoluteness, Determination

Lower Trigram: Qian (Heaven) – strong force, strongly advancing
Upper Trigram: Dui (Joy) – words, cries of warning

The Judgment: Resoluteness. Declare it in the court of the king crying out. There is danger. Notify the city. It is not beneficial to approach the enemy but beneficial to have someplace to go (undertake something; do something else).

This is a hexagram about resoluteness or maintaining determination in working towards your goals despite any problems and troubles you might encounter. It is actually the veiled story of remaining resolute and never giving up in order to survive through various military assaults. It is about persevering in the face of death so that you hold onto life and don't die. In the first line you suffer injury to your feet, and so resolutely advancing on a military campaign at this time would guarantee harm and distress rather than victory. In the second line you are attacked with night assaults, which is a time of yin, but you need to remain resolute and not worry. In the third line you become wounded on the forehead and get soaked by rain but resolutely maintain your determination to stay alive and move forward. In the fourth line you become haggard and can hardly continue walking but you resolutely continue forward. In the fifth line we have the image of a stubborn weed in the center of the road that cannot be killed despite being constantly trampled upon by carts and people, and this symbolizes the resoluteness you need to survive a war. In the last line we have the counsel that if you are not warned about potential dangers during war then being both blind and resolute can result in your death. This is why the Judgment says that you should notify everybody of existing dangers so that people can avoid them.

1. Injured toes. Advancing will not be victorious but distressful.

2. There are cries of alarm (apprehensive screams). In the evening and during the night there are enemy attacks. Do not worry.

3. Wounded on the forehead. It is ominous. The wounded gentleman resolutely moves onward alone. Meeting rain, if he gets soaked it will be infuriating but this is not a problem.

4. There is no skin on the buttocks. Walking is halting (staggered) like pulling a sheep. Regrets disappear. Listen to the words but do not believe them.

5. Purslane so resolute (stubborn weeds) in the center of the road. There is no trouble.

6. There are no cries of warning. In the end this is ominous.

43.1: Yang at the first line at the beginning of the Qian Great Force trigram, which represents great strength and strong action. **"Injured toes [wounded in the front of the foot]. Advancing is not victorious but distressful."** Because this is the lowest line or gradient of the hexagram it refers to the feet as well as someone who is weak. Here the Qian Great Force trigram represents a force pressing you to move forward, but you are injured so are not fit to advance. The lowest level of demonstrating resoluteness is to advance while being slightly injured, which means while suffering some sort of handicap. This is symbolized in this line by having injured toes (feet) but still walking forward. A similarity appears in opposite hexagram line 21.1 where you strip off the legs of a couch while in the reverse hexagram line 44.1 you fasten something to a brake so that there is no movement whatsoever. The need to advance while injured represents a problem that indisposes you so you must remain determined in order to pass through the difficulty. It represents setting off to battle when you are weak and injured, and thus you won't be victorious.

43.2: Yang at the second line in the middle of the Qian Great Force trigram. This is also the bottom line of an inner Qian Great Force trigram. **"There are cries of alarm [apprehensive screams] during the evening and night due to enemy attacks. Do not worry."** The enemy attacks are the result of the two Qian Great Force trigrams that manifest as assaults especially since this is the strong middle line of the lower Qian trigram. Cries of alarm appear during the two times of the evening and night due to these assaults. A similarity appears in opposite hexagram line 23.1 where there are disputes and arguments. This line, 43.2, requires an even higher degree of resoluteness than the first line to shoulder these attacks because you must persevere through evening and nighttime enemy attacks that *represent strong yin conditions*. There is nothing to fear, however, as this is a yang line in the center of two other yang lines. Hence, you simply resolve to pass through such temporary difficulties and you will survive.

43.3: Yang at the third line at the top of the Qian Great Strength trigram. This is also the middle line and bottom line of an inner Qian Great Strength trigram. **"Wounded on the forehead. It is ominous. The wounded gentleman resolutely moves onward alone. Meeting rain, if he gets soaked it will be infuriating [irritating, distressing, not pleasurable] but not a problem."** The third line of the hexagram, which is the top line of the bottom trigram, usually indicates some type of destruction or deterioration because the trigram is ready to change into another, and that change of state tends to be destructive. Similarly, in reverse hexagram line 44.3 a man has difficulty walking due to having no skin on his buttocks but he keeps going, while opposite hexagram line 23.3 has a man being flayed. In the first line your foot was hurt (personal troubles), then you faced enemy attacks at night (yin conditions), and now your forehead is wounded and you flee to meet miserable conditions perhaps because of another military assault due to all the Qian trigrams. Each line has symbolized an increasing level of difficulty as well as growing resoluteness required to pass through the troubles. Staying determined (resolute) throughout these problems is like walking alone and becoming caught in a rain storm where you get soaked and become dripping wet, which is a sign you were ill-equipped or unprepared for the journey. Although these poor conditions cause you to become angry, annoyed, distressed or just irritated in the end there is no real trouble in this because you are still alive and pass through the situation without major injury. Walking alone probably means that many of your comrades died but you are a survivor who escaped only with a head injury. Thus you continue proceeding ahead with determination, which is the meaning of resolution and perseverance. You just keep plowing ahead despite whatever difficulties you encounter. This perseverance is a manifestation of the great strength of five consecutive yang lines in this hexagram and the influence of three Qian Great Strength trigrams overlapping this line.

43.4: Yang at the fourth line at the beginning of the Dui Joy-Talking trigram, which represents eloquence and the mouth. This is also the middle line of an inner Qian Great Strength trigram and top line of an inner Qian Great Strength trigram. **"The buttocks have no skin on them. Walking is hard going [herky-jerky, staggered, or haltingly difficult] like pulling a sheep. Remorse will vanish. Listen to the words but do not believe them (because they are untrustworthy)."** The buttocks have no skin on them so a haggard man walks with difficulty. In opposite hexagram line 23.4 a man's skin is stripped away also, and in reverse hexagram line 44.4 a man has no skin on his buttocks so has difficulty moving forward.

The haggard man has been beaten up because of warfare but is a survivor despite his wounds and depletion. In this line your resoluteness surpasses whatever was required within the previous three lines since its intensity increases with every line. A haggard man hobbles along even though it is difficult for him to walk. His walking is extremely halting as if he were pulling an uncooperative sheep, but he keeps going despite his wounds (because of two inner Qian Great Strength trigrams). Obviously he is injured, but eventually all this trouble and remorse will pass. It just so happens that the custom of leading a sheep in war was akin to raising the white flag of surrender. This is at the beginning of the Dui Talking-Joy trigram so due to its influence you might hear beautiful, eloquent words from military commanders perhaps about how your situation will improve, how the war is almost over, how the other side will surrender, etcetera but you should know better about such pep talks from experience. As a seasoned soldier you know better than to believe in whatever you hear *because talk is unreliable*. "Words you hear should not be believed."

43.5: Yang at the fifth line, in the middle of the Dui trigram. This is also the top line of an inner Qian Great Strength trigram. **"Stubborn strong weeds in the center of the road. No trouble."** In the fifth line we should finally see some form of success or perfection from remaining resolute, and the analogy used is that of stubborn weeds that just won't die no matter what happens to them. An individual who has been resolute on some undertaking is like strong, stubborn weeds in the center of a road that you cannot kill despite all the people and carts plowing over them and crushing them. This is a symbol for a soldier who resolutely holds onto life, never gives up and just won't die. They just keep holding on with perseverance, which is the influence of the Qian trigram, and therefore survive due to remaining resolute. The entire hexagram tells us about the importance of resolving to live no matter what and surviving means you suffer no trouble.

43.6: Yin at the sixth line at the top of the Dui Mouth (talking) trigram and hexagram. **"There are no cries of warning. This ends ominously [ultimately disastrous]."** You should be warned when danger is near otherwise there will be disaster, and in warfare this is an omen of death. The Judgment aptly says, "Declare it in the court of the king crying out. There is danger. Notify the city." This is the only yin line in the hexagram and it is stacked on top of five strong yang lines. For each of the yang lines there was suffering, struggle and sometimes military assault. The message of this line is that you need warnings to avoid military assaults in order that you don't die (and thus remain resolute).

In terms of the construction of the hexagram and its expression in this line, there is a Qian Great Force trigram below and a Mouth (Dui Talking trigram) above, and if the mouth does not warn of that dangerous impending force then "in the end it is ominous."

HEXAGRAM 44

Gou - Meeting, Going to Meet

Lower Trigram: Xun (Wind) – wood, motion, penetrating, destructive
Upper Trigram: Qian (Heaven) – great strength, creative, strong action

The Judgment: Meeting. The girl is strong. Do not marry the woman.

This hexagram is in the shape of a woman's body and is actually about seeking (going to meet) a sexual partner. In the Judgment a man is warned against marrying a woman who is too strong for him, which actually means avoiding a partner who is sexually exhausting. The lines say that a man should remain independent or celibate for as long as possible otherwise he will engage in excessive sexual activities that will cause him to become physically depleted. This is a common theme in Chinese Taoism and Chinese medicine. In the first line you really want to meet someone (engage in sex with either your wife or a different partner) because your sexual desire is strong, but you are weak and depleted like a skinny, lean pig. You need to practice celibacy and restrain yourself even though desire is raging so you are like a pig that needs to be tied up so it cannot jump about helter-skelter (have sex). In the second line you have accumulated some fish in a wrapper, which means recovered inner energy, but it is still not safe to engage in sex because you are not over the stage of depletion entirely. In the third line you engage in excessive sexual activities, so your buttocks are now raw and you have difficulty walking due to depletion. In the fourth line you are truly sexually depleted and totally deficient in inner energy. In the fifth line the sexual activity has resulted in pregnancy - a baby descends from Heaven. The sixth line shows a couple copulating with locked horns, which means expending an extensive amount of energy in sexual activity.

1. Fasten to a metal brake. Persevering (in waiting rather than going anywhere) is auspicious. If you go somewhere this will be inauspicious. You must tie up an impetuous lean pig so that it cannot rage around (jump about helter-skelter).

2. The wrapper (packet) contains fish. There is no trouble. It is not beneficial to have audience.

3. There is no skin on the buttocks. His steps are hobbled. Danger exists. No great trouble.

4. The wrapper (packet) contains no fish. Rising up will bring misfortune.

5. Willow leaves cover (wrap) a gourd containing a pattern. Something descends from Heaven.

6. Locking their horns. Distress. There is no trouble.

44.1: Yin at the first line and at the bottom of the Xun Wind trigram, which represents movement. **"Tie (yourself) to a metal brake. Persevering (in not going anywhere) is good fortune. Movement to go somewhere will be inauspicious. You must tie up an impetuous lean pig so that it cannot rage around [jump about helter-skelter]."** The Xun Wind Movement trigram is like sexual desire, perhaps with your wife or swelf-gratification, but you should not do anything. You are like a skinny, lean pig so you are depleted and do not have sufficient energy at the moment even though you experience sexual desire. You are told to persevere in remaining celibate, which is the meaning behind "binding yourself to a metal stake." If you go somewhere this will be inauspicious, i.e. produce misfortune. Thus, "You must capture (tie up) an impetuous lean pig so that it cannot pace around helter-skelter" in sexual activity.

44.2: Yang at the second line in the middle of the Xun Wind trigram, and in this line we will see the wind aspect of leaking, penetration or movement in some way. This is also the bottom line of an inner Qian Great Strength trigram. **"The wrapper contains fish. There is no trouble. It is not beneficial to have audience."** If we consider that line one might refer to rising sexual desire due to the Xun Wind trigram then in this line the desire is stronger, as is the desire to go and meet someone for a sexual encounter (as per the name of the hexagram). In the previous line the pig was too thin, but now you have some fish (which normally represents resources or wealth). Here fish in the wrapper refers to semen in a man's sexual organs together with increased vitality (thus fertility), and the Qian trigram lends inner strength to his particular situation. However, he *can resist the pull of sexual desire* because the line says there is no trouble. It is not favorable for him to "have audience," which means to meet a woman for a sexual encounter because sex at this time would drain his energy. As future hexagram 33.2 says you should tie up the piglet's legs with yellow ox hide so that it cannot run around.

44.3: Yang at the third line at the top of the Xun Wind trigram. This is also the middle and bottom lines of two inner Qian trigrams. **"There is no skin on the buttocks. His steps are hobbled. Danger [peril, adversity] exists but there is no great trouble."** In the previous line you were advised *not to meet* other parties but you now insist on going ahead and doing so because of the force of the two Qian trigrams pushing and empowering you and the Xun trigram enticing you. Opposite hexagram line 24.3 states that you have repeated returns due to danger, so you probably tired yourself out through sexual activity. You therefore are tired, depleted and have difficulties walking, which is what happens after men exhaust themselves in sexual activities. The line says that "Danger exists but no great trouble" because you can recover your energy through abstinence. If we consider that the Xun Wind trigram refers to sexual desire and we are at the destructive third line overlaid by two Qian great strength trigrams then this interpretation makes sense, and is consistent with the previous lines. It suggests that the man succumbed to his strong sexual desires and depleted himself sexually since depletion has sapped his energy, which is symbolized by having difficulty walking and wearing out his buttocks.

44.4: Yang at the fourth line, at the beginning of the Qian Heaven trigram. This is also the middle of an inner Qian trigram and top line of an inner Qian trigram. **"The wrapper (packet) contains no fish. Rising up will bring misfortune."** Fish symbolize abundance and a man's internal treasure. Here the man has totally exhausted himself due to the presence of three overlapping Qian trigrams. He has become sexually depleted. Perhaps the woman is too strong as the Judgment warns, but in any case "his packet does not contain fish any longer." This is a stage of debilitation or *misfortune* where his energy is sapped and thus he has to rest rather than "rise up" and repeat his performance. When you have lost all your internal energy it becomes easy to get sick so misfortune is avoided through the self-control of restraint.

44.5: Yang at the fifth line in the middle of the Qian Heaven trigram. This is also the top line of an inner Qian Great Strength trigram. **"Willow leaves cover a gourd (melon) containing a pattern. Something drops [falls] from Heaven."** This line is the lord of the hexagram that usually represents someone or something of high status. The man and woman meet, have sex, and now the woman becomes pregnant - "Willow leaves (the pregnant woman's body) cover a gourd containing a pattern." This is certainly the symbol of a baby or fetus for "This fate descends from Heaven." Hence the fifth line shows that the woman conceived a baby, while the opposite hexagram line 24.5 is about a magnanimous return.

44.6: Yang at the top at the end of the Qian trigram of great strength, and the end of the hexagram. **"Locking their horns causes distress. There is no trouble."** This is the top line of the upper Qian trigram, which is a position where the yang energy tends to be destructive. In the previous fifth line the woman conceived a baby but in this line they are locking horns, which could mean two things. First, it could be a double entendre with sexual suggestiveness for *very active* copulation since the horn is a phallic symbol. Second, it could represent a couple arguing, fighting or contending with each other since the top line can be destructive. If "locking horns" represents fighting (possibly due to there being a pregnancy) then there will be distress, but it is natural for a couple to argue now and thus there is "no trouble." If "locking horns" means sexual intercourse again then the "distress" represents *very active* sexual activity, which isn't any trouble. Future hexagram line 28.6 says that a man wades in the shallows that go over his head that is ominous but no problem, and this has sexual connotations. I personally do not feel this line represents a couple fighting because most every line leads to the top gradient intensity of "meeting," or sexual intercourse.

In terms of the overall construction of the hexagram and how it is reflected in this line we have a Xun Wind trigram beneath a Qian Great Strength trigram, and thus the struggle of locking horns is the Xun trigram while the fact that there is no trouble afterwards is the Qian Heaven trigram.

HEXAGRAM 45

Cui - Gathering Together, Assembling

Lower Trigram: Kun (Earth) – union with another, gathering together
Upper Trigram: Dui (Joy) – happiness, trust, crying

The Judgment: Gathering Together. Success. The king goes to his ancestral temple. Beneficial to see a great (important) man. Success. Beneficial to continue onwards. Sacrificing a great ox is auspicious. Beneficial to have a destination (goal).

The hexagram is an image of a large lake in the earth that is fed by many streams of water, and this represents how men accumulate into one large group. The lines in this hexagram are about different types of gatherings and the various stages of gathering together with others. In the first line a friendly relationship may have ups and downs but you can renew a disjointed relationship with old friends that has gone fallow just by contacting them. In line two you can then can enjoy a prolonged gathering and the cherished feeling of closeness with others. The third line is a yin example of gathering together because of a sad event while the fourth line is a yang example of gathering together. Finally there is a prime state of many people gathering together around you due to your (powerful, wealthy or influential) position that attracts them. In the sixth line the gathering is over and people must part so they are unhappy but this is the natural way of things. It is possible that this hexagram is like hexagram 30 by telling the story of progressing through life where initially a boy and girl like each other and eventually get married, attend the funeral of a dear one, give birth to a child, the man eventually gains a position, and eventually there is a funeral for a spouse.

1. If there is an accord (trust or sincerity) but one does not carry through to the end, then disorder and gathering will alternate. If one calls out then with a single grasp of the hand there would be laughter. Do not worry. To go forward is no trouble.

2. Prolonged auspiciousness (in gathering together). There is no trouble. With sincerity even a vegetarian (small) offering is

beneficial.

3. A mournful gathering. There is nothing beneficial. Going is without blame, just a small amount of distress.

4. Greatly auspicious (gathering). There is no trouble.

5. People gather around due to your position. There is no trouble. If there is no confidence (trust) in you, prime (high-minded) enduring persistence will cause remorse to vanish.

6. Weeping, sniveling and sniffling. No trouble (misfortune).

45.1: Yin at the first line and at the beginning of the Kun Gathering trigram that symbolizes the earth element, acceptance and the congealing, conglomeration or assemblage (massing) together of diverse elements. In Chinese culture the earth element is considered an agglomeration of all the other elements within it – fire, water, wind and space (metal) – so here it represents an assemblage or gathering together of individuals. **"If there is accord (trust or sincerity) with one another but one does not carry through to the end, then disorder and gathering will alternate (in the relationship). If one calls out then with a single grasp of the hand they can laugh again. Do not worry. To go forward is no trouble."** The first line of the Kun Assembly trigram is weak hence there is a very relationship that fluctuates with ups and downs. It is as if a couple is seeking union but there is indecision and lack of a commitment. However, if any of the two extend contact to the other another during a break in the relationship then with one handclasp they will renew their bonds and be smiling and laughing together again. Basically, two individuals can have a deep, sincere relationship but experience a temporary separation. However, if they call out to one another then their separation can be healed in an instant. This is the lowest level of gathering together, represented by a yin line, where the assembly is weak or inconsistent. The inconsistency of togetherness is due to the yin nature of the line and the fact that the bottom of the Kun Earth trigram is the lowest or weakest degree of agglomeration or massing together.

45.2: Yin at the second line in the middle of the Kun Assembly trigram. This is also the bottom line of an inner Gen Mountain trigram. **"Prolonged auspiciousness (from gathering together). There is no trouble. With sincerity even a vegetarian (small) offering is beneficial."** This is possibly the marriage of a couple. You assemble together due to the agglomerative influence of the strong middle line of the Kun trigram and stay together for a long time because the Gen Keeping Still trigram projects the influence of accumulation and non-movement. Thus we have the potential of marriage and gathering together is natural under these forces. Marriage accords with the influences and represents prolonged auspiciousness. When the couple loves one another then wealth does not matter, nor do you have to spend lavishly on a wedding so even just a small sacrifice is beneficial.

45.3: Yin at the third line at the top of the lower Kun Earth trigram. This is also the middle line of an inner Gen Mountain trigram and bottom line of an inner Xun Wind trigram. **"A mournful gathering (with sighs and lamentation). There is nothing beneficial. Going is without blame, just a small amount of distress."** People here assemble together due to the agglomerative nature of the Kun Assembly-Massing trigram and accumulation influence of the Gen Mountain trigram. It is an unhappy mournful gathering and since the Kun trigram often signifies corpses or burial perhaps this is a funeral. Most likely it is the funeral of one of the parents of the couple because this hexagram is portraying one's progression through life and such things will happen as a yin type of gathering. We have the image of grief and lamentation because this is the third yin line in a row. The basic idea of line two was that you will stay together for a long time, and since this is the third consecutive yin line of a trigram there is a strong manifestation of yin, which is that there is a temporary gathering that is sorrowful or sad just before the next phase of life that occurs after the transition to the upper trigram.

45.4: Yang at the fourth line, and at the beginning of the upper Dui Joy trigram. This is also the middle line of a Xun Wind trigram and top line of a Gen Mountain trigram. **"Great auspiciousness. No harm."** The lower Kun trigram of three yin lines is gone and this is the beginning of the upper Dui Joy trigram so it is greatly auspicious that you have made the transition to this happiness trigram. The previous yin line showed sorrow at a gathering but this yang line represents happiness, probably because of *the birth of a baby to the couple, which is auspicious*. A baby would account for the presence of the Xun Wind trigram (birth and new life) and Dui Joy trigram, and the Gen trigram would represent the gathering of people together or even the future of the baby. The fourth line of a hexagram often shows a successful achievement of the hexagram's theme where a perfect accomplishment is seen in line five, and that's what we see here. A baby would be an addition to the family, that increases the size of the gathering.

45.5: Yang at the fifth line in the middle of the Dui Joy trigram. This is also the top of an inner Xun Wind trigram. **"People gather together due to your (favorable) position [rank]. There is no trouble. If there is no**

confidence (trust) in you, through prime (high-minded) enduring persistence your regrets will vanish." This line is probably referring to the husband acquiring some stature or even leadership position in his community as he grew older. The fifth line is the lord of the hexagram, usually involves an individual of high status, and portrays a perfected form of the message of the hexagram. The superior status individual is represented by the middle line of the Dui Talking trigram, and it is a person who can bring people together because of his favorable rank or position. Therefore people gather around him. People typically surround individuals who have wealth, power, status or influence. Nonetheless a leader will not necessarily be able to depend upon this following unless he earns their trust and allegiance. When people have no confidence in you (the disintegrating nature of the top line of the Xun Wind trigram) then you have to continue being alone by yourself but still manifest your virtues and open welcome. "If they have no confidence in you then persevering on your own is necessary. Regrets will then vanish." Line 16.5 similarly says, "Continue as you are doing. Long-lasting illness, but you will not die" while line 46.5 says, "Determined persistence at ascending is auspicious. He ascends the stairs." The fifth line is basically saying that people will gather around you because of the status you have achieved in life but if they don't trust you or like you enough to want to associate with you then that's fine. You do not have to convert them for as the Judgment states, just continue onwards by yourself to your destination (goal).

45.6: Yin at the sixth line, at the top of the Dui Mouth-Talking trigram and ending the hexagram. **"Sobbing, sniveling and sniffling. No trouble."** The entire hexagram was about gathering people together, and now there is a yin line where tremendous sorrowful appears, so perhaps this is the death of a spouse. There is "Weeping and wailing" or "Sighing, sobbing and sniveling" because the Dui Mouth-Talking trigram is at a top destructive line. Naturally it is sorrowful when friendly groups depart or when there is the death of the spouse so "This is blameless." I think that the entire hexagram is about the passage of life like hexagram 30. In this hexagram, initially there is a boy and girl who eventually get married, attend the funeral of a dear one, give birth to a child, eventually the husband rises in status over time and possibly becomes someone important or admired, and then there is a funeral for a spouse.

In terms of the overall hexagram and how it is reflected in this line, the three yin lines of the lower Kun trigram come through as the sighing, sobbing and sniveling while the upper Dui trigram comes through as there being no trouble to this because this is the natural cycle of life and death.

HEXAGRAM 46

Sheng - Ascending, Rising and Advancing, Pushing Upwards, Advancement

Lower Trigram: Xun (Wind) – ascending upwards, motion, offering
Upper Trigram: Kun (Earth) – king, Mount Qi, stairs, darkness

The Judgment: Ascending Upwards. Supreme success. Use to see a great person. Do not worry. Proceeding to the south is auspicious.

The hexagram is an image of a seed or spouting vegetation that must pierce through the earth as it grows upwards towards the sun and sky. This is a hexagram about the stages of ascension, or path of making steady progress to rise upwards in life. The ambition to improve your situation is not a form of materialistic corruption but the basis of human progress whereby you better yourself and the world. Each line represents an increase in the level or degree of ascension with the message of the hexagram being that ascension is so important in life that even when you cannot see what lies ahead you should continue trying to make improvements in yourself and your circumstances since this betters everything. In the first line you start advancing strongly. In the second line you offer thanks to Heaven for your advance and ask for help in achieving more. In the third line your advancement has reached a stage where you encounter no more obstructions, so the pursuit of progress encounters no obstacles. In the fourth line your advancement has reached the status of regality where your deeds or progress matches with the ancestors of the Zhou dynasty. In the fifth line you are advised to keep advancing by persistently continuing to take small steps of progress. In the last line you are advised to keep working at ascending even if you encounter gloomy situations or cannot see the future clearly.

1. Really ascending. Greatly auspicious.

2. If you are sincere even just a small sacrifice (offering) is beneficial. There is no trouble.

3. Ascending upwards into an empty (deserted) city.

4. The king makes an offering on Mount Qi. Auspicious. No trouble.

5. Determined persistence is auspicious. He ascends the stairs.

6. Ascending in the dark. Striving unceasingly is beneficial.

46.1: Yin at the bottom at the start of the Xun Wind trigram. Therefore there is penetrating movement like the wind element, and in this case the direction is upwards since the hexagram represents ascending or ascension. **"Indeed truly ascending [advancing upwards]. Greatly auspicious."** In this line, someone low in status starts their ascent from the bottom gradient. Ascension, advancement or improvement starts at the very first line of the Xun Wind trigram, and this is greatly auspicious since the meaning of the hexagram is that rising is blessed. Hence we have great good fortune due to the wind element moving upwards (rising or ascending) rather than an image of bad fortune you might expect because the line is yin.

46.2: Yang at the second line in the middle of the Xun Wind trigram. As a yang line we should expect movement and good fortune especially since this is also the bottom line of an inner Dui Joy trigram. **"If you are sincere even just a small sacrifice is beneficial. There is no blame."** The principle of the line is that even though your resources are modest you can still advance. Why is someone making an offering? They are giving thanks to Heaven and also asking for help to keep the increase going that started in line one. Future hexagram line 15.2 states, "Expressing one's humility," which means one does not have many resources but still shows their sincerity. Because they are starting from such a low level they don't have much to offer Heaven, but as long as they are sincere a humble offering is enough. The activity of ascension or rising involves progressing upwards step by step. The ascension is due to the Xun Wind trigram and the sincerity of the offering is due to the presence of the Dui Joy trigram.

46.3: Yang at the third line where you reach the top of the Xun Wind trigram. This is also the middle of an inner Dui Joy trigram and bottom line of an inner Zhen Thunder trigram. **"Ascending [rising] into an empty city."** Initially I thought the proper translation was "ascension into an elevated city" because your progress has caused you to reach a higher/better state of existence, your status increases due to reaching an elevated city, and so forth. However, a better option is "ascending into an empty city" where your advancement has reached a stage where there are *absolutely no obstructions to your progress*, which should make you joyous (Dui trigram). Your advance seems effortless. In Chinese warfare the "empty city ruse" made famous by Zhuge Liang is that a besieged city is emptied of residents and soldiers so that it becomes undefended. A conquering general can claim it without effort, but is initially wary of claiming the city fearing it might be an ambush. Here your progress is so strong that you advance without encountering any opposition so the empty city simile is appropriate. "Empty" would also match with the fact that the next three lines are yin (empty). Effortless progress mirrors the fact that in the fourth line a king travels to a mountain to offer thanks for his advance.

46.4: Yin at the fourth line at the start of the upper Kun Earth trigram. This is also the middle of an inner Zhen Thunder trigram and top line of a Dui Joy trigram. **"The king makes an offering on Mount Qi. Auspicious (a sign of good fortune), and no harm."** Here we have an image of a mountain, which represents the earth element of the Kun trigram, and there is also a king because the *Yijing* often uses the Kun trigram to represent a king or royalty since he rules over many people. At this line you have progressed past the empty city to a mountain (Mount Qi) that is the site of the ancestral temple of the lords of Zhou, which appears in the line due to the presence of the Kun Earth trigram and thunder in the sky (Zhen trigram). At this level of progress a king makes a sacrifice to honor his ancestors or to give thanks to Heaven for the progress of ascension, which is a reflection of the Dui Joy trigram.

46.5: Yin at the fifth line in the middle of the Kun Earth trigram and top line of an inner Zhen Thunder trigram. **"Determined persistence [perseverance at ascending] is auspicious. He ascends the stairs."** Any ambition to better your own condition and persist in advancement step by step is auspicious. The stairs probably mean the stairs leading to the temple on Mount Qi from line four, which is represented by the Zhen Thunder trigram since it is situated on a mountain (touching Heaven). This fifth line is lord of the hexagram and represents a perfected form of its main message, which is that one must continually work at rising or progressing upwards in gradual steps, which are indicated by the "stairs." By ascending the stairs it also says that you will reach a position of progress or prominence, which is also seen in line 45.5 (people gather around you due to your rank) and 48.5 (the well is fed by a cold spring so all people use it). You should always keep at the task of ascension, which means pushing forward to improve yourself and your situation and should persevere even if you meet difficulties. The difficulties are due to the earth element trigram of three yin lines that represent obstructions.

46.6: Yin at the top of the Kun Earth trigram and top line ending the hexagram. **"Ascending [advancing upwards, rising] in the dark. Unceasing determination is beneficial."** Even though you cannot see what lies ahead because of darkness, which means you are pushing forward blindly without awareness of the hazards that are ahead, you must persevere in pushing onwards. *The message is not to rest.* The darkness or gloom is caused by the extreme yin of the Kun trigram's three yin lines. It means pushing forwards blindly unaware of the future. If you are in a dangerous, dark, gloomy or hazardous place then don't dilly dally but keep moving. Here you are pushing upwards in the darkness before dawn. Even when you cannot see what lies ahead because you are in the dark you should keep making efforts to make progress (in life). The proper course of action is to get out of the overbearing yin, which at this top line is the most destructive part of the upper Kun trigram. To do so you must be unremittingly persevering by not pausing, not stopping, and *by unceasingly working at progressing* and then yin has the potential to turn to yang.

In terms of the construction of the hexagram and how this is reflected in this top line there is a Xun Wind trigram beneath a Kun Earth trigram, and thus the beginning of the line shows the wind element's function of "determined continuance" in rising upwards while the advice for progressing through the obstructive nature of the Kun Earth trigram is to "Ascend the stairs."

HEXAGRAM 47

Kun - Burdened, Oppression, Exhaustion, Entanglement

Lower Trigram: Kan (Water) – dark valley, wine, trouble, difficulties
Upper Trigram: Dui (Joy) – mouth, talking, food and drink

The Judgment: Burdensome Oppression. Success. Perseverance will bring the great person auspiciousness. No trouble. Whatever is said is not believed.

This is a hexagram about distress and exhaustion due to being burdened by a confining political position (government office). It is about suffering hardship, difficulty, affliction, adversity or exhaustion due to accepting a government position that will bring you wealth, but will also entangle you with all sorts of troublesome problems and distressful responsibilities. Each line represents a different type of distress such as mental depression or sexual exhaustion, overeating and mental worries, being weighed down by problems, harassment by others, political entanglement and so on. In the first line an individual occupies himself with sexual activities to the point of overindulgence because he isn't employed, or he is suffering from depression because he cannot secure a position. In the second line he has the good fortune of finally gaining a government position and then mentally suffers even though he enjoys the perks of wine and food that come because of the job. In the third line he becomes oppressed by difficult situations encountered due to his position, and he carries the weight of worry without being able to share them with others. In the fourth line he becomes worried because officials are going to come and investigate how he handled affairs in his position. In the fifth line he is threatened with mutilating criminal punishment for his misdeeds by high officials but somehow escapes punishment. In the sixth line he is inescapably entangled in difficult circumstances and realizes that although any and all actions will cause regret he must do them anyway to move ahead, does so and leaves the hexagram of oppression. The Judgment reminds us that when we face oppression, adversity or obstructions then words often won't help us get out of the situation and it is only perseverance that will bring good fortune.

1. The buttocks become entangled by a tree stump. He enters into a dark valley and for three years is not seen.

2. Oppressed (entangled) by food and wine. A man with scarlet kneepads arrives. It is beneficial to offer a sacrifice. To start upon a military campaign is inauspicious (leads to misfortune) but no blame.

3. Trapped in rocks, stuck in brambles. Entering into his home he does not see his wife. Misfortunate.

4. Coming slowly, slowly. Oppressed by a bronze carriage (the conveyance of the aristocrat). Distress, but there is an end.

5. Nose (to be) cut off, feet (to be) cut off. He is oppressed (threatened) by the man with crimson kneepads, but slowly gains release. It is beneficial to make a sacrificial offering.

6. Entangled in creeping vines he trips. This is called, "Making a move causes regrets." He suffers regrets. Marching to war is auspicious.

47.1: Yin at the bottom at the beginning of the Kan Water trigram. **"The buttocks become entangled by a tree stump. He enters in to a dark valley and for three years is not seen."** The first possible interpretation is that the man's buttocks are oppressed by a tree stump because he passively sits on it. In this interpretation the dark and gloomy valley means depression or melancholy where the man is discouraged because he cannot escape his circumstances. He is depressed because no one wants him – he cannot secure a government position. Reverse hexagram line 48.1 says that the well is muddy and no one wants to use it so perhaps he is oppressed with emotional turmoil because he cannot get appointed. Yet again, this line could simply mean that someone gets entangled within an adverse situation and simply cannot extricate himself since no one sees him for three years, but that is an excessive amount of time for the initial line of a hexagram that should exhibit the lowest level of intensity for adversity. A third interpretation is that this image has the erotic implications of sexual intercourse due to the conjunction of buttocks, a tree stump (the penis), deep valley (vagina) and the water of the Kan trigram. In this case the meaning is that an individual becomes preoccupied with indulgence in sexual intercourse for quite some time, which is why no one sees him for three years (which actually means enjoying himself until the fourth line). This causes exhaustion so the man is *oppressed by pleasure* at this bottom line.

Future hexagram line 58.1 accordingly speaks of harmonious joy, which lends credence to this interpretation while opposite hexagram line 22.1 is talking about walking to a wedding (which in this case could symbolize sex or a job dealing with people). This entire hexagram is about oppression and exhaustion, and in the first and the second lines of the hexagram the oppression is self-afflicted arising due to mental and emotional states rather than harassment, burdens or troubles. To me it is a toss whether this refers to oppression by pleasure that preoccupies the man and causes exhaustion since line two is also to be "oppressed by food and drink," or depression for not being employed.

47.2: Yang at the second place in the middle of the Kan Water trigram. This is also the bottom of an inner Li trigram. **"Oppressed by (entangled in) eating and drinking, a man with scarlet kneepads arrives [to award him an office]. It is beneficial to offer a sacrifice. To start upon a military campaign [marching to war, proceeding, advancing] leads to misfortune but no blame."** Entangled with food and drink (the Kan Water trigram), distressed/oppressed with food and drink or preoccupied by food and drink symbolizes luxury and plenty, which is a function of the Li Celebration trigram. You already have these luxuries when your ruler burdens you with a high position, which will increase them, and since you are preoccupied with them *the oppression or burden is internal.* Scarlet knee bands (a type of legging) were worn by high minister government officials, grand dukes or princes. Someone wearing those bands arrives, which means that the individual is offered a government position. Future hexagram line 45.2 accordingly says, "Prolonged auspiciousness (from gathering together)." This job offer of an official position is a good fortune that always leads to good wine and food, and the good fortune is why one should offer sacrifice (thanks) to Heaven. However, this line is saying that a government position will actually be a burdensome oppression but there is no blame in taking the position. The position entails trouble, which is why it says, "Campaigning [marching to war, setting forth, proceeding] is inauspicious" because undertaking this position entails job burdens that will oppress you. The fact that wine and food oppress him in this line lends weight to the interpretation of the first line as being an image of getting lost (becoming entangled) in the enjoyment of sexual intercourse, namely oppressed because of enjoyments. Then again, because he has such luxuries available but is oppressed inwardly this line also lends credence to interpreting the first line as mental funk or depression for not having any position, in effect being a water well that no one wants to use.

47.3: Yin at the third line at the top of the Kan Water trigram. This is also the middle line of an inner Li trigram and bottom line of an inner Xun

Wind trigram. The yin nature of the line means misfortune and the fact that the subject has to face the troubles alone. **"Being weighed down [oppressed, trapped, oppressed by] by rocks, stuck in brambles [resting on thorns and thistles]. He enters his home and his wife is not there. There is misfortune."** Here the new official travels a rocky road of difficulties and his job responsibilities are like a load of boulders on his shoulders and brambles he must walk through. Future hexagram line 28.3 accordingly says that a ridgepole sags, which normally happens from too much weight or pressure. Escaping these troubles he returns home to rest but doesn't (refuses to) see his wife, who would normally give him comfort, so he cannot share his troubles with her. The one person he should be able to depend upon for relief isn't there to share his woes and so he suffers the distress by himself. The severe distress is due to the line being the top of the Kan trigram, which is often its most destructive placement, and this is also first line of a destructive Xun Penetrating Wind trigram. The comfort he would normally find at home (the Li trigram) is overwhelmed by these two negative influences. This is an increase in the level of adversity compared to the first and second lines.

47.4: Yang at the fourth line (indicates movement), and it is at the first line of the upper Dui Talking trigram. This is also the middle line of an inner Xun Wind trigram and top line of an inner Li trigram. **"Coming very slowly, beset (with adversity) by a bronze-fitted carriage (the conveyance of the government official or aristocrat). Distress, but it will end."** Carriages are for the rich, feudal lords and for government officials. A carriage with government officials is slowly coming for him, which causes distress. "Coming very slowly" might refer to the fact they are coming to investigate or charge him for infractions he committed over time in his position so his worry is distressful. Officials may be coming to charge him for misconduct as we will see in line five. The charges and his distress would reflect the presence of the Dui Mouth-Talking trigram and Li Burning trigram, and the slow coming of the metal carriage (Li trigram) would be a reflection of the presence of the strong Xun Penetrating Wind trigram that represents troubles and movement.

47.5: Yin at the fifth line, and in the middle of the Dui trigram. This is also the top line of an inner Xun Wind trigram. **"Nose (to be) cut off, feet (to be) cut off. Oppression by the man with crimson kneepads and then slowly gains release [extricates himself to get free]. It is beneficial to make a sacrificial offering."** Here the individual encounters a man (official) with *crimson* kneepads who threatens him with severe physical mutilation as a criminal punishment for his deeds. Crimson kneepads were the insignia of the feudal lords who could meet out punishments, but crimson leggings were also worn by the public official in charge of criminal punishments. A lord – who might have been the individual slowly approaching in the carriage – can threaten you with the penalty of amputation while the penalty official will actually do this. The crimson leggings basically indicate a man who can mete out severe punishment for any infractions or misdeeds that the official performed in his office, or simply because he falls out of favor. The fifth line usually shows a fine example of the meaning of the hexagram. In the second line we saw *scarlet* kneepads, which were worn by high ministers or princes, whom the individual encountered while enjoying food and drink. That line symbolized oppression by good fortune. The threat of this oppression reflects the power of the Xun Penetrating Wind trigram whose top line is usually very destructive. "He slowly gains release" means that the individual (official) gradually extricates himself from the predicament. Future hexagram line 40.5 accordingly says, "The superior person becomes untangled." Next, "It is beneficial to make a sacrifice" appears as advice either to ask for heavenly assistance to escape punishment or to give thanks to Heaven for help rendered. The oppression is so severe that he should definitely have made offerings to Heaven to request help in securing his release because Heaven is the only entity powerful enough to help someone in such dire straits. This line is basically the highest level of oppression yet where an individual is threatened with severe and lasting punishment (oppression), which is the overall meaning of the hexagram.

47.6: Yin at the top line of the Dui Joy trigram, and finale of the hexagram. **"Entangled in [encumbered by, bound by] creeping vines he trips. This is called, 'Making a move causes regrets.' He suffers remorse (for doing so). Then he continues marching forward, which is auspicious."** You are entangled in a situation that constitutes some form of oppression. You know that your actions to resolve the entanglement will cause further trouble but you must do so anyway and consequently suffer distress. Hence, "Action causes regret." You must take action because it is the only remedy for relief from the adversity, and you actually have the strength to break free. That being the case, your actions eventually produce good fortune for as the Judgment states, "Perseverance will bring the great person auspiciousness." The hexagram is complete so the time for oppression is moving to a close and with your active efforts that will happen.

In terms of the construction of the hexagram and how it is reflected in this top line, the Kan Difficulty trigram is beneath a Dui Joy trigram so we find an entanglement with troubles (Kan) in this line preceding action that leads to auspiciousness, namely the joy of relief (Dui).

HEXAGRAM 48

Jing - The Well

Lower Trigram: Xun (Wind) – minnows, leaking, destructive
Upper Trigram: Kan (Water) – well, a frigid cold spring

The Judgment: The Well. One can change the town but cannot change the well. It neither decreases nor increases. There is coming and going to and from the well. If the rope does not reach to the bottom of the well or the jug breaks then misfortune.

This hexagram is about the rehabilitation of a village well used for drawing water. By progressive steps a poor well of undrinkable water becomes rehabilitated so that it can eventually serve the people with fresh, cool, clear water. Its rehabilitation can represent the restoration or renewal of buildings or other infrastructure as well as people. In the first line the well is so undrinkable that even animals refuse to use it. In the second line it becomes damaged through age and misuse because no one takes care of it. In the third line people realize that the well could be repaired with the result that everyone could use it and thereby benefit. Therefore, in the fourth line the well is repaired by becoming lined with bricks. In the fifth line the well is renewed and now it flows with clear cool water because it is fed by cold springs. In the sixth line it is well-accepted by the public and becomes commonly used by everyone after its rehabilitation. In one sense the well can represent a person who is initially useless but who can become rehabilitated, or even an institution or other city infrastructure. In some cases it can even represent a country's king. The Judgment reminds us that there is coming and going to and from a well, which is the center of village activity, and if it becomes damaged then everyone suffers.

1. The well is muddy and not drinkable. The old well has no game coming to it.

2. The well is deep, shoot at the minnows. The bucket is worn out (battered) and leaks.

3. The well leaks and is not drinkable. It makes my heart pained because it can be used for drawing water. If the king were wise (bright) then all together would share its blessings.

4. The well is bricked (tiled). There is no trouble.

5. The well is frigid, fed by a drinkable cold spring.

6. The well is well-received (by the people). Do not cover it. There is trust in it. Supreme good fortune.

48.1: Yin at the bottom, and at the beginning of the Xun Penetrating Wind trigram. **"The well is muddy and the water undrinkable. No game [animals] comes to this old well."** The Xun Penetrating Wind trigram appears as a destructive force of deterioration in this line. The meaning is plain. There is nothing to be gotten at this well, neither water nor game. It is abandoned because it no longer provides good water – the water is soiled and stagnant. A well is useless when it no longer benefits creatures or people so no one will bother to take care of it, maintain it and so it will deteriorate. One takeaway from the line is that you should take an inventory of all your resources and see that they are working and sound.

48.2: Yang at the second line in the middle of the Xun Wind trigram. This is also the bottom line of an inner Dui Lake trigram. **"He shoots (arrows) to kill fish at the bottom of the deep well. The dipping bucket is broken [worn out, battered, cracked] and leaks."** The meaning of this line is not to misuse your resources because doing so can lead to their destruction. The Chinese were known to put minnows in their well to help keep the water fresh through movement, and sometimes put bigger fish in the wells. However, a well should be used for drinking water rather than for storing fish. If you shoot at fish in a well you will certainly damage both the bucket and the well. Shooting fish at the well hole is a lousy way to entertain yourself and certainly a way to damage the well. When a well is misused it will deteriorate so the principle being transmitted is to take care of property (and infrastructure) so that it doesn't get harmed and become useless. In addition to this direct damage, over time the bucket will crack with age, get beaten up and eventually leak so you must take care of your equipment that will naturally deteriorate over time. The leaky bucket is a symbol of the destructive nature of the penetrative wind element (Xun trigram). The destruction to the well is caused by people in this line, and the Dui Water trigram refers to the bucket whose shape is like an open mouth filled with water just like a lake.

48.3: Yang at the third line at the top of the Xun Wind trigram. This is also the middle line of an inner Dui Lake trigram and bottom line of an inner Li Fire trigram. **"The well leaks and is not drinkable. This pains my heart because it can be used and water taken from it. If the king were wise [bright] then all together would share [receive] its blessings."** The well leaks because of the deterioration over time caused by the presence of the penetrating destructive wind element. The leaking occurs at the most destructive line of the Xun Wind trigram that normally represents penetration and leakage. Its water is not drinkable because it needs to be dredged so that the water becomes pure. The line notes that the well could still be used (if repaired) because of the presence of the middle line of the inner Dui Lake trigram, which is its strongest line. "If the king were wise (Li Bright trigram) then all would share the blessings" means that if the well were fixed (dredged and relined) because the king issues a command to do so (fix the country's infrastructure) then all could use it and then everyone would benefit and become happy (Li trigram). The king appears in this line due to the presence of the Li Sun trigram and represents leadership that decides to repair the broken infrastructure. In one sense, the king also represents the well via his ability to provide refreshment as source of water to his people, and it is only until he uses his power to fix something obvious that he becomes useful to the people again. The king should not let available resources go to waste, which comes down to issuing the right mandates to repair vital resources and infrastructure such as wells, roads, bridges, schools, and so forth.

48.4: Yin at the fourth line at the beginning of an upper Kan Water trigram. This is also the middle line of an inner Li Fire trigram and top line of an inner Dui Lake trigram. **"The well is bricked [lined with bricks or tiles]. There is no trouble."** This is a yin line influenced by the presence of the Kan Water trigram and Dui Lake trigram so the topic is a water well that is newly bricked up due to the influence of the Li Fire trigram (bricks are earth baked in a kiln or dried in the sun). The basic idea is that repairing infrastructure or refurbishing old assets can make them come alive again so that everyone can use them and benefit. The ruler in line three is also being reformed or rejuvenated himself by finally working for the people. The fourth line of a hexagram often shows a successful resolution of the difficulties seen in the third line, or a successful achievement of the hexagram's theme where a perfect accomplishment is seen in line five, and that's what we find here.

48.5: Yang at the fifth line in the middle of the Kan Water trigram. This is also the top line of an inner Li Elegance trigram. **"The well is fed by a cold stream. Drink."** The refurbished well now has clear, cold spring water to drink. The fifth line is lord of the hexagram and usually shows a perfected form of its ideal message and an individual of high rank, which in this case is a superior well. Here there is a yang line of good fortune in the middle of the Kan Water trigram so the well water is not ordinary but perfect. There is a frigid stream feeding the well, so its water is clear, cool and pure for drinking (Li Excellence trigram). This is an example of an ideal well *after being repaired* where everything now is perfect. In a way it represents an ideal ruler of the people who is a source of life and refreshment to the populace.

48.6: Yin at the top of the Kan Water trigram, which symbolizes a well, and the end of the hexagram. **"The well is accepted (by the people). Do not cover it. There is trust [faith, confidence] in it. Supreme good fortune."** The well (Kan trigram) is accepted by the people because it supplies all who come to it. Therefore people daily draw water from the well and use it freely. "Do not cover it" means do not hinder its usage because "There is trust [faith, confidence] in it" since it is so well-received. This is a fine well, which thus summarizes the message of the hexagram. The well also symbolizes a ruler who has reformed himself to now do more beneficial deeds for the people so that they accept him gladly and develop faith in him.

In terms of the construction of the hexagram and how it is reflected in this line there is Xun Wind trigram beneath a Kan Water trigram, and thus in this line we see a well (Kan trigram) and all the hustle and bustle of people using it (Wind trigram).

HEXAGRAM 49

Ge - Revolution, Transformation, Instituting Change

Lower Trigram: Li (Fire) – yellow, military affairs, overthrowing
Upper Trigram: Dui (Joy) – mouth, talking, trust

The Judgment: Revolution. On a *si* day there will be trust. Supreme success. It is beneficial to keep continuing. Regrets vanish.

The hexagram bears the images of a fire beneath a lake of water (that symbolizes a great mass of people), which would result in the transition to boiling water, hence this is a hexagram about instituting change and *transformation*. The big lesson here is that you must drum up lots of support before you try to change anything significant in society that has a large footprint of consequences because there might be opposition. You not only need people's help to institute the changes you want but need the public to accept those alterations, which will require securing the cooperation of many people. In the first line you must strengthen yourself and your forces before you start to institute revolutionary changes. In the second line you must wait until the timing is right before you can start making changes and you must spend at least half of your time making preparations before you try to institute them. In the third line you must start communicating to the proper parties (such as the public and elites) about what you are trying to do in order to develop confidence in you and your plans. In the fourth line, after you win trust and confidence in your plans from the necessary people you can start to institute the changes you want. In the fifth line, at first you can make the sweeping changes you want that are as bold and clear as a tiger's stripes, but later in a sixth step you should only institute changes or clarifications that are small and precise like a leopard's spots and not try to make any new big changes. This is one way to summarize the steps for instituting radical change. The Judgment reminds us that a revolution can only happen when the time is right after belief (trust or confidence) has been established in one's promises of change, and it is beneficial to keep pushing ahead trying to transform situations for the better.

1. Strengthen it using a yellow ox's hide.

2. On a *si* day (when the time is right) you can overthrow. Campaigning (marching forth to war) then is auspicious and produces no troubles.

3. Campaigning (marching forth to war) is ominous. It is dangerous to continue. When change has thrice been discussed then there will be trust (confidence).

4. Regrets have vanished. Trust (confidence) is established. Changing the mandate (instituting the changes) is auspicious.

5. The great person's changes are (dynamic, strong, clear and distinctive) like a tiger's stripes. He is publicly trusted even before divination is consulted.

6. The superior person's changes are like a leopard's spots. Lesser people only change their countenance. Campaigning (marching forth to war) is ominous. Auspicious to settle down.

49.1: Yang at the first line and at the bottom of the Li Fire trigram. **"Strengthen it (yourself and your plans) using a yellow ox's hide."** He becomes firm and strengthened because he is bound with (by, in) yellow ox hide, which is used to strengthen something by wrapping it. The advice is that before making the attempt to institute great changes you must first fortify (strengthen) yourself. At the dawn of a great change (revolution), which is symbolized by the first line of the Li Fire trigram since fire destroys the old (or because its flickering represents changes), you must consolidate and strengthen your forces, network of relationships, helpers, etcetera. This strengthening is symbolized by binding yourself or your resources with the hide of a yellow ox. Since opposite hexagram line 50.1 (a cauldron is overturned) and future hexagram line 30.1 (sensation in the toes) want you to move, this warning to first strengthen yourself is appropriate. The ox is typically a docile, patient creature so another possible interpretation is that this is not the right time to try and make revolutionary changes so you should restrain yourself through moderation and patience. One should sit tight and not move. Reverse hexagram line 3.1 states that it is beneficial to settle down instead of continuously running around, which would accord with this interpretation whereas 50.1 and 30.1 are against this. Since line two reiterates this message of waiting the "refrain from action" interpretation is less preferred than making preparations and strengthening yourself since this accords with the Li trigram whereas waiting does not.

49.2: Yin at the second line that is the middle of the lower Li trigram and beginning line of an inner Xun Wind trigram. **"On a *si* day [when the time is right] you can overthrow [institute reforms that make changes that abolish the old]. Campaigning then is auspicious and produces no troubles."** In this line the overthrowing of the old (revolution) is due to the influence of the Li trigram while campaigning or marching to war picks up the influence of the Xun Penetrating Wind trigram as well as the Li Military trigram. According to the Chinese calendar of earthly branches, the *si* day is the sixth branch out of a total of twelve so it is just prior to the midpoint of the 12-day week. Afterwards the week starts moving towards its termination and then a new week commences. The meaning of the line is that you should start instituting changes at a proper moment *after first making sufficient preparatory efforts*, which are made during the first part of the week, and afterwards you can work to spread those changes from the middle of the week to the end of a cycle. Half of your time should be spent in preparations and half in instituting changes. In other words, only when the timing is right/ripe *after first making appropriate preparations* can you launch a military campaign and march to war. You have to prepare first and wait until everything is ready in proper alignment (because you prepared) to maximize your chances for success. Only after this is done can you institute reforms (that "burn" the old – Li trigram) because you must first make sufficient prior preparations otherwise revolutionary changes will probably be unsuccessful.

49.3: Yang at the third line, which is at the top of the bottom Li trigram. This is also the central line of an inner Xun Wind trigram, and bottom line of an inner Qian Great Strength trigram. **"Marching forth to war [campaigning] is ominous. It is dangerous to continue. When change [revolution, overturning] has thrice been discussed, then there will be trust (confidence in your plans)."** The second line told you that you could institute changes (go to war) on the *si* day that corresponds to the third of six hexagram lines, hence now, but this line says not to do so because your preparations are still not complete – you have not drummed up enough support. All three trigrams and the yang nature of the line suggest marching to war but the line warns against doing this despite the strong presence of testosterone (Li, Xun, Qian, yang) until everyone is on board with the project so that it has total support. Thus the *Yijing* is super-emphasizing the principle of *making sufficient preparations and drumming up support before trying to institute big changes*. Before a revolution can succeed you need to persuade people to support it and that requires education and communication. This warning is so strong that it goes against the nature of the line, and the lesson is that it is safe to proceed only if you can win the cooperative support of the elites and public. This line isn't about warfare but about advancing to institute the changes you want, and a military campaign is used as an analogy. It probably is *not about* a revolution to overthrow a ruler because no ancient Chinese ruler would allow any book to exist that might recommend his overthrow and in ancient China the change of government was due to military conquest rather than a people's revolt. "Marching forth to war is ominous" means that moving forward to force changes on people will not succeed when they don't yet understand what you are doing and why. They'll put up resistance and won't accept any rash actions that have not been explained. Governments typically first run public relations campaigns to win public approval and acceptance of their plans before instituting radical changes. When talk of revolution (abolishing the old) has made the rounds three times then you will win the trust and cooperation of others because the people will have accepted the idea after being convinced. "Three times" just means *several times rather than three times*, but refers to the three consecutive yang lines of the hexagram starting with this line so that you are successful in the fifth line. Reform must be discussed and deliberated several times before you win the trust of the people and then you can confidently act due to their consent.

49.4: Yang at the fourth line at the beginning of the upper Dui Talking trigram. This is also the middle line of an inner Qian Great Strength trigram and top line of an inner Xun Wind trigram. With such strong impelling forces we should see forward progress made in this line. **"Regrets vanish. Trust (confidence in you and your policies) is established. Changing the ordinances (instituting the changes) is auspicious."** In the third line you talked about making changes and in this line you've won people's trust and confidence so you can start instituting them. "Regrets have vanished" means that opposition has disappeared. You won the people's allegiance, they believe in you and your plans so your disappointment disappears, and you can now go ahead with the reforms you want to make and change the existing ordinances. In the fourth line of a hexagram we often find a successful achievement of the hexagram's theme but a more ideal, model or perfect accomplishment is usually seen in line five, which is the case here.

49.5: Yang at the fifth line in the middle of the upper Dui Talking trigram, and as the top line within an inner Qian Great Strength trigram. **"The great person's changes are (dynamic, strong, clear, and distinctive) like a tiger's stripes. He obtains the public's confidence [inspires their trust] even before divination is consulted."** The subject of the fifth line is usually someone significant of high status since this line is the lord of the hexagram. Thus this individual is compared to a tiger because of the supreme placement of this line and its yang nature within a Qian Great Strength trigram. The stripes we see on a tiger – an animal of great strength, energy and purpose – are clear and distinctive. The supreme leader's changes are similarly extremely clear, broad and obvious like a tiger's stripes, and therefore people believe in him and follow him with their sympathetic support of trust and confidence. He is sure in his heart that his cause is correct so *he does not need to resort to divination in order to know what to do*. A tiger represents his power and strength and he makes big, bold changes (the Dui Talking trigram) that are as clear as a tiger's stripes. A great man doesn't need a divination to tell him what to do nor does he need confirmation that his changes are appropriate. Because of his greatness he is trusted by others, has their approval, and can proceed with his innovations.

49.6: Yin at the sixth line at the top of the Dui trigram and top of the hexagram. **"The superior person's changes are like a leopard's spots. Lesser people only change their countenance. Campaigning [advancing now] is ominous. Auspicious is to now remain where you are."** The fifth line represented someone who was lord of the hexagram, but this line is simply that of a superior person. This person institutes changes near the end of the revolution that are not as bold, broad and sweeping as a tiger's stripes. Instead they are small, clear and precise like a leopard's spots because that is all that can be digested by the public at this time. The great changes were accomplished earlier in line five, and now is the time for small details such as *clarifications*. Clarifications are a symbol for the Dui Talking trigram. The ancient Chinese believed that the colored specks of a leopard changed with the seasons. In this line the leopard's spots symbolize the period after the revolution when the major changes (practical reforms) were instituted and the principles that motivated them have already been articulated and disseminated. Petty people understand the writing on the wall and superficially comply with the new changes, but they only make an outward show of it, thus they "change their face only." Their adherence, obedience or allegiance is only skin-deep hence it only goes as far as their countenance. *Since one cannot gain any more than outer acquiescence at this ti*me you must abide in the present state without making any more new big changes. Advancing now at new ventures will bring misfortune. You must work to solidify the situation and consolidate your position rather than move ahead to new objectives, which is why, "To move forward now will be disastrous. Staying as you are brings good fortune."

In terms of the composition of the hexagram and how it is reflected in this line there is a Li Fire trigram beneath a Dui Mouth-Talking trigram, and so the changes have already been made in the Li trigram and now is the time to just make verbal clarifications that are the Dui trigram.

HEXAGRAM 50

Ding - The Cauldron, The Alchemical Vessel, Establishing the New, Transforming the Fortune

Lower Trigram: Xun (Wind) – wood, motion, penetrating, destructive
Upper Trigram: Li (Fire) – brilliance, elegance, shining, light, clarity, mind

The Judgment: The Cauldron. Supreme auspiciousness. Success.

The hexagram has the image of putting wood into a fire to cook food. This hexagram is called "The Cauldron" because its shape looks like a cauldron. The broken lines at the bottom suggest legs, upper yin lines suggest cauldron handles, and middle yang lines suggest the body of the vessel. When food is cooked by fire it undergoes a transformation and the actual meaning of this hexagram is also about transforming or changing something - your fortune, which is also a sacred matter. In ancient times a cauldron was used to cook sacrificial offerings to induce blessings from Heaven for some type of beneficial change. The sacrificial offering was used in requests to transform a situation and create good fortune in order to correct or banish bad fortune. Hence the cauldron is like an alchemical vessel. That is why this hexagram is a commentary on the steps required to change your bad fortune. In the first line you overturn a cauldron to get rid of the stale stuff inside, which means taking steps to eliminate the vestiges of the old bad fortune. Hence, in order to change the fortune of being childless to continue your lineage you take a concubine to obtain a son. In the second line you start doing everything you need to do to change your fortune and must ignore the neighbors and naysayers who speak against you and your efforts. In the third line you suffer difficult problems to changing your fortune but despite the difficulties everything works out in the end. In the fourth line you suffer an accident that causes great shame, perhaps due to incompetence in your efforts at transformation, but you continue with your efforts to change your fortune. In the fifth line finally things are turning your way and in the sixth line, because you persevered, everything has turned around to become beneficial because the fortune has been successfully changed. Thus the Judgment says "Supreme auspiciousness." Since overturning a cauldron (as in line one) was often used in Chinese history to represent the overturning of a dynasty, this hexagram could also be retelling the history of the conquest and subsequent control of the Shang dynasty in establishing the state of Zhou, and this historical perspective is provided.

1. The cauldron is overturned with its feet turned upwards. Beneficial to expel what was bad. One takes a concubine to get a son. No blame.

2. The cauldron has been filled. My enemy has an illness but it cannot reach me. Auspicious.

3. The ears (handles) of the cauldron come apart (crack off). Its movement is blocked. The fat (plump) pheasant meat inside is not eaten. In the countryside the rain diminishes. Regrets, but in the end auspicious.

4. The legs of the cauldron break. It overturns spilling the duke's stew. Ominous.

5. The cauldron has yellow (golden bronze) ears and a bronze (metal) carrying pole. Beneficial to continue at persevering.

6. The cauldron has a jade carrying pole (lifting bar). Greatly auspicious. There is nothing not beneficial.

50.1: Yin at the first line of the lower Xun Wind trigram. **"The cauldron is overturned with its feet turned upwards. Beneficial to expel what was bad. One takes a concubine to get a son. No blame."** Here in the first line the wind element starts penetrating the situation to help transform the bad fortune and you act to "get rid of the old." The cauldron is overturned with its feet pointing upwards so that you can empty out the stale stuff inside and dump out that stagnant material. This is like the thunderbolts that occur in line one of opposite hexagram 51. You are trying to change the situation or fortune by first getting rid of any old garbage in order to clean out old matters since you want to break with the old. You therefore have to get rid of any vestiges of the old fortune that were spoiling your circumstances or holding you back. For example, when the new Zhou regime took over the state of Shang it had to get rid of the remnants of the old administration in order to change the dynasty. To emphasize this advice, the analogy is provided of someone who takes a concubine (yin) for the sake of having a son to change the situation of having no heirs. In Chinese culture it was very important to have male heirs and if you could not continue your lineage it was acceptable to have children from someone other than the primary wife to secure the continuation of one's lineage. Basically, overturning a sacrificial vessel and expelling its crusted contents shows a firm resolve to purge the old order while taking a concubine is for the purpose of trying to have a son so that there is a new generation, i.e. a new fortune (or dynasty). Incidentally, overturning the cauldron is also a Chinese analogy for overthrowing a meritless dynasty in order to throw out an evil ruler and install a new virtuous king. Thus, this cauldron turned upside-down might symbolize the overthrow of the Shang dynasty and its evil King Di Xin by King Wen (Ji Chang) of the state of Zhou. King Wen could not conceive a child with his primary wife, the daughter of the Shang King Zhou Di Xin, so she was demoted and a secondary wife became the primary wife in order that he could gain a son as heir. This history is probably reflected in this line.

50.2: Yang at the second line of the lower Xun Wind trigram, and it is the bottom line of an inner Qian Heaven trigram. **"The cauldron has been filled [is stuffed with food]. My enemy has an illness but it cannot reach me [affect me, cannot do me harm]. Auspicious."** The fact that the cauldron is filled with food means it is being used for cooking, which suggests that the alchemical transformation of your fortune is proceeding and going well. Cooking means that you are transforming the food, hence you are changing or transforming the bad fortune (so that, for instance, enemies cannot harm you). In other words, the ceremony of using the cauldron for cooking means that you are making definite progress in altering your fortune for the better. This progress reflects the stirring power of the Xun Wind trigram and the benefit of the Qian Heaven trigram. In ordinary life, when your fortune starts changing for the better some people around you may develop ill-will because you start changing and advancing, which is a mental affliction like jealousy. Therefore it says that your enemies have an illness (which reflects the Xun Penetrating Wind trigram) but they cannot approach you to do you harm hence there will be good fortune as your positive changes proceed. One can comment in many ways about the sacrificial cauldron being full (due to the presence of the Qian trigram) and therefore evil fortune can no longer approach you because the ceremony has produced protection (opposite hexagram line 51.2 also states that you will not lose your valuables), but the real message is that the work you are doing to change your fortune is succeeding. It is also provoking a negative response in others that you should ignore. In terms of history, this image of a full cauldron might symbolize the growing power of King Wen in the state of Zhou before he toppled the Shang where the enemies were Zhou's border states that were jealous of its accomplishments but could not match Zhou's might so could not hurt it.

50.3: Yang at the third line of the hexagram, which is the top line of the Xun Wind trigram. This is also the middle line of an inner Qian Heaven trigram and bottom line of an inner Dui Lake-Mouth trigram. **"The ears [handles] of the cauldron come apart (crack off). Its movement is blocked. The plump pheasant meat inside is not eaten. In the countryside the rain diminishes. Regrets, but in the end auspicious."** Basically, the old negative yin fortune is undergoing a transformation, which is the entire purpose of ceremoniously using the cauldron to change the fortune from yin to yang. There are three yin conditions: the cauldron's ears come off and it cannot be moved or it is just very difficult to move the vessel, the food inside isn't eaten, and the rain in the countryside diminishes. These problems symbolize that *obstructions are being encountered as you work to move/change the fortune*. For this yang line the images seem yin, but they lead to yang in the end because eventually there will be good fortune courtesy of the Qian trigram. The cracked cauldron ears that block the cauldron's movements might be due to the destructive nature of the Xun trigram and certainly reflect the damage that would be caused by the opposite hexagram (51.3): "Violent crashing thunderbolts." The food also isn't eaten since you are only at the first line of the Dui Mouth trigram that isn't high enough to reach the mouth at the top Dui line, and it doesn't rain either where the rainfall reduction represents scarcity. This line is at the top of a destructive Xun Wind-Wood trigram and the wood is being burned to heat the fire underneath the cauldron to cook the food, which is why there appears mention of diminished rain water. In terms of history, the cauldron that has lost its handles may symbolize the death of King Wen (Ji Chang) before his rebellion is completed. However, his son King Wu was eventually able to complete the conquest of the state of Shang. The cauldron handles being broken can also represent the officers of the old Shang regime that must be replaced before the fat pheasant meat can be eaten, which means before the benefits of new regime can be enjoyed. In this case the diminishing frontier rain storms probably refers to border incursions that diminish after the greatness of Zhou's victory.

50.4: Yang at the fourth line of the hexagram, which is the bottom line of the new upper Li trigram. This is also the middle line of an inner Dui Mouth trigram, and top line of an inner Qian Heaven trigram. **"The legs of the cauldron break. It overturns spilling the duke's stew. Ominous."** This is a higher, more destructive form of the third line. Instead of the ears of the cauldron coming off its legs accidentally break. In the third line you simply do not eat the contents of the sacrificial vessel whereas here they spill out. Opposite hexagram line 51.4 says, "Thunderstorm and then mud." In the third line, the rains diminish. Here the duke's meal, which looked delicious, is lost. You possibly suffer this accident due to incompetence and it causes you great shame, but you must continue with your efforts to change your fortune despite this negative event that represents a setback. How can this be a yang line? Because yang activity occurs – you are engaged in performing yang activity through cooking, which means transforming your fortune, but trouble occurs because sometimes things go awry during your efforts. In terms of the line's construction, the Li Fire trigram at the upper trigram instead of beneath the cauldron is a problem so the cauldron breaks and spills. This also happens due to the destructive nature of the top line of the Qian Great Force trigram. As usual, the cauldron itself is represented by the Dui Mouth trigram. In terms of history, a cauldron with broken legs might symbolize the three-year rebellion led by the three brothers of King Wu after he died (two years after the conquest of Shang) while King Wu's young son, Prince Song (King Cheng of Zhou), was looked after by another brother who served as his regent (the Duke of Zhou). The three brothers rebelled in favor of the surviving Shang heir Wu Geng whose story is in line 17.6. The rebellion was led by the third son of King Wen, Guanshu Xian. In other words, support for the new order fails and this is symbolized by the cauldron's legs breaking. However, the rebellion was defeated by the Duke of Zhou (fourth son of King Wen), King Cheng was placed on the throne, and the remnants of the now twice-defeated Shang were put under the rule of the Marquis of Kang, who was another relative of the deceased King Wu. The Marquis of Kang appears in hexagram 35.

50.5: Yin at the fifth line of the hexagram that is the middle line of the upper Li Fire-Brilliance trigram. This is also the top line of an inner Dui Mouth trigram. **"The cauldron has yellow ears (golden bronze) ears and a bronze carrying pole. Beneficial to continue at persevering."** The fifth line of a hexagram usually shows a perfected from of its message and an extraordinary individual of high status which in this case becomes an exceptional cauldron. You are in a yin situation, but the cauldron has yellow ears and is hauled on a bronze carrying pole. The image is basically saying that the sacrificial vessel (offering) is exceptional, which is usually the case of some great personage in the fifth line. Its exceptional nature is a result of the Li Brilliance trigram and the fact that it is a cauldron is the Dui Mouth trigram. The exceptional cauldron vessel means that the changes you desire in your fortune are finally manifesting in a positive way. Therefore it will be advantageous to persevere with your efforts until the changes are complete. In terms of history this fine cauldron - newly cast for the state of Zhou with bronze handles and a golden carrying pole - probably symbolizes the one brother who served as regent and took care of his nephew, the future King Cheng, before he became king. This was Zai of Dan, or Duke of Zhou, under whose rule peace returned to the kingdom. He would be represented by the bronze carrying pole. The cauldron has good handles and a strong carrying pole so it can be used. The cauldron's carrying pole represents the king whereas the handles represent governing officials.

50.6: Yang at the sixth line at the top of the upper Li Brilliance-Fire trigram, and the top of the hexagram. The hexagram looks like a cauldron, and this line represents its top line, which is probably a pole. **"The cauldron has a jade carrying pole. Greatly auspicious. There is nothing not beneficial."** Some translate this line as the cauldron having jade handles but the Mawangdui text reads as a jade pole. Whether the cauldron has jade handles or jade carrying pole this is the manifestation of the Li Brilliance trigram. The precious jade basically indicates great good fortune, which means that the fortune has finally transformed (a new dynasty has taken over) and everything is beneficial now. The fact that there is a pole means you can move the cauldron to a new location like a ruler changing things within the state (also implying that your fortune has changed), and jade ears mean the same thing so that altogether there are multiple confirmations of the successful transformation of your fortune. "Nothing not advantageous" also means that your fortune has been successfully changed due to all your efforts. The efforts started in line one where you got rid of the old garbage and started doing whatever was necessary to change your situation, which is now advantageous. In terms of history, this hexagram line may symbolize King Cheng who ascended the throne several years after his father's death (King Wu) and reigned for over forty years. This was one of the most peaceful reigns of the Zhou dynasty hence the cauldron's carrying pole (the ruler who carries the state) is made of jade that does not corrode while bronze does.

In terms of the composition of the hexagram and how it is reflected in this line we have a Xun Movement trigram below and Li Brilliance trigram above, so the line first speaks of the "jade carrying pole" to denote the movement potential of the Xun trigram and the jade and auspiciousness denote the Li trigram.

HEXAGRAM 51

Zhen - Thunder, Lightning Strike, Shock

Lower Trigram: Zhen (Thunder) – thunder, lightning, shock, movement
Upper Trigram: Zhen (Thunder) – thunder, danger, lightning strike

The Judgment: Thunder comes – Crack, crack! Afterwards laughter and talk – Ha, Ha! The shock terrifies for a hundred miles but he does not let there be a spill from the sacrificial cup.

This hexagram of thunder and lightning represents powerful, terrifying situations that we cannot control yet we can control our reactions to them. The hexagram of thunder, which is composed of a doubled trigram, is about dealing with dangerous situations that arise and cause shock, fright or even destruction. While some compare this hexagram to an earthquake or military invasion there is also the very strong possibility that this hexagram is secretly describing *arguments between a husband and wife* but I'm not going to focus on this interpretation because once you know this you will be able to decipher the lines yourself in this vein. The Judgment reminds us that even during frightful cases of shock there are things needing to be done (household duties) during those emergencies and we must complete them. In the first line an unexpected event occurs causing shock and terror, like an argument, but after the situation passes everyone forgets about it and returns to having a good time. In the second line the shock of a more dangerous situation arises (such as a thunderstorm, earthquake, flood or military invasion), which causes you to abandon your belongings and flee. In the third line the intensity of danger increases because you are caught in the middle of a violent thunderstorm, which is like being caught in the middle of a battle or violent physical argument, and so you run away to escape harm's way. In the fourth line a thunderstorm ceases and afterwards there is mud everywhere indicating that the storm has caused a legacy of problems all over. In the fifth line a thunderstorm arises and despite its occurrence there are still things that need to be done and duties to perform so you must attend to them despite the danger. This means you must maintain your concentration during the commotion. The sixth line is a commentary on violent, dangerous or explosive situations in general that are symbolized by a thunderstorm. During such situations you should not launch any new ventures because you must attend to managing the current situation. You might escape harm but the neighbor may not. If the danger occurs very close to you couples will end up discussing the matter perhaps to apportion some type of blame. This is like a wife exploding and scolding a husband because of something he did that affected her but not him.

1. Thunder comes – terrifying, terrifying! Afterwards there is laughter and talk – ha, ha! Auspicious.

2. Thunderbolts. Danger. He relinquishes his treasures and flees to the high hills (to escape). Do not pursue what is lost. In seven days you will retrieve it.

3. Terrifying thunderbolts. Shocked into moving. No trouble.

4. Thunder and then mud.

5. Thunder comes and goes dangerously (thunderbolts are flying here and there all around so alarmingly). There is no loss. Tasks (activities) must still be performed.

6. The thunderbolts are so menacing. He looks around him with trembling apprehension. An expedition is inauspicious. The thunderbolts do not hit him but strike a neighbor. No trouble. In a marriage there is criticism (arguments about some matter).

51.1: Yang in the first place at the bottom of the Zhen Thunder trigram. **"Thunder comes – terrifying, terrifying [with thunder comes fright and terror]! Afterwards there is laughter and chatting - ha, ha! Auspicious."** The lightning strikes, which symbolize a powerful force that produces fright and alarm. After the storm people forget about the danger they went through and the fright again turns into laughter and talk - ha, ha! Good fortune because the disaster passes without harm. So at first there is a thunderous shock and upset that horrifies everyone, like a contentious argument, but afterwards the mood changes to happy laughter, gaiety, conversation, gossip and glee. A shocking event causes concern but is dismissed after it passes and things return to normal. For instance, husband and wife can have a fierce argument and then laugh afterwards as things return to normal. Historically speaking, the Zhou conquerors can be compared to this line because they descended upon the Shang like thunderbolts but left most lords to rule in their territories, thus things returned to normal after they conquered a region.

51.2: Yin in the second place in the middle of the Zhen trigram and as the bottom line of an inner Gen Mountain trigram. **"Thunderbolts. Danger. He relinquishes his treasures and flees to the high hills (to escape). Do not pursue what is lost. In seven days you will retrieve it."** The Zhen thunderstorm is dangerous. He is worried so much that he abandons his valuables and runs to safety by fleeing to the high hills (Gen trigram) to escape the danger. The Gen Accumulation trigram also stands for accumulated treasure and in this line he leaves his possessions where they are. He doesn't have to pursue whatever he left behind because it will be regained in seven days, meaning that after the emergency everything will return to normal so he can come back and reclaim it. Seven days refers to a cycle or period of time rather than seven days. In a hexagram of six lines sometimes each line represents a day and "after a week" represents the next subsequent line so it basically means after the emergency and its aftermath subside. The thunderstorm, thunderbolts or lightning strikes are the manifestation of the Zhen trigram while the goods he accumulated and hill he runs to are a reflection of the Gen Mountain trigram. Maybe a man left the house due to an argument and just had to get away from it all to clear the air and let things calm down.

51.3: Yin in the third place at the top of the Zhen trigram, as the middle line of an inner Gen trigram, and as the bottom line of an inner Kan trigram. **"Terrifying (violent crashing) thunderbolts [frightening booming thunder]. Shocked into moving [excited into taking action]. No trouble."** This is the top line of the Zhen Thunder trigram so there are violent crashing thunderbolts in a tremendous thunderstorm that represents a very dangerous and terrifying situation which makes one distraught. We know the situation is dangerous because the line bears the influence of the Kan Danger trigram and the top line of the Zhen trigram is destructive as well. The fright is so great that the individual is spurred into taking certain protective actions, which is also a reflection of the Zhen trigram's influence toward movement. In the opposite hexagram, line 52.3 shows that an individual strains himself to keep from moving. The Zhen trigram basically represents a natural stimulus to action so if you are moved to act during danger this is good rather than a mistake. Hence, "Violent crashing thunderbolts. If shocked into moving (excited into action) no fault." The thunder comes in a terrifying manner making one distraught, but there is no destruction in the end due to the influence of the middle line of the Gen Keeping Still trigram holding things together. You might think of this line as an argument between husband and wife that turns physical with dishes thrown everywhere, or it is just violently loud, but it is resolved in the end.

51.4: Yang in the fourth position at the bottom of the upper Zhen trigram.

This is also the middle line of an inner Kan Water trigram and top line of an inner Gen trigram. **"Thunderstorm followed by mud."** The thunder is the Zhen trigram whereas the mud is the Kan Water-Abyss trigram. A thunderstorm followed by mud means the storm left a big mess making it difficult to clean up the situation afterwards. Mud is a dirty aftereffect that also makes it difficult to move, which is a reflection of the inner Gen Mountain trigram. The line basically is saying that after the thunderstorm the individual is surrounded by unfortunate messy circumstances (mud). This is like an argument between husband and wife that leaves messy consequences that are hard to clean up.

51.5: Yin at the fifth position of the hexagram in the middle of the upper Zhen trigram. This is also the top line of an inner Kan trigram. There are two ways to translate this line: **"Thunder comes and goes dangerously [thunderbolts are flying here and there all around alarmingly]. There is no loss. Tasks must still be performed (things must still be done)."** The line reflects the presence of the Zhen Thunder trigram and Kan Danger trigram. Danger exists all around but one must still perform their duties properly. This fifth line is the lord of the hexagram so it should show a perfected from of its overall message. The basic idea is that during a thunderstorm – an emergency or time of alarm – there is danger but you must still attend to affairs properly. Therefore an individual must come and go amidst the thunder, despite the peril, because tasks still need to be performed since there are things to do yet. Thus he does not let the situation rattle him so that he incurs loss but continues doing everything that needs to be done. In the reverse hexagram line 52.5, for instance, an individual controls their talking despite the presence of impulsive energy. In this line things still need to be done and ordinary affairs need to be completed properly. This is the meaning of the hexagram in general that also appears in the Judgment, namely that the shock may terrify for a hundred miles but you should not let any wine spill from the sacrificial cup or ladle. You must keep concentrating on doing what needs to be done despite the temporary alarm. This is like fighting between husband and wife and yet even though there is tension you still must continue with household tasks and duties for life must go on.

51.6: Yin at the sixth place at the top of the upper Zhen Thunder trigram that completes the Thunder hexagram. **"The thunderbolts are so menacing. He looks around him with trembling apprehension [terror, panic]. An expedition [launching a new venture] is inauspicious. The thunderbolts strike a neighbor, not himself. No trouble. In a marriage there is criticism."** The dangerous situation (Zhen trigram) is so menacing and devastating that he looks around himself with trembling apprehension, even panic or terror. To start moving forward on a new venture at this time (campaigning) is just the wrong time to be starting anything. The danger hits one's neighbor but you escape harm. The "neighbor" may symbolize the wife who experienced something unpleasant while the husband escaped harm (perhaps the problem was his fault so he better not start something new for awhile) and he has to fearfully listen to her complaints, which were the storm. In this interpretation there are unpleasant words and criticism between spouses about the situation because perhaps one of you should be criticized for causing this mess. Since line 52.6 is the opposite of this one and features eminent stilling or wordlessness, it makes sense that this line shows some bickering and criticism such as apportionment of blame. Typically there is one line of the six in a hexagram that reveals the true story line, and this one mentions a couple suggesting that it is indeed about a husband and wife. If we take this as the meaning then in one way the entire hexagram can be viewed as the story of arguments between husband and wife.

In terms of the composition of the hexagram and how it is reflected in this line, there is a Zhen trigram beneath a Zhen trigram and so in this line there are thunderbolts and trouble that cause marital discord.

HEXAGRAM 52

Gen – Mountain, Keeping Still, Stillness, Accumulation

Lower Trigram: Gen (Mountain) – keeping still, stopping
Upper Trigram: Gen (Mountain) – keeping still, stopping

The Judgment: Keeping Still. He keeps his back still (meditation) so that he no longer feels (forgets the feeling of) his body. He goes into his courtyard and lets go of thoughts about his self. There is no trouble.

The image of mountains in this hexagram represent stillness and detaching one's mind from various problems or impulses that arise in life. This hexagram is very similar to hexagram 31 where a man gives in to sexual desire. However, in this case *you resist sexual desire (by remaining motionless like a strong mountain)* despite the fact that it seems to be gnawing at you or cutting up (cleaving) your body, which means it is tormenting you. The man resists sexual desire through the discipline of *trying to forget/ignore his physical feelings and by cultivating a mentally empty state of eminent stilling so that the fire of lust does not grab him*. The Judgment teaches us that an individual can practice meditation to forget their body and empty their thoughts so that their mental troubles decline and in the overall hexagram the focus is similarly on emptying out so that you can refrain from sexual urges. Each line in the hexagram represents a greater degree of stilling than in the previous line. Following a typical *Yijing* pattern, the intensity of restraint starts at the feet, which symbolize the lowest degree of restraint, and it increases as the lines ascend to the head. In the first line you do not move your feet to avoid getting into trouble, which equates with resisting sexual desire, and are reminded to retain this determination. In the second line you do not move (to initiate sexual activity) even though you feel the torment of sexual desire in your body that afflicts you like experiencing the pain of having your flesh cut apart. In the third line you strongly want to engage in sexual activity but successfully refrain even though the discipline of restraint strains your will. In the fourth line you do not move your body and thereby avoid sexual activity by keeping still and averting trouble. In the fifth line, which represents the ideal representation of the hexagram's message of restraint, you order your speech carefully despite strong impulses and that reserved speech avoids error and regret. The meaning is that sexual impulses are stirring you to act in a certain way but you transcend them. You resist their negative pull and control yourself through discipline to act in an elevated manner despite the impulses and desires impelling you. In the sixth line we have mention of the highest form of stilling, which refers to meditation, that enables you to deal with sexual desire. The Judgment also speaks of meditation as a solution to the problem of detaching from impulses that might impel you with sexual desire being just one example.

1. Stilling his feet. There is no trouble. It is beneficial to remain determined over the long-run.

2. Stilling the calves of his legs. He does not raise aloft his cut flesh. His mind is not happy.

3. Stilling his waist (midsection). There is straining of the muscles of the spine. Danger. His heart suffocates.

4. Stilling his torso (the trunk of his body). There is no trouble.

5. Stilling his cheeks (jaws). His words are well-ordered. Regret disappears.

6. Eminent stilling. Auspicious.

52.1: Yin at the first line of the hexagram and the bottom of the Gen Mountain trigram, which naturally means the discipline of stilling or no movement. **"Stilling his feet. There is no trouble. It is beneficial to be remain determined over the long-run."** Any sexual desire that arises in the body always starts small and this is symbolized by a stirring in the lowest gradient level of the body which are the feet. "Stilling his feet to remain motionless and not move forward in activity averts trouble." Keeping the feet motionless means not moving despite impulses to act. Not moving your feet therefore means not giving into the first inklings of sexual desire that accost you. "It is favorable to be permanently determined" means to keep resisting the pull of sexual desire because it does not just arise and disappear immediately but tends to linger and attack people for quite some time.

52.2: Yin at the second line of the hexagram as the strong middle line of a Gen trigram and as the first line of an inner Kan trigram. **"Keeping his calves motionless. He does not raise aloft his cut flesh (to reduce the discomfort). His mind is not happy (because he is suffering in pain and discomfort)."** Sometimes you have to restrain yourself from acting even if it causes you discomfort such as when you are refraining from giving into sexual desire. This individual is being burned by pain yet cannot change his position to relieve himself of the hurting. Thus he is not happy or at ease. His disciplined restraint is a manifestation of the Gen Keeping Still trigram while his unease and distress is the influence of the Kan trigram.

52.3: Yang at the third line of the hexagram, the top line of the Gen trigram, middle line of an inner Kan trigram, and beginning line of an inner Zhen Thunder trigram. **"He keeps his waist still [keeps a check on the loins]. There is straining of the muscles of the spine. Danger. His heart suffocates."** This level of restraint is higher than that required in the third line which simply caused discomfort. Now you are suffering great internal turmoil from sexual desire. In this case resisting sexual impulses is requiring even more discipline since sexual desire has reached the hips/loins which are being kept still even though lust is prevalent. The strength of the desire explains why the spine is affected (it is "cleaved open" because desire pulls him forward while restraint pulls him back) and the heart feels suffocated ("the heart is smoked") due to the forced abstinence to resist the driving impulses. In this line the disciplined restraint is a manifestation of the Gen Keep Still trigram, the *extremely strong* sexual desire is a manifestation of the Kan trigram and Zhen trigram since it wants to make the man move, and danger also arises due to the presence of the Kan trigram.

52.4: Yin at the fourth position at the bottom of the upper Gen trigram. It is also the middle line of an inner Zhen trigram and top line of an inner Kan trigram. **"Stilling his torso [the trunk of his body]. There is no trouble."** This is a yin line at the bottom of the Gen Keeping Still trigram so it represents non-movement despite the influence of the Zhen trigram. Hence, he "stills his torso." He maintains his composure and does not act on the sexual impulses afflicting him. If you put the lust of sexual desire aside (stilling the torso) and can ignore the impulsive feelings then there will be no trouble, meaning that you will avoid sexual activity including self-gratification. There is no trouble in staying chaste with celibacy and refraining from sexual activity because this is the proper thing to do.

52.5: Yin at the fifth line of the hexagram, the middle line of the upper Gen trigram, and the top line of an inner Zhen trigram. **"Stilling his cheeks (jaws). His words are well-ordered. Regret disappears."** The fifth line of the hexagram usually presents a perfected form of its overall message and in this case it talks about being careful with one's speech. However, it is really about being careful to restrain your impulses and desires and act in a more elevated manner instead of letting animal desires control you. Talking sparingly and orderly means to control oneself rather than just give into lower impulses. A man trains to watch his words carefully and speak in a measured, controlled and elevated fashion because he wants to rise above his animal nature and enter the realm of majestic, consummate conduct. Consequently his speech is in proper order; he doesn't just say whatever he wants but controls his impulses and elevates his word play. Similarly, this means that he carefully restrains (Gen trigram) his sexual impulses and desires (Zhen trigram) while channeling his energies in a more elevated fashion than sexual release. "The causes for regret disappear" or "occasions for repentance will disappear" because being careful in avoiding impulsive behavior avoids offending others and doesn't create a situation where you get into trouble. You only have to do this for a short while before the impulses will pass. Careless talking represents the Zhen trigram while speaking carefully (controlling one's impulses and channeling them in a higher fashion) represents the Gen trigram. This is the message being transmitted by the hexagram which provides us with a method for accomplishing this in the Judgment. The Judgment states, "He keeps his back still (meditation) so that he no longer feels (forgets the feeling of) his body. He goes into his courtyard and lets go of thoughts about his self. There is no trouble."

52.6: Yang the top of the hexagram and top of the Gen Keeping Still trigram. One of the many meanings it symbolizes is resting and meditation. The highest form of keeping still is inner tranquility. **"Eminent stilling. Auspicious."** "Eminent" means the presence of a consummate positive quality. *Here "eminent stilling" represents inner mental peace instead of just physical non-movement.* True inner tranquility is often compared to the majesty, dignity and nobility of a mountain because a mountain is known for stillness and has deep, thick roots that make it unshakable.

In terms of the hexagram's construction and how it is reflected in this line, there are two Gen Keeping Still trigrams on top of each other which comes through as "eminent stilling" instead of just "stilling" or "stilling, stilling."

HEXAGRAM 53

Jian - Gradual Development, Progressive Advancement, Step-by-Step Growth, Gradual Progress in Life

Lower Trigram: Gen (Mountain) – stopping, boulder, land
Upper Trigram: Xun (Wind) – trees, advancing, pregnancy, feathers

The Judgment: Gradual Development. A maiden marries. It is beneficial to continue onwards.

Using the image of a wild goose that gradually migrates from the water to a hilltop, and the challenges of a married couple to conceive a child, this hexagram is about gradual progress in a person's life as they grow beyond being a child and gradually pass through the common trials of life as they develop into adulthood. When you are young it is common to be involved in foolish, dangerous things before you grow up and start getting serious about wanting to advance yourself. Thus the first line is about a young child who unthinkingly does dangerous things such as swim in deep waters. A subsequent stage of development is to leave those foolish, dangerous activities behind but then devote yourself – as young adults do – to a different type of oblivious play and fun such as eating and drinking happily, which in the second line is symbolized by a goose eating and drinking happily. This might even represent a marriage. Finally you grow enough to enter the realm of maturity, and here life involves real troubles and dangers you must face yourself because you are not a child any longer and no one is protecting you. You must protect yourself. This is symbolized in the third line by a goose that advances onto the land, a man who is called to war, and a woman who experiences pregnancy but loses the baby. Therefore you realize that you must protect yourself to produce security in life, and in the fourth line a goose accordingly seeks a safe place to roost. Finally you advance to a stage of progress in the fifth line symbolized by a goose standing on the top of a hill, which represents life accomplishment, and by a woman who finally gets pregnant after much unsuccessful effort which is her major accomplishment. Lastly, in the sixth line you exemplify an honorable, respected elder who reaches the pinnacle of success and becomes a model for society.

1. The wild goose advances to the shore. Dangerous for a young son. There are words spoken. No trouble.

2. The wild goose advances onto some boulders. Eating and drinking and honking happily. Auspicious.

3. The wild goose advances to the land. A husband sets forth on a campaign (marches to war) but does not return. The wife is left pregnant but does not give birth. Ominous. It is beneficial to defend yourself against bandits.

4. The wild goose advances to the trees, and now finding a (suitable) place to roost. There is no trouble.

5. The wild goose advances onto a mound (the top of a hill). For three years the woman cannot get pregnant but in the end nothing prevents it. Auspicious.

6. The wild goose advances to the high ground. Its feathers can be used for a (ceremonial) headdress. Auspicious.

53.1: Yin at the first line of the hexagram, at the bottom of a Gen Mountain trigram. **"The wild goose advances to the bank. The young son experiences danger. There is a lot of talk [gossip, scolding, criticism]. No trouble happened."** It could be that "a wild goose advances to the shore" to reach the protection of the river bank. It might have just finished swimming around on its own oblivious to any problems, or there were no problems and it was simply tired, or it was escaping danger and so on. The future hexagram line 37.1 says that a house should be gated for protection, and here a child's life must be protected because children are ignorant and foolish. Thus, when it says that a young son is experiencing danger he was probably left to run around untended doing whatever he wants such as swimming in a river (which is dangerous for a young child) like the solitary goose that has no supervision or protection. This leads to danger. Because this is the Gen Keeping Still trigram the young boy should not be free to swim around like an independent goose but must be watched carefully to avoid getting into danger. "There is a lot of talk" means there is a lot of scolding about some danger the child got into (due to lack of supervision) as well as disciplinary criticism of the child. Despite the peril there is no blame because no drowning or accident occurred - just criticism. It is proper to correct a young child to prevent dangerous activity in the future because this hexagram is about safely advancing in life from childhood to adulthood. Basically, this lowest and weakest line of the hexagram represents a young child (the status of a beginner) who will gradually grow into a position of eminence but he starts out small and must be protected from doing dangerous things.

53.2: Yin at the second line of the hexagram in the middle of the Gen Mountain trigram, and as the bottom line of an inner Kan Water trigram. **"The wild goose advances onto an outcropping of boulders. Eating and drinking and honking happily. Auspicious."** Here the goose climbs out of the river (Kan trigram) onto some boulders (Gen trigram) in the river, which means escaping from the dangerous currents of life because it is happy and well provided for. Once on the rocks the goose celebrates by eating and drinking (Kan trigram) happily. This is like young children or young adults who play fully without knowing about any of the dangers or hardships of life because they don't have to face its currents as adults must do. To stop swimming and come out of the water (the Kan Water-Danger trigram) is due to the influence of the middle line of the Gen Mountain trigram that represents stillness and land. The middle line of a trigram usually demonstrates its natural characteristics strongest whereas the top line usually shows a tinge of destruction since it is the extreme point of the trigram where it starts changing into another.

53.3: Yang at the third line of the hexagram at the top of a Gen Mountain trigram, as the middle line of an inner Kan Danger trigram, and as the bottom line of an inner Li trigram. **"The wild goose advances across the land. A husband goes forth on a campaign but does not return. The wife is left pregnant but does not give birth. Ominous. It is beneficial to defend yourself against bandits."** Future hexagram line 20.3 talks about observing the ups and downs of one's own life. There are various difficulties or dangers in life that appear in this line that are a manifestation of the middle line of the Kan Danger trigram. The wild goose advances across the land, perhaps to a plateau or hill since the Gen Mountain trigram is present. For geese it is dangerous to live too far away from water since those places are open to attack and have no food. Advancing across the land represents traveling through life. Following this are three scenarios that indicate the dangers of loss and separation in life. A husband marches off to war but does not return is a situation of becoming separated from the wife. He is probably killed. A pregnant wife who does give birth is becoming separated from her unborn child, and also represents death. Perhaps she could not get enough nourishment to feed the growing child because the next sentence says it is beneficial to drive away bandits, robbers or plunderers (fighting them is the Li trigram) who try to steal your food and possessions, which is another type of loss or separation. These are examples of the sufferings of life and cases where people experience separation, loss, death, the hardship of obtaining food and the need to protect themselves. These are all adult concerns of the dangers of life (Kan trigram) whereas in the previous two lines we saw the happy activities and unconcerned mindset of children. One is warned in this line to bolster their defenses against marauders and robbers who would rob you of your possessions. This is the stage of adulthood where you can no longer be oblivious to the dangers of life.

53.4: Yin at the fourth line of the hexagram as the first line of the upper Xun Wood-Wind trigram, the middle line of an inner Li trigram and top line of an inner Kan trigram. **"The wild goose advances to the trees and now finds a (suitable) place to roost. There is no trouble."** Wild and domestic geese do not roost sleeping in trees because their bodies are too large. However, the goose advances to the trees (Xun Wood trigram) and finds a suitable place to roost (Li trigram) among them. This represents finding a suitable place away from danger where one can find peace in life and rest. There is safety since the Li (Fire) and Kan (Water) trigrams cancel each other with the Li trigram being stronger. The idea of this line is to make further progress in life and move to a new safer and settled stage of existence beyond that of the bottom trigram.

53.5: Yang at the fifth line of the hexagram as the middle line of the upper Xun Wood-Wind trigram and top line of an inner Li trigram. **"The wild goose advances onto a mound. For three years the woman cannot get pregnant. In the end nothing prevents it. Auspicious."** The fifth line of a hexagram usually shows a perfected form of its message or meaning. Here a wild goose finally leaves all the dangers and troubles behind and advances onto a mound or hill that is elevated, which means a man finally achieves something in life such as accumulating wealth or renown. The journey to this elevation is similar to a woman finally getting pregnant after trying for so many years, which is also achieving something significant (a baby). These are analogies for life using the story of a goose advancing from water onto land until it finally attains elevation, and the story of a woman struggling to get pregnant who eventually succeeds. Having passed through so many dangers and troubles one finally starts to taste success and the beauties of life. The advancing to the mound represents the Xun Movement trigram while the celebration of getting pregnant represents the Li trigram.

53.6: Yang at the sixth line as the top of the Xun Wood-Wind trigram completing the hexagram, and representing it. **"The wild goose advances to the high ground [a hill, the summit, the heights]. Its feathers can be used for a (ceremonial) headdress. Auspicious."** The top line of this hexagram represents the extreme of good fortune in life, like a tree that has grown strong and tall, which you achieve after all your life struggles. The gradual advance in step-by-step progress has reached its peak – the summit or heights that represent the pinnacle of success in life. The goose advancing to high ground symbolizes a man who rises to achieve something great in life by making something out of himself. Now everybody accords him status because the goose's feathers are used in a ceremonial headdress in some ancient dances. He receives respect for his life after a long progression of trials. The Judgment says that a woman marries (so that the cycle of life continues) and should experience the normal progression of life, which is symbolized in this hexagram, and now we have reached the peak of attainment.

In terms of the construction of the hexagram and how it is reflected in this line there is a Gen Mountain trigram beneath a Xun Wind trigram, and so the sentences start off with reaching a high ground (Gen trigram) where the feathers (Xun Wind trigram) are used for a headdress.

HEXAGRAM 54

Gui Mei - Marrying Maiden

Lower Trigram: Dui (Joy) – marriage, concubine, younger sister,
Upper Trigram: Zhen (Thunder) – motion, agitation, stabbing

The Judgment: The Marriageable Maiden. Marching to war (to set forth on an undertaking) brings misfortune. There is nothing for which this is beneficial.

On the surface this hexagram seems to be about marriageable girls and the dangers of mismatched marriages. However, like hexagram 17 it is actually about the tale of Ji Chang, Duke of the West, who later became known as King Wen. King Wen is credited with creating the sixty-four hexagrams, their sequence and the Judgments of the *Yijing* while imprisoned by King Di Xin of the Shang dynasty. His second son later became King Wu of Zhou, who overthrew the Shang dynasty by defeating the Shang army at its capital, and thus became the first king of the Zhou dynasty. King Wen's son, King Wu, is credited for creating the line statements of the *Yijing*. In this hexagram the Shang ruler King Zhou Di Xin gave his daughter in marriage to Ji Chang (King Wen) as his principal wife. When she produced no offspring the Lady of Shu - a secondary wife - was raised to the rank of principal wife. She became the mother of King Wu (the Duke of Zhou). In the first line a maiden is given in marriage with a younger sister; these two include the princess daughter of Shang King Di Xin and the secondary wife, the Lady of Shen. In the second line a blind man becomes able to see but retains his perseverance, which refers to the imprisonment of King Wen and his determination to topple the Shang dynasty. In the third line a maiden with her maid go to marry but then the maid is replaced by her sister, which is the story that the princess daughter of King Di Xin was sent back to her home to return with her "younger sister," the Lady of Shen, who was to become the secondary wife. In the fourth line a maiden does not marry on the approved auspicious date so must marry later on a different auspicious date. In the fifth line the king's daughter is given in marriage but she is not as splendid a bride as the secondary wife, the Lady of Shen. In the sixth line the woman holds up a basket without any fruit in it, symbolizing that she will not be able to give birth to children (which correctly summarizes the story of the princess of Shang), and the husband King Wen slaughters a sheep without any blood, which also symbolizes the inability to produce an heir. The Judgment basically warns not to get married if the match is not beneficial.

1. A maiden is given in marriage along with a younger sister. The lame becomes able to walk. Marching to war (a military campaign) is auspicious.

2. The blind man becomes able to see (is cured). It is beneficial for a person in the dark to stay determined.

3. A maiden is given in marriage along with a concubine but goes back and returns with her younger sister.

4. The marrying maiden postpones the marriage date (stays unwed beyond the appointed time). She will be late in marrying but the time will come.

5. The sovereign Di Yi gives his daughter in marriage. The embroidered sleeves of the princess's garments are not as splendid as those of her younger sister's sleeves. The moon is almost full. Auspicious.

6. A woman holds up a basket, but there is no fruit in it. A man stabs a sheep, but no blood flows from it. There is nothing beneficial.

54.1: Yang at the bottom line of the hexagram and Dui Young Woman trigram. **"A maiden is given in marriage along with a younger sister. The lame becomes able to walk (is cured). Marching to war is auspicious."** In ancient China it was common for high officials to marry two sisters plus one of their nieces. A younger sister who follows her elder sister into a marriage becomes a junior wife. Not being a full wife is a deficiency like lameness, so she is likened to a lame person who is able to walk but not as effectively as others. She has the duties of a wife but not the status of a wife and because she has no power she cannot have a direct influence on how the household is run. Though in an inferior status ("lame") nevertheless she is able to get by and move forward. Here the situation probably refers to the story of Ji Chang (King Wen) from hexagram 17 who married a daughter of King Di Xin and a second wife or "younger sister" from Shen, who is probably Taisi. This younger sister or subordinate secondary wife was probably the mother of the eventual King Wu who launched a war against Di Xin to topple the Shang dynasty. That eventual military expedition is even mentioned in this line. Hence this fits the story line of a lame individual who has a reversal of fortunes and becomes able to walk. A lame man is cured (becomes able to walk) means his limitations have been removed, which would the case with Taisi's status if she became the primary wife or her son eventually became King Wu.

54.2: Yang at the second line in the middle of the Dui trigram and the second line of an inner Li trigram. **"The blind man becomes able to see. It is beneficial for a person in the dark to stay determined."** Many interpretations would say that the recluse in this line (man in the dark) stands for an unmarried individual, and he should stay unmarried because once a blind man can see (Li trigram) the character of a potential wife (Dui trigram) he can decide on whether to marry or not, and should refrain from a mismatch by remaining single (a person in the dark or solitary individual). Another interpretation is that because he cannot see what lies ahead he should not marry. However, once again this line probably refers to the story of King Wen from hexagram 17. King Wen was imprisoned by King Di Xin whereupon he then became the *solitary* "man in the dark" (blind man), and after he was released ("a blind man becomes able to see") he began plotting the overthrow of the Shang dynasty. This line retells of his determination to topple the Shang state through the phrase "a person in the dark (the prisoner Ji Chang) stays determined."

54.3: Yin at the third line, at the top of the Dui trigram, as the middle line of an inner Li trigram and bottom line of an inner Kan trigram. **"A maiden is given in marriage along with a concubine, but goes back and returns together with her younger sister."** There are multiple girls in this line because the line is yin and the Dui and Kan trigrams represent femininity. At first a marriage match is made with a maiden and her maid (a "lady in waiting" who will become a concubine), and then the concubine is replaced by the younger sister, which is a disguised way of indicating the secondary wife or Lady of Shen. This is the top line of the Dui Joy trigram so there is marriage that represents the Li Celebration trigram as well, but there is a tinge of not-quite-rightness due to the presence of the Kan trigram (which accounts for the turning back and then returning). Basically the daughter of King Di Xin was sent back to her home to return with her younger sister, the Lady of Shen, who was eventually to become the secondary wife.

54.4: Yang at the fourth line at the bottom of the upper Zhen Thunder trigram, the middle of an inner Kan trigram and top line of an inner Li trigram. **"The marrying maiden postpones the marriage date (stays unwed beyond the appointed time). She will be late (tardy) in marrying but the time will come."** The maiden should be marrying because of the presence of the Li Celebration trigram, but the Kan Danger trigram predominates so she misses the marriage date (Zhen Thunder trigram) because of some type of delay. Basically, the girl skips or misses the auspicious time selected for the marriage so has to wait for another auspicious time for the wedding to take place.

54.5: Yin at the fifth line, which is the ruler of the hexagram, at the middle of the upper Zhen Thunder trigram and top of an inner Kan trigram. "**The sovereign Di Yi (the last Shang king Di Xin) gives his daughter in marriage. The embroidered sleeves of the princess's garments were inferior to those of her younger sister. The moon is almost full. Auspicious.**" The fifth line of a hexagram often shows individuals of high status, and in this case we have images of a king and his daughter, namely King Di Xin and his daughter. In the fifth line we also often see a perfected form of the message of the hexagram, and in this line we see the story of a royal bride being upstaged by her younger sister. The normal interpretation would be that even if you marry royalty nothing is perfect and there is always someone better. This is why the bride is symbolized by an "almost full moon." However, what this is actually saying is that the King's daughter is inferior to her "younger sister," the Lady of Shen Taisi. Di Xin's princess daughter was not able to produce an heir but Taisi was. According to tradition, after a certain period of time remaining barren the secondary wife became the primary wife so Taisi replaced the princess as the primary wife. This is why the sentences refer to "the moon is almost full," which means that the time is almost up for the princess to produce an heir before the princess loses her position as the primary wife. In this line the pomp and ceremony of the marriage is a representation of the Zhen Thunder trigram while the moon appears due to the presence of the Kan trigram.

54.6: Yin at the sixth line, completing the hexagram, at the top of the upper Zhen trigram. "**The woman holds a basket empty of fruit [nothing is in it]. The man stabs a sheep but no blood flows. There is nothing beneficial.**" Let's interpret this line without reference to the Ji Chang King Wen story and then turn to it afterwards. The image of this line, which is at the top destructive line of a Zen Thunder trigram, is that of a fruitless marriage from the standpoint of both parties. The fruit basket was supposed to be a gift for father-in-law and mother-in-law, but the basket was empty of fruit symbolizing there is no fertility. There will be no pregnancy because the wife cannot conceive. In actual fact, the Shang princess who married King Wen was unable to conceive and was replaced by a secondary wife. A sheep is normally sacrificed for the ancestors at Chinese weddings and its meat used in the feast. However, it can also be used in sacrifices such as asking for an heir, which King Wen would certainly do when his wife could not conceive. Here the man stabs a sheep (which symbolizes impregnation) but no blood flows, which represents the inability to produce an heir. In this marriage there is nothing that symbolizes good fortune or fruition, which at the top line of the hexagram represents the extreme of mismatched conditions for both parties. The bride is barren (cannot conceive) and the groom has no seed (is infertile).

In terms of the construction of the hexagram and how it is reflected in this line there is a Dui trigram beneath a Zhen trigram, so the image includes a woman holding a fruit basket (Dui trigram) while the man sacrifices (Zhen trigram) a sheep.

HEXAGRAM 55

Feng – Affluence, Abundance, Seeking Prosperity

Lower Trigram: Li (Fire) – lord, Big Dipper, noontime
Upper Trigram: Zhen (Thunder) – motion, agitation, fate change

The Judgment: Affluence. Success. The king approaches you. Do not worry (have no fears). It is appropriate for the middle of the day.

This is a hexagram about seeking prosperity and abundance, and it reminds us that prosperity and affluence are part of your fortune where the timing is determined by Heaven. Prosperity and abundance are matters of fate so they cannot appear in someone's life until the fate unlocks. That is why this hexagram doesn't talk very much about how to achieve prosperity but only about how it is blocked by being screened off or obstructed … until the time is right *if it is your fated fortune to achieve it*. Hence the Judgment says that the king approaches you in the middle of the day that represents good fortune coming when the time is appropriate (which is noontime when the sun is brightest). In the first line an individual meets someone of similar rank who helps him achieve temporary prosperity. In the second line his prosperity is blocked and therefore he isn't accepted by others due to being poor until they approve of his personality. In the third line the intensity of factors obstructing his prosperity increases and he breaks his arm trying to free himself from this situation. In the fourth line this struggling effort has done him some good because the situation improves a bit and he meets the helpful person of the first line. In the fifth line his good fortune can now finally appear because his fate has changed for the better. The line might even be announcing a coming baby. The last line is a reminder that if you attain the prosperity you seek but have no one to share it with then you will be lonely, which essentially says that there is no such thing as prosperity and abundance without relationships.

1. He meets his noble counterpart. Though it be only for ten days it will (be a week) without harm. Going forward there will be elevation (he will rise).

2. The curtains are so abundant (shielding the sun so that you are able to be) that at midday he can see the Big Dipper. Going forward will be met with mistrust and harm. Through sincerity you can inspire approval. Auspicious.

3. The screens are so abundant (the obscurity is so great) that mid-day appears as darkness. He breaks his right arm. No blame.

4. The curtains are so abundant (shielding the sun so that you are able to be) that at midday he can see the Big Dipper. He meets with the ruler of Yi. Auspicious.

5. There comes a pattern (the fortune changes). There is celebration and praise. Auspicious.

6. Abundant his rooms. Screened is his house. He peers through the doors (peeks into the rooms) but is lonely because there is no one. For three years he sees no one. Ominous.

55.1: Yang at the first line of the hexagram that is the bottom of the Li Elegance trigram. **"He meets his noble counterpart. Though it be only for ten days they can stay together without harm. In going forward there will thereafter be elevation [progress]."** Translating this line is problematical. There is an opportunity to meet a noble counterpart like King Wu meeting an ally, but only for a short period of time. He goes forward and seizes the opportunity. He meets another lord who matches with him and starts associating with someone who will help him rise. Opposite hexagram line 59.1 (rescuing requires the strength of a strong horse) and reverse hexagram line 35.1 (progressing but held back) state that you have been held back and need someone with power, wealth and status to help you. Meeting a noble partner that helps you is due to the brilliance of the Li trigram and the yang of the first line. Since this is the bottom line followed by a yin line this good fortune is temporary because it only lasts one cycle. Hence the sentences, "Though it only be for ten days (the ten-day Chinese week of earthly branches) they can be together without harm. Doing so will be rewarding because afterwards going forward there will be elevation." The elevation, which is once again the Li trigram and yang of the line, will come in the form of good fortune such as wealth and affluence because the noble ally gave you ideas and possibly some initial help, but he didn't "burn you" as befits the Li trigram, which is why it was mentioned that "they can be together without harm."

55.2: Yin at the second line of the hexagram that is the middle line of a Li hexagram, and the bottom line of a Xun Wind trigram. **"The curtains are so abundant (shielding the sun so that you are able to be) that the Big Dipper is seen in the middle of the day. Going forward will be met with mistrust [suspicion, doubt] and harm [enmity, disapproval]. Through sincerity you can inspire approval. Auspicious."** Here the thick (or abundant) curtains represent conditions preventing your prosperity from manifesting (being achieved) because the curtain hides or obscures things. Your abilities are hindered so they aren't being recognized or actions are being hindered so they are not producing results. Circumstances stand in your way. They hide, obscure or prevent your good fortune so completely that it is like shielding the sun to produce darkness in the middle of the day and it is so dark that you can even see the Big Dipper. If you try to do anything during such a non-prosperous state (when you are poor) you will be looked down upon by others and treated with disdain, enmity and ill-will. If you try to join the lord's group you will be treated with suspicion as a newcomer until you can prove yourself. By displaying sincerity towards others you will eventually gain their trust so good fortune comes from being friendly. Your prosperity here is the strong middle line of the Li Brilliance trigram but it is obscured or damaged by the Xun Penetrating Wind trigram and the fact that this is an unfortunate yin line. The good fortune and elevation from meeting with your lord and counterpart in the previous line only lasted one cycle so in this line you meet with deficiency since time ran out.

55.3: Yang in the third place of the hexagram that is the top of the Li Fire trigram, the middle line of an inner Xun trigram and bottom line of an inner Dui trigram. **"The screens are so abundant [obscurity is so great] that mid-day appears as darkness. He breaks his right arm. No blame."** The screens are so thick in obstructing (obscuring) his prosperity that it is like darkness at mid-day, which is an eclipse of the sun that blocks its light, so you could reword the first sentence as, **"Prosperity is screened so thickly that it is like mid-day brightness appearing as darkness."** Despite these adverse circumstances, which constitute a *more intense, stronger set* of obstructions than those in the previous second line, the next line is yang. With great effort he struggles to get out of this terrible situation and is working so hard that he breaks his right arm. It is proper behavior to act this way so there is no blame. Now that you will next move into the upper trigram your good fortune can arise.

55.4: Yang at the fourth line, at beginning of the upper Zhen Thunder trigram, in the center of an inner Dui Joy trigram, and as the top line of an inner Xun Wind trigram. **"(There is obstructive screening due to) abundant curtains so thick that at midday he can see the Big Dipper.**

He meets with the Yi ruler. Auspicious." The curtains (obstructions) obscuring his good fortune are so thick that it is like the midday sun dimming and the sky becoming so dark that you can see stars in the sky (the Big Dipper). The second line was like this while the third line was total darkness, but now it is getting lighter again (since you moved to the upper trigram) so the fortune is changing for the better. Hence, he fortuitously meets a lord who is of like mind and an equal counterpart. This might be the same individual in line one or someone different but we cannot tell. Opposite hexagram line 59.4 also says that a dispersion leads to an accumulation but people do not expect this, so at this time the man finally meets someone who can help him. Future hexagram line 36.4 talks about a lord finally having a meeting of minds with one of his ignored officials. Thus he is encountering circumstances that will help him succeed so he meets the lord of similar mindset to achieve progress. The situation is changing for the better and the screening/obstruction of his prosperity still exists but is diminishing. The top destructive line of an inner Xun trigram causes the destruction/hampering of prosperity, and the fact that he meets a lord of the state of Yi (eastern barbarians) who was kind to the shepherd brothers Hai and Heng (see 34.5) is a way of saying that his fortune is becoming better. Wang Hai was an ancestor of the Shang ruling house and was the leader of the nomadic Zi clan who led their flocks to pasture in the state of Yi. He is said to be the first domesticator of cattle and sheep in ancient China. His people took handouts from the Yi people whose ruler was very hospitable and generous to Hai and his brother Heng. Hence the meaning of this would be that he met a very generous and hospitable lord who helps him and changes his fortune for the better. Another possible translation is that "He meets with his counterpart (equal) lord," which is less likely, because the word *Yizhu* is employed that could mean a foreign, vulgar, ignorant, calm, mild, level-headed, plain, placid, of like-kind, of equal-rank lord/master, or it could mean the leader of the Yi people. Both translations lead to the same conclusion that the fortune is changing for the better.

55.5: Yin at the fifth line, as the center of the upper Zhen Thunder trigram and as the top of an inner Dui Joy trigram. **"There comes a pattern [the fortune changes]. There is celebration and praise. Auspicious."** The fifth line usually shows an auspicious (perfected) manifestation of the meaning of the hexagram, and in this case prosperity and abundance finally appear. *"A new pattern arises"* means that the fortune changes because a new pattern is like a new life or baby (see 44.5), which one would certainly celebrate. In this case that sudden change to prosperity is due to the influence of the Zhen trigram. In future hexagram line 49.5 a great man institutes dynamic changes that are as broad, strong, clear and distinctive as a tiger's stripes and this accords with the change in fortune. The "new pattern" is one of prosperity and recognition. There is an uplifting of spirits and celebration where the joy is the manifestation of the Dui Joy trigram. Hence there are blessings and rejoicing, congratulations and praise. The Judgment says there will eventually be success in achieving abundance, which is like a king approaching, so have no worries about this because you will eventually achieve it when the time is proper. The time of achievement is represented by noontime since that is when the sun is brightest and highest overhead.

55.6: Yin at the sixth line completing the hexagram and at the top of the Zhen Thunder trigram, so the fortune of prosperity is accomplished but subject to the destructive nature of the Zhen trigram. **"Abundant his rooms. Screened is his house. He peers through the doors [peeks into the rooms] but is lonely because there is no one inside. For three years he sees no one. Ominous."** The many rooms means that there is prosperity in the dwelling; he has become rich so there is abundance in the rooms and his rooms are abundant. However, this individual either screens (cuts) himself off from his family or he simply has no one to enjoy prosperity with. The house is deserted. "He peers through the doors of the prosperous house and peeps into the rooms but he sees no one inside." His family is absent so his wife and children don't share in the blessings with him. Such bad fortune of solitary loneliness is due to the destructive nature of the top line of the Zhen Thunder trigram. I have known many rich people who at the end of their lives said that their greatest fortune was their family and relationships rather than their wealth, and I have read countless autobiographies where tremendously rich people have written that the real wealth of their life has been their friendships and family rather than money or material things.

In terms of the construction of the hexagram and how it appears in his line there is a Li Prosperity trigram beneath a destructive Zhen Thunder trigram, so in this line there is first mention of the many rooms symbolizing prosperity and then mention of the emptiness felt because of the misfortune that there is no one to share it with.

HEXAGRAM 56

Lu – The Wanderer, The Traveler

Lower Trigram: Gen (Mountain) – stopping, camp, accumulated goods
Upper Trigram: Li (Fire) – burning nest, pheasant

The Judgment: Wandering Travel. Small success. Constancy in traveling is auspicious.

This hexagram has an image of a fire on a mountain that travels from place to place, hence it is used to discuss traveling. This hexagram is about events that can happen to you during the wandering of adventure travel. In the first line you either don't start out with enough money or just get preoccupied with trivial, unimportant things and thereby bring misfortune on yourself. In the second line you set up lodgings along the way and are lucky enough to get a good servant to help you. The third line reminds us that misfortune sometimes happens during travel with an example being that you might accidentally burn down your lodgings and lose your servant, thus showing that travel disasters can happen. In the fourth line you stop at another resting place, replenish the goods you lost and buy an axe for protection. In the fifth place you see a pheasant, shoot at it, but lose one arrow. You win some renown for your trip even though not everything went perfect, and because of the trip you are recognized and rewarded by the ruler and gain some ideas of what to do with your life. In the last line you lose your lodging again along with many valuables. This would be the normal interpretation of this hexagram but an alternative interpretation is that it is retelling the history of the ancestors of the Shang dynasty – Wang Hai and his brother Heng – while they pastured their flocks of sheep as guests of the king of Yi.

1. He travels meagerly. This invites disaster onto himself.

2. The traveler approaches a camp (to lodge). He embraces (conceals) his wealth (belongings). He obtains a trustworthy young attendant.

3. The traveler burns down his camp (accidentally through negligence). He loses his young attendant. Persistence (in

carelessness) is dangerous.

4. The traveler stops at a resting place. He obtains goods and an axe. His heart is not happy.

5. He shoots at a pheasant, one arrow misses. In the end, he wins praise and a mandate.

6. A bird's nest is burnt up. The traveler at first laughs but later he weeps and wails. He loses an ox at Yi. Ominous.

56.1: Yin at the first line of the hexagram and Gen Accumulation trigram. There are two ways to translate the first part of this line. **"He travels meagerly [without sufficient money or provisions]. This invites disaster [calamity] onto himself."** To travel meagerly without sufficient funds or provisions is a reflection of the Gen Accumulation trigram since it stands for saved funds, and we find a focus on funding matters in all three lines of the bottom trigram to settle upon this interpretation of the line. Meager funds means a lack of sufficient funds for traveling, like hoboing, and if you travel without having sufficient money you will of course incur difficulties. Movement for this individual should be difficult because the Gen trigram also symbolizes being stationary or keeping still, which makes it difficult to travel. This line probably refers to the story of Wang Hai and his brother Heng who were leaders of the nomadic Zi clan. They were ancestors of the Shang ruling house so they appear frequently in the hexagrams (see 34.5 and 55.4). They fell into trouble because of their poverty-stricken lifestyle that was relieved due to the kindness of the Yi ruler. He treated them like dignitaries and allowed them to shepherd their sheep in his territory but as a result they turned to an intemperate lifestyle that destroyed them, hence they invited calamity onto themselves.

56.2: Yin at the second line of the hexagram, middle line of the Gen Mountain trigram and beginning line of an inner Xun Wind trigram. **"The traveler approaches a camp (for lodging). He embraces/conceals his wealth (belongings). He obtains a trustworthy young attendant."** It makes no difference whether the lodging is a camping spot, inn or other lodging or resting place. The traveler stops for a while in a safe place and gains a servant. Due to the wind element there is travel to a location, but due to the Gen Keeping Still trigram the traveler lodges at an inn or camping site. In order that he isn't robbed he conceals his belongings, which are also a reflection of the Gen Accumulation trigram. Banditry was common in ancient China so he keeps them close by embracing them, which is a Chinese idiom. He obtains a young attendant to run around and do things for him, which reflects the presence of the submissive wind element at the lowest line of its inner trigram. Continuing with the story of Wang Hai and his brother, they were invited into the land of Yi to pasture their flocks and probably gained the assistance of a shepherd boy.

56.3: Yang at the third line of the hexagram that is the top line of the Gen Mountain trigram, middle line of an inner Xun Wind trigram and bottom line of an inner Dui Mouth trigram. **"The traveler (accidentally) burns down his camp (through carelessness). He loses his young attendant. Keeping on this way (of carelessness) is dangerous."** Here there is the destruction of the camp burning down due to negligence since it says that the traveler is responsible. Making a fire was part of any camp and here it goes out of control through negligence leading to loss. This is a typical accident that can happen when traveling where through carelessness your own comfortable situation can end tragically. Its destruction is a reflection of the destructive nature of the Xun wind element. "The traveler burns down his camp (the Gen Mountain trigram). He loses his young attendant (the Xun Wind trigram)." To continue with such careless negligence is dangerous. Hence, "Perseverance in being this way (carelessness or recklessness) is dangerous." Opposite hexagram line 60.3 aptly states, "If one is not moderate-like with cautious restrictions there will be lamentations and sighs," while reverse hexagram line 55.3 states "The obscurity is so great that mid-day appears as darkness and he breaks his right arm." Continuing with the story of Wang Hai and his brother, Hai loses his herds when he dallies with the queen of Yi and then loses his life and the livestock. In effect, he burns down his own lodge. Heng reported his dalliance with the queen to guards who then killed Hai by cutting up his body, and then Heng fled the comfortable life in Yi back to his homeland without the flocks.

56.4: Yang at the fourth line of the hexagram, at the bottom of the upper Li trigram, as the middle line of an inner Dui trigram, and as the top line of an inner Xun Wind trigram. **"The traveler stops at a resting place. He obtains (gets or purchases) valuables and an axe but his heart is not happy [at ease]."** Here the traveler has to replenish the items he lost in the previous line because of the fire. In the *Yijing* an axe usually represents activity or command authority, but he might be purchasing the axe to protect/defend himself because he feels unsafe (not at ease) since it is a weapon. He also is certainly not happy having to spend his funds to purchase these items (because the cost hits you more heavily when you are traveling) so his mind is not at ease. No one wants to spend unbudgeted money during traveling especially when you don't have much money. In this line the purchasing of goods is the yang nature of the line, the goods he purchases represent the Li trigram, and his heart is uneasy because of affliction to the Dui Joy trigram being attacked by the Xun Wind trigram. Continuing with the story of Wang Hai who is now dead, after returning home Heng raises an army (the axe) and returns to Yi to recover the recover the tribe's lost sheep, but when the king forgives him he stays, settles down in Yi because of the enticing lifestyle, and resumes his intemperate lifestyle. Thus he went home, stopped at that resting place and raised an army (axe) but his heart is not at ease.

56.5: Yin at the fifth line of the hexagram this is the center of the upper Li Pheasant trigram and the top line of an inner Dui Mouth trigram. **"He shoots at a pheasant losing one arrow. Eventually he wins praise [renown] and a mandate."** The pheasant represents the Li Brilliance trigram, and shooting at it means that the traveler spent some resources trying to achieve some desired objectives on his trip but wasn't always successful. Shooting at a pheasant means seeking a government office. The fifth line symbolizes a perfected form of the message of the hexagram so it symbolizes his adventure trip in general that cost him some resources, but afterwards it wins him fame, praise and renown from other people. What else does he receive? A mandate or command, which could be an offer from a ruler for an office because his talents are recognized, or just a commendatory decree. A "mandate" can also refer to a personal direction on what to do in his own life because of what he learned during his travels. Reverse hexagram line 55.5 similarly states, "There comes a pattern [the fortune changes]. There is celebration and praise." In the end, he obtains praise due to his travel achievements, expanded his mind due to his travels, perhaps gains recognition and an office, and develops some clear ideas on what to do for his future. In this line the pheasant represents the Li Brilliance-Fire trigram and the praise he receives is the Dui Mouth trigram that is also the mandate. Continuing with the story of Heng (the ancestor of the Shang people), he does not return home with the flocks so the Zi clan installs a new king - Shang Jia Wei who was the son of Wang Hai who was killed. Shang Jia Wei then crosses the river and destroys the Yi kingdom, which is shooting at the pheasant and winning the throne. The line of the Shang kings descends from Shang Jia Wei, *which is the mandate*. This story appears in the *Yijing* in several places, as does the history of the overthrow of the Shang dynasty partly because the author wanted to justify the morality behind the toppling of the Shang state and therefore emphasized the immoral behavior of even the Shang ancestors. The consistent message of the *Yijing* is like a PR campaign for the Zhou dynasty where the message is: "Shang is bad, Zhou is good. Shang is evil, Zhou is virtuous."

56.6: Yang at the sixth line of the hexagram that is the top of a Li Brilliance trigram. This is the end of the hexagram and in this case it talks about traveling in general. **"A bird's nest catches fire. The traveler at first laughs, but later he weeps and wails. He loses an ox at Yi. Ominous."** The bird symbolizes the traveler and the nest his camp. Some translators logically have "A bird disorders its nest," "A bird's nest becomes disordered," or "A bird destroys its nest." Alternatively, to reflect the fact that this is *the top destructive top of the Li Fire trigram*, some translations have "A bird burns its nest" but it is impossible for a bird to do this whereas "A bird's nest burns up" could happen due to a fire as in line three. "The traveler at first laughs, but later he weeps and wails" because his trip has been making him happy but now he is crying since he loses everything due to the burning of the nest/camp and "losing an ox at Yi." Once again, this line probably refers to the story of Wang Hai (an ancestor of the Shang ruling house) who lived a life of ease by traveling to the neighboring land of Yi where he and his brother started pasturing their cattle and sheep. Due to unfortunate involvements with the Yi people Hai lost his life and livestock, which is because he was enjoying himself so much ("the traveler at first laughs") that he burned his own nest through acts of sexual indiscretion with the Yi king's consort that caused his own death ("he weeps and wails"). Later his son Shang Jia Wei went to Yi, destroyed the kingdom, and became the ancestor of the kings of the Shang dynasty. Therefore the line reminds us of the history, "He lost an ox in Yi. Ominous," which could also refer to the original death of Wang Hai, the loss of his flocks, and everything that it led to producing. Normally you would take this line as a warning of undertaking travel that is fun until through carelessness you lose everything but the alternative interpretation shows that it could simply be retelling history.

In terms of the composition of the hexagram and how it is reflected in the sentences of this line there is a Gen Mountain trigram beneath a Li Celebration trigram, so the line first mentions a nest (Gen Stillness-Stopping trigram) and next laughter (Li trigram) that turns into weeping and loss as in military warfare (Li trigram).

HEXAGRAM 57

Xun – Wind, Gentle Influence, Penetrating Influence

Lower Trigram: Xun (Wind) – incessant moving, penetrating, divining
Upper Trigram: Xun (Wind) – pregnancy, penetrating, axe

The Judgment: Gentle Influence. Success through what is small. It is beneficial to have a destination (goals). It is beneficial to meet with a great man.

This is a doubled hexagram about the wind element that sometimes represents our vitality, life force or Qi energy. The lower trigram represents the wind element as thinking and the upper trigram represents the wind element as doing, so "wind following wind" is an image of compliance where actions follow thoughts. As with all the doubled hexagrams, the last line represents a state of excess where the element suffers some type of destruction because the hexagram is completed and will transform into some new state - some new hexagram. Success in this hexagram is attained through thinking, which is the "what is small" (wind element) mentioned in the Judgment. The Judgment advises you to talk with a great man (of many accomplishments) about understanding the situation you are in and deciding what to do. Thinking enables people to successfully accomplish their undertakings, which the *Yijing* refers to as "going somewhere" or "arriving at a destination." In the first line the mental activity of going back and forth thinking about some topic is symbolized by soldiers who must advance and retreat, which is like the incessant movement of the wind, and the relevant advice is to stop any excessive spinning of thoughts and to instead cultivate a stable mind (or activity). In the second line something is bothering you so the *Yijing* advises using thinking and contemplation to fathom out circumstances or influences not yet understood in order to comprehend the situation and possible outcome. This is why the Judgment says to meet with a great man, which is someone accomplished in great deeds. In the third line you are warned against thinking so much that you cannot stop thinking; excessive thinking will be detrimental in causing mental distress (unrest). In the second upper trigram we move to doing (actual physical activity) so you now successfully catch three different types of game on a hunt after having used thinking and planning in the lower trigram. In the fifth line you are told to keep on doing what you were doing in pursuing accomplishments, which means to remain persistent rather the subject to the fluctuations of the wind element. You are also warned that your good fortune will only last for a limited time because all situations are impermanent, and transitoriness is the essential nature of the moving wind element. Good fortune is transitory so the situation is destined to change just as the wind always changes its power, speed and direction. Finally, in the last line we are presented with wind stirring beneath the bed as the most intense level of the wind element – a sign of Qi life force stirring positively (after the success of the fifth line) that will then result in sexual activity and a consequential loss of a man's treasure. In Chinese culture his treasures or valuables are his semen (Jing) and his Qi energy, which is represented by an axe used to do things. There is a very good chance that many of the lines are veiled references to sexual activity which is normally engaged in when a man's Qi (vital energy) rises. Qi is symbolized by the wind element, and sexual activity in this hexagram can be represented by the Li, Dui or Xun trigrams, or combinations thereof.

1. Advancing and retreating. Steadfastness (ability to remain constant) is beneficial for a military man.

2. Wind under the bed. A large number of shamans and diviners are used. Auspicious. No trouble.

3. Repetitious (incessant) wind. Distress.

4. Regrets disappear. During the hunt (in the field) three kinds of game are caught.

5. Persistence will bring good fortune. Regrets will disappear. There is nothing that is not beneficial. There is no beginning but there is an end. From three days before a *geng* day to three days after a *geng* day. Auspicious.

6. Wind under the bed. He loses his valuables and his axe. Persistence is inauspicious.

57.1: Yin line at the first line, at the bottom of the Xun Wind trigram that represents gentle penetrating wind. **"Advancing and retreating. A soldier's steadfastness (ability to remain constant) is beneficial."** Advancing and retreating, which is the nature of the wind element, is an analogy for movement (activity) and for thinking. The wind element and the Xun trigram can represent either thinking or the activity of doing something that involves movement. An individual who advances and retreats (yin), going backwards and forwards, is mentioned here to represent someone who is constantly thinking about something by tossing the topic back and forth in their head, and so their reversals symbolize the wind that is always changing directions. This is unlike the stability of line 58.1 where there is contentment and stable harmony just from being with someone. This individual is like someone who is spinning thoughts back and forth in their head without achieving any progress, or like someone who keeps reversing their activities. Such an individual should develop the steadfastness of a soldier, *which means concentration and stability*, and stop thinking so much or reversing their position so much. It's beneficial to cultivate the constancy and firmness of a soldier because this steadfastness means progress in a single consistent direction. The steadfastness of a soldier basically symbolizes stability or concentration rather than the act of tossing thoughts back and forward around in the head. Advancing and retreating can also stand for sexual activity, and a soldier's steadiness would then mean celibacy or sexual restraint that calms one's life force or Qi. Celibacy is one way to accumulate Qi energy within your body versus losing it through sexual dissipation, so this is an alternative interpretation of the line that will also match with line six. If we take this as the meaning, which is quite possible, then opposite hexagram line 51.1 would entail sexual innuendos ("Thunder comes [sexual desire]. Terrifying. Afterwards there is laughter and gaiety") as would inverse hexagram line 58.1 ("Harmonious joy").

57.2: Yang at the second line in the middle of the Xun Wind trigram and at the bottom line of an internal Dui Talking trigram. **"Wind under the bed. A large number of shamans and diviners are used. Auspicious. No trouble."** At this line some wind has appeared beneath a bed, which is sometimes translated as a couch or platform. Beds are made of *wood*, which is another synonym for the wind element, and the fact that wind has appeared below the bed symbolizes a greater accumulation of the wind element (such as one's life force) than in the first line. Specifically there are some influences stirring that are making someone restless so that they cannot sleep, and this could be *either a rise in a man's vitality or his thinking*. Due to the Dui Talking trigram it is probably that you keep thinking about some matter, perhaps tossing and turning in the bed since the wind is having an influence on the bed, and you need to discuss the matter with others. Diviners and shamans are normally called in to analyze events ("divine the omen or event") and give advice so they represent the Dui Talking trigram and the act of analysis – thinking about any hidden influences, determining their meaning and projecting their possible outcome. There will be good fortune and no error from this because this is the purpose of thinking, which is to understand a situation so that you can determine what to do. Something has happened that is making you uneasy and you use the powers of your thinking, which is the wind element or "the small," to try and divine the meaning, implications and best course of action. If we take this as having sexual implications (Qi stirring under the bed causes sexual activity) it could also refer to a resulting pregnancy, and then the priests and fortune tellers would be called in to divine the future of the baby.

57.3: Yang at the third line at the top of the Xun Wind trigram, at the middle line of an inner Dui Talking trigram, and at the bottom line of an inner Li trigram. **"Repetitious (incessant) wind. Distress."** This line symbolizes far too much thinking that causes distress, namely mental unrest that is an increase in the wind element over the second line. There is too much thinking – incessant thinking – because the third line of the Wind element represents destructive mental motion and the strong middle line of the inner Dui trigram represents talking (and thus thinking or yapping as well). You therefore have two influences producing excessive thinking or stirring of the wind element, or even of the life force Qi. Line 58.3 also refers to enthusiastically thinking too much about future joys, so this complementary hexagram suggests excessive thinking and planning. Additionally, the inner Li trigram represents fire, which in turn stands for intellectual thinking or brilliance, so the over-abundance of thinking in this line is enormous. In the first line of the hexagram you were told to stop spinning thoughts that go back and forth and concentrate instead of continually flipping around, or to stop incessantly reversing your (plan of) actions. In the second line you were told to start using your thinking to comprehend an unsettling situation, and now you are being told not to engage in overthinking. Whenever we have a trigram its bottom line is usually a diluted or weak form of the meaning of the trigram, its middle line is usually a solid representation of its essence, and the top line usually embodies some destructive tinge of its qualities because the element of the trigram reaches an extreme and is about to (be destroyed because it is about to) transform into something else. We also have that here – excessive thinking meaning too strong of a wind element, especially as the next trigram is wind as well. If we take this as a continuation of the sexual innuendos it would refer to lots of worry and discussion on the coming baby, which would produce concern or distress to new parents. Or, it could represent very active sexual activity because the Dui trigram represents a young woman. Both interpretations would take into account the Xun trigram, Dui Joy trigram and Li trigram.

57.4: Yin at the fourth line, at the bottom of the upper Xun Wind trigram, middle line of an inner Li trigram, and top line of an inner Dui Joy trigram. **"Regrets disappear. During the hunt (in the field), three kinds of game are caught."** Now we have shifted to the upper trigram and left the realm of thinking to move into the realm of actual physical activity. Both realms of thinking and activity are represented by the wind element since it symbolizes movement. Here the individual goes hunting, probably with bow and arrow (the wind element of the Xun trigram), and he doesn't just make a catch but bags three types of different game from the hunt. He becomes enthusiastically happy for his success, which is due to the combination of the inner Li and Dui trigrams. All that preparatory thinking in the lower trigram has born fruit because it has finally been turned into positive action that has produced successful results. The great bounty of "three different types of game" (fish, fowl and mammal) is due to the influence of the thinking in the lower three lines of the first trigram along with the combination of the inner Li Brilliance-Celebration trigram and Dui Joy trigram. If we continue with the interpretation of the Wind (Qi or Life Force) hexagram as meaning the pregnancy of a baby, this line might refer to all the things that need to be purchased or done before its arrival which the man must collect in the field as preparation.

57.5: Yang at the fifth line in the middle of the Xun Wind trigram and at the top of an inner Li trigram. **"Persistence will bring good fortune. Regrets will disappear. There is nothing that is not beneficial. There is no beginning but there is an end. From three days before a *geng* day to three days after a *geng* day. Auspicious."** If you keep doing the positive activity that you started in the previous line – thinking and then acting – this will lead to good fortune and your regrets will disappear. In a hexagram about the ever-changeable wind element one would expect to see advice to remain persistent rather the subject to the vagaries of the wind element that would blow you this way or that way in thoughts or behavior. The lower trigram was preoccupied with thinking, you then switched to action in the fourth line, and now in this line you have the potential of gaining more if you keep acting appropriately. Some translate part of this line as, "Nothing at first [which symbolizes the wind element as well as thinking without doing] but you have it in the end" but I believe the better translation speaks to the transitory impermanence of events that is a feature of the ever-changing wind element since a time period is given. "There is no beginning but there is an end" is like saying no one knows where the wind originates or where your initial thoughts come from about some matter or even when something first started. The wind element of thinking eventually manifests as activity and then disappears after you accomplish something, but those accomplishments only last for a short while because our world is characterized by impermanence. The good fortune will only last temporarily since this is the nature of reality (which is the essential feature of the ever-changing wind element). Since the good fortune of the Xun trigram can only be temporary this is symbolized by lasting only until week's end. In the Chinese heavenly stems calendar the third day after the *geng* day is the *gui* day, which is the end of the ten-day week, and this is when the good fortune ends. The good fortune commenced at mid-week because it started three days before the *geng* day (day seven of the ten-day Chinese calendar) so it appeared at approximately mid-week to represent starting *after* all your prior thinking and planning (and prep-work). The fifth line of a hexagram usually represents some perfected stage of the hexagram's overall meaning. In this case the meaning is to capture the wind element; you should get some ideas, continue working to achieve them, eventually things will turn beneficial for you, there will be a temporary gain that is auspicious, but it will only last a short while for that is the nature of impermanence (and the wind element that constantly shifts and moves). If we continue with the sexual interpretations then this line might refer to the expected due date of a baby that should be given birth between such and such a date. This would take into account the Xun Qi trigram and Li Celebration trigram, and a new life would certainly represent the fifth line theme of a hexagram concerning Qi, our life force. In other words, the hexagram is about the Xun trigram, or wind element. It can either represent thinking and activity (since they are the movements of consciousness or the body) or our life force, namely our Qi. Both interpretations are provided.

57.6: Yang at the sixth line at the top of the upper Xun Wind trigram. **"Wind under the bed. He loses his valuables and his axe. Persistence is inauspicious."** There are several ways to interpret this line. Two wind trigrams stacked together in this hexagram represent a large amount of wind movement. The hexagram therefore represents a profusion of too many stirring activities or thinking. Continuing this way is inauspicious (misfortunate) because this inundation can cause you to make mistakes and lose everything. The remedy is to pursue stability, concentration and a steady course of action because continuously over-thinking or continually changing your behavior will produce misfortune. You can experience loss just as the lines suggest. A second explanation is that the wind (life force) penetrating beneath the bed represents stirring forces such as sexual desire because your life force (your Qi the symbolizes the Xun trigram) has become over-abundant. This is the top line of the upper Xun Wind trigram and top trigram lines tend to be destructive. It is also the highest intensity of the wind element, which also represents a man's life force. In Chinese culture a man's treasure is his semen or Jing, and an axe represents his Qi energy or ability to do things because he has strong vitality. Hence, this top line might mean that a man's stirring vitality at its strongest prompts him to engage in sexual activities, whereupon he loses his valuables (semen or Jing) and isn't interested in doing any activities (use his axe) due to the loss of Qi energy since he has to rest. This interpretation is not far-fetched due to the fact that reverse hexagram line 58.6 speaks of seductive joy (in referring to sex), opposite hexagram 51 can be taken as a symbol of sexual intercourse, and future hexagram line 48.6 says that the well is accepted by the people and should not be covered (which is a sexual innuendo as well). The line advises that you should not remain preoccupied with sex ("continuing on this way is misfortunate") because such an excess degrades one's health. Chinese medicine specifically warns against an excess of sexual indulgence.

In terms of how the composition of the hexagram is reflected in this line, the lower Xun trigram is wind stirring (penetrating) beneath the bed and the upper Xun trigram is the destructive fate of losing your valuables so "wind penetrates beneath the bed and he loses his valuables," which may refer to sexual orgasm.

HEXAGRAM 58

Dui - Joyousness, Joyful, Happiness, Self-Indulgence; Peace Negotiations

Lower Trigram: Dui (Joy) – joy, contentment, pleasure
Upper Trigram: Dui (Joy) – joy, pleasure, gratification

The Judgment: Joy. It is beneficial to persevere.

For this hexagram I wish to offer two translations because of the usefulness of the more modern texts. The first translation would be a traditional *Yijing* translation that most people would have in their libraries. It takes the Dui trigram as meaning Joy that gives us an opportunity to transmit the findings of modern psychology on the topic. The second will be a Mawangdui translation (which is what I normally use) based on interpreting the Dui trigram as Talking or Negotiations. I think you will find it useful to compare the two versions.

For the first translation this hexagram has the image of two lakes that might be replenishing each other. Lakes tend to nurture and refresh people with good feelings such as joy. This is one of the eight doubled hexagrams whose theme is the Dui trigram of joy, gratification and pleasure. In the lower Dui trigram we have natural joys and in the upper Dui trigram we have a more active pursuit for pleasurable joys. In the first line we have the natural state of pleasure or contentment, which is the passive pleasure of feeling good because of being in harmony with other people, situations or even oneself. Next you experience sincere laughing or bubbling happiness joy rather than just the pleasurable harmony of contentment as in line one. When you start seeking for pleasure this disquiet will cause unrest so the third line warns about the coming joys in the subsequent upper trigram that are possibly errant pursuits. In the upper trigram we then have warnings about putting too much emphasis on seeking joy or pleasure because the pursuit can be harmful. In the fourth line, over-thinking about future pleasures will throw you out of balance into a state of constant uneasiness. The entire hexagram concerns joy, and in the fifth line you are warned not to "place your confidence" in deteriorating joys or pleasures because they don't last. Lastly, we have the mention of seductive, enticing, tempting joy without any commentary. The line represents an extreme type of joy – probably sexual pleasure – that can become harmful from overindulgence like everything else in life.

1. Harmonious joy. Auspicious.

2. Sincere joy (delight). Auspicious.

3. Joy to come. Inauspicious.

4. Deliberating over joy one is not at peace. By avoiding the illness there will be happiness.

5. Placing confidence in disintegrating (deteriorating, impermanent) matters is dangerous.

6. Seductive joy.

58.1: Yang at the first line at the bottom of the Dui Joy trigram. **"Harmonious joy (inward harmony). Auspicious."** Modern psychology says that the low-intensity pleasures of life include harmony, comfort, amusement, satiation, and relaxation. The harmonious joy of this line, which is a feeling of contentment, comfort and inner harmony, appears because this is the lowest level of joy or pleasure. The harmonious pleasure you feel from being together with other people, being in harmony with situations, or just feeling an inner harmonious pleasure due to the contentment of being are what this line symbolizes. This is a peaceful, non-excited, passive form of pleasure or happiness that is the lowest gradient of joy within these six lines.

58.2: Yang at the second line in the middle of the Dui Joy trigram, and as the bottom line of an inner Li trigram. **"Sincere joy (inward sincerity). Auspicious."** The good fortune of this line comes from experiencing a higher intensity of joy than in line one – sincere, happy joy such as gladness, good cheer, sparkle, ebullience and fun (which modern psychology identifies as moderate-intensity pleasurable emotions) – rather than the passive internal pleasurable feeling of inner harmony. This stronger type of more active joy not only expresses the strong middle line of the Dui trigram but picks up the brightness of the Li trigram too. This matches with future hexagram 47.2 where a man is enjoying food and wine and in opposite hexagram line 51.2 a cauldron is full of food and transforming someone's fortune so that harm cannot come to the individual.

58.3: Yin at the third line within the bottom Dui Joy trigram, as the central line within an inner Li trigram, and bottom line of an inner Xun Wind trigram. **"Coming (expecting) joys."** As a general rule this third line of joyousness should represent a greater intensity of joy than in the previous lines but also suffer from a tinge of destruction. Initially I thought this third line should be translated as, "Chasing after (seeking) joys. Inauspicious," where the principle was that enthusiastically running around *seeking joy, chasing after whatever can give thrills or pleasure*, would likely result in misfortune. The idea is that desiring delight brings misfortune. However, the author of the *Yijing* could easily have written this as chasing joy, pursuing joy or attracted to joy so I dropped that interpretation. The *Yijing* often has lines that refer to the following one or two subsequent lines in the hexagram. What makes the most sense to me therefore is that "Coming joys" follows this pattern and refers to enthusiastically *expecting* the actual joys of the upper trigram. This makes sense since paired hexagram line 57.3 is about incessantly thinking about some topic and the next three hexagram lines are destructive joys so this translation fits. We know this line is inauspicious because it is a yin line, it is the top line of the Dui trigram where a top line is usually destructive, it is the bottom line of a Xun Moving Wind trigram that can be destructive, and it is the middle line of an inner Li Fire trigram that can burn you or just represent an excessive amount of brilliance. To station oneself in an unsettling expectation of future joys – which is a higher state of excited ebullience than the prior lines – is deleterious and thus inauspicious.

58.4: Yang at the fourth line, which is the bottom line of the upper Dui Joy trigram, the middle line within an inner Xun Wind trigram, and the top line within an inner Gen Stillness trigram. **"Deliberating over [considering, weighing] joy one is not at peace. By avoiding the illness [eliminating your affliction] there will be happiness."** If you keep thinking about pursuing pleasures then your mind, according to the interpretation provided for line three, will have no peace but will become restless and uneasy. You can only find true contentment and inner peace, which are the truest form of happiness, by reducing such expectations. In other words, someone who is constantly deliberating over seeking joys and pleasures, weighing matters by tossing them about endlessly in their mind, will not experience peace. By destroying their inner harmony they will also destroy their potential for joy. Deliberating over joy produces an unsettled mental state of restlessness and unease that borders on the injurious because it can lead you into harm's way. The Xun Wind trigram is here leading to an incessant deliberation over delightful expectations – which is a higher intensity of joyousness than previous lines – while the warning not to do this reveals the influence of the Gen Keeping Still trigram.

58.5: Yin at the fifth line that is the central line with the upper Dui Joy trigram and the top line within an inner Xun Wind trigram. Therefore we should expect a negative (yin) image that combines the strong concepts of joy (Dui trigram) with the penetrative but destructive influence of the wind element (Xun trigram). We should also expect this fifth line, as lord of the hexagram, to reveal the basic core nature of the Dui trigram. **"Misplacing trust in disintegrating [deteriorating, decaying, impermanent] matters is dangerous."** The pleasures/joys we seek in life are all impermanent or transitory and hence they are unsatisfactory since they are temporary. Once the external stimulus is gone the positive emotions we experienced fade away leaving behind little trace. Furthermore, rarely do they lead to elevation. They usually just produce some degree of temporary gratification and afterwards the unsatisfactory cycle of desire and stimulus repeats itself again. To misplace one's trust in such things is to focus your life or even existence on transitory pleasures that cannot give you real happiness, and thus "placing confidence in deteriorating matters is dangerous" and foolish. If an individual does not stop constantly thinking about joyous pleasures then they might become addicted to the pursuit of unsatisfactory transitory influences rather than real inner contentment. The principle of impermanence and deterioration comes from the two Xun trigrams and the message is that you cannot depend upon transient pleasures destined to disintegrate so doing this is perilous. You should not lose yourself to pleasures that bring no lasting peace or contentment.

58.6: Yin at the sixth line at the top of the Dui trigram and the hexagram. **"Seductive joy."** This top line represents the highest-intensity level of joy or pleasure in the hexagram that modern psychology refers to as bliss, ecstasy, thrills, euphoria, and elation. However, the *Yijing* refers to "seductive pleasure" or "seductive joyousness," which probably means sexual pleasure or sexual bliss. Why? Because this line should represent the most intense form of human pleasure since it is the hexagram's top line and all of the adjectives cited can refer to sex. Furthermore, the hexagram is composed of two Dui trigrams that symbolize young women, open mouths and happiness that can also refer to sex. In paired hexagram line 57.6 we had an excess of wind energy under the bed where the individual loses his valuables (Jing or semen) and energy (axe), thus suggesting sex once again. Hence, "seductive joyousness" probably refers to sex.

- - o - -

For the second translation more focused on the Mawangdui manuscript, this hexagram has the image of two mouths talking to each other and their topic is negotiations revolving around the war between the Shang and Zhou. The lines tell the progression of talks for establishing peace between the conquering Zhou and the conquered Shang. In the first line we have reconciliation talks between the two parties. In the second line we have discussions on exchanging captives or prisoners of war. In the third line we have pending negotiations, or more talks to come. In the fourth line we have the sides talking in negotiations and pondering matters but nothing is settled yet. The key is to hammer out the issues, and specifying matters is like confining an illness so people become secure from the disease. In the fifth line is the warning that trusting in the peace talks is putting faith in something that will wear away, which indeed happened because the Shang people later rebelled. In the sixth line the talks are concluded so we have established peace and a lasting satisfaction.

1. Reconciliation (peacemaking) talks. Auspicious.

2. Prisoner of war talks. Regret disappears.

3. Pending negotiations. Ominous.

4. There are peace negotiations but nothing is settled yet (they ponder peace but are not yet serene). If they establish security from illness there will be happiness.

5. Trust in something that strips away (disintegrates over time). This is dangerous.

6. Lasting satisfaction (drawn out joy).

58.1: Yang at the first line at the bottom of the Dui Talking trigram. **"Reconciliation (peacemaking) talks. Auspicious."** The Shang and Zhou talk about ending the war.

58.2: Yang at the second line in the middle of the Dui Talking trigram, and as the bottom line of an inner Li Military trigram. **"Prisoner of war talks. Regret disappears."** The meaning is obvious. The reason these are talks about captives is due to the presence of the Li Military trigram.

58.3: Yin at the third line within the bottom Dui Talking trigram, as the middle line of an inner Li Military trigram and bottom line of an inner Xun Wind trigram. **"Pending negotiations. Ominous."** Here there are still more negotiations necessary because we are at the top of the Dui Mouth trigram and the mouth, being a yin line, is still open. Naturally the topic is the aftermath of the war (Li trigram). Because matters are not yet settled (Xun Moving Wind trigram) this omen of unsettled issues means there are points of contention that may never be settled to anyone's true satisfaction. This might lead to the continuation of the war at present or the breakout of warfare in the future even after peace is established. A later rebellion proved that this would happen.

58.4: Yang at the fourth line, which is the bottom line of the upper Dui Talking trigram, the middle line within an inner Xun Wind trigram, and the top line within an inner Gen trigram. **"There are peace negotiations but nothing is settled yet (they ponder peace but are not yet serene). If they are secure from illness there will be happiness."** There is more negotiation, which is a reflection of the Dui Talking trigram. The topic is a peace settlement to end the war due to the presence of the Gen Stillness trigram that represents peace. "If a disease is confined the outcome will be happiness" appears due to the presence of Xun Wind trigram because wind in Chinese medicine refers to sickness. Confining or limiting any fighting or issue disagreements will be a happy outcome for all. Delimiting the end results of certain issues in negotiation is the same affair under a different name.

58.5: Yin at the fifth line, which is the middle line in the upper Dui Talking trigram and the top line within an inner Xun Wind trigram. **"Trust in something that disintegrates (over time). This is dangerous."** Most translators would render this line as something to do with flaying, but flaying is an analogy for something that gets stripped away or is worn away through gradual stripping and thus deteriorates over time. Therefore this is *not about flaying captives* by slowly stripping away their skin. It is about misplacing trust in the peace agreement, which is dangerous because peace between the parties will probably degrade over time. It could also concern (trusting) the strategy of stripping away at the various items requested by the Shang by denying their various requests. It is common sense that either of these avenues is dangerous. They are an outcome of the destructive line of the Xun Penetrating Wind trigram that is present. My previous translation of line 58.5 bears relevance: "Misplacing trust in disintegrating [deteriorating, decaying, impermanent] matters is dangerous." This would suggest that the better translation is "Trust in something that strips away (disintegrates over time). To have such trust is dangerous."

58.6: Yin at the sixth line at the top of the Dui Talking trigram and the hexagram. **"Lasting satisfaction (drawn out joy)."** Here a peace settlement has likely been successfully negotiated so people are expecting long-term peace.

HEXAGRAM 59

Huan - Dispersing, Dissolution

Lower Trigram: Kan (Water) – danger, dissolution, dispersion
Upper Trigram: Xun (Wind) – dispersal, sweating, bleeding, crying out

The Judgment: Dispersion. The king approaches his temple. It is beneficial to ford the great river. It benefits to persevere.

This hexagram has an image of wind blowing over water that tends to disperse and drive apart any objects on its surface. Similarly, this hexagram is about sacrificing yourself to deal with a dangerous situation that imperils people and that requires a dispersal of you and your self-interest. In the first line is the lesson that helping others during an emergency usually requires great strength, resources, stamina, etc., which is symbolized by "possessing the strength of a horse." When the disaster is too great, however, everyone's first impulse is to save themselves by running to safety (support) so this is what happens in the second line. The third line indicates that when the situation permits you might be able to forget about yourself and your self-interests and nobly act to help others, which would make you a hero. In the fourth line there is the lesson that a disaster can cause people to scatter and lose connection with one another but afterwards groups will gradually coalesce and assemble together once again so you should not worry about temporary separations caused by an emergency or calamity. In the fifth line is the lesson that to really help people during great troubles, difficulties or calamities you must give generously of yourself to assist others, and this type of assistance is better than making an offering in a temple. This is basically the commentary on dispersion other than the lesson of the sixth line that when you have passed through some disaster or calamity it is best to remove yourself as far away as possible from it if there is a chance that it will happen again.

1. Help rescue (during a dangerous state of dissolution) using strength like that of a horse. Auspicious.

2. Amid the dispersion he races to his support (for security). Regret disappears.

3. Dispersing oneself (discarding any regard to one's own self or interests). There are no regrets.

4. His group disperses. Supreme good fortune. Dispersion (dissolution) leads to (a gathering, accumulation, or unification like) a mound. This is not what one would ordinarily expect.

5. Dispersing sweat, he greatly cries out (disperses a great roar). He dispenses the accumulations in the royal granaries (in order to provide help). There is no trouble.

6. Dispersing (wiping off) his blood stains, he departs to far away. There is no error.

59.1: Yin at the bottom of the Kan Trigram, which means danger. **"Help rescue (during a dangerous state of dissolution) using the strength of a horse. There will be good fortune."** The basic idea of this hexagram is that there is a situation of dispersion, dissolution or scattering (caused by an emergency or calamity like a flood), probably dangerous, and people must be rescued. This first line states that being able to rescue others from a dangerous situation requires ability such as great strength like that of a horse. To rescue others you don't need a strong horse but the strength of a horse which means strong ability, energy, strength, resources or *strong spirit*. There are various alternative ways to translate this line but they all deal with this same basic idea. The danger of the situation comes from the fact that this is a yin line at the beginning of the Kan Danger trigram and very beginning of the hexagram so rescue is possible because the danger from dissolution isn't yet severe.

59.2: Yang at the second line in the middle of the Kan Water-Danger Trigram. This is also the bottom line of an internal Zhen Thunder trigram that means shock or movement. **"Amid the dispersion [dissolution, gushing flood] he races to his support (for security). Regret disappears."** During the dispersion/dissolution (that is like a Kan trigram flood of water) he hurries to whatever supports himself and offers security. This might be people, a safe place or contrivance. Because this is the first line of an inner Zhen thunderbolt trigram that represents a calamity he will naturally run to safety due to the shock, and his secondary concern will be to help others *after he first takes care of himself*. Hence I would take the meaning of the line to be that he rushes to support himself first rather than support others (due to the inner Zhen trigram and strong middle line of the Kan danger trigram), which is natural, and in the third line he then focuses on helping others once his own safety is secured. First save your own life before you can save others. "Regret disappears" because this is a yang line where safety/support is available within the dangerous situation.

59.3: Yin at the third line that is the top (extreme) of the Kan Water-Danger trigram. This is also the middle line of an inner Zhen Thunder trigram and bottom line of an inner Gen Mountain trigram. **"Dispersing his self [dissolving one's selfishness, forgetting one's body and interests] there are no regrets."** Dispersing oneself in order to help others in danger means discarding any regard to your own personal safety, possessions or interests. It means surrendering your egotism and selfishness. If you were trying to save yourself from danger then "dispersing yourself" might mean running to find safety but in this case the individual is probably acting as a hero and forgetting their own safety and interests in the process of aiding others in distress. In both cases, the virtue of foregoing selfishness and materialism are a way to help others in a dangerous situation of dissolution where lives and property are getting destroyed.

59.4: Yin at the fourth line, at the bottom of the upper Xun Wind trigram of scattering. This is also the middle line of an inner Gen Accumulation trigram and top line of an inner Zhen Thunder trigram. **"His flock [following, group, fraternity, congregation, crowd] disperses. Supreme good fortune. Dispersion (dissolution) leads to a mound (gathering, collection, accumulation, or reunification). This is something beyond ordinary people's expectation."** Basically, the *dispersion of your group* is a natural event during an emergency where people rush to secure their own safety. If you want to help people then you have to abandon your selfishness and parochialism, which is dispersing yourself and your group. Naturally there is a dispersal of people in this line who scatter due to the influence of the Xun Wind trigram and the impetus of the inner Zhen Thunder trigram that would also scatter people in fright during a calamity. However, the line says that after the danger and subsequent dispersal eventually groups of people will afterwards pull together again like mounds (accumulations of earth) that form on a plain. This alludes to the influence of the inner Gen Mountain-Accumulation trigram. In other words, groups reform again after people disperse due to a panic. Ordinary people would not have thought this is possible – it is beyond their understanding or expectation – because they cannot see the inner trigrams ruling situations, and therefore would never expect that a great dissolution could lead to accumulation due to the unseen inner Gen trigram.

59.5: Yang at the fifth line in the middle of the upper Xun Wind trigram that sits atop the lower Kan trigram of danger. This is also the top line of an inner Gen trigram. **"Dispersing sweat, he greatly cries out [disperses a great roar]. He dispenses [scatters afar] the accumulations in the royal granaries (in order to provide help). There is no error."** This line is the lord of the hexagram so it should involve a remarkable individual. In being the middle line of the Xun trigram it should strongly represent the nature of the wind element, and it should also represent the perfected message of the hexagram due to being its fifth line. *Due to struggle and a great exertion of effort* the man sweats, and then greatly cries out (disperses a great roar), both of which are an expression of the wind element. To help the people he also disperses his accumulated belongings, which are what he amassed over time representing the inner Gen Accumulation trigram. In order to accomplish this feat of great helpfulness he needs to use tremendous effort, which is why he is sweating blood and making a great effort of shouting (Xun trigram). Sweating blood and shouting are emphasized because this is a dangerous situation and he is trying extremely hard using all of his energy and power to help others. The line teaches us to forget (disperse) your own selfishness or self-interest to help people in times of difficulty and danger and is like a lesson for the ruler and powerful elites of a state. In fact, the Judgment of the hexagram is that a king goes to a temple to make a sacrifice, and that it is beneficial to cross a great river (perform a great deed). By doing this great deed of dispersing his goods to help others he is crossing the great river, and this is actually more beneficial than making a sacrifice at a temple. There is no error in this.

59.6: Yang at the sixth line at the top of the Xun Wind trigram. **"He disperses (wipes off) his blood stains. He departs to far away (to separate himself from the dangers just concluded). This is no error."** In this line you wipe off your blood, bloody wounds or bloody stains. You have just been through a hell of a lot of danger. Perhaps this was a battle where you "scattered your own blood." Now you separate yourself from that horrible situation to leave those troubles behind and go away. Thus, "He dissolves his blood stains (bloody wounds are gone), departs and stays far away from things (to separate himself from the past danger). There is no error in this. Keeping at a distance or going away is without blame."

The top line also summarizes the hexagram's overall construction of a Kan water trigram sitting below a Xun wind trigram (to scatter or move away) because you "wipe away the blood" (Kan) from the dangerous situation (Kan) and "depart to far away" after the calamity (blood being lost).

HEXAGRAM 60

Jie - Restraints, Regulations, Limitations, Boundaries

Lower Trigram: Dui (Joy) – mouth, courtyard design, sighs
Upper Trigram: Kan (Water) – danger, trouble, difficulties

The Judgment: Bitter Restraints. One cannot continue this way.

The hexagram has an image of a lake holding water, which is a limited space that restrains the water within its boundaries. This hexagram is about imposing boundaries, limitations, or restrictions on people, situations and so forth to restrain them. From the lowest line to the top line of the hexagram we see an increasing degree of restrictions where they become progressively more bitter or severe. At the lowest line you voluntarily place restrictions on yourself as appropriate and through that self-discipline thereby avoid troubles in your life. In the second line you are reminded that there are situations where you should break those self-imposed limitations otherwise there will be misfortune. In the third line there is a warning that behavior should always be moderate like the golden mean, and in the fourth line you are living peacefully with self-restraints. In the fifth line the advice is to live with just the perfect amount ("sweet spot") of self-restraint so that you don't become tired from the self-discipline, which is why in the last line you are warned not to subject yourself to bitter, overly repressive self-restraint because you cannot maintain this over the long run and it will lead to misfortune.

1. Not going out the door into the courtyard. There is no trouble.

2. Not going out past the courtyard gate. Ominous.

3. If one is not moderate (in behavior due to restrictions or due restraint) there will be sighs. There is no trouble.

4. Peaceful moderation. Success.

5. Sweet moderation is auspicious. This practice leads to elevation.

6. Bitter moderation. Persistence is ominous. Regrets will pass.

60.1: Yang at the bottom line at the first line of the Dui Mouth-Talking trigram. **"He does not go out the door into the courtyard. There is no trouble."** A man restrains himself by not passing beyond the inner courtyard that is right outside his door, or he could also be inside a temple since they have courtyards and represent self-discipline. A courtyard is built in the shape of a head with mouth, or Dui trigram. Both your home and a temple are a safe haven so by not leaving their vicinity to become involved in the outside world (by not abandoning the rules of self-discipline, ethics, propriety, etc.) you avoid trouble. Not stepping out of the house or temple equates with not experiencing any troubles because you restrain yourself through the self-discipline of boundaries. In fact, not to go into the courtyard symbolizes restraint so the line basically means "avoid troubles through self-restraint." In other words, you will avoid trouble, fault, blame, error or regret if you don't become involved in situations, i.e. don't leave the house or temple, which also means if you don't abandon proper behavior.

60.2: Yang at the second line in the center of the Dui trigram (that represents talking, breaking free, and stepping forward) and at the first line of an inner Zhen Thunder trigram. **"He does not go out past the courtyard inside the gate [past the gate of the house that is in front of the yard]. Ominous."** This line is the opposite of the first line. The inner Zhen thunderbolt in this line threatens misfortune (ominous), and in keeping with the yang line there should be movement and activity but there is not. Instead the man stays inside the perimeter of his courtyard and refuses to leave (or act) to enter the public world, which he *should do* because of the Zhen trigram danger. In this line you must relax your restraint because you cannot be forever inflexible. Sometimes you must break the rules or violate the boundaries such as in line 59.2 of the opposite hexagram where in an emergency a man runs for protection. In the case of emergency or threatening influences, not going out past the courtyard gate when you should leave is an omen of misfortune for staying.

60.3: Yin at the third line of the Dui Mouth trigram, and it is the first line of an inner Gen Mountain-Stillness trigram. Thus one would expect to see images of talking and stillness, which we have: **"If one is not moderate there will be sighs. There is no trouble."** There should be restrictions in this line because of the influence of the Gen Keeping Still trigram while sighs and crying are mentioned due to the presence of Dui Mouth-Lake trigram. In the first line of the hexagram the self-discipline of restraining yourself was a way to avoid trouble, in the second line not acting (restraint) was considered wrong, and the third option of moderation appears in this line. The principle being taught is captured in the saying: "No limitations means lamentation; observing no regulations (rules) means sighs will follow." In this line you do not show any sign of moderate discipline or due restraint as suggested is necessary by the presence of the Gen Keeping Still trigram, in which case there will be regret because you go against the influence of the trigrams. Therefore we have lamenting and sighing as a result, which is an expression of the presence of the Dui Mouth trigram, and there is no one to blame but yourself because you exceeded the principle of moderation (self-discipline) symbolized by the inner Gen trigram. If you don't practice any self-restrictions or limitations – if you don't observe due restraint – you'll end up being sorry for your behavior and will have cause to regret. Therefore the lack of self-control means eventual lamentations. Basically a lack of restraint, which means a lack of moderation and self-control, leads to distress and then sorrow (sighs) and lamentation in consequence.

60.4: Yin at the fourth line, at the first line of the Kan Danger trigram and at the central/middle line of an inner Gen Keeping Still trigram. **"Living peacefully [contentedly, serenely, calmly] with self-restraint."** or **"Serene with the limitations. Success."** Here you contentedly submit to self-restraint and handle this with ease. You are naturally attentive to self-discipline. Success! Abiding by limitations is now easy. Why can you peacefully live with self-restraint and experience ease? Because this is the strong middle line of an inner Gen Non-movement trigram, which means that limitations are naturally followed. Also, the influences of the Kan Danger trigram can be avoided by being attentive to regulations. You can secure your safety through the self-discipline of restraint so you do so. The result will be success and good fortune ("Prosperous and smooth") which refers to the subsequent fifth line of good results. The principle presented is that in order to prevent troubles in life you should become perfectly content with various behavioral restraints and naturally follow them with ease because they will enable you to avoid harm and attain eventual success in life. Temperance and self-discipline – calmly restraining yourself and accepting limitations because that is the best thing to do – is the success of self-cultivation in achieving consummate conduct that cannot be faulted. Commentators might say that the meaning of this line is that accepting self-limitation is easy when it derives from the cultivation of your character, but the actual cause of restraint is that this is the strong middle line of inner Gen trigram.

60.5: A yang line at the fifth place as the middle line of a Kan Danger trigram and top line of an inner Gen Keeping Still trigram. The circumstances are dangerous because you are within the middle of a Kan Danger trigram, but this is its yang line that often gives the possibility of good fortune. You are also at the top line of a Gen trigram that represents limitations, keeping still or non-movement. Hence the lines: **"The sweet amount of moderation will bring good fortune. This practice leads to elevation."** In the opposite hexagram the message of line 59.5 is to give of yourself as much as possible to save others. *Here you must instead restrict yourself by employing just the right amount ("sweet spot") of restraints or limitations to experience good fortune.* That amount of restraint, of course, is moderate rather than overly severe so the tax on your self-discipline is not overwhelming. It entails the sweet spot or "just perfect level" of moderation that produces good fortune. This is the fifth line of the hexagram so this is the general meaning or advice of the hexagram in perfected form. In proceeding through life you need to practice self-discipline and personally subscribe to a sweet level of acceptable constraints in order to experience good fortune by thus avoiding errant behavior.

60.6: Yin at the sixth line, the top of the Kan Danger trigram. **"Bitter moderation. Perseverance is ominous. Regrets will pass."** It is uncomfortable to live for a long time under overly restrictive restraints. The Judgment of the hexagram is "Bitter limitations. One cannot continue this way," and in this line we learn why, which is because they will end up producing misfortune. Severe, excessively harsh restraints should be avoided or abandoned. In reverse hexagram line 59.6, for instance, the individual leaves to get as far away as possible from past troubles. Basically, the continued enforcement of extremely harsh, difficult, bitter, overboard self-limitations will produce misfortune because they can cause severe irritation and a reactive desire to break free so you cannot persevere in regulating yourself this way. After removing them such problems will go away. This is the top line of the hexagram so it represents negativities due to the extreme of limitations, especially since this is the top line of a destructive Kan Danger trigram.

This line also reflects the overall construction of the hexagram where the Dui Joy trigram is beneath the Kan Danger trigram and hence joy is suppressed by excessive restrictions that produce unease (misfortune), but once bitter restraints are removed the regrets or discomfort will pass.

HEXAGRAM 61

Zhong Fu - Inner Sincerity, Inner Trust, A True Relationship

Lower Trigram: Dui (Joy) – solitary repose, drinking wine, singing, talking
Upper Trigram: Xun (Wind) – straying horse, pheasant, bird cry

The Judgment: Inner Sincerity. Pigs and fishes bring good fortune. Beneficial to ford the great river. Favorable augury (good fortune).

This hexagram has an image of wind blowing across a lake. This will disturb its surface but not its depths, and deep waters represent deep sincerity or friendship between people. This hexagram is about seeking or establishing sincere relationships (unity) with others. The lines therefore demonstrate gradated levels of sincere relationships. In the Judgment, pigs and fishes represent wild animals you must catch rather than domesticated animals. They were offerings given to spirits by people of low rank who could not afford sheep or oxen, and common people would eat together sharing their suckling pigs and fishes in banquets on special occasions. Fish also represent fertility and pigs represent babies or small children, so together they represent a closely knit family or inner sincerity between people. Since this hexagram represents the development of sincere wholehearted relationships the first line starts off with an individual experiencing internal peace (sincerity) or contentment because no one else is around. He experiences the inner peace and tranquility of a solitary existence. In the second line we move to a familial relationship where the family members harmoniously share good times together, which represents a stronger degree of relationship between people. The third line shows that even good relationships might turn adversarial at times, and that people will fight and temporarily break with one another. In the fourth line a horse bolts away from its teammates thus demonstrating the temporary disunity of the third line due to arguments or disagreements. In the fifth line the parties reunite and are bound together again (because the disagreement was a temporary phenomenon). It reminds us that it is the sincerity between parties that binds people together in relationships. In the final top line we see the example of a bird's call reaching heaven representing the fact that using boastful, empty words to produce unity among people will end up in dissipation.

1. Enjoying peace (in solitary repose), good fortune. If there is another then it will be disquieting.

2. A crane calls in the shade, and its young harmonize with (respond to) it. "I have a fine chalice of wine. Together we will drain it."

3. He makes an enemy. Sometimes drumming, sometimes stopping, sometimes weeping, sometimes singing.

4. The moon is almost full. A horse in the team strays off. There is no trouble.

5. There are captives tied up (bound) together. There is no trouble.

6. A pheasant's cries ascend to Heaven. Persistence is ominous.

61.1: Yang at the first line at the bottom of the Dui trigram. The Dui trigram usually represents a lake, joy, happiness, pleasure, mouth, pot, water, young girl and talking with others. **"Enjoying peace (solitary repose) is auspicious. If there is another then you will not be at ease [there will be no inner peace or tranquility]."** A personal experience of inner peace due to no other human relationships being present is "auspicious." It is a reflection of the Dui Joy trigram. What would destroy such inner calm, peace and composure would be the presence of other individuals since they would constitute a disquieting distraction. Their presence will unsettle your mind and interrupt your peace and tranquility even if they are close relationships. The idea of inner repose is like a calm lake (Dui trigram) whereas another person interrupting this tranquility is like the talking aspect of the Dui trigram that represents disturbance.

61.2: Yang at the second line within the Dui trigram, and at the first line of an inner Zhen Thunder trigram. **"A crane calls in the shade [from a hidden secluded place], and its young harmonize with it [call in reply]. 'I have a fine chalice of wine to share with you.'"** This line represents an increase in the feeling of close human relationships ("sincerity") because there is an empathic response to a crane calling its chicks, which represents familial relations. They wish to be together and will enjoy that familial joy of togetherness that is symbolized by drinking wine together. The calling crane represents the Zhen Thunder trigram. The young replying in harmony to the calling reflect the Dui Joy-Talking trigram. Drinking the wine also reflects the Dui Joyousness (and Mouth) trigram since it is an enjoyable experience shared with others.

61.3: Yin at the third line within the Dui trigram. This is also the middle line of an inner Zhen Thunder trigram, and bottom of an inner Gen Keeping Still trigram. We will see all three trigrams reflected within the image of the line. **"He makes an enemy [adversary]. Either he beats a drum or he stops. Either he weeps or sings."** Future hexagram line 9.3 says that cart and axle separate (showing a disagreement) while husband and wife their roll eyes at each other. This is in accord with the interpretation of making an enemy from the people within line two. These four sounds – drumming, stopping, singing, crying – are sounds you hear during military activities, which means that the two parties start fighting or arguing. The opposite hexagram line 62.3 also warns, "He does not pass him. Be on guard against him. Otherwise one might be injured. Ominous." Somehow you were with a group of people in line two and had an argument since this is the third destructive line of the Dui Talking trigram. The confrontation occurs at the strong middle line of the Zhen Thunderstrike trigram. Because this is the center of the Zhen Thunder trigram there is the beating of a drum. Because there is an influence of an inner Gen Keeping Still trigram then sometimes the drumming stops. Because this is the mouth of the Dui trigram there is singing, or weeping because it is the third destructive line of the trigram.

61.4: Yin in the fourth line as the first line in the upper Xun Wind trigram. This is also the middle line within an inner Gen Mountain trigram, and top line within an inner Zhen Thunder trigram. **"The moon is almost full. A horse in the team strays off [runs away, disappears]. There is no trouble."** Because the situation has turned confrontational you or someone else runs away from the group. "The moon is almost full" appears because this is the second of two yin lines and a third yin line would create a trio of pure yin to accurately represent the full moon. The reference to the moon represents cyclical change. It denotes a cyclicality where the loss of the horse is temporary because it will naturally return on its own (due to the cyclicality). It means that the friendship of the previous lines has temporarily broken (due to the argument in line three) but later it will return to normal again. This fourth line of the hexagram is the bottom line of an upper Xun Wind trigram, which symbolizes the horse and the fact that it runs away. The loss reflects the top destructive line of the inner Zhen Thunder trigram. Hence, overall this fourth line represents an abrupt transition after the lower Dui Talking trigram where there was a strong argument and fallout between two parties. This new upper Xun Wind trigram results in a big change of state where one party moves away from another – hence the windy movement (running away) of the horse. In terms of the topic of sincerity, after the previous altercation in the third line there is some loss of unity, relationship or a "loss of sincerity" but it is no great trouble since it is just temporary.

61.5: Yang at the fifth place as the center line of the upper Dui trigram, and as the top line of an inner Gen Mountain trigram. **"Captives are tied up together. There is no trouble."** The captives in this line are horses who are tied together. One ran away in line four due to arguments and returned of its own accord (as per the cyclicality of the moon denoting an eventual return). Then the parties made up with one another because they became tied up as a group again - bound together. The sincerity between the parties creates a unity bond like a tether. This line expresses a perfected form of the general meaning of the hexagram just as the fifth line usually does. There is a phrase, "Being sincere, binding follows," which means that sincerity between parties links them together in wholehearted allegiance to one another and this is the basis of a deep friendship (relationship). This is due to the top line of the Gen trigram that represents non-movement together with the central line of the Dui trigram that represents the unity of people enjoyably being together.

61.6: Yang at the top line of the hexagram, and at the top of a Xun Wind trigram signifying movement. **"The cry of the pheasant rises to Heaven. Persistence is an omen of coming misfortune."** A famous Chinese saying runs, "The cock's cry flies to Heaven while he himself stays on earth." In this case its cries would represent empty words and lofty rhetoric about unity, closeness, brotherhood and so on rather than words reflecting the real inner sincerity and commitment that truly binds some people together. It probably represents a degree of exaggerated phrases that dissipate into the sky, and whose empty promises lead nowhere because the hexagram is complete and change is now destined to occur. Opposite hexagram line 62.6 even says, "A flying bird gets caught in a net" whereas in this line one's efforts to use golden words rather than establish a real bond between people is a fake overreaching whose fraud is an omen of misfortune. The presence of the wind element (Xun trigram) appears in the image of a bird crying out its call. The subject should take a proper measure of himself because the extreme of overreaching will produce misfortune.

In terms of the overall construction of the hexagram, which means in terms of the meaning of the top and bottom trigrams stacked upon one another, this is reflected in this line through the image of a golden pheasant crying (Dui trigram) and trying to simultaneously reach Heaven while flying (the Xun trigram).

HEXAGRAM 62

Xiao Guo - Trying to Exceed One's Smallness

Lower Trigram: Gen (Mountain) – stopping, keeping still
Upper Trigram: Zhen (Thunder) – danger, shooting arrows, calamity

The Judgment: Trying to exceed one's smallness. Success. It is advantageous to persist (persistence furthers). You can accomplish small goals but not great deeds (small things are possible, big things are not). A flying bird leaves behind its song: "One should not strive too high; one should remain low." Greatly auspicious.

This hexagram has the image of a bird flying (thunder) above a mountain, and warns us to play it safe rather than try to rise too high. Specifically, this hexagram is about trying to meet other people (for favors) when your status isn't high enough. Each line of the hexagram represents someone with a lower status trying to meet (pursuing) someone of much higher status. In the words of the Judgment, someone is trying to exceed their own smallness. In the first line a small bird flies towards some destination, which symbolizes trying to accomplish a great feat (meeting someone of higher status), but the small one cannot meet the greater one. The flying produces misfortune. In the second line a man tries to meet his grandfather but is only able to meet his grandmother, which is like someone trying to meet his king but only able to meet a lower-level minister. In both cases they cannot meet the higher status individual they want. In the third line you are warned about meeting the minister rather than your lord whom you want to meet, and told to make sure you don't get injured because of him. In the fourth line you meet with him and are again warned to be careful and cautious in the meeting; perhaps it entails bribes. In the fifth line some expectations for rain don't pan out – meaning that circumstances should produce what you want to occur but the previous meeting is not producing any results. However, a duke (representing the minister) shoots some fowl with a tethered string and retrieves what he wants (through his relationships). In the sixth line there is the reminder that if you, being small, try to accomplish a great deed (fly off to some destination) without (paying for?) the assistance of a higher counterparty then this will result in disaster. The Judgment accordingly reminds us to attempt only small accomplishments.

1. A flying bird, thus ominous.

2. He passes by his grandfather but meets his grandmother. He does not reach his lord but meets his minister. There is no trouble.

3. He does not pass him. Be on guard against him. Otherwise you might be injured. Ominous.

4. There is no trouble. Meet him instead of passing him by. Going is dangerous so one must be cautious. Do not perpetually continue as you are doing long-term.

5. Dense (heavy) clouds are there but no rain comes from the western border. The duke shoots a stringed arrow and retrieves prey from a pit.

6. Not meeting but passing by the other without encounter. A flying bird gets caught in a net. Ominous. This is called a catastrophic calamity.

62.1: Yin at the first line of the Gen Keeping Still trigram. **"A flying bird, with it will come misfortune."** Here a bird trying to fly from one place to another, which is an analogy for trying to meet someone, is unsuccessful. The misfortune is due to flying (trying to get to some destination) when the line is under the influence of the Gen Keeping Still trigram that represents non-movement. Hence, you are trying to go against unfavorable circumstances and you accordingly produce misfortune. Why are we using a flying bird instead of some other image? Because a bird symbolizes something small that attempts the greatness of flying, i.e. soaring in the sky to go somewhere (meet someone). The idea of the hexagram is that one should not try to attempt something great because your status is small.

62.2: Yin at the second line of the Gen Mountain trigram and at the beginning of an inner Xun Wind trigram. **"He passes by his grandfather but meets his grandmother. He does not reach his lord but meets his minister. There is no trouble."** He fails to meet the one he wants to meet and instead meets someone of secondary status. In this case that lesser individual – a grandmother or minister rather than king – is represented by the yin nature of the line. How could you be successful in meeting someone of much higher status since this is a yin line as well as the strong central line of the Gen Stillness trigram? However, there is no fault to the effort because the attempt appears due to the presence of the Xun Wind trigram that causes movement.

62.3: Yang at the third line and at the top of the Gen Mountain trigram. This is also the middle line of an inner Xun Wind trigram and the bottom line of an inner Dui Talking trigram. **"He does not pass him. Be on guard (protect, defend yourself) against him. Otherwise you might be injured. Ominous."** The Gen Mountain trigram stands for stopping and the Dui Mouth trigram represents talking while the middle line of a Xun Penetrating Wind trigram represents harm. You cannot pass by the minister (go around him) to meet the ruler therefore you should not refuse to meet him (the minister of line two), but since the minister is an underling who may misunderstand or misrepresent what you want (or might even take advantage of your request since Chinese officials were known to do so) you must guard yourself in the meeting. Otherwise you might become injured due to his shortcomings, which is indeed possible because the subsequent Zhen trigram represents thunder and shock and the last line of the lower trigram often bodes of destruction. Hence there is therefore a warning to be on guard with what you say (Dui trigram). Perhaps someone will injure you from behind, such as the minister, since there are two yin lines previous to this one and the next trigram is the assault of the Zhen Thunder trigram. You must take precautions when meeting someone of lower rank than your desired target because they will often refuse to pass on the message to the individual of higher rank, or misrepresent it, and they certainly won't present your case with your own degree of fervor. Furthermore, your requests might entail the necessity of bribes or favors so much caution is in order.

62.4: Yang in the fourth place at the start of a Zhen Thunder trigram. This is also the middle line of a Dui Joy trigram, and the top line of a Xun Wind trigram. We might expect some measure of success since this is a yang line. **"There is no trouble. Meet him instead of passing him by. Going [proceeding] is dangerous so there must be caution [exercise care]. Do not perpetually continue as you are doing long-term [persist in acting this way]."** This line marks the beginning of the new Zhen upper trigram which represent power so he meets with the minister instead of the lord he originally desired. "He does not pass by the other but meets him. Going forward to do this means danger" since this is a powerful person. Let's not even go into the necessity for gifts and bribery, which are a dangerous undertaking. "One must therefore be cautious and on guard" addresses this concern (because this is a Zhen Thunderbolt trigram). Although you want to secure the benefit you want, the line advises: "Do not continually act this way in meeting with the minister (and perhaps using bribery) because you must be overly cautious and protect yourself."

62.5: Yin at the fifth place in the middle of the Zhen Thunder trigram, and as the top line in an inner Dui Lake trigram. We usually see an individual of exalted position in the fifth line achieving some degree of success or perfection related to the meaning of the hexagram. Here we have a prince and he is hunting, which is Zhen Thunder activity. **"Dense [heavy] clouds on the western border but they don't produce rain. The duke shoots a stringed arrow (harpoons a bird) and retrieves his prey from a pit."** You met with the minister in line four and now have expectations that aren't panning out. That's because the situation is like clouds that should produce rain but do not. This line is at the top of an inner Dui Lake trigram that represents water, and the *western* region is normally represented by the Water trigram so rain is expected, i.e. you expect the minister to deliver especially if you had to bribe him. Clouds that do not rain against expectations means that you should be getting what you desire but nothing is happening. In other words, any expectations you developed from the previous activity of meeting with the minister did not transpire. After all, the meaning of the hexagram is that you are small but trying to exceed your smallness by meeting someone greater than yourself to get something significant. Because this line is the lord (ruling line) of the hexagram it contains an exalted personage, and it also falls under the influence of the Thunder trigram. Therefore there is the image of a duke performing a "thunderous" activity – he shoots an arrow to which a string has been attached so as to make retrieval easy and he hits some prey. These tethered arrows were used to hunt fowl to keep them from flying away with the arrow. This means you pull on your strings to the official that you contacted to get what you want, *or he uses his connections and pulls on the strings to get what you want*. The official is probably the one represented by the duke who retrieves his prey from a pit, which means the palace or a pit of dangerous intrigues and manipulations. You are too small to do this. Only someone great can do so.

62.6: A yin line at the top of the hexagram, which is at the top of the Xun Wind trigram. **"Not meeting, but passing the other by without encounter. A flying bird gets caught in a net. Ominous. This is called a catastrophic calamity [disaster]."** This is a self-incurred disaster because of someone small trying to achieve what only the more powerful can achieve such as in line five. The activities of the bird (the small man) cause self-inflicted injury and misfortune. Because of the Xun wind element there is the image of a flying bird and the fact that someone passes by another without meeting. There are several possible explanations. The first possibility is that he did not meet the minister again but tried to do things on his own (without being great enough) another time so he created a self-inflicted calamity by becoming netted in some difficulty. The trouble arises because his status just is not great enough since he is "small." The second possibility is that he may owe the minister some payment for what he did since it was successful but refuses to meet with him to pay up and then lands in trouble. Chinese history records several tales where individuals who did not want to pay an official for doing a favor got into trouble. Don't ever try to cross a big boy.

In terms of the structural composition of this hexagram and how it appears in this line, the lower Gen Accumulation trigram means that the parties should not pass by one another while the upper Zhen Thunder trigram produces a lightning strike and produces the catastrophic calamity.

HEXAGRAM 63

Ji Ji - After Completion, After Fording the River

Lower Trigram: Li (Fire) – curtain, military conflict, Exalted Ancestor
Upper Trigram: Kan (Water) – danger, trouble, water

The Judgment: After fording the river. It is beneficial to persevere. In the beginning the situation is auspicious but in the end chaotic (disorder).

In the *Yijing* a great undertaking, difficult task, important enterprise or big accomplishment is signified by the expression "crossing a great river." Crossing or fording a river can be either a minor but difficult stage in a large undertaking or the major event in itself. Using the analogy of crossing a river, this hexagram steps through the phases of a military invasion to conquer a territory and then emphasizes the steps you must take afterwards. It warns against a military victory turning sour in the end because not enough effort went into managing a conquered territory afterwards. The Judgment states that after completing a great task you must keep working hard because after completion the situation can turn chaotic. In other words, after your military accomplishment you should work to solidify your gains. The lines in the lower trigram are about the various inconveniences involved in accomplishing the great feat whereas the upper trigram is about what you should do after completing the task, which requires securing matters through good administration and management. After the great task is accomplished *the focus should be on making sure that your achievement doesn't deteriorate into chaos*. You should also give thanks and despite the newly won confidence from your success you should be focusing on good administration of the territory just conquered instead of immediately launching into another difficult project or you will become submerged in water over your head. In the first line there are some minor but inconsequential difficulties at the initial phases of a military invasion. In the second line your forces get bogged down and invasion plans discovered. In the third line you begin the assault of the enemy territory. In the fourth line you become very careful about the safety of your troops. In the fifth line you conquer the enemy and give thanks to Heaven *but are not sufficiently focusing on the administration of the region just conquered*. In the sixth line you are warned to administer the conquered territory well and not get involved in any new campaigns at this time.

1. The wheels drag. The tail gets wet. There is no trouble.

2. The lady loses the curtain of her carriage. Do not chase after it. In seven days you'll get it back.

3. The High Ancestor attacked the Land of Ghosts (*Guifeng*). In three years he conquered it. Inferior men ought not be utilized (in such a great task).

4. A jacket padded with silk wadding rips (into tatters). Be careful all day long.

5. The eastern neighbor slaughters an ox (as sacrifice). However, it is not as good as the western neighbor's modest offering in really bringing the blessing.

6. His head gets wet (becomes drenched in water). Danger.

63.1: Yang at the first line, at the bottom of the Li Fire trigram. **"The wheels drag. The tail gets wet. There is no trouble."** When you start out on a big venture, such as crossing a river, little problems will happen at the start. This is natural, so the problems are of no special consequence because they are just little annoyances and minor irritations to be expected. For instance, the wheels dragging in mud might mean that a carriage or cart must be dragged out of the mud because it accidentally got stuck. While horses drag it out of the mud its wheels will leave a trail. Or, perhaps the wheels drag because brakes are being applied so that you proceed slowly but cautiously. Future hexagram line 39.1 says that going forward leads to lameness, which means that you probably got stuck and had to be pulled out of the mud which is why the wheels of the carriage were dragging. There are several possible meanings that usually entail the idea of a minor step in a journey needing some type of correction. The difficulties are not dangerous here at the beginning steps of the crossing. Since this is all happening within the Li Fire trigram there is no doubt that *what is being symbolized is the start of a military operation*, especially since it is mentioned in line three. A fox is also mentioned because it raises its tail when crossing a stream and will get its tail wet if it is not careful, which is an annoyance. The necessity of raising the tail indicates that you need to be careful in these initial steps, and the fact that the tail gets wet shows that something goes wrong. None of the problems you encounter at this stage are severe or fatal but just small irritations and thus, "There is no trouble" because the problems aren't a big deal.

63.2: Yin at the second line in the middle of the Li Elegance trigram, and at the beginning of an inner Kan Danger trigram. **"The lady loses the curtain of her carriage. Do not seek it. In seven days you'll get it back."** The fact that a woman loses a carriage curtain – while the carriage is struck in the mud – means that she becomes exposed and a woman is used because she represents a yin condition. It is probably that your military operations have become exposed or put in a compromising position. This military step is influenced by the Li trigram and by the Kan Danger trigram, so losing the privacy of your invasion plans means that your strategy has been revealed. Or the loss of the veil (curtain of a carriage) could mean that you lose something in moving forward and simply become inconvenienced and embarrassed (due to being revealed). Here the degree of trouble is greater than in the first line because you are progressing further into the undertaking. Primarily it is still just a loss of secrecy and some minor equipment for moving forward that consequently results in a bit of trouble and discomfort. Future hexagram line 6.2 says "Unable to win the lawsuit. Retreating he returns home" that in this case means he cannot launch a surprise attack any longer so he should cool his jets until he formulates a new strategy and gets back on track, which is the same as the woman retrieving her carriage curtain after a while. The meaning of "in seven days" means that a cycle of events (a short period of time) must play themselves out before you can formulate a new strategy that your enemy does not know about, which then takes us to the next hexagram line.

63.3: Yang at the third line at the top of the Li Fire-Brilliance trigram. It is also the central line of an inner Kan Danger trigram, and the first line of an inner Li trigram. **"The High Ancestor attacked the Land of Ghosts [*Guifang*, Land of Gui, Demon's Territory]. In three years he conquered it. Inferior men ought not be utilized (to attempt such a thing)."** Here the High Ancestor is the title of King Wu Ding of Shang who reigned about two hundred years before the conquest of Shang by the Zhou (1324-1266 BCE). The Land of Ghosts (*Guifang*) or Demon's Territory, was northwest to the ancient Shang state and populated by people whom the Shang regarded as barbarians. Traditionally these were the Rong, Di, Hu, Xunyu, Xianyu, Xianyun or Xiongnu peoples. They are mentioned in line 8.3 and symbolized by the Kan Danger trigram. King Wu Ding conquered these people after three years of conflict, which means three hexagram lines that take us to a military victory in line five. This is definitely a dangerous undertaking requiring superior men so inferior men should not be used as military leaders in the operations (symbolized by the Li trigram) although infantry will naturally be sacrificed as expendables. In those days infantry did most of the fighting while nobles guided battles by issuing orders from their chariots, which are probably the carts or carriage of the first and second lines. After this troublesome region has been conquered the hexagram warns not to hand its administration over to inferior men. Inferior men ought not be used as leaders in either the military conquest or subsequent administration. The whole message of this hexagram is that succeeding in difficult tasks requires *men of talent*.

63.4: Yin at the fourth line, at the first line of the upper Kan Water-Danger trigram. This is also the middle line of an inner Li Brilliance trigram and top line of an inner Kan Danger trigram. **"A jacket [short coat] padded with silk wadding rips [into tatters]. Be careful [be on guard, watchful] all day long."** Now that you are busy fighting to conquer *Guifang*, the Demon's Territory, your expensive jacket gets ripped into tatters, which means that your men are getting killed. The beautiful jacket (Li trigram) stuffed with silk padding rips and turns into tatters (the doubled Kan trigram) to represent the death of your soldiers. Hence, to remain careful in wearing it all day long means being careful in protecting your troops.

63.5: Yang at the fifth line in the center of the upper Kan Danger trigram, and at the top line of an inner Li trigram. The fifth line as lord of the hexagram usually shows some perfected form of the meaning of the hexagram, and since this is a yang line we see that. **"The eastern neighbor slaughters an ox as sacrifice but the western neighbor makes a smaller offering and really receives a blessing."** There are two ways to interpret this. Most interpreters would default to a superficial explanation and say that the lesson here is that genuine sincerity when thanking Heaven (for "crossing a river" or defeating an enemy) is much better than an ostentatious display. After the great achievement you don't have to make an ostentatious show of display and hence the modest offering that "does not brag" is the one that receives the blessings due to its sincerity. My preferred interpretation takes into account that the fifth line should summarize the hexagram's main message in some sense, and this line should also show the victory promised in line three. The interpretation should not be about a sacrifice or gratefulness to Heaven but the fact that lots of work was required to achieve the great feat of conquering the land of *Guifang* and many people were killed in the process. Those soldier deaths were the "sacrifices" of the eastern neighbor, or Shang, but the little effort made afterwards in administering the conquered territory *is what truly produced the benefits or blessings that were being sought*. For instance, after the Zhou conquered the Shang dynasty King Wu ordered the Shang people to move to the Luoyang area where they were put under strict supervision. The Shang people eventually rebelled! Therefore do not neglect good management after conquering this territory ("after completion") or there will be trouble in some way. If you don't continue to hold down the territory then there will be the misfortune of rebellion and revolt later that requires more fighting again, which is what happened to the Zhou conquerors of the Shang people. Along this line of interpretation eastern and western don't just represent the Shang (eastern) and *Guifang* (western) but are also like the sun that rises in the east, symbolizing the beginning of the project, and its setting in the west symbolizes its completion or accomplishment *where the more important aspect is now managing the conquered territory well*, otherwise everything will fall apart so that all the lives lost and efforts expended were in vain.

63.6: Yin at the sixth line at the top of the upper Kan Water-Danger trigram and the line strongly shows the influence of this trigram. **"His head gets wet (becomes drenched in water). Danger."** The focus of this hexagram is on "after completion." The image of the line is of a man who becomes submerged under water (Kan trigram), which could lead to drowning because most men in ancient China could not swim. You should not wade into water too deep for yourself. The meaning is that a man now becomes involved in difficulties that inundate him because of acting imprudently after the victory so *he becomes "in over his head" due to poor administration when he didn't handle the affairs adequately*. The hexagram warned the eastern neighbor who made an ostentatious display of thanks (symbolizing the efforts spent for accomplishment) that they must put a lot of effort into handling affairs after the conquest of *Guifang* but they did not do so and hence now he is sinking. At this sixth line the war has already been completed and the situation has transformed into an aftermath of chaos, rebellion and revolt because you used inferior men to handle governing affairs and they let things turn into tatters. The pride of achievement may tempt you into another great undertaking but at this time you should avoid get involved in anything else since that is beyond your present capabilities since you are inundated with troubles. *Paired hexagram line 64.6 aptly warns not to drink and lose your head in over-confidence so that you consequently do something stupid.*

In terms of the construction of the hexagram and how it is reflected in this line, there is a Li trigram at the bottom symbolizing the great accomplishment (crossing a river) and then the Kan Danger-Water trigram on top that represents the chaos or deterioration that may happen afterwards – remember that a revolt did historically happen. Thus "the head becomes drenched in water" if you do not focus on proper administration, which summarizes the message of the hexagram in the Judgment: "After fording the river it is beneficial to persevere. In the beginning the situation is auspicious but in the end chaotic (disordered or dangerous)."

HEXAGRAM 64

Wei Ji - Before Completion, Not Yet Across the River

Lower Trigram: Kan (Water) – abyss, pit, danger, trouble, difficulties
Upper Trigram: Li (Fire) – brilliance, elegance, shining, light, clarity, mind

The Judgment: Before Completion. The young fox, when nearly across the river, gets its tail wet. Nothing is beneficial.

This hexagram is primarily about the difficulties involved in accomplishing some great endeavor *before its completion*, and those preliminary troubles are illustrated through the analogies of a fox crossing a stream and people crossing a river in a chariot that both represent marching to war. The meaning of this hexagram is juxtaposed against hexagram 63 where mismanagement caused a rebellion after a great war was concluded whereas in this hexagram the emphasis is put on a slow and steady preparation for war while the end result is success and celebration. The hexagram's Judgment warns that before you complete the crossing usually nothing goes well just as in the previous hexagram. The steps necessary for a positive end result are primarily found in the lower trigram while the upper trigram contains various possibilities about what can happen afterwards. In the first line you get started at an endeavor and a fox's tail becomes wet due to carelessness. In the second line you get slowed down because your carriage gets stuck in the river mud. In the third line you learn you must make suitable preparations for the hard part of the endeavor (i.e. engaging in battle) by first completing some difficult preliminary steps (such as crossing a river). Only after all of this preparation work is fully completed are you finally ready in the fourth line to attack the undertaking (enemy) with great energy and fervor. Once successful (the fifth line), your glory of accomplishment will tend to evoke not just praise and recognition from others but their allegiance. Lastly, the sixth line shows that having achieved the great accomplishment, which means winning the war, you can now celebrate but if you indulge yourself and lose your head (a sound perspective) this will certainly lead to trouble. In the 63rd hexagram, which is paired with this one, you ended up in trouble at the end because you didn't keep an eye on managing affairs afterwards.

1. His tail gets wet. Distress.

2. The wheels drag. Steadfast persistence is auspicious.

3. Not yet across (the water). Marching to war is inauspicious (it is a bad time to attack). It is beneficial to cross the great river.

4. Steadfast persistence (in your efforts) is auspicious. Regrets are gone. The Thunderer (Zhen) attacked *Guifang* (The Demon Territory). After three years he receives an award from the great kingdom.

5. Continuous persistence (in your efforts) is auspicious. No regrets. The superior man's glory evokes the response of confidence from others. Auspicious.

6. He drinks wine with confidence. There is no trouble (for this indulgence). But if he allows his head to get wet (becomes drunk) he will lose touch with reality (and fail in what is right).

64.1: Yin at the bottom line within the lower Kan trigram of water. **"His tail gets wet. Distress."** This describes the fate of a young fox that gets his tail wet when trying to cross a stream. If a fox gets its tail wet during the middle of a deep crossing it could drown because a tail the becomes heavy with water will pull it down, hence it always raises its bushy tail. However, in this case the fox's tail gets wet and begins to drag him under so there is distress. The meaning is that during the initial activity of some great task it is common for something to go wrong and start taking you under because you are trying to go too fast or attempting too much at the start or it is just that accidents happen. Be more cautious. The line is actually describing potential danger at the start of a military campaign where the presence of the Kan Water trigram comes through as water and danger.

64.2: Yang at the second and central line within the lower Kan trigram of water, and it is the bottom line of an inner Li trigram. **"The wheels drag. Steadfast persistence [keeping on] is auspicious."** Here the wheels of a chariot end up dragging in the mud of the river bottom and the chariot leaves behind a trail as it is dragged free by a team of horses. Previously a fox got his tail wet and now a chariot's wheels drag in movement so the line says to stay determined in pushing forward. Even at the beginning of the next line he is not yet across the river so despite this slow down he must maintain his persistence. Once again the Kan trigram comes through as the water/mud and difficulty while the Li trigram appears in the fact that this is a military expedition.

64.3: Yin at the third line within the lower Kan trigram of water. It is also the bottom line within an inner Kan trigram as well as the middle line of an inner Li Fire trigram. **"He is not yet across the river. It is a bad time to attack. It is advantageous to ford the great river."** In this line you are crossing the stream but not yet across so it is *unfavorable to launch an attack because of your precarious position*. This comes from there being two Kan Water-Danger trigrams. Your troops must completely cross a river before they can engage in battle, which means that you are still in a stage of preparations and should not initiate major actions until completed. If you launch a military attack now while still in the middle of a precarious, vulnerable position it will result in misfortune. You must first complete any necessary preparations because of the excessive Kan trigram dangers. Therefore it is not yet advantageous to initiate new actions, i.e. launch a military assault. The doubled Kan Water-Danger trigram manifests in this line as danger and the actual river while the Li Fire trigram represents marching to war, which is put on hold until you cross over into the upper trigram where some of the water element now suppressing the fire element disappears. First have the troops finish crossing the river and then you can advance and begin to fight. This hexagram is about "before completion" so the principle being stressed is to adequately prepare before an invasion.

64.4: Yang at the fourth line, which is the first line within the upper Li trigram, the middle line of an inner Kan trigram, and the first line within an inner Li trigram. Previously we were in the lower Kan trigram but now we have just advanced into the upper Li Fire trigram of fiery activity and warfare so there is a marked change of state. **"Steadfast persistence in your efforts is auspicious. Regrets have vanished. The Thunderer (Zhen) attacked *Guifang* (The Demon Territory). After three years he receives an award from the great kingdom."** This line might reference an event in Chinese history about 150 years before the founding of the Zhou dynasty where a three-year campaign was led against *Guifang*, a barbarian territory of non-Chinese tribes. The attack was launched by a general or lord called Zheng, which means Thunderer or Thunderbolt. Some translate this as "Like thunder he attacks *Guifang*" but there is actually an individual being named for launching the war rather than "he attacked with/like thunder." This is possibly the Zhou Duke Ji Li who fought against the Gui Rong tribe, and who (according to the *Bamboo Annals* chronicle of ancient China) eventually received a tremendous reward of land, horses and riches from the Shang king for his victory. In the third line you crossed the river and now you continue moving forward with long-term persistence to conquer *Guifang*, so the regrets for waiting have vanished and you start making headway in military progress due to the doubled Li Military trigram. You eventually conquer the barbarian region of *Guifang*, which is certainly a difficult feat because a Kan Danger trigram is involved. This takes three years of efforts, so after three lines we should find a celebration of the conquest in the sixth line of the hexagram.

64.5: Yin at the fifth line in the center of the upper Li trigram, and the top line of an inner Kan trigram. **"Steadfast persistence is auspicious. There are no regrets. The superior man's glory [radiance, brilliance] evokes the response of confidence [trust, allegiance] from others. Auspicious."** In this line you are clearly winning and obtain glory from your battle victories, however, continuous effort is required to complete the conquest. The Kan trigram affecting this yin line testifies to the difficulties of the task while the Li trigram stands for military activities. The fifth line of a hexagram usually displays a perfected form of the message of the hexagram, and often involves an individual of elevated status. In this case the superior man becomes elevated – by winning the trust, allegiance and admiration of the people – because of the glory of his battle accomplishments. The Li trigram comes through as a superior man who wins glory ("radiance") for his brilliant military victories, and thus he develops a following of admirers. The theme of the hexagram is "before completion" or "prior to wining the war," and this hexagram simply puts forward the principles of preparation and the need for strong perseverance through many military engagements over three years before finally winning completely in the end.

64.6: Yang at the sixth line, and at the top line of the upper Li trigram. **"He drinks wine with confidence. There is no trouble (for this indulgence). But if he allows his head to get wet (becomes immersed or drunk) he will lose touch with reality (and fail in what is right)."** Here you start feasting and celebrating with wine due to your success, and there is no fault in this self-congratulatory deed. However, if you get drunk after you achieve some great deed then you might let the celebratory praise and congratulations go to your head. If everyone is applauding you while you are drunk then you can easily lose touch with reality and start making administrative mistakes that could imperil the new conquest. You might begin to think you can accomplish anything or you are now special and allowed to do things not permitted. You can lose your head just as Alexander the Great did in killing the Macedonian general Cleitus in a drunken fury. In this case, however, we are talking about long-term drunkenness so that you lose your good judgment and no longer handle ordinary matters properly and thus you fail in what is right. Due to self-deception you will fail to do what is correct and great problems will then arise from your own making. Even a state can fail due to hubris if it lets its prosperity go to its head. "Allowing your head to get wet" is not just a symbol of getting drunk but a symbol of excessive pride, arrogance, haughtiness and hubris clouding your judgment *afterwards* because your head swells from your successes, which here is represented as intoxication due to drinking wine, and then you will fail to take care of necessary matters appropriately. The warning is not to fall prey to arrogant over-confidence that will pull you into *large* judgmental and behavioral mistakes that affect the state.

In terms of the construction of the hexagram and how this is reflected in this sixth line there is a Kan Water trigram beneath a Li Fire trigram, and thus we see the image of drinking (Kan) during a celebration (Li) with the warning not to let his head get wet (Kan) because it might possibly leading to some sort of destruction (Li Fire trigram).

SUMMARY AND CONCLUSION

I have tried to provide you with some major additions to our understanding of the *Yijing* by revealing special patterns that rule the lines along with various historical references that appear within the hexagrams.

All subsequent translations of the *Yijing* should reference its inner structure of overlapping trigrams because they certainly explain why certain "random" phrases and images suddenly appear in the lines.

There are at least five major patterns that structure the content of the lines and the trigrams are one of these patterns. If you reference the reverse, opposite and future hexagrams for certain lines this will at times also help improve future translations and interpretations. You must also remember that a special focus of the hexagrams is retelling the history of the Shang and Zhou dynasties and focusing on topics such as military invasions, the challenges faced by government officials, sex and sexual desire, the phases of life, marriage, raising children, self-improvement, and commentaries on certain life situations.

The contents of the sixty-four hexagrams are usually just commentaries on special topics that cleverly follow a special pattern, and because they were so full of insightful content they were turned into a form of divination. However, the sequence of events or story line laid out in each hexagram is certainly not fated as a pattern that must absolutely occur because the commentary of six lines is just a clever creation – out of countless possible – that follows the general structural pattern of the *Yijing* in terms of yin and yang, trigrams, and hexagram gradients.

Hopefully this revelation of patterns, and my attempts at providing *Yijing* translations (that could certainly be improved given more time), will provide enough insight that future translators will produce better and better translations over time.

ABOUT THE AUTHOR

Bill Bodri is the author of several investment, marketing, health and self-help books including the following:

Breakthrough Strategies of Wall Street Traders
Super Investing
Hard Yield Investments, Hard Assets and Asset Protection Strategies
Bankism

Culture, Country, City, Company, Person, Purpose, Passion, World
The Art of Political Power
The I Ching Revealed

How to Create a Million Dollar Unique Selling Proposition
The Claude Hopkins Rare Ad Collection
Move Forward
Quick, Fast, Done

Visualization Power
Sport Visualization

Detox Cleanse Your Body Quickly and Completely
Look Younger, Live Longer
Super Cancer Fighters

Neijia Yoga
Arhat Yoga
Buddha Yoga
Bodhisattva Yoga
Neijia Yoga
Color Me Confucius

The books that would best accompany this one would be:

Culture, Country, City, Company, Person, Purpose, Passion, World (super-duper highly recommended),
Color Me Confucius
Move Forward, and
Quick, Fast, Done.

www.ingramcontent.com/pod-product-compliance
Lightning Source LLC
Chambersburg PA
CBHW070419010526
44118CB00014B/1821